Praise

Disarmament in the ti.... ... ...

"An absorbing account of how the US verified the key agreement that ended the Cold War. Should be read and absorbed by all who wonder how we can overcome the rush to war today."

—JACK MATLOCK, former US Ambassador to the Soviet Union

"Ritter's riveting personal history of nuclear arms control as seen from the inside, with its intense personal and institutional conflicts, could not come at a more propitious moment. Ritter is telling us that America's dispute with Russia today must not prevent the renewal of serious arms talks, with all of their difficulty."

—SEYMOUR HERSH, Pulitzer Prize-Winning Investigative Journalist

"Scott Ritter's book could not be timelier. He transports us back to an era where the world stood on the brink of a nuclear apocalypse. With an intimacy and eye for detail that only comes from having experienced the events he describes firsthand, Ritter walks us through the threat posed to the world by intermediate-range nuclear missiles, and the amazing work done by the American inspectors and Soviet factory workers tasked by their respective governments to eliminate them. In the process, Ritter and the characters in his narrative help create the conditions for one-time enemies to learn to live together in peace."

—DANIEL ELLSBERG, author of *The Doomsday Machine: Confessions of a Nuclear War Planner*

"Scott Ritter's page-turner focuses on his role as inspector monitoring Soviet implementation of the US-Russia INF treaty of 1987—a near-miraculous agreement under which an entire class of short- and intermediate-range nuclear missiles was actually destroyed. . . . Scott gives us a fascinatingly intimate account of the bumpy on-site road to effective inspection/verification. Bumpy even in the presence of the mutual trust existing at the time. That trust is now squandered. God help us."

—RAY McGOVERN, former senior CIA analyst for Soviet/Russian affairs

DISARMAMENT
in the time of
PERESTROIKA

* * * * *

Arms Control and the End
of the Soviet Union

A Personal Journal

SCOTT RITTER

Clarity Press, Inc.

ISBN: 978-1-949762-61-7
EBOOK ISBN: 978-1-949762-65-5

In-house editor: Diana G. Collier
Book design: Becky Luening

Library of Congress Control Number: 2022935660

Clarity Press, Inc.
2625 Piedmont Rd. NE, Ste. 56
Atlanta, GA 30324, USA
https://www.claritypress.com

Table of Contents

*This book is dedicated to the memory of George M. Connell
and Douglas M. Englund, two ardent Cold Warriors
transformed into Pioneers of Peace*

*Douglas Marz Englund
1940–2017*

*George Murdoch Connell
1942–2015*

Good Defeats Evil

*Zurab Tsereteli's statue, "Good Defeats Evil," outside
United Nations Headquarters. The dragon is made of parts
taken from SS-20 and Pershing II missiles.*

*"Yet when I hoped for good, evil came;
when I looked for light, then came darkness."*

JOB 30:26

I HAD HEARD ABOUT IT long before I first laid eyes on it. Entitled "Good
Defeats Evil," the bronze sculpture was of Saint George on horseback, slaying
a Dragon that was made from missile parts—a quintessential depiction of
disarmament. The massive bronze statue (standing some 36 feet high and
weighing in at 40 tons) had been presented to the United Nations by the Soviet
Union on the world organization's 45th Anniversary on October 24, 1990. It was
the work of Zurab Tsereteli, a renowned artist from the Republic of Georgia,

and commemorated the landmark Intermediate Nuclear Forces (INF) treaty, signed by US President Ronald Reagan and Soviet General Secretary Mikhail Gorbachev on December 7, 1987.

Tsereteli's installation made use of metal bits and components from decommissioned US Pershing II and Soviet SS-20 missiles. These two missiles were the *yin* and the *yang* of the INF treaty. The Soviet deployment of the road-mobile SS-20, armed with three nuclear warheads, had, in 1979, tipped the nuclear balance of power in Europe to Moscow. The US had responded by deploying the Pershing II missile, which could reach Moscow from its launch sites in West Germany in less than 8 minutes, threatening the Soviets with nuclear annihilation.

Previous arms control treaties sought to limit the number of missiles in the respective arsenals of the US and Soviet Union. The INF treaty was different—it banned these missiles, and others like them, altogether. The Pershing II and SS-20 became the symbols of the INF treaty, paired together as a reminder of both the evil man could create, and the ability of man, if he had the will, to overcome that evil.

On the morning of September 23, 1991, I took advantage of my presence in New York City to examine Tsereteli's sculpture up close and in person. I left the Helmsley Hotel and walked down 42nd Street, toward First Avenue. The sun was out, the sky was blue, and New York City was laid out before me in all its glory. I paused before crossing First Avenue, admiring the line of flag poles that fronted the United Nations compound, the colorful banners of its many member countries snapping in the breeze. Tsereteli's statue was installed in a park just inside the gate to the UN compound.

Good defeats Evil. I agreed with the sentiment behind the title but was uncomfortable with the certainty it conveyed. The cause of disarmament was a pure one—of that there was no doubt. This was especially true regarding the INF treaty, where inspections, begun in July 1988, were at the time of my visit still ongoing and would continue until 2001, when the 13-year period set forth in the INF treaty expired.

The INF treaty, however, was more than a simple black and white construct. Like any experience derived from the human condition, it was far more nebulous in character, created from a palette of differing shades of grey. This was especially the case when observed from the Soviet perspective. The INF treaty was implemented during a time of great change in the Soviet Union. The deployment of the SS-20 missile represented the high-water mark of the Soviet missile production facilities involved in its manufacture. The elimination of the SS-20 missile under the terms of the INF treaty, conversely, signaled the start of a period of steady economic and—given the hand-in-glove relationship between Soviet defense industry factories and the communities that supported them—social decline.

The principal Soviet defense facility involved in the manufacture of the SS-20 missile was the Votkinsk Machine Building Plant, situated in the city of Votkinsk. Nestled near the Kama River, at the foothills of the Ural Mountains, Votkinsk was located some 700 miles east of Moscow, in a region that had been closed to foreigners for decades. American weapons inspectors, of whom I was one, were charged under the provisions of the INF treaty with conducting verification inspections at the Votkinsk Missile Final Assembly Plant. To accomplish this mission, we established a permanent presence in Votkinsk, which provided us with a unique window on the changes taking place at the factory, in the city of Votkinsk and its surrounding environs, and in the Soviet Union as a whole.

From this vantage point, we had a ground-eye view of the struggles brought on by the effort to convert the Soviet over-reliance upon missile production into sustainable civilian industry. Complicating an already Sisyphean task were the internal political struggles taking place throughout the Soviet Union, brought on by the transformative policies of Glasnost (the ability of every Soviet citizen to openly discuss economic and political policy) and Perestroika (the actual restructuring of the Soviet political and economic system) advanced by Soviet General Secretary Mikhail Gorbachev.

The socio-economic drama that unfolded in parallel with the job of installing a monitoring facility outside the gates of a Soviet missile factory was not some academic exercise, but rather an intimate journey into the lives of flesh-and-blood people who, prior to the implementation of the INF treaty, were conditioned to look upon one another as enemies.

Disarmament in the time of Perestroika seeks to capture the history of these two intertwined narratives from the personal perspective of those involved.

It is the backstory to the drama captured in Zurab Tsereteli's statue, without which it would be incomprehensible—little more than a collection of missile fragments and bronze.

SCOTT RITTER
Delmar, New York

PROLOGUE

The Missile Crisis

John Sartorius (left) and Sam Israelit (right) pose with a 6-axle missile-carrying railcar,
Votkinsk Portal Monitoring Facility, March 10, 1990.

"If you can keep your head when all about you are losing
theirs and blaming it on you."

IF..., RUDYARD KIPLING

The Device

WASHINGTON, DC. JANUARY 12, 1990—The Intermediate Nuclear Forces
(INF) treaty was signed on December 8, 1987 by President Ronald Reagan and
Secretary General Mikhail Gorbachev. The treaty eliminated the short-range
(500–1,000 kilometers/310–620 miles) and intermediate-range (1,000–5,500
kilometers/620–3,420 miles) missiles in both the US and Soviet arsenals. By
January 1990 we were well into the second year of treaty implementation, with
the initial on-site inspections having begun on July 1, 1988. The treaty had been
ratified in the US Senate by an overwhelming 93–5 vote, surviving the delaying
tactics and so-called "killer amendments" of Senator Jesse Helms, a Republican
from North Carolina who was vehemently opposed to arms control of any kind,
especially when it involved the Soviet Union.

The significance of seventeen and a half months of successful implementation of the landmark treaty seemed to escape Helms and his staff. One staffer, a former Marine and CIA officer named David Sullivan, was particularly driven in his efforts to focus Senatorial angst against the INF Treaty. Every letter sent by Senator Helms to US government officials which dealt with the INF Treaty was prepared by David Sullivan himself, often using as background highly classified information leaked to him by sympathetic former colleagues inside the US intelligence community.

Sullivan had a checkered career. As a CIA employee in 1978, he had been caught leaking classified information to Richard Perle, who at that time was a staffer for Senator Henry "Scoop" Jackson (D-Washington), a staunch opponent of arms control. The CIA Director at the time, Stansfield Turner, was appalled at the leak, which involved extremely sensitive intelligence derived from NSA communications intercepts. Sullivan resigned from the CIA before Turner could fire him. But like a cat with the proverbial nine lives, David Sullivan was soon afterward able to land back on his feet, quickly getting a job as a staffer for Senator Lloyd Benson, and later Jesse Helms.[1]

With Sullivan digging up all the dirt possible on what he viewed as the "flawed" implementation of the INF Treaty, Senator Helms was able to continue his program of active resistance to arms control and disarmament. The North Carolina Republican had tried his best to derail the INF Treaty ratification process and having failed, was looking to use the specter of Soviet cheating under the INF as a vehicle to stop an even more ambitious disarmament efforts being negotiated at that time between the US and the Soviet Union.

Helms seized, in particular, on CargoScan, a 9-million electron volt state-of-the-art X-ray device (referred to in the treaty language as a non-damaging radiographic imaging system), an important item of equipment central to the inspection verification mission of US inspectors stationed outside the main gates of the Votkinsk Machine Building Plant. The lengthy process involved in making it operational proved to be a boon for Sullivan and Helms.

The purpose of CargoScan was to permit inspectors to image the second stage of the long-range SS-25 missiles. These, which had been inserted into launch cannisters, had precluded visual inspection as they exited the Votkinsk Machine Building Plant. CargoScan provided an essential verification task needed to confirm that the launch cannisters did not, in fact, carry the banned intermediate-ranged SS-20 missile; the first stage of the SS-25 was virtually identical to that of the SS-20, making the second stage the key distinguishing feature.

Under the terms of the INF Treaty, CargoScan was supposed to be operational no later than six months after the treaty entered force. However, the CargoScan equipment was not ready for shipment to Votkinsk until the fall of 1989, nearly a year behind schedule. Even as the various components comprising the CargoScan system were being installed, disputes over the technical characteristics of the system, centered around its configuration and the data expected to be collected, prevented the Soviets from certifying CargoScan as operational, and in doing so, provided grist for the Sullivan-Helms arms control alarm mill.

"I have just been reliably informed that despite my urgent and repeated exhortations," Helms wrote in a January 12, 1990 letter to President George H. W. Bush, homing in on his main point of argument, "the CargoScan system will not reach its initial operating capability until as late as February 14, 1990. I am also told that the main reason for this extraordinary tardiness is an endless series of questions raised by the Soviets about the CargoScan systems—questions designed to delay its operation." Helms closed his letter with a not-so-veiled threat: "I respectfully request that you expedite the operational capability of the INF CargoScan…these Soviet-inspired delays raise questions about Soviet intentions that could become issues in any START ratification process."

Helms' letter was the hot ticket item at the headquarters of the On-Site Inspection Agency (OSIA), a Department of Defense organization specifically created to oversee the implementation of the INF Treaty.

I prepared to redeploy to the Soviet Union in mid-January for another tour of duty at the Votkinsk Portal Monitoring Facility. US inspectors stood watch outside the gates of the Votkinsk Final Assembly Plant where the Soviets assembled SS-25 missiles before shipping them via railcar to the Strategic Rocket Forces of the Ministry of Defense. This was going to be my seventh rotation into Votkinsk since the treaty entered into force on July 1, 1988. In the intervening time I had been involved in virtually every aspect of the Votkinsk inspection mission—except CargoScan. Now, through the luck of the draw, I was going to be in the proverbial hot seat when this overly technical piece of equipment, so central to the success of the portal monitoring mission, was due to be made operational.

In many ways, I was responsible in large part for at least some of the delay in bringing CargoScan to Votkinsk. When CargoScan was approved for use at Votkinsk, it existed only in theory. To turn theory into reality, the actual device had to be assembled and tested at the Technical On-Site Inspection (TOSI) facility located at Sandia National Laboratory on Kirtland Air Force Base, just outside Albuquerque, New Mexico. The TOSI facility was the test bed for the various technologies that were used by the US inspectors at Votkinsk. CargoScan was but the latest in a series of on-site inspection technologies to be developed at Sandia, then shipped to Votkinsk.

While this was happening, US and Soviet negotiators were meeting in Geneva to hash out the agreed upon parameters regarding the operation of CargoScan. On December 8, 1988, they finally published same as part of a Memorandum of Agreement (MOA) addressing various technical issues that were not covered in the treaty text—one week *after* the treaty-mandated deadline for CargoScan to be installed and operational.

Even with a completed MOA, the details surrounding the installation of CargoScan, as well as bringing it into a state of operational readiness, were not yet finalized. This task was placed in the hands of the inspectors and their Soviet counterparts at the Votkinsk Factory. A lack of formal documentation regarding the various components was a problem. CargoScan was a "one-off" system, and no such documentation existed. As a result, the inspectors were held prisoner by the timeline set by the Sandia engineers, their Air Force contract supervisors, and the various technicians from the companies that produced the CargoScan system's components. As documents were produced at the TOSI facility, they were sent to Votkinsk, where they were shared with the Soviets, who invariably raised questions, requiring the documents to be returned to Sandia for clarification. This drawn-out process slowed the construction at Votkinsk, as the Soviets were loathe to greenlight anything until they were certain it operated solely within the technical parameters permitted by the treaty.

By July 1989, this process of system integration had progressed enough for Sandia to declare CargoScan ready to be shipped to Votkinsk and put into operation. I had been scheduled to travel to the TOSI facility since April 1989 to be trained on the system. Other commitments, however, kept bumping me from the training schedule. For a while it looked like I was going to have to receive my initial operator training on the job, after CargoScan had been installed and made operational.

This was not to be. In early July 1989, I picked up the phone in my cubicle at OSIA Headquarters to find Colonel Doug Englund, one of the co-Directors for Portal Monitoring at the time, on the other end. Doug said he was visiting Sandia National Laboratory. "Pack your bags," he said. "I need you to fly to Albuquerque for CargoScan familiarization training."

Doug was not being trained, but rather was conducting a final inspection of the CargoScan system before it was to be dismantled, transported, and reassembled in Votkinsk. I was confused as to what my role was, so I simply followed Doug as he was led through the TOSI set up by the Sandia staff. Any confusion I might have had about my purpose there, however, would soon evaporate.

"You guys do realize that we're thousands of miles away from the nearest Radio Shack," Doug told them. "If this thing breaks, the Soviets don't stop producing missiles. From a compliance verification standpoint, CargoScan has got to work perfectly, every time."

The Sandia representatives provided Doug with what appeared to be a well-rehearsed line to a clearly anticipated issue: "Don't worry," the head Sandia staff member said. "It's idiot proof."

Doug's eyes twinkled, a hint of a smile forming on his otherwise expressionless face. "Yes," he replied, "but is it *Marine* proof?"

The senior Sandia representative looked at me and nodded his head. "Of course."

Suddenly, I knew exactly why I had been summoned to accompany Colonel Englund.

"Let's run the system through its paces," Doug said. "Captain Ritter will serve as the operator."

I tried to interject that I had not been formally trained on the operation of CargoScan, but a Sandia staff member brushed my objection aside. "No worries," he said. "Just follow the instructions in the manual."

"It's *idiot* proof," Doug added, smiling.

I took a seat at the console, and we began implementing a scenario where a railcar carrying a missile would be scanned by the CargoScan system. I followed the instructions as they appeared in the manual, pushing the designated buttons on cue.

Everything was going fine until Doug interjected, "We have a breach of the safety zone," he said. "One of the Soviet factory workers has accidentally opened the gate, potentially exposing himself to lethal doses of radiation."

I flipped through the manual to the page for emergencies, and then followed the instructions for shutting the system down. Midway through my efforts, the entire CargoScan computer froze. One of the Sandia representatives took my place at the console and tried to reboot the system, but to no avail. Other Sandia experts gathered around, reviewing the steps I had taken to see if I had inadvertently deviated from procedure and caused the system to freeze.

It was soon clear that I had done nothing wrong—I had followed the procedures as written. But there was a flaw, a step that had been left in the procedures that should have been taken out. Moreover, it was a step that an experienced operator would have known was wrong and would not have implemented—at least that is what the Sandia representatives were saying in their defense.

"There is no room for error in Votkinsk," Doug countered. "Maybe an idiot would have known not to push that button. But Marines follow orders and execute the process as it is written. You said the system was 'Marine proof.' Clearly it is not."

The frozen computer would take more than a month to fix, pushing CargoScan even further behind schedule, and costing millions of dollars. I expressed concern that I would be blamed for this delay. My fears were put to rest as Doug and I drove away from the TOSI facility.

"I've always been told that when you have a difficult job to do, you send in the Marines," Doug said. "And I always thought that that was a load of horse manure."

Doug looked at me and smiled. "They told me CargoScan was ready, so I decided to send in the Marines." He laughed. "You did fine." He chuckled under his breath. "'Marine proof,' my ass."

The Great American Novel

WHEN I WAS FIRST assigned to OSIA, it was to fill an "intelligence analyst" position. The OSIA Director, General Lajoie, eliminated it. The message was clear—OSIA was an inspection agency, whose sole mission was to implement the provisions of the INF Treaty.

It was *not* in the business of intelligence collection.

This did not mean that OSIA did not need intelligence support. We did. The Defense Intelligence College (DIC), located on Bolling Air Force Base and operated by the Defense Intelligence Agency (DIA), was responsible for organizing tailored training for prospective inspectors on the recognition of treaty limited items—the missiles and launchers that were scheduled to be eliminated under the treaty.

Likewise, the CIA's Arms Control Intelligence Staff (ACIS), responsible for supporting the intelligence community's role in formulating arms control policy, was given the task of coordinating intelligence community briefings regarding the various sites that were to be inspected. This would include the production of site diagrams that would be carried by the inspectors during the conduct of their mission.

Dr. David Osias, a career DIA official, had been detailed to the CIA as the Director of ACIS. He had extensive experience in intelligence analysis (much of it in technical areas relating to arms control, ballistic missiles, and nuclear weapons). He and his small staff of dedicated analysts and intelligence managers oversaw ACIS's work in monitoring Soviet compliance with and OSIA's implementation of the INF Treaty.[2] Osias and his staff were fully engaged in the dual tasks of helping guide the INF Treaty through a very contentious Senate ratification process and organizing to support the OSIA inspection effort with pre-inspection briefings and post-inspection debriefings.

Within OSIA, the Inspection Division had a well-established relationship with the intelligence community for pre-inspection support. This sharply contrasted with Portal Monitoring, responsible for the establishment of the Votkinsk Portal Monitoring Inspection Facility (VPMF), a full-time presence of US inspectors who would man a technologically advanced monitoring and verification facility, of which CargoScan was a part, outside the gates of the Votkinsk Final Assembly Plant. Portal Monitoring's pre-implementation coordination with ACIS was virtually non-existent. This was due more in part to operational reality than organizational malfeasance; the personnel assigned to Portal Monitoring were too busy trying to define the scope and scale of their mission, let alone what, if any, intelligence support they would require from ACIS.

There was, however, a modicum of coordination. In May 1988, for instance, ACIS sent a briefing team to OSIA to provide insight into what they knew and did not know about what was going on in Votkinsk. Such briefings were, by their very nature, extremely sensitive; a memorandum from the former Director of the CIA, William Casey, to the Chief of ACIS, dated December 19, 1983, referred to "gaps" in the ability of the US intelligence community to carry out this important task. While the specific nature of these "gaps" were classified, they were apparently significant enough to warrant the attention of the Director, who was concerned not only about "deficiencies," but also the costs and timelines associated with the unspecified "capabilities" designed to overcome them.[3]

One of the problems we encountered in our effort to learn more about Votkinsk was the fact that at the time of the briefing we were still in our temporary offices in the Coast Guard headquarters building. It was not cleared for certain arms control-related programs, which had their own classification designations and levels of compartmentalization. As such, the ACIS presentation was a disjointed affair, with the briefers dancing around certain issues.

Two products, both classified at the Secret level, were left for our temporary retention so we could better familiarize ourselves with the place we were going to inspect. One was an imagery-based study prepared by the Joint Air Reconnaissance Intelligence Centre (JARIC), a British imagery analysis organization. The analysis contained in this report was surprisingly detailed and, as it turned out, accurate, regarding Soviet missile production in Votkinsk.

The other I initially thought was a parody—a study prepared by an independent contractor, Sierra Pacific, which examined various scenarios by which the Soviets could smuggle missiles out of the Votkinsk Final Assembly Plant under the noses of the inspectors. Two such scenarios were featured. The first involved tunneling, the second the use of dirigibles which would fly under the cover of darkness and lift missiles out of the factory to an off-site location a few kilometers away for transfer to ground equipment and subsequent transport. Neither scenario seemed plausible, but their mere existence underscored the extent to which the detractors of the INF Treaty would go in their quest to undermine the treaty's viability.

There were two main intelligence issues regarding monitoring the missiles exiting the Votkinsk Final Assembly Plant. The first dealt with a possible follow-on to the SS-25, the second with covert SS-20 production. From a monitoring standpoint, a follow-on to the SS-25 was not really our business. It was assumed that once such a missile entered production the Soviets would declare it and provide enough technical information to enable the inspectors to differentiate it from an SS-20.

The second, however, represented the heart and soul of our monitoring mission. In their declaration made as part of the INF treaty, the Soviets had provided a detailed breakdown of the number of SS-20 missiles in their inventory. According to press reports published prior to the ratification of the INF Treaty, several analysts within the intelligence community had taken umbrage at the number of SS-20 missiles declared by the Soviet Union—650. While ACIS found that number believable, the DIA held that the Soviets had produced upwards of 1,000 SS-20s.

The DIA was also the source of analysis supporting possible cheating scenarios, including one theory built around the alleged existence of a covert force of SS-20 boosters intended to launch nuclear devices into the atmosphere over Soviet territory. These purportedly would then be detonated, creating a so-called "dome of light" which would destroy US warheads as they re-entered the atmosphere. For this theory to work, however, the Soviets would have had to produce up to 350 additional SS-20 missiles above and beyond the numbers declared. (This fight became politicized when the detractors of the INF Treaty in the US intelligence community—and there were many—leaked intelligence about the "dome of light" to the Senate, prompting Senator Jesse Helms to write a letter to William Webster, the Director of the CIA, in January 1988 expressing his concerns.[4])

To better support the OSIA mission, ACIS piggy-backed a support team onto OSIA's Field Office–Europe's "Gateway" facility, located in a remote corner of the Rhein Main Air Force Base, outside of Frankfurt, West Germany. "Gateway" was a two-story building, the ground floor of which contained its administrative offices. It housed the personnel who coordinated the considerable work of managing Soviet inspections of INF-related locations throughout Europe. For most inspectors, however, "Gateway" came to symbolize what was located on the second floor. To get there, one had to physically leave the OSIA-controlled first floor of the structure and climb a set of stairs on the exterior of the building leading to the second floor. There, at the top, you were "buzzed" in through a locked door before entering the workspaces of the ACIS support team.

The ACIS presence at the Frankfurt Gateway was a classic intelligence operation. Here, analysts scampered to put together information on the various sites in the Soviet Union related to the INF Treaty using sensitive sources of information, and later helped retrieve information from the inspectors via a formal debriefing process upon their return. The walls of the ACIS "Gateway" were covered in maps of the Soviet Union and photographs of various Soviet missile hardware. Once the inspections were under way, mementoes collected during the various missions were also on display: the formal officer caps, fur *shapkas* (hats), and various *znachki* (little commemorative pins the Soviets had a penchant for producing and collecting).

The Gateway facility was still under construction when the Votkinsk advance party, of which I was a member, assembled in Frankfurt in mid-June 1988. Since we were not yet "inspectors," the advance party travelled to Moscow commercially, via Lufthansa. Our return trip was different—we rotated out with the first baseline inspection teams onboard a dedicated US Air Force C-141. By this time Gateway had transformed into a hub of beehive-like intensity and tempo, with 100% of the effort focused on prepping the next baseline inspection team and debriefing the team that had just returned.

I made a concerted effort to make myself available to the Gateway staff for debriefing, only to find that Votkinsk did not factor into their thinking—half the Gateway personnel I approached were unfamiliar with the Portal Monitoring mission and were surprised that I was in Frankfurt. Upon return to OSIA Headquarters, I reached out to ACIS about the lack of support, only to be told that the US intelligence community did not view the Portal Monitoring mission as having much intelligence value, and as such was low on their priority list dominated by the short-term inspection missions that defined the baseline inspection period.

While as inspectors, we had no mandate to carry out "intelligence collection" beyond those tasks permitted by the treaty, we were expected to know the treaty inside and out, and to ensure that the Soviets were not violating their treaty obligations. The collection of additional "intelligence" was limited to that which we could acquire through serendipity—if we could see it during normal inspection activity, then it was fair game. But if we had to do anything to gain access to information beyond that which was permitted under the treaty, then it was prohibited.

Anyone who thought that the "serendipity" rule was simply political cover for James Bond-style covert action would have been disappointed by reality. There was no room for any deviation from that guideline, and anyone who stepped over that line was either immediately subjected to corrective action or released as an inspector. Indeed, in July 1988, during the initial rotation of inspectors to Votkinsk, an inspector with a past affiliation to the CIA collected water samples in the vicinity of the Votkinsk Final Assembly Plant, believing—wrongly—that they would contain run-off from the factory that could reveal information about the composition of Soviet solid rocket fuel. When the inspector tried to turn in the samples at the Frankfurt Gateway, they were destroyed without further evaluation, and he was returned to his parent organization and banned from further involvement as an inspector. The Votkinsk Final Assembly Plant was just that—an assembly plant, with no production processes involving solid rocket fuel manufacturing taking place on its premises.

My effort to obtain copies of the Votkinsk factory newspaper, *Trudovaya Vakhta,* was another example of targeted "serendipitous" intelligence collection. The feeling within ACIS was that this newspaper would provide analysts within the Office of Soviet Analysis, the Directorate for Intelligence's premier analytical unit on all matters pertaining to the Soviet Union, with unique insight into the inner workings of the Votkinsk Machine Building Plant, including the names and functions of various departments within the plant organization, and the identities of personnel assigned to these departments.

There were rare sightings of copies of this newspaper at various locations in the city of Votkinsk. I tried going to the town library, using my interest in Russian history as an excuse, to see if there was an archive that could be accessed. There was, but the librarian, apparently well steeped in operational security, questioned my need to see current copies of the factory paper if I were, as I had claimed, merely researching the Russian Civil War.

Later, in my wanderings through town, I discovered that a copy of the paper was posted on a bulletin board inside the House of Culture. When I returned the next day to do a more substantive reading, however, I found the paper removed, never to be posted there again. The KGB, it seemed, was on to me. I never did obtain a copy of the factory paper.

I had better luck when it came to observing the work being done at the Votkinsk Final Assembly Plant. Following the first few rotations, I sought to formalize the process of recording all traffic in and out of the factory. We maintained a log of this traffic as a matter of course, but this only listed the type of vehicle (truck or railcar), identifying number (license plate or railcar number), and date and time of activity. I took a standard reporter's notebook and began recording more specific details, such as what was contained inside the railcars when they exited the facility, and what we observed on the backs of trucks entering the facility.

I cleared my intent to collect this information, and to have other inspectors collect the same information when I was not on duty, with Colonel George Connell. Connell approved the effort, with the caveat that we should be discreet in our observations and always keep the log under the control of a duty officer. He called the project "the Great American Novel" (or GAN, for short), and successive logbooks were all marked accordingly.

I began paying particular attention to the plant locomotive, and as part of the GAN project I began tracking its movements inside the facility as it moved from building to building, shuttling railcars about. I would make these observations from the temporary inspection building, as well as when I walked the perimeter of the facility, and then plot them on a diagram of the facility. I then spent countless hours (of which we had an abundance while on duty) comparing these plots with the arrival and departure of various missile components, until a pattern emerged.

I made the plant come alive in my mind's eye, visualizing the missile assembly cycle, and getting a feel for what the normal pulse of the Votkinsk Final Assembly Plant was in terms of SS-25 missile production. In this manner,

I was able to assess that the plant had the capacity to produce around 60–65 missiles per year, with a surge capability of no more than 80–85. I wrote this up in a formal analytical paper and, in the fall of 1988, delivered it to ACIS for their evaluation.

My paper set off a firestorm in the intelligence community. The missile production rate I assessed was not, in and of itself, controversial, mirroring that contained in the British JARIC imagery analysis. My assessment, however, was derived from a more current and populated data set, incorporating direct observations regarding the arrival and movement of missile components and a more comprehensive timeline of railcar movement inside the factory made on a continuous basis over a sustained period. ACIS pushed to have the report incorporated into its overall analysis of Votkinsk's production capacity, which it hoped would strengthen its case that the Soviets were complying with the INF treaty, since my data helped weaken the DIA's theory of accelerated production schedules for the SS-20 needed to sustain the notion of a covert force of up to 350 undeclared missiles.

My report also woke ACIS up to the intelligence potential of the Votkinsk Portal Monitoring activity. ACIS beefed up its Votkinsk team, which was consolidated into what became known as the Treaty Monitoring Management Office. During my rotations back to OSIA Headquarters I found myself to be a frequent visitor to CIA Headquarters to discuss my observations in greater detail with the staff there, and with other CIA analysts. By this time, we had opened a few missiles for visual inspection, and the detailed drawings that were generated by these events were of great interest to ACIS analysts.

As much as ACIS liked my report on the Votkinsk SS-25 assembly process, the same could not be said of DIA, whose assessments formed the foundation of speculation regarding the existence of a covert SS-20 missile force. Soon after ACIS published my paper, I found myself summoned to a "meeting of the minds" at DIA Headquarters, convened by an Air Force Brigadier General who was joined by a bevy of Colonels, Lieutenant Colonels, and civilians of varying seniority. This collective challenged my assessment and demanded that I change the conclusions. I pointed out that my assessments were drawn solely from my analysis of observations that I had personally made at the Votkinsk Final Assembly Plant, and that while they were free to disagree with my conclusions, unless they had a specific problem with my methodology, the facts were what they were, and the report would remain as written.

The Brigadier then reminded me, in his best Brigadier voice, that I was sticking my nose where it did not belong. Strategic assessments, he said, were done by teams of qualified analysts who worked for equally qualified managers, and their product influenced defense budgets worth hundreds of millions, if not billions, of dollars. My analysis, he noted, as well meaning as it was, was not worth the paper it was printed on. He (rightly) questioned my pedigree—barely a year ago I was junior company grade officer serving as the intelligence officer of a Marine field artillery battalion with zero experience with Soviet intercontinental ballistic missiles. Now I was writing analysis that could have a deep impact on issues pertaining to the strategic nuclear balance between the US and the Soviet Union. For the good of the country, he said, and for my own best interests, I should have the paper withdrawn.

The DIA team was exploiting both my patriotism and professional insecurities, and I was of half a mind to accede to their demands—to pull the paper until I could confirm its findings with additional information. But when the General invoked my "best interests," I perceived it as a threat, and the Marine in me took umbrage. I reminded the Brigadier, and the others assembled in the conference room, that I was there voluntarily. I pointed out that I worked for OSIA, and that I took my orders from Brigadier General Roland Lajoie, the Director of OSIA, and no one else outside the OSIA chain of command. I also pointed out that I was a Marine, and as such my "best interests" were the sole prerogative of the Marine Corps, which, I added, saw fit to assign me to OSIA. I excused myself, and left the building, convinced that my short career as a weapons inspector was finished.

I had little time to think about my confrontation with DIA, as I rotated back to Votkinsk for a tour that spanned the 1988 Christmas holiday and lasted through the end of January 1989. This trip was marked by a surge of SS-25 missiles, which exited the Final Assembly Plant in the first two weeks of January—nine in total. All these missiles had been completed, or nearly completed, by the end of December 1988, but their transport had been delayed, perhaps because of the holiday. We did not open any of these missiles (that decision was made by ACIS, which would make the call at the time the missile declaration was made by the Soviets). The purge of missiles, however, emptied out the factory of all missiles and missile components, allowing, for the first time since inspections were implemented, a direct cause-effect relationship to be assessed between what was going into the factory, and what was coming out.

While I was deployed in the Soviet Union, David Osias, together with his Votkinsk manager, Karen Schmucker, had initiated a process which resulted in the Director of the CIA, William Webster, writing me a classified letter of commendation. "What you did for us (ACIS) in INF," Karen later told me, in explaining the decision to go forward with the letter, "made the difference between that part of the operation being successful or an embarrassment."

General Lajoie presented the letter to me in a quiet ceremony in the OSIA operations room. "The dedication and total professionalism which you displayed to evoke such high-level recognition is truly impressive," he wrote in a cover letter to the award. "All of us at OSIA are proud of your accomplishment and express our gratitude for the distinction that your achievements bring to the On-Site Inspection Agency." The CIA letter of commendation was copied to several very senior government officials, and was placed in my official file at Headquarters, Marine Corps.

In a hand-written note to Colonel Connell, General Lajoie, while stating that I was to be "commended" for my actions, he emphasized that "we need to make sure that these efforts remain low key & passive." Regardless of the level of enthusiasm shown by the CIA, intelligence collection was *not* in the OSIA mission statement.

Despite the high-level recognition from the CIA Director, there continued to be fallout from the Votkinsk production analysis paper. The DIA questioned the ability of an inspector to make the kind of detailed observations I had made. As a means of rebuttal, OSIA sent several intelligence community analysts to Votkinsk as "short time" duty officers. For OSIA, it was a "win-win" arrangement—OSIA got some much-needed relief in terms of deployment tempo while the intelligence analysts got an opportunity to see Votkinsk first-hand and confirm that the potential for serendipitous collection was real.

Those in the intelligence community who doubted the findings of my paper, however, had one last trick up their sleeves. OSIA had a safe full of "Great American Novels," chock-full of the minutia that had been observed by duty personnel operating out of the Votkinsk Data Collection Center (DCC). To confirm the intelligence value of inspector observations, ACIS contracted with a well-known beltway national security consulting company, Science Applications International Corporation (SAIC), to do a detailed assessment of the data contained in the Great American Novel collection.

I was proud of the effort that had gone into making the GAN a reality. By this time, we had implemented well-oiled procedures where all inspection personnel on duty would record everything they saw regarding movement in and out of the factory. The result was a data-intensive logbook. With Colonel Connell's permission, I turned over more than a dozen volumes of the GAN to ACIS and awaited the findings.

SAIC held on to the GAN volumes for several months. Then, in the late summer of 1989 (after my CargoScan adventure at TOSI), I was summoned to a briefing at an off-site location near Dulles Airport, where ACIS reported on the SAIC findings. In short, after taking more than a hundred thousand dollars of taxpayer money, SAIC concluded that the information in the GAN was of little or no intelligence value. According to ACIS, SAIC believed the data was too fragmentary, too haphazardly collated, and too innocuous to be of any use by anyone.

I was outraged by the result. I had a proprietary interest in the viability of the GAN as a source of raw data possessing intelligence value. Now ACIS was telling me that this was not the case. I asked the ACIS analyst who had headed up this effort what he wanted to do with the dozen or so volumes of the GAN that

SAIC had returned. "They belong to you," he responded. "We have no further interest in them."

I took the copies of the GAN back to OSIA Headquarters, where I put them in a safe. Although they were technically unclassified, ACIS treated them as "Secret" because they contained observations that were protected under the terms of the treaty. I then packed my bags and returned to Votkinsk.

Over the course of the next six weeks, I poured over the copies of the GAN stored in the Duty Officer's desk in the Vokinsk Data Collection Center, trying my best to correlate what I was seeing enter the plant with what I observed exiting the plant. Complicating this analysis was the fact that there were at least two distinct missile systems being produced simultaneously by Votkinsk— the SS-25 and the *Kourier* small ICBM. Differentiating what containers were associated with which missile was a challenge.

I had an analytical breakthrough in early October. I had tracked an empty missile cannister entering the facility, followed by five additional railcars carrying a specific range of containers which I equated to being affiliated with a single SS-25. In my notes I predicted the following: "Railcar 368-98054 will exit on 1 or 2 October with an SS-25."

On October 2, 1989, at 1 PM in the afternoon, railcar 368-98054 exited the Votkinsk Final Assembly Plant carrying an SS-25 missile.

Using similar cause-effect methodology, I estimated that another railcar, 368-99714, would exit the plant on October 12, 1989, carrying a *Kourier* small ICBM. At 9.20 PM, it did exactly as I predicted.

I was able to repeat this predictive cause-effect analysis throughout my tour. There was, however, some "slop" in the data, which implied I was missing something. One of the correlations I had made was that SS-25 missiles were shipped out in railcars that fit a certain numerical pattern (368-98xxx), while the railcars used to transport the *Kourier* appeared to have their own unique numerical pattern (368-99xxx). My biggest problem was that I had a mix of components and railcars in the Final Assembly Plant that did not fit either pattern—basically a *Kourier* missile transport railcar mixed with SS-25 component-carrying railcars.

Then something happened that made me question my entire analytical "breakthrough"—an SS-25 missile exited in a railcar with the 368-99xxx number sequence that I previously had only associated with railcars carrying the *Kourier* small ICBM. Fortunately, this missile was designated by ACIS to be opened, allowing further investigation.

During cannister opening events, the inspectors get to stare at the front end of the SS-25 missile, with the third stage and post-boost vehicle front and center in their field of vision. By this time, each inspector had developed their own routine regarding what they were looking for. The most important thing was to confirm the existence of a third stage—if the missile had that, it was probably not an SS-20 (although only by imaging the second stage using CargoScan would hardliners, who believed that the Soviets could produce elaborate third-stage mockups to disguise an illegal SS-20, truly be satisfied).

Inspectors would then go through a mental checklist of the repeatable observables—the four thrust vector devices, centering rings and pads, rivet patterns, and so forth. I had, by this time, been put in charge of training personnel assigned to Votkinsk regarding the priorities for observations made during cannister openings, so there was a uniform approach to data collection.

As was the case with previous missile viewings, I ran through my personal observation routine and in doing so, found an anomaly—an approximately 18-inch-long metallic strip inserted midway on the side of the post-boost vehicle. It appeared to have been riveted onto the body of the missile and lay flush with the surface. By this time, the other inspectors were well versed in the drill; upon our return to the DCC, I sketched out the basics of what I had observed in the Great American Novel, and then had each of the inspectors involved in the cannister opening review it. To a person, they had seen the same thing as I had, and we all agreed that this metallic "bar" had never been observed on earlier cannister openings.

During my outbound rotation through Frankfurt, I provided the Gateway debriefers a description of what had been observed. Upon return to OSIA Headquarters, I was immediately summoned by ACIS to brief them on my findings at their offices in CIA Headquarters. After listening to me and looking at the detailed sketch I had made of the anomaly, Karen Schmucker sent me down the hall to meet with an analyst who specialized in telemetry. He surmised that the anomaly could be a slit antenna used to transmit telemetry related to some sort of testing program.

Armed with this insight, I made my way to another part of the building, where the Office of Imagery Analysis (OIA), the CIA's in-house photographic interpretation unit, was located. There I spoke with the OIA analyst responsible for monitoring the Plesetsk missile test facility, where the SS-25 and other missiles had undergone their flight testing. He had a checklist of visual "cues" that served as indicators that a missile test was imminent. While a cursory examination of available imagery revealed nothing suspicious, the analyst thanked me for the heads up—he would monitor the situation closely.

Back at OSIA Headquarters, I juggled my normal responsibilities with intensive analysis of the Great American Novel. I was scheduled to return to Votkinsk in mid-January 1990, and I wanted to nail down the predictive pattern analysis I had been working on before my next rotation. After three weeks of work, straddling the Christmas and New Year's holiday, I finally was able to distill the data into a repeatable formula and put it down in a report which was forwarded to ACIS right before my departure for Votkinsk. In short, my paper showed that, using the data contained in the GAN, I was able to predict, with near certainty, the number and type of missiles being assembled inside the Votkinsk Final Assembly Plant, and the date when these missiles would depart the factory.

Simply put, I had broken the code about the Votkinsk Final Assembly Plant's production cycle.

The Phone Call

I ARRIVED IN VOTKINSK in early January 1990, and like everyone else at the Portal Monitoring Facility, was caught up in the drama surrounding CargoScan. Site preparation for receiving CargoScan had been underway since January 1989, with the Soviets pouring 1,000 metric tons of concrete, and installing over 4,500 feet of conduit and 17,000 feet of electrical wire to construct the 2,640 square foot shelter that would house the giant x-ray equipment and protect those operating it from harmful radiation.

The modules containing the x-ray devices and support systems began arriving in early October 1989, with the final placement of the equipment taking place on November 16. By early January 1990, installation and testing had progressed to the point that CargoScan was considered safe to power up. A team of radiation safety specialists were dispatched to Votkinsk to carry out a radiation survey, which was completed by January 13, 1990. At that point it was deemed by the US side that CargoScan had reached operational capability.

There was, however, one major catch—the Soviets believed that the system, as installed, did not conform to the specifications set forth in the Memorandum of Agreement (MoA). The Soviet core objections were that the shutter to the actual imaging device was not non-transparent when operating at the established x-ray dose rate used during actual imaging operations, meaning that CargoScan would be capable of imaging an object even when the shutter was shut. Moreover, the Soviets held that the scan area proposed by the inspectors exceeded the area established under the MoA, and that the width of the irradiated area was greater than that specified in the MoA. Finally, the Soviets noted that there were no procedures in place regarding the erasure of any image taken that exceeded the specifications set by the MoA, and as such they could not permit operation of CargoScan until such a procedure had been finalized and agreed upon.

The Soviet and US diplomats who negotiated the MoA in December 1988 had spent the next ten months in Geneva, Switzerland wrangling over the extremely complicated issues surrounding the installation and operation of CargoScan before deeming the task too hard and punting the matter to the Votkinsk factory personnel and OSIA inspectors on site, who were authorized to develop local procedures to resolve the myriad of outstanding issues. This meant that the personnel who were originally mandated to carry out the more perfunctory tasks of maintenance and basic operation of CargoScan in Votkinsk were now responsible for coming up with extremely complex technical solutions to problems that had not been envisioned when the MoA was written.

There were two categories of inspectors in Votkinsk. The INF Treaty allowed for 30 inspectors to be onsite at any given time. OSIA was responsible for filling five of these slots with officers who would serve as Site Commander and Deputy Site Commander. The OSIA officer who was most familiar with not only the operations of CargoScan, but also the technical minutia of the MoA which outlined the technical specifications of how CargoScan would be permitted to be operated under the terms of the INF treaty, was an Army First Lieutenant named John Sartorius. John assumed this responsibility unwillingly—the field grade officer who was supposed to be the technical lead, and who had sat in on the technical discussions carried out in Geneva, Switzerland, had proven not to be up to the task, prompting the OSIA leadership to pass this burden on to John who, in typical fashion, then exceeded all expectations.

The other category were civilian contractors, part of a contingent hired by Hughes Technical Service Company (HTSC) to provide an on-site presence of 25 personnel to maintain and operate the Votkinsk Portal Monitoring Facility. The technical lead for HTSC on CargoScan was a young engineer named Sam Israelit, whose formal job description was "construction supervisor." Sam had performed yeoman's work throughout the entire CargoScan installation process and was intimately familiar with every aspect of the system, making him the go-to guy for coming up with a response to the Soviet concerns. He was ably assisted by another HTSC employee, Jim Lusher, whose knowledge of CargoScan's technical intricacies were second to none.

Sam and John, with the support of Jim Lusher, quickly became the brain trust that OSIA and HTSC turned to in their work with their Soviet counterparts on the development of the local CargoScan operating procedures. Thanks in large part to their efforts, CargoScan was deemed ready for operation by mid-January 1990. Only the Soviet objections prevented this from occurring.

Like everyone else on site, Sam and John were under extreme political pressure to get CargoScan up and running—Senator Helms' January 12, 1990 letter weighed heavy on them, and upon us all. While both Sam and John believed that the Soviets were technically and legally correct in their objections, the instructions from OSIA Headquarters were to brush the Soviet concerns aside, and instead to cobble together a system of "local understandings" and "interim procedures" which created the perception of addressing the Soviet concerns without resolving the identified problems.

This approach almost worked. With Sam and John as the guiding force, the inspection team, headed up by the Site Commander, an Air Force Lieutenant Colonel named Mark Dues, engaged in a constant series of meetings with their Soviet counterparts, submitting draft procedures for the safe operation of CargoScan while providing detailed technical reasoning for keeping the US parameters in place. Operating under strict instructions from OSIA Headquarters, Mark Dues pressed the Soviets to "arrive at a mutually satisfactory timetable to come to an understanding on local procedures, implement them on an interim basis, and commence full operations," noting that it was the US intention "that the first missile to exit the plant in February [1990] be subject to imaging" by CargoScan.

At a meeting on January 31, 1990, Anatoli Tomilov, the head of Department 162 (the entity within the Votkinsk Machine Building Plant organization responsible for dealing with US inspectors), let it be known that contrary to the US position, the Soviets did not consider the CargoScan system to be operational, and that they would refuse to allow any SS-25 missile departing the Votkinsk factory to be imaged by CargoScan until all their concerns had been satisfied. In a final effort to reach a mutually acceptable understanding, the US inspectors, together with their Soviet counterparts, carried out a mock-inspection on February 2, 1990, using a 6-axle railcar carrying a simulated SS-25 missile, which ran CargoScan through its entire operational cycle. At the end of this mock inspection, the inspectors prepared a report which detailed the procedures—many of them developed locally—necessary for the safe operation of CargoScan in a manner which would conform to the intent, if not the letter, of the MOA.

At the conclusion of the mock inspection, Mark Dues and Anatoli Tomilov met and agreed that the interim procedures that had been developed from the mock inspection were sufficient to be used to image an actual SS-25 missile. The two of them drafted up a written statement which declared that CargoScan would be declared operational as of February 9, 1990, and any missile which left the Votkinsk Final Assembly Plant on or after that date would be subject to inspection using CargoScan in accordance with the agreed upon interim procedures. The agreement noted that "both sides will continue seeking resolution through higher channels" of differences which existed regarding outstanding technical issues, while allowing the agreed upon interim procedures to be in force until resolution of these issues was received. This agreement, drafted on February 2,1990, was to take effect on February 5, 1990.

The inspectors and their counterparts at the Votkinsk Final Assembly Plant had turned the table on those officials who had put the task of resolving the CargoScan problem in their hands to begin with. The interim procedures were heavily caveated with annotations which explained that before they could be finalized, they would need to be certified as correct by diplomats from both the US and Soviet Union. In the meantime, however, CargoScan would be made operational, presenting the diplomats with a *fait accompli*. Any decision to modify the CargoScan procedures, and thus further delay CargoScan, would be on the shoulders of these diplomats.

While Sam and John struggled to create the conditions under which CargoScan could be made operational, I continued to monitor the movement of missile components into the factory. It quickly became clear to me that much of what I was observing fit the pattern of the "anomaly" observed the previous November—the SS-25 with the suspected antennae modification that was shipped out in a 368-99xxx railcar. According to my calculations, the Soviets had enough components to assemble three of these "anomalous" missiles, but were apparently delaying their departure, since they failed to be shipped out based upon what I had assessed to be the normal "pulse" of factory operations. (In addition to the three "anomalous" missiles, I assessed that there were several normal SS-25 missiles, as well as at least one *Kourier* missile, inside the plant, either completing assembly or waiting to be shipped.)

The dispute over the operational status of CargoScan seemed to be the most likely cause—we had, since mid-January 1990, declared that we were ready to scan the next missile out of the facility. The Soviets appeared to want to avoid a confrontation and were holding off on shipping any finished missiles from the plant until both sides agreed that CargoScan was indeed operational.

But something was amiss. During the January 31, 1990, meeting with US inspectors, Anatolyi Tomilov had expressed concern over the impending US measurement of an actual SS-25 second stage using CargoScan, declaring that the Soviet side must be shown the US side's methods for determining measurement tolerance levels. Tomilov noted that there were going to be "differences" between what was going to be measured by CargoScan, and what the Soviets had declared as the missile measurements in the MoA, and that he wanted both sides to be prepared when this occurred.

The agreement reached between Mark Dues and Anatoli Tomilov to begin imaging missiles on February 9, when seen in the context of Tomilov's comments regarding the existence of non-standard second stages on at least some of the missiles ready to be shipped out of the Votkinsk Final Assembly Plant, caught my attention. It appeared to me that the Soviets, through this agreement, had created a window where non-standard missiles could be shipped out of Votkinsk without being subjected to CargoScan inspections. This window would open at the stroke of midnight on February 5, and close at the same time on February 8.

I was convinced that the Soviets did not want the US to use CargoScan on these three "anomalous" missiles and, as such, would use the three-day gap between February 6 and February 8 to ship them out of the factory. Moreover, I strongly believed that these concerns should be communicated to OSIA Headquarters.

What I had to say, however, could not be communicated over the phone line in the DCC—the Soviets were monitoring every word. Back in 1988 I had instituted a "duress" code with Colonel Connell, where if I said a specific phrase over the DCC line, it meant that I would be travelling to Moscow, where I would use a secure line in the Embassy for communications. This system had never been used—until now. I dialed Colonel Connell using the duty officer phone, and we spoke about routine matters. In the middle of the conversation, I used the duress phrase. Connell did not skip a beat, causing me to wonder if he had picked up on the code.

After I hung up, I approached Mark Dues and told him I had to go to Moscow. I was not scheduled to fly to Moscow until later that month as part of the normal rotation, and my intervention meant I would be bumping someone else off the list. In short order, Mark added me to the rotation, and that night I found myself on a Yak-42, winging my way to the Soviet capital.

Under normal circumstances, the Moscow rotation, which comprised an OSIA officer and an HTSC inspector, would arrive in Moscow in the evening, and check into accommodations at the Ukraina Hotel located in downtown Moscow, reserving Sunday for business at the Embassy. This was not, however, a normal situation, and as soon as I checked in at the Ukraina Hotel, I made my way to the US Embassy, just a short walk away. The Marine manning the gate recognized me from a photograph that had been taped on the wall of his post, saluted smartly, and buzzed me in without question. "Welcome back, Sir," he said. "Someone will be here shortly to escort you."

To my relief, Colonel Connell had, in fact, picked up on the duress phrase, and had called ahead, arranging for me to gain access to a secure phone. The Marine placed a call on an internal Embassy phone, and within a minute I was greeted by a man in civilian attire, who shook my hand without introducing himself. He led me up several flights of stairs, until we came to a door guarded by more Marines. This was the most secure part of the Embassy, home to the CIA Moscow Station and other secretive intelligence activities. Once inside, I was led to a specially constructed enclosure—the "bubble"—inside of which was a chair and a desk, on which was a STU-III secure phone.

Safely ensconced inside the "bubble," I dialed the number for OSIA, and then activated the cryptological "key," scrambling the signal to a level that permitted conversations of up to "Top Secret." On the other end was Colonel Connell. I got straight to the point. "The Soviets have three missiles inside the plant that appear to be different from both the SS-25 and the partitioned railcar" (the term "partitioned railcar" was given to railcars carrying the *Kourier* small ICBM, which was named after a specific inspection procedure that had been agreed upon with the Soviets back in the fall of 1988).

I explained to Connell my analysis regarding anomalous data suggestive of a third missile type being shipped from Votkinsk and informed him that this information had been previously shared with ACIS, together with the methodology used to make this prediction. "I believe," I said, "that the Soviets could take advantage of the window created by the agreement to start CargoScan on February 9 to get these missiles out."

Citing the Soviet statements of January 31, in which they suggested that the results of a CargoScan image of a second stage may not conform with the measurements provided for in the Memorandum of Understanding, I told Connell that I assessed that the Soviets most likely would not want these missiles scanned. "If they do not exit these missiles by February 9," I said, "then we are looking at the possibility of a crisis, since the Soviets will likely want to exit these missiles without CargoScan being used." I paused. "I wanted to give you a heads up so you can plan accordingly."

Connell listened carefully. I had fully expected to be questioned in detail as to how I was reaching these conclusions, and even chastised for playing "Chicken Little," claiming the sky was falling when it was not. Instead, Connell simply repeated what I had told him, asked me if I had anything else to add, and then thanked me before hanging up. Connell immediately briefed General Lajoie, and then informed ACIS.

By this time, Votkinsk had become an important intelligence target for ACIS, which brought in a senior arms control expert named John J. Bird to head up an expanded staff of analysts, including an entire team dedicated to Votkinsk, in an expanded version of the TMMO now known as the "Treaty Monitoring Center," or TMC. Bird concurred with my assessment that the Soviets could rush the missiles in question out of the Votkinsk Final Assembly Plant before CargoScan became operational. Based upon this concurrence, and with Connell's recommendation, General Lajoie decided on the spot to cancel the on-site agreement regarding the February 9 CargoScan start date. It was also decided that Connell would fly out to Votkinsk to personally ascertain the scope of the problem, as well as try to keep the operation of CargoScan on track.

Crisis

TO SAY THAT the Soviets were upset by the decision to nullify the agreement regarding making CargoScan operational on February 9 was an understatement. In a sternly worded memorandum delivered to the inspectors on February 7, Anatoli Tomilov made it clear that, going forward, the Soviets were going to take a hard line regarding the technical issues of disagreement. "I have taken into consideration your verbal declaration of February 6, 1990," Tomilov wrote, "that the American memorandum S02-Feb 90, signed by you (i.e., Mark Dues) on February 5, is groundless."

Tomilov then stated that the "protracted conversations at recent meetings" regarding the criteria for the operation of CargoScan "have not moved us forward." Tomilov then requested that the US side provide "satisfactory explanations" on how to resolve the existing Soviet concerns. "I hope," Tomilov concluded, "that the American side will make every effort, as has the Soviet side, that the first inspection cycle using CargoScan apparatus does not lead to a conflicting situation." The only way to avoid such an outcome, Tomilov wrote, was for "the completion of an agreement on the criteria for a successful inspection."

But the fact of the matter was that, in the eyes of the Soviets, Lieutenant Colonel Dues had lost all credibility as a negotiating partner who operated in good faith. While John Sartorious, Sam Israelit, and Jim Lusher continued to work to come up with possible solutions to the Soviet objections, it was clear that no progress could be expected until Colonel Connell arrived on site and took over the negotiations.

Connell arrived in Votkinsk on February 14 as part of a mid-week rotation that saw Mark Dues depart, replaced as Site Commander by Army Lieutenant Colonel Roy Peterson. To maintain the OSIA brain trust regarding local discussions with the Soviets, Connell had John Sartorious, who was originally scheduled to rotate out with Mark Dues, remain in Votkinsk for the duration of Connell's visit. John's replacement, Air Force Captain Stu O'Neill, had arrived with Connell, providing the site with three veteran duty officers (John, Stu, and myself), a rare occurrence.

Colonel Connell arrived with a very straightforward agenda—the US was going to insist on using CargoScan on the next missile exiting Votkinsk, and unless the Soviets wanted to create a situation where the US side would be compelled to declare a treaty "ambiguity," creating a diplomatic crisis and empowering those who had been lobbying against the successful implementation of the INF treaty, there needed to be some movement on resolving the outstanding issues.

In response to OSIA dispatching Colonel Connell, the Soviets had the Defense Industry representative for Votkinsk, Lev Kokurin, travel to Votkinsk to participate in the talks. While the Soviets showed a willingness to work with Roy Peterson to overcome the remaining issues in dispute, they made it clear that the spirit of compromise that had existed on February 5, when the deal worked out between Mark Dues and Anotoli Tomilov was signed, was no more. Colonel Connell noted that both sides had agreed to make CargoScan operational on February 9, meaning that the procedures that had been agreed to on February 5 should still be valid at the present time. Why, he asked, couldn't the next missile exiting the plant be inspected using CargoScan?

Kokurin expressed his amazement that the US failed to execute the February 5 agreement, given the emphasis that it had placed on making CargoScan operational. Kokurin observed that it seemed to him like the US was deliberately creating conditions designed to keep CargoScan from going online and manipulating these conditions so that it would look as if the Soviets were the party responsible for failing to comply with the treaty.

Connell stated that he sympathized with the Soviets about what had happened regarding the agreement, noting that while Mark Dues had indeed negotiated the deal, it was subject to final review and approval by OSIA headquarters.

Here, Connell was surprisingly forthcoming, telling Kokurin that General Lajoie "had concerns that a number of missiles might leave the plant between the date of the agreement (February 5) and February 9, when CargoScan was scheduled to go online." Connell again asked why, if they had an agreement that would have allowed CargoScan to become operational by February 9, could they not simply use that same agreement structure today, and allow the US side to image the next missile to leave the plant?

Kokurin responded by noting that when the US backed out of the agreement, the agreement was voided. As far as the Soviets were concerned, they were back to square one, with the US needing to answer to the satisfaction of the Soviet side the remaining outstanding issues before CargoScan could be declared operational. Before the first day's meeting concluded, Connell reiterated his opening point—the US was going to insist on imaging the next missile to exit the plant, and if the Soviet side refused, then the US side would have no choice but to declare an ambiguity and follow the procedures outlined in the treaty for such occasions.

For the next three days Sam Israelit and John Sartorius were engaged in a series of seemingly endless meetings with their Soviet counterparts to resolve the remaining issues. On February 16, the two sides carried out a repeat of the mock inspection of February 2, using a 6-axle railcar carrying an empty cannister that, while smaller than that used for an SS-25 missile, allowed the two sides to operate the CargoScan system under as realistic conditions as possible. One of the major problems facing Sam and John was the fact that while the treaty and the MoA relied on the inviolability of words, they were dealing with the reality of physics. Simply altering the language of the MoA could not overcome issues involving radiation, energy, and time-distance relationships.

CargoScan Operating Schematic

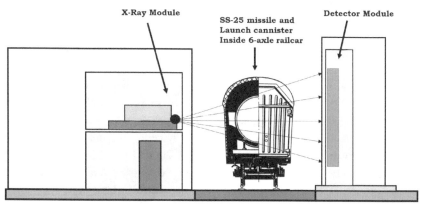

Figure One: CargoScan operating schematic

Sam Israelit received permission to call engineers at Varian, the company that produced the digital detectors used in the CargoScan imaging system, to come up with a working solution to the issue of scanning dimensions and power requirements. Following these conversations, Sam and John produced detailed schematics to explain the science behind the US position to the Soviets. Despite the herculean effort of all involved, by the time Colonel Connell was scheduled to leave Votkinsk, on the evening of February 19, the two sides remained unable to bridge the gap on critical points of disagreement.

The final meeting between the US and Soviet sides before Connell's departure proved to be an exercise in futility. While Anatoli Tomilov called for additional technical meetings to resolve the remaining outstanding issues, Connell was very blunt as to what the US position was: "CargoScan is ready." The US would insist on being able to image the next missile leaving the plant, Connell said. If the Soviets refused, an ambiguity would be declared.

Recognizing the inevitability of this outcome, Connell asked the Soviets to begin working with the inspectors on the specific wording should be included on any inspection report involving a CargoScan-related ambiguity to lessen the impact of what would assuredly be "a strained moment" for both sides. "We must resolve our differences unemotionally," Connell concluded.

Connell and his party left for Moscow that evening, taking John Sartorious with them. One of the last instructions given by Connell to Roy Peterson was to begin drafting boilerplate language that would be used in the event an ambiguity was eventually declared.

In the days that followed, Sam Israelit did his absolute best to come up with solutions to the technical issues raised by the Soviets. On February 27, Anatoli Tomilov delivered a final consolidated list of the Soviet concerns. The next day, February 28, Sam Israelit conducted what amounted to a *tour de force*, responding with great precision and technical detail to each point that the Soviets had raised. Even Anatoli Tomilov was impressed, agreeing that many of the solutions proposed by Sam would appear to be acceptable to the Soviets.

But then the meeting turned somewhat ominous. Tomilov turned to Roy Peterson, and asked him directly: "Does the US side consider CargoScan to be operational?" Peterson responded affirmatively.

Tomilov stated that, despite the progress that had been made, the two sides could not seem to come to a final agreement regarding CargoScan. He noted that while the US agreed to certain things during a meeting, in the end the result was always the same—the US insisting that CargoScan was operational, and the Soviets maintaining that it was not. "I might have to send out a missile today to resolve this problem," Tomilov announced. He told Peterson that it was not necessary for the US side to continue wasting time providing answers to the Soviet proposals, because in the end these amounted to little more than mere suggestions for solving problems created by the US side.

On that note, the meeting adjourned, leaving the US inspectors wondering if Tomilov was bluffing about the missile.

Thursday, March 1, 1990, began pretty much like every other day that had transpired since the US initiated portal monitoring inspections back in July 1988. At 7 am, the day shift, with Stu O'Neill serving as duty officer, took over from the outgoing night shift. Safety checks were conducted of the site, logs opened and maintained, and duty rosters were exchanged with the Soviet side. A steady flow of vehicles entered and exited the main gate of the Votkinsk Final Assembly Plant, each of which was dutifully monitored and recorded by the inspectors.

The normalcy came to a halt when, at 2.20 PM, the Soviet duty officer delivered a declaration notifying the US inspectors that a 6-axle railcar with a missile was going to exit the portal at 2.50 PM.

Tomilov, it turned out, had not been bluffing.

Stu notified Roy Peterson of the declaration, and then called OSIA headquarters per standard operating procedure, informing the duty officer there of the missile declaration. The Soviets had exited dozens of SS-25s from the portal since inspections had begun, all without incident. This one, however, would cause an international incident.

Because the US and Soviets were still working on resolving the outstanding technical issues regarding the operation of CargoScan, the Soviets had positioned a 6-axle railcar containing an empty cannister in the CargoScan area to assist in measurement tests. If the US were to be using CargoScan to image the declared missile, however, the test railcar needed to be removed. At 2.33 PM, Stu formally issued this request, only to be informed by the Soviet shift leader that the request had been refused. Stu notified Peterson, who immediately called the Soviets and demanded that the test railcar be removed within ten minutes. The Soviets failed to comply.

At 2.50 PM, the Soviets exited a 6-axle railcar, number 368-99565, from the portal. When I saw the number, my heart jumped—it was one of the "anomalous" missiles I had predicted the Soviets would seek to exit without being imaged by CargoScan.

Stu oversaw the measurements of the railcar and the missile cannister it contained by the team of duty inspectors, and then notified the Soviets of his intent to scan the missile, as permitted under the terms of the INF treaty, using CargoScan.

The Soviets refused to permit the missile to be scanned by CargoScan.

By this time, OSIA headquarters had been mobilized, and Colonel Connell was standing by, waiting to see what happened next.

With Stu busy coordinating with OSIA headquarters, I was called upon to assist Lieutenant Colonel Peterson in interfacing with the Soviets. For me, the most critical thing was to keep things calm. I met with the Soviet shift leader, Yevgenii Efremov, with whom I had had a good working relationship that dated back to the very first inspections conducted in early July 1988. (Indeed, Efremov had invited me to his home on New Year's Eve a little more than a year ago to help ring in the New Year.) We greeted each other, and quickly established that the unfolding events were out of our control, and that we would do our respective jobs as we were instructed, with no malice or anger toward one another.

The first thing we did was to agree to move the railcar to an environmentally controlled building purpose-built by the Soviets for carrying out visual inspections of missiles inside the launch cannister. The treaty allowed for eight such inspections per year. By moving the railcar into the inspection building, I was not committing to carrying out one of the eight allocated visual inspections— that was a decision made by OSIA, in coordination with ACIS, once they had been notified that a missile was leaving the factory. Rather, both Efremov and I were cognizant of the reality that we might be in for a long standoff, and given the frigid temperatures, it made more sense to get it out of the weather.

At 4 PM, I joined Roy Peterson in a meeting with Efremov and Tomilov, where we reiterated our request to scan the declared missile-carrying railcar using CargoScan. The Soviets refused. At 6 PM we reconvened, and for the next 45 minutes tried in vain to get the Soviets to change their minds.

At 7 PM I took over from Stu O'Neill as the night duty officer. Almost immediately I was confronted by the Soviets trying to send a locomotive to the inspection building, where it presumably would hook up to the 6-axle missile-carrying railcar and exit the Votkinsk Final Assembly Plant premises. On Colonel Peterson's orders, I refused to turn the signal light at the first checkpoint outside the factory gate "green." By keeping it "red" I was forcing the locomotive to hold in place.

Roy Peterson continued to meet with Tomilov to get the Soviets to agree to allow CargoScan to be used to scan the missile-carrying railcar, but to no avail. Finally, at 7.37 PM, Tomilov announced that the Soviets would remove the railcar from the environmentally controlled inspection building in five minutes time. Peterson relayed this information to Connell, who informed Roy that the US government had issued a formal request to Soviet authorities in Moscow for a 48-hour delay so that the issue could be discussed at higher levels. Tomilov received the information and left to consult with his superiors.

At 12.33 am on the morning of March 2, with the locomotive still halted at the traffic light, I contacted Efremov to ask of what Tomilov's response was. Efremov informed me that Tomilov had gone home for the night. I advised Efremov that it seemed clear that no decision regarding the movement of the railcar was going to be made that night, and that, in the interest of not interfering with the functions of the plant, I proposed that the locomotive be returned to the facility, and that all non-missile related rail traffic be allowed to proceed without delay. Efremov agreed. We also agreed to lock and seal the environmentally controlled inspection building, effectively freezing the missile-carrying railcar inside until a final decision was made.

The 48-hour delay turned into 72, then 96, and still no word came down from either Moscow or Washington, DC on how to proceed. Roy Peterson, Stu O'Neill, and I, accompanied by Sam Israelit, continued to meet with Tomilov daily to narrow the scope of the issues keeping the Soviets from declaring CargoScan operational, but to no avail. We heard rumors from the Soviets about a special delegation of CargoScan experts and policymakers from both the US and Soviet sides being dispatched to Votkinsk sometime around March 11 for the purpose of resolving the outstanding issues once and for all, but nothing from OSIA.

I continued to believe that the Soviets were going to exit the three "anomalous" missiles I assessed were in the plant before any final agreement was made, to keep them from being scanned and avoiding a broader discussion about the 2nd stage discrepancies alluded to by Tomilov on January 31. The longer the impasse dragged on, however, the more it appeared that the Soviets were planning on holding tight until the rumored delegation arrived.

Then, on March 7, during one of our routine meetings discussing the fate of CargoScan, Tomilov presented the US side with a memorandum, titled "Levelling of Economic Sanctions against the American side for the delay of SS-25 missiles caused by the CargoScan system's lack of readiness for inspection procedures in accordance with the MoA."

The memorandum reiterated the Soviet position regarding the various discrepancies that prevented them from declaring CargoScan operational. The memorandum then declared that the Soviets were declaring the US side to be in violation of the INF treaty, in so far as the US inspectors had impeded and delayed the inspected facility's operations, "causing significant economic damage to the Votkinsk Machine Building Plant."

The memorandum noted that "because only one missile may be located in the inspection area at any one time, [the US side is] delaying the exit of six additional missiles that have been loaded in railcars and ready for departure."

This number correlated well with my own accounting, which held that the Soviets had three "anomalous" missiles (two inside the plant, and one secured in the environmentally controlled inspection building), four normal SS-25 missiles, and one *Kourier* small ICBM ready to be shipped from the plant (the Soviet number did not include the *Kourier*, which was not a declarable missile under the INF treaty).

The memorandum went on to warn the US inspectors that "economic sanctions of 165,000 rubles for each of the seven non-treaty-limited SS-25 missiles that have been delayed will be levied against the American side to compensate for the damage caused to the Votkinsk Machine Building Plant."

During the discussions that followed the delivery of this memorandum, Tomilov noted that the sanctions would likely be harsher—for every hour of delay experienced, the US side would be billed $1,000. The proposition of the US paying sanctions of any amount was rejected out of hand by Roy Peterson.

I was scheduled to rotate out of Votkinsk on March 8. My departure would mean that there were no OSIA officers on site who had experienced the full scope and scale of the technical discussions that had transpired between the US and Soviet sides since early January 1990. To rectify this, Colonel Connell ordered John Sartorious to return to Votkinsk after only a little more than two weeks at home. John cut short his vacation plans and headed back to the Soviet Union.

John and I wished each other well when our paths crossed at the airport in Izhevsk. John proceeded to Votkinsk, while I flew on to Moscow, and then to the US, arriving in Washington, Dulles in the afternoon of March 9, a Friday. I checked in with Colonel Connell, who was preparing to depart the US for Votkinsk late Saturday night, March 10, to join up with the CargoScan delegation. "Your theory is going to hell in a handbasket," he told me, referring to my prediction about the three "anomalous" missiles being spirited out of the plant to avoid being scanned by CargoScan.

I pointed out that the missile that was sitting in the environmentally controlled inspection building was one of the "anomalous" missiles, saying "I still believe that the Soviets are going to get these missiles out before CargoScan goes operational."

"But Tomilov says he has seven missiles ready to go," Connell noted. "Are they going to try and push through all seven?"

"Only three have anomalies that would be detected by CargoScan," I replied. "I think they will exit those three and leave the rest."

"The clock's running," Connell said, not convinced. "Go home. Enjoy your weekend. I'll see you when I get back."

I was paged at 6 am the next morning, March 10. I called the number on my pager and got the OSIA operations center. "Colonel Connell needs you to come into the office," I was told by the duty officer. "There's activity in Votkinsk."

Just an hour before, the Soviets had announced that they were going to remove the missile carrying railcar located in the environmentally controlled inspection building and ship it out of the plant. When queried by Roy Peterson as to why the Soviets were taking this action when the CargoScan delegation was due to arrive in two days' time, Tomilov replied that the Votkinsk factory was experiencing a financial crisis, in so far that it could not pay its employees until it was paid for the missiles it produced, and that this payment would not happen until the missiles were received by their respective customers.

The Soviet action set in motion a frenzy of activity, with the US Ambassador to the Soviet Union, Jack Matlock, sending formal protests to various Soviet officials, and Secretary of State James Baker calling Soviet Foreign Minister

Eduard Shevardnadze. On site, the inspectors and the Soviets undertook a lengthy kabuki dance, dragging out the various inspection related activities to buy time for the powers that be to intervene and stop the ongoing crisis that was reaching a point of no return. It became apparent, however, that a decision had been made by the Votkinsk factory leadership to go through with the exiting of the missile without allowing CargoScan to be used. This decision had the backing of the Ministry of Defense Industry, and there was little either the Ministry of Foreign Affairs or the Ministry of Defense could do about it. (The senior Soviet representative to the Special Verification Commission, Ambassador Strel'tsov, once quipped that "General Medvedev's [the Soviet equivalent of General Lajoie] authority ends at Izhevsk airport [where inspectors would land before being driven to Votkinsk].")

Around midnight on March 9 the US inspectors, overseen by Stu O'Neill, began the process of opening the launch cannister inside the railcar and conducting a visual inspection of the missile inside. After the cannister opening, Stu once again requested that the missile be imaged using CargoScan; once again the Soviets refused. Photographs were taken of the railcar outside of the CargoScan enclosure, to make a record on the ambiguity. Then, at 2.23 am on the morning of March 10, the railcar exited the Votkinsk plant, under US protest.

"That's one," I told Colonel Connell.

Later that day, the Soviets declared two more missile-carrying railcars—398-99730 and 368-99748—both associated with the "anomalous" missile. Both missiles exited the Votkinsk Final Assembly Plant without being imaged by CargoScan. Both were declared as ambiguities by the US inspectors.

"That's two and three."

Connell stared at me for a full minute, before shaking his head. "Well, you've made a believer out of me," he said. He later backed that statement up with a pointed comment in my annual fitness report: "Top notch analytical skills," Connell wrote. "Excels at integrating all-source data to make deadly accurate predictions of near-term events at Soviet missile production facility."

No more missiles exited the factory. Connell flew out to Moscow that night.

The US and Soviet Union were in a full-fledged crisis, and those who were opposed to US-Soviet arms control, like Senator Jesse Helms and David Sullivan, were drawn to the controversy like sharks to blood. The future of the INF treaty was on the line, as well as the viability of a strategic arms reduction treaty. The possibility of mankind living in a world where the threat of nuclear annihilation did not hover like an ever-present plague seemed to be dissipating before our very eyes.

We could have avoided this crisis by simply sticking to the terms of Mark Dues' February 5 agreement. But we were there to do a job, and that job included inspecting the contents of railcars capable of carrying prohibited missiles as they exited the Votkinsk Machine Building Plant. Allowing three missiles assessed

Soviet 6-axle train with SS-25 missile onboard exits Portal
without being inspected using CargoScan, March 10, 1990.

as being of an "anomalous" character to exit the plant without insisting on our inspection rights would have played directly into the hands of the likes of David Sullivan and Senator Jesse Helms, who believed the inspections to be incapable of detecting Soviet violations.

"Trust but verify" was more than a presidential quip; for the US inspectors working in Votkinsk, it was a way of life.

CHAPTER ONE

A Rendezvous with History

The entrance to the Votkinsk Final Assembly Plant, February 1988.

"Study the past if you would define the future."

CONFUCIUS

The Funeral

MOSCOW, DECEMBER 23, 1984—It was his fifth funeral in four years, and the protocol was the same for each—in the center of the Hall of Columns in the House of Unions, the body of an old man lay in a coffin mounted on a high floral-draped catafalque, his face illuminated by a small spotlight. Black-clad Soviet officials lined up on either side while a line of citizen-mourners slowly shuffled past. In the background, the strains of Tchaikovsky's *Pathetique* symphony played softly. The smell of fresh cut fir trees filled the air, a byproduct of the evergreen sprigs that adorned the room. The lights of the hall were set low, its crystal chandeliers covered with black mourning crepe.[1]

As a senior member of the Communist Party of the Soviet Union, Vladimir Gennadievich Sadovnikov would have been invited the attend these funerals, regardless. But the 56-year-old engineer was much more than that—as the Director of the Votkinsk Factory, he was part of an elite group of military industrialists who had dominated Soviet socio-economic life since late 1964, following the ouster of Nikita Khrushchev as the First Secretary of the Communist Party, who was then replaced by a coterie of Politburo members led by Khrushchev's deputy, Leonid Brezhnev.

That was twenty years ago. Now those who plotted against Khrushchev were dropping like flies. Alexei Kosygin, one of the three key anti-Khrushchev putschists (the others being Brezhnev and Nikolai Podgorny), was the first, passing on December 18, 1980, at the age of 76. Brezhnev was next, dying on November 10, 1982, at the age of 75. Brezhnev was replaced as First Secretary by Yuri Andropov, the former head of the KGB. But Andropov lasted less than a year and a half, passing on February 9, 1984, at the relatively young age of 69 (there would have been a sixth state funeral, with the death of Podgorny on January 12, 1983, at the age of 79, but Podgorny had been removed from the Politburo by Brezhnev in 1977, and as such did not rate a full state ceremony).

Logically, the death of so many men clustered around the central levers of power would be cause for alarm. The fact that Yuri Andropov's successor, Konstantin Chernenko, was himself ill and withdrawn as a leader only magnified the concern. But Sadovnikov had not panicked while attending any of these previous funerals, because he was always in the presence of a man who, since assuming the position of Minister of Defense in 1976, was the real power in the Soviet Union—Dmitri Fyodorovich Ustinov. When Brezhnev had suffered a massive stroke in 1977, severely reducing his ability to make decisions, Ustinov was one of four other men who had governed in his name.

But now here Ustinov was. Dead.

For more than 43 years, Ustinov had played a larger than life role in the affairs of the Soviet Union.[2] Plucked out of relative obscurity by Joseph Stalin on June 9,1941, the then 32-year-old Director of the Bolshevik Factory in Leningrad was offered the position of People's Commissar for Armaments only two days after his predecessor, Boris Lvovich Vannikov, had been arrested, charged with "failing to carry out his duties" (a common charge that could be made with little or no supporting evidence).[3] When war broke out less than two weeks later, the young Commissar Ustinov found himself in the center of a maelstrom, trying to produce armaments for the war effort while simultaneously evacuating critical factories threatened by the German advance to safety east of the Ural Mountains.

The success of the evacuation and the reestablishment of the Soviet defense industry earned Ustinov the title "Hero of Soviet Labor," and gained the favor and trust of Joseph Stalin (who called Ustinov "Redhead," in reference to his ginger locks) and the Soviet leader's inner circle. Moreover, the forced dislocation of Soviet industry radically transformed the composition of Soviet economic power elites, with the old cadre either killed, captured or displaced by the war, and a new generation rising in their stead, building industrial cities in the Soviet hinterland that were totally dependent upon military industry for their economic and social survival. The vertical integration of virtually every aspect of existence into a system controlled by a factory director was matched by a similar consolidation of authority into a handful of individuals working from Moscow—including Dmitri Ustinov.

It was Ustinov who had plucked Sadovnikov from his position as Chief Engineer at the Izhevsk Mechanical Plant in June 1966, promoting him to the position of Director of the Votkinsk Factory. Prior to this promotion, Sadovnikov was but one of many aspiring military industrialists who came of age in the years following the Second World War. Born in 1928 in the Republic of Tatarstan, Sadovnikov received his engineering degree from the Kazan Aviation Institute in 1953 before being dispatched to the Ukrainian city of Dnepropetrovsk, where he was put to work as a member of Mikhail Yangel's design bureau, part of the Yuzhny Machine Building Plant (Yuzhmash), responsible for designing air-to-air missiles. In 1958, the responsibility to produce air-to-air missiles was transferred to the Izhevsk Mechanical Plant in Udmurtia, and Sadovnikov, by that time the head of the air-to-air missile design bureau, followed. By 1960 he had organized his own design bureau and had been promoted to the position of Chief Engineer for the entire plant, the position he held when Ustinov reassigned him to Votkinsk.[4]

The Votkinsk factory, founded in 1759, was in an eponymously named city nestled in the foothills of the Ural Mountains some 1,300 kilometers (800 miles) east of Moscow. Since its inception, the Votkinsk factory had served first as a metallurgical and later as an industrial center, reaching prominence in the mid-19th century for innovations in the manufacture of steel. Later, during the Second World War, it served as a major military production center that absorbed the manufacturing infrastructure of defense factories evacuated from Kiev ahead of the advancing German armies.[5]

When Sadovnikov arrived at Votkinsk, the factory was involved in two separate missile production efforts. The first was the ubiquitous SCUD-B, originally the brainchild of Viktor Makeev, a missile designer responsible for developing a new family of tactical ballistic missiles derived from the German V-2 of World War II infamy, later known in the West as the SCUD-A. Makeev oversaw the construction of several prototype SCUD-Bs in 1957–1958, but Ustinov decided to dedicate Makeev to the task of developing submarine-launched ballistic missiles, and production of the SCUD-B was transferred from Makeev's factory in Zlatoust to the Votkinsk factory, marking Votkinsk's first foray into ballistic missile production.[6] The SCUD-B missile proved to be a boon for the Votkinsk factory. Missile flight tests began in 1959, and in 1964 the system was accepted by the Soviet military. For the next 25 years the Votkinsk factory produced thousands of these missiles for both domestic use and export.[7]

For the second missile production effort, Ustinov drew on the work of an innovative designer of solid fuel missiles, Aleksandr Nadiradze. Nadiradze had previously been the Chief Designer of a design bureau headed by Vladimir Chelomey, where he had overseen the development of high-altitude research rockets. Chelomey, however, was adamantly opposed to the use of solid rocket fuel in ballistic missiles, citing safety and reliability issues. When Nadiradze's design for a mobile solid-fuel missile was approved by Ustinov in 1961, Chelomey balked, and Nadiradze was given control of his own bureau to bring the design to fruition. Since then, Nadiradze had become the godfather of Soviet solid fuel ballistic missile design.[8]

Nadiradze's new solid fuel missile, known as the *Temp-S* (better known in the West as the SS-12 SCALEBOARD), represented a new direction in solid fuel rocket design, and as such Nadiradze needed his own dedicated missile assembly facility, separate from those used by the competing design bureaus. It was here that Dmitri Ustinov's master plan in having the Votkinsk factory become involved in missile manufacturing through the SCUD-B program now reached fruition—on September 5, 1962, Resolution No. 934-405 of the USSR Council of Ministers, sponsored by Ustinov himself, authorized Nadiradze to begin full-scale development of the SS-12 missile system. Included in that order were instructions that missile assembly would be carried out at the Votkinsk factory.[9]

The SS-12 missile proved to be a huge success for Nadiradze, who was awarded the Order of Lenin—the highest decoration for civilians in the Soviet Union—for his work. This recognition was extended to all those institutions affiliated with the program, including the Votkinsk factory. The first flight test of the missile took place in March 1964, and by 1967 the SS-12 was operationally deployed with the Soviet Army. But the SS-12 was an intermediate-range missile; Nadiradze had yet to break into the rarified air of ICBM designers. Until that occurred, both Nadiradze and the Votkinsk factory would be lesser players in the Soviet Defense Industry game.

They would not have long to wait for that opportunity. Ustinov's decision to put Sadovnikov in charge of Votkinsk was driven by the fact that the USSR Council of Ministers had, the previous March, signed a decree authorizing the Ministry of Defense Industry to begin development, together with the Nadiradze design bureau, of a new solid-fuel ballistic missile, known in the Soviet Union as the *Temp-2S* and in the West by its NATO designator, the SS-16.[10]

Little is known about the initial research and development phase of what would become the SS-16 missile. However, shortly after the Council of Minister's decree in March 1966 which initiated the program, Vladimir Sadovnikov was transferred from Izhevsk to Votkinsk, where he took over as the factory director. One of his first tasks was to build a new dedicated missile final assembly plant on the outskirts of Votkinsk, away from the center of town, where the existing missile production facility, Machine Building Plant No. 235, was located. The new missile being envisioned by Nadiradze was bigger than the SS-12, and the dangers posed by any accidental fire or explosion was too great to permit assembly in the center of the city.

The initial flight test of the SS-16 took place on March 14, 1972 at the "Research Proving Ground for Missile and Space Weapons USSR Ministry of Defense," located near the village of Plesetsk, in Arkhangelsk Oblast, some 800 kilometers (500 miles) north of Moscow. The target area was the Kura Missile Test Range on the Kamchatka Peninsula in the Soviet Far East, some 5,700 kilometers (3,550 miles) away. The test was a success. Votkinsk had landed its first major ICBM contract, and the Nadiradze bureau had scored its first major victory in the highly competitive world of Soviet ballistic missile design. On September 9, 1976, in recognition of his achievement in designing and producing the SS-16 ICBM, Alexander Nadirazde was awarded the title "Hero of Socialist Labor." Joining him in this recognition was Vladimir Gennadievich Sadovnikov, the Director of the Votkinsk factory.

The personal success enjoyed by Sadovnikov regarding the SS-16 was shared with the workers of the Votkinsk factory through the awarding of a second "Order of Lenin." But Sadovnikov went further, rewarding the workers and their families as only the Director General of a major Soviet military industrial factory enterprise could—he brought natural gas to the city of Votkinsk for the first time. This was a complex operation, requiring the laying gas supply pipelines throughout the city, and individual gas lines into the homes designated to be supplied. The Votkinsk factory paid for every expense associated with this task.

In February 1977, the task of connecting Votkinsk to the Northern Lights pipeline, which transported natural gas under high pressure from the Vykhtyl gas fields in northern Russia to Moscow, and onwards to Minsk, was undertaken. This was an auspicious occasion, made even more so by the fact that a team of specialists was going to do the tie in on a live pipeline—the first time an operation of this complexity and danger was ever attempted in the Soviet Union. Sadovnikov, aware that there was the possibility of an accident that would result in the crew being killed, insisted that he be physically present when the tap was conducted—if men were going to risk their lives to supply his city and factory with natural gas, then he would share the risk. The operation went off without a hitch, and Sadovnikov's name was spoken with reverence by the grateful citizens of Votkinsk.

Little could either Sadovnikov or the citizens of Votkinsk know that their new-found prosperity was living on borrowed time. The job of the Votkinsk factory was to build ballistic missiles. But by 1977, the Soviet Union and its arch enemy, the United States, were nearly ten years along in negotiating a system of arms control intended to curtail the work of the Votkinsk factory, and other facilities like it in the Soviet Union and United States.

This diplomatic experiment faltered at first. On July 1, 1968, then-US President Lyndon Johnson was able to help push through the nuclear non-proliferation treaty (NPT), which was signed by the United States and the Soviet Union, along with 59 other countries. The signing of the NPT opened the door for even more ambitious arms control dialogue. On August 19, 1968, the Soviets indicated that they were ready to receive President Johnson in Moscow for a major summit where arms control would lead the agenda. One day later Soviet tanks rolled into Czechoslovakia, crushing a reformation movement in that country that had become known as "the Prague Spring." Johnson labeled the Soviet action in Czechoslovakia "an aggression," the arms control summit was cancelled, and Johnson left office with his dream of checking the arms race unfulfilled.

Johnson's successor, Richard Nixon, came into office hampered by the same realities that had previously constrained his predecessor when it came to US-Soviet arms control—Vietnam, the Middle East and China. But any hesitation about the urgency of opening meaningful negotiations with the Soviets evaporated when, in January 1969, Nixon was briefed on the current iteration of the Single Integrated Operations Plan (SIOP)—the US nuclear war plans. Confronted with the fact that the US had only one plan for nuclear war, which, if executed, meant that more than 80 million Soviets, and at least that many Americans, would die, Nixon embarked on a renewed diplomatic effort which culminated in US and Soviet negotiators sitting down across from each other in Helsinki, Finland, on November 19, 1969, initiating a process that would come to be known as the Strategic Arms Limitations Talks, or SALT.

From the perspective of Alexander Nadirazde and Vladimir Sadovnikov, the SALT negotiations were of interest in so far as they involved complex theories on the numbers and types of missiles that would be permitted in each nation's arsenals. The SS-16, with its single warhead, was at a disadvantage, since these counting formulas favored missiles capable of carrying multiple warheads. (Although its warhead dispensing bus was designed to be capable of delivering three independently targeted warheads, the SS-16 was only tested with a single warhead, and operationally deployed in the same configuration.)

Moreover, the US was proposing an outright ban on mobile missiles, which would outlaw the SS-16 before it reached operational viability. In the end, the Soviets and their American counterparts agreed to place caps on the total number of ICBM's each side could have but left mobile missiles on the table. This agreement was codified on May 26, 1972, when Richard Nixon joined

Leonid Brezhnev gathered in the Hall of Saint Vladimir inside the Kremlin's Grand Palace to sign the interim SALT agreement.

The Missile

THE INTERIM SALT AGREEMENT created problems for the Soviets that had not been foreseen. The deficiency in their existing intermediate-range force structure, and the failure of Soviet defense industry to field any viable replacements, left the Soviets vulnerable to NATO nuclear forces. To compensate, the Soviets had re-tasked some 120 silo-based ICBMs that had been allocated to cover targets in China to an INF role, re-targeting them to cover strategic targets in Western Europe. However, these missiles were counted as ICBMs under SALT, and as such their continued service in an INF role put the Soviets at a severe disadvantage when it came to its overall strategic force.

Dmitri Ustinov was in a unique position to initiate policy in response to the new reality imposed by the interim SALT agreement. As such, Nadiradze had been given a heads up by Ustinov in 1971 to begin design work on a new intermediate-range missile. Less than a year after the interim SALT agreement was signed, on April 28, 1973, the Central Committee authorized full scale development of what would become the *Pioneer* missile, known in the West as the SS-20 SABER.

The fact that the SS-20 was derived from the same foundational technology as the SS-16 greatly simplified the design and production of the missile. The SS-20 incorporated the first two stages of the SS-16, along with its post-boost vehicle and warhead dispensing bus. Given the similarities between the two missiles, the decision was made to use the same mobile launch platform as the SS-16. This greatly simplified the assembly work being done at Votkinsk, since the specialized tools and equipment used on the SS-16 were compatible with the SS-20.

The flight test program for the SS-20 was conducted simultaneously with final phase of the SS-16 flight test program, with some 20 test flights conducted between September 21, 1974 and January 9, 1976 from the test launch facility at Kapustin Yar (the initial SS-20 test flight took place from the old V-2 test location, a nod to the roots of the program). The SS-20 passed all its technical and operational tests, and in August 1976, the first SS-20 regiment, equipped with nine launchers, was deployed. Votkinsk began serial production of the missile at the same time.[11]

The decision to deploy the SS-20 missile came in the aftermath of the Vladivostok Summit, held on November 23–24, 1974, between President Gerald Ford (who had replaced the disgraced Richard Nixon in 1973, who had been forced to resign from his office due to the fallout from the Watergate scandal) and the ailing Leonid Brezhnev. The interim SALT agreement was due to expire in 1977, and both the US and Soviet sides were anxious to cement a follow-on agreement, SALT II, that would both preserve the gains made in the initial interim agreement and expand the scope and scale of arms limitations and reductions. While the Ford-Brezhnev summit failed to produce a new treaty, it did result in the exchange of confidential memoranda detailing several points of agreement which emerged from the Vladivostok meeting, noting that these agreements would enter into force in October 1977, and remain in force until December 1985.

Dmitri Ustinov sought to double down on the SS-20's strategic importance by authorizing Nadirazde to undertake a major upgrade, resulting in what was, in effect, a completely new missile known as the *PioneerUTTKh* (UTTKh stands for Improved Tactical and Technical Characteristics). More than simply an adaptation of the first two stages of the SS-16, as was the case with the

Soviet SS-20 missile being fired from its mobile launcher.
Photo Credit: Soviet MoD

original variant of the SS-20, the *PioneerUTTKh* incorporated all new rocket motors possessing a greater diameter than the originals, a new equipment section containing upgraded guidance and control, and an all-new warhead delivery bus that allowed for far greater accuracy than the original *Pioneer.*

The Council of Ministers decree authorizing Nadiradze to proceed with development of the *PioneerUTTKh* was signed on July 19, 1977. By 1979 Nadirazde and the Votkinsk factory were ready to begin flight testing of the new missile, with the first launch taking place in August 1979, continuing through August 1980 with a total of ten successful launches. The *PioneerUTTKh* was accepted by the Soviet Strategic Rocket Forces in April 1981. Under the direction of Ustinov, Sadovnikov and the Votkinsk factory were tasked with an aggressive production schedule. By the end of 1981, some 180 of the new missiles had been produced, part of a plan that called for more than 600 missiles to be delivered to the Strategic Rocket Forces by 1987.

In 1981, his work on the *PioneerUTTKh* earned Sadovnikov his second Gold Star as a "Hero of Socialist Labor," as well as another "Order of Lenin." Both awards were presented by Ustinov himself. Moreover, these projects cemented the relationship between Ustinov and Sadovnikov. The Minster of Defense had travelled to Votkinsk to oversee the work on these missiles so often that a special Dacha (a Russian colloquialism for a summer house, in this case an exceptionally elaborate one intended for year-round use) was constructed on the outskirts of the city for Ustinov and his entourage to rest and relax during their stay.

Even in this time of prosperity, Ustinov sought to shield Nadiradze and the Votkinsk factory from the vagaries of arms control. The election of President Jimmy Carter in November 1976 brought an end to the domination of American arms control by Henry Kissinger, the long-serving diplomat who had labored in both the Nixon and Ford White Houses as National Security Advisor and Secretary of States. Carter was keen on advancing arms control with the Soviet Union, which meant formalizing the SALT II interim agreements that had been made in Vladivostok back in 1974 into treaty form.

During years of long and tedious negotiations, Ustinov had shielded the work being done by Nadiradze on mobile missiles from the cutting block, resisting all American efforts to ban them. But the deployment of the SS-20 had complicated that effort. The CIA's 1976 National Intelligence Estimate on Soviet Strategic Nuclear Forces noted that "the similarity between the two systems will make it difficult for us to determine whether the Soviets are deploying SS-X-16 ICBMs with the SS-X-20 launch units" (the "X" designator indicating a missile system still under development). US negotiators, taking their cue from the CIA and fearful of a "breakout" scenario which had the Soviets convert existing SS-20 missiles into ICBM-capable SS-16 missiles, indicated that the only way a SALT II accord would be verifiable using technical means (i.e., satellites) was for the Soviet Union to agree to ban the SS-16 missile in its totality, ensuring that any observed mobile missiles would only be of the SS-20 variety.

Ustinov had no choice but to agree to this provision. But he sought to preserve as much of the work of Nadiradze and the Votkinsk factory as possible. His first decision, contrary to the negotiated provisions of the SALT II treaty then underway, was to maintain the SS-16 missile in the Soviet inventory, although at reduced numbers—to 42 missiles, as opposed to the 100 or so missiles approved under the plan authorized by the Central Committee. Several regiments of SS-16 ICBMs were maintained in great secrecy in the Plesetsk region, and the missiles produced by Votkinsk were put into "combat storage." The mobile launchers for the SS-16, which should have been eliminated under the provisions of SALT II, were instead diverted to the SS-20 program, since they used the same vehicle.

The SALT II negotiations, however, opened the window for a new mobile ICBM project. The Nadiradze bureau had submitted a proposal for a new mobile ICBM, the *Topol*, or SS-25 SICKLE, which was approved by the Council of Ministers on July 19, 1977. The SS-25 missile was an upgrade to the SS-16 and was derived from the same technological line as the SS-16/SS-20 missile, incorporating many of the upgrades that were put into the *PioneerUTTKh* missile. However, the SALT II treaty then under negotiation called for a ban on the deployment of new missile systems. Ustinov was able to insert into the treaty text a provision allowing for the development of a new "light ICBM," so long as its performance characteristics did not exceed 5% of the missile system it was intended to replace.

To acknowledge that the SS-25 was an extension of the SS-16/SS-20 family would simply recreate the verification problem that led to the banning of the SS-16 in the first place. Instead, Ustinov designated the new SS-25 as the RT-2PM, indicating that its lineage was derived from a totally different missile system, the RT-2M, or SS-13 SAVAGE. In 1973 the Nadiradze bureau had been given the task of taking over the modernization of the SS-13 from another design bureau, KB Arsenal. In 1974, Nadiradze incorporated numerous technological innovations, especially in motor case design and solid fuel composition, into the SS-13 upgrade, fielding a new missile, known by its Soviet designation as the RT-2M. This modification was done independent of the Votkinsk factory, which at the time was fully committed to the SS-16/SS-20 development effort. However, by designating the SS-25 as a follow-on to the SS-13, Ustinov's sleight of hand preserved both the SS-25 as well as guaranteed Votkinsk's continued economic prosperity.

Missiles meant money, and money meant Sadovnikov could advance the interests of his factory, its workers, their families, and the other citizens of the city of Votkinsk. There was a tremendous amount of competition for the resources of the state when it came to the defense industry, and not every factory or design bureau had profited the way Votkinsk and the Nadirazde Bureau had.

The reason for their success rested in part on the high quality of their product. But Votkinsk was getting more than its fair share of defense contracts, primarily because Ustinov kept funneling projects its way.

There was a growing recognition within the Soviet leadership, Sadovnikov knew, that the products from factories like his were contributing to an increasingly dangerous atmosphere between the United States and the Soviet Union. Ustinov himself had been a realist about nuclear weapons. "Could anyone in his right mind speak seriously of any limited nuclear war?" the Minister of Defense was quoted as saying in the July 25, 1981 issue of *Pravda.* "It should be quite clear that the aggressor's actions will instantly and inevitably trigger a devastating counterstroke by the other side. None but completely irresponsible people could maintain that a nuclear war be made to follow rules adopted beforehand, with nuclear missiles exploding in a 'gentlemanly manner' over strictly designated targets and sparing the population."[12]

But Ustinov's support for the deployment of the SS-20 missile in the late 1970s had resulted in an American response—the deployment to Europe of advanced Pershing II and ground-launched cruise missiles which the Soviets viewed as an existential threat. "The American Pershing and cruise missiles scheduled for deployment in Europe," Ustinov told a meeting of Warsaw Pact defense ministers in October 1983, "are part of this strategy to reach superiority over the Warsaw Pact countries and to conduct a nuclear first strike."[13]

Ustinov's speech was delivered at the height of the annual US-NATO military exercise known as REFORGER (for Return of Forces to Germany). The 1983 iteration of this exercise, known as "Autumn Forge '83," was particularly robust, involving tens of thousands of troops and thousands of armored vehicles and aircraft simulating large-scale conventional conflict with the Warsaw Pact, culminating with a two-week command post exercise, Able Archer, which rehearsed, in extremely realistic fashion, NATO plans for the use of nuclear weapons against the Warsaw Pact and the Soviet Union.

The Autumn Forge '83 exercises caught the attention of the Soviet Union like none other. "The dangerous nature of the military exercises by the US and NATO in recent years commands attention," Ustinov told *Pravda* on November 19, 1983—two weeks after Able Archer concluded. "These exercises are characterized by an enormous scope, and they are becoming increasingly difficult to distinguish from a real deployment of armed forces for aggression."[14]

The Soviet General Staff shared Ustinov's conclusions, noting in an after-action report published on February 2, 1984, that "In 1983, [the exercises] took place on such a scale and were so close to the real combat situation that…it was difficult to catch the difference between working out training questions and actual preparation of large-scale aggression." The article noted that the 1983 exercises were a rehearsal for a "limited nuclear war" initiated by NATO.

The Soviet Union, Ustinov noted in the remarks published by *Pravda*, would not stand idle in the face of such threats. "The sharp exacerbation of the international situation," Ustinov wrote, "is making even higher demands on the level of preparedness of the Soviet Armed Forces, on the improvement of their management and on their technical equipment."

The "technical equipment" included the missiles Sadovnikov produced in his factory. Indeed, the entire Soviet SS-20 missile force—the product of the Votkinsk factory—had been placed on "combat alert" during the Autumn Forge exercises. The Chief of the Soviet General Staff, Marshall Nikolai Ogarkov, was in the hardened underground national command post during the final phase of the exercise (i.e., Able Archer), and was receiving intelligence updates every six hours. The commander of the Soviet Strategic Rocket Forces, Marshall Vladimir Tolubka, was also monitoring the NATO exercises.[15]

Soviet doctrine at that time was known as "launch-under-attack," which would involve unleashing the totality of the Soviet strategic nuclear force in an all-encompassing retaliatory strike the moment it was concluded that a nuclear attack had been initiated against the Soviet Union. This strike would blanket Europe and the United States with more than 12,000 nuclear warheads, including the more than 900 150-kiloton warheads carried by the more than 300 SS-20 mobile launchers which were, at that time, in service.

The decision to launch, once given, could be delivered to the Soviet nuclear arsenal within thirteen seconds.

In mid-July 1982, prior to the Autumn Forge '83 and Able Archer, US and Soviet arms control negotiators had sat down across from one another in Geneva, Switzerland, for preliminary talks over intermediate-range nuclear forces (INF).[16] The US decision to deploy Pershing II and cruise missiles to Europe in response to the Soviet deployment of SS-20 missiles created a sense of urgency for these talks, but the atmosphere was less than positive. President Ronald Reagan had just put forward a new negotiating position built on the premise that the US would forgo the deployment of its weapons to Europe if the Soviet Union got rid of its SS-20 arsenal. Ustinov, in an article in *Pravda* published on the eve of the talks, rejected this offer. "This 'zero option,'" Ustinov declared, "is intended to force 'unilateral disarmament' on the Soviet Union."

On November 23, 1983, with negotiations at an impasse, the Soviet delegation walked out of talks with the US concerning the reduction of intermediate-range nuclear forces, a move supported by Ustinov. The Soviets likewise ended their participation in Strategic Arms Reduction Treaty (START) talks on December 8, 1983. Sadovnikov, as the Director of the Votkinsk factory, had been monitoring the negotiations, always alert for anything that might impact the factory's economic interests. With the termination of arms control talks, Sadovnikov no longer had to worry—the missiles would continue to roll off the production floor of his factory, and orders for more missiles would keep coming in.

But the Autumn Forge '83 crisis forced a clear recognition on the part of both the US and Soviet Union that the status quo was unsustainable. Pershing II missiles began arriving in Europe in November 1983. With a speed of nine times the speed of sound, the missiles could strike Moscow within 6–9 minutes of being launched, something the future General Secretary of the Soviet Union, Mikhail Gorbachev, likened to having "a loaded pistol pointed at our head."[17] Even President Reagan recognized this reality, noting in his address to the United Nations General Assembly on September 24, 1984 that the US and Soviet Union needed "to extend the arms control process to build a bigger umbrella under which it can operate—a road map, if you will, showing where in the next 20 years or so these individual efforts can lead."

Normally arms control-related matters such as crafting a response to Reagan's statement would be handled by Ustinov. But shortly after the US President spoke, the Soviet Minster of Defense fell ill. In his absence, the Foreign Ministry moved forward on the issue of arms control. On the sidelines of the 1984 General Assembly debate, President Reagan met with Soviet Foreign Minister Andrei Gromyko, during which the two discussed Reagan's "umbrella" concept for arms control talks. The two men agreed to begin working on a process for future arms control meetings, and by November 22, 1984, US and Soviet officials announced that they would resume arms control talks early the next year, on January 7, 1985.

Ustinov's passing was sudden and unexpected. On September 27, 1984, he first presided over an awards presentation for General Secretary Chernenko, whom Ustinov personally decorated with the "Hero of Socialist Labor." Afterwards, Ustinov attended a military-political meeting, where he complained of illness and was taken to the hospital. Ustinov was diagnosed with untreated pneumonia which had turned into sepsis. By December it was determined that he would require surgery, but once the doctors opened him, they were presented with a plethora of health issues, including sclerosis and other signs of organ failure. During the surgery Ustinov started bleeding profusely, and eventually succumbed. He was 76 years old.

At the foot of Ustinov's casket lay 40 red velvet cushions, on which his medals and awards were displayed—a diamond-studded marshal's star, his medal as Hero of the Soviet Union and his two orders of Hero of Socialist Labor, 11 Orders of Lenin and dozens of other medals representing a lifetime of service to the Soviet Union.

But for Sadovnikov, Ustinov was more than just a cluster of medals. He was a mentor, a friend, and the source of the Votkinsk factory's lifeblood—contracts for missiles destined for the Soviet Army.

The Treaty

USTINOV'S DEATH was not announced through normal channels. Instead, Mikhail Gorbachev, who in 1978 became the youngest member of the Central Committee of the Communist Party at age 47, and was widely believed to be the heir apparent to the ailing Konstantin Chernenko (Gorbachev was chairing meetings of the Politburo in Chernenko's absence), made the announcement while on a trip to the United Kingdom, where he was trying to improve relations between the two countries. "We have had a great and tragic loss," Gorbachev announced in a statement released to reporters. "The Minister of Defense, Marshal Dmitri Ustinov, our old friend and comrade-at-arms, has passed away."[18]

Gorbachev cut his trip to the UK short in order to return to Moscow for Ustinov's funeral. Before he left, however, he expressed his frustration at the current state of relations between the Soviet Union and the United States. "It is especially important," Gorbachev said, "to realize that the arms race cannot and is not capable of ensuring the security of the state."[19]

These words weighed heavily on military industrialists like Vladimir Sadovnikov. Arms control had been an ever-present reality during the entirety of his tenure as Director of the Votkinsk factory. But the theory of disarmament had always been offset by the reality of the defense needs of the Soviet Union, which, from the standpoint of those who built ballistic missiles, had been defined by Dmitri Ustinov. Sadovnikov never had reason to waver in his confidence that, as long as Ustinov was Defense Minister, the Votkinsk factory would have plenty of work.

The January 7, 1985 meeting in Geneva between Secretary of State George Shultz and Foreign Minister Gromyko took place as scheduled. While there continued to be wide gaps between them, the two diplomats agreed that they would seek a way to halt the arms race, inclusive of a resumption in negotiations to reduce their respective strategic- and intermediate-range nuclear weapons. Sadovnikov had heard such talk before, and yet his factory kept producing missiles.

Then on March 10, 1985, Konstantin Chernenko died. Once again, Vladimir Sadovnikov found himself traveling to Moscow to attend a state funeral. Normally, upon the death of a General Secretary, the Central Committee would take several days to announce a successor. This had been the case following the deaths of both Brezhnev and Andropov. But in the case of Chernenko, his replacement was announced a mere four hours and fifteen minutes after the public was notified of the General Secretary's passing.

In his acceptance speech, Mikhail Gorbachev made it clear that his priority would be the economic development of the Soviet Union. "We are to achieve a decisive turn in transferring the national economy to the tracks of intensive development," he announced. "We should, we are bound to attain within the briefest period, the most advanced scientific and technical positions, the highest world level in the productivity of social labor."[20]

These words meant little to Sadovnikov, if for no other reason than the Votkinsk factory already operated at the highest level of scientific and technical achievement when it came to the production of ballistic missiles. As he listened to Gorbachev's speech, however, it became clear that the development the new General Secretary was speaking of did not include the Votkinsk factory and its missiles. Gorbachev referenced the renewed arms control talks then underway in Geneva. The Soviet Union, Gorbachev declared, sought "real and major reduction in arms stockpiles, and not the development of ever-new weapons systems."

The Votkinsk factory was in the business of developing these "ever-new weapons systems"; Gorbachev was now openly talking of doing away with the life's work of Sadovnikov and the engineers and workers he employed—even though they were a long way from reaching an agreement, if indeed such lofty goals could be accomplished. The SALT talks had dragged on for decades, and the scope and scale of the work at the Votkinsk factory had only increased. The SALT agreements dealt with arms limitations, not reductions, and could be verified via so-called "technical means"—spy satellites and other means of remote information collection. Reductions were a whole different issue, one requiring a level of compliance verification unobtainable in the past—on-site inspections involving an American presence on the ground—which the US required if for no other reason than the Soviet Union had always objected in principle to that very notion. There was no reason to think the US could convince the Soviet Union to accede to this level of intrusion on its sovereignty any time soon.

But change was in the air. In Geneva, the senior US negotiator, Ambassador Max Kampleman, tabled a US demand that any future arms control treaty between the US and Soviet Union include on-site inspections. His Soviet counterpart, Ambassador Viktor Karpov, did not reject the US position out of hand. "We will try to make an agreement that will be verifiable by both sides, not only by the United States but by the Soviet Union," Karpov told reporters afterwards. "You can be sure of that."[21]

Karpov's comments were made on March 12, 1985. Two days later, Mikhail Gorbachev delivered the eulogy for Chernenko as his body was buried beside the walls of the Kremlin, near to where Ustinov's ashes had been interned a mere three months prior. When Chernenko's coffin was set down, facing the Kremlin mausoleum, Gorbachev and the other leaders of the Soviet Union mounted the mausoleum to pay their respects. Unlike the previous burial ceremonies following state funerals, no members of the military accompanied him, a fact that was not lost on the likes of Sadovnikov and the other military industrialists in attendance.

For Votkinsk these were heady times. In addition to sustaining its aggressive production of the *PioneerUTTKh*, Ustinov, prior to his death, had tasked Nadirazde and Votkinsk to develop a further modification of that missile, known as the *Pioneer-3*. These would be deployed to the Soviet Far East, near the Bering Sea town of Chukotka, targeting US early warning radars in Alaska and North Dakota, an intelligence gathering radar located on Shemya Island in the Aleutians, and the US nuclear missile submarine base in Bangor, Washington.

In concert with the Chukotka *Pioneer-3*/SS-20 modificazion effort, Nadiradze was charged with producing an even more advanced missiles system intended to counter the planned deployment into West Germany of advanced Pershing II intermediate-range missiles. Based upon the second and third stages of the *Topol*/SS-25 and incorporating the three-warhead dispensing bus of the *Pioneer-3*/SS-20, Ustinov envisioned a new missile—known as the *Skorost*—which would be forward deployed into the Warsaw Pact for the sole purpose of targeting the Pershing II and GLCM INF systems being deployed by the US.

The *Skorost* existed in more than just theory—Nadiradze had been working on the concept since 1982. On November 23, 1983, based upon this preliminary work, Ustinov directed that Nadiradze take the concept from the drawing board to fruition in the shortest time possible. The Ministry of Defense published the technical and tactical requirements for the missile in December 1983, and Ustinov pushed through Council of Minister approval on January 9, 1984. By April 1984 the VPK had approved the production and deployment schedule of the *Skorost* system. The unprecedented speed at which the *Skorost* went from concept to approved operational system—six months—is demonstrative of not only the seriousness with which Ustinov treated the need to respond to the US INF deployment, but also his absolute authority when it came to defense matters, especially those involving ballistic missiles.

The Chukotka/*Skorost* deployment scheme was Ustinov's gambit for bringing the INF issue to a head. By simultaneously threatening the West Coast of the United States and the US INF systems in Europe, Ustinov hoped to force the US back to the negotiating table, where the Soviet deployments could be offered up in exchange for the removal of the US INF systems. The goal was to return the military balance to where it was before the US deployed the Pershing II and GLCM to Europe. It represented a dangerous escalation of the sort that the Soviets were normally reticent about undertaking. But Ustinov alone was calling the shots, and there was no system of checks and balances in place to counter him.

In parallel to their work on Ustinov's Chukhotcha/*Skorost* initiative, Nadiradze and the Votkinsk factory continued their efforts regarding the SS-25 ICBM. The initial flight test of an SS-25 missile was conducted from the Kapustin Yar test facility on October 27, 1982. It was a failure. Nadirazde worked to resolve the problems identified in that test before launching a second test missile, this time from Plesetsk, on February 8, 1983. This test was a success, and serial production of the SS-25 was anticipated to begin in early 1985.

At the time of Ustinov's funeral, the Votkinsk factory was continuing to produce the SS-20 missile, at a rate of around 65 per year, as well as a short-range missile, known as the *Oka*, or SS-23 SPIDER, of which 60 or so were moved off the production line every year. But more, newer projects were in the works—the SS-25 was due to enter serial production the next year, and the ink was barely dry on the resolution of the USSR No. 696-213, dated July 21, 1983, regarding the design of an even newer ICBM, the *Kourier.* This missile was so secret that NATO did not have a designation for it. Derived from consultations with the commander of the Strategic Rocket Forces, V. F. Tolubko, who was monitoring the US development of a small ICBM known as the Midgetman, the *Kourier* was built around advances in solid fuel technology and would use powerful lightweight carbon filament motors in which a modern solid fuel mixture would be cast—a departure from the cartridge method employed by Nadiradze's previous designs. The Nadiradze Design Bureau had just completed the conceptual work on this new missile when Ustinov died.[22]

The nation buried its hero, and showed the appropriate level of adulation, renaming the city of Izhevsk "Ustinov" in his honor. Dmitri Ustinov had, over the course of more than 43 years of work at the senior-most levels of the Soviet defense industry, accumulated so much power and influence that his death left a huge vacuum. Because of the paralysis Ustinov's death created in the stolid Soviet system, Mikhail Gorbachev (who took over as General Secretary in March 1985, following the back-to-back deaths of Yuri Andropov and his successor, Konstantin Chernenko) was able to fill this void with relative ease. One of his first acts as General Secretary was to appoint a new Secretary for Defense Affairs, Lev Zaikov. Zaikov was a former military industry plant director, and an able politician in his own right, having served as the mayor of Leningrad, and that city's party chief.

Gorbachev's next act was to stop Ustinov's Chukotka/*Skorost* scheme, which the new Secretary General viewed as unnecessarily provocative. All preparations for deploying the *Pioneer-3*/SS-20 to Chukotka were halted, and the *Skorost* program was stopped in its tracks. Nadiradze and Sadovnikov had been pushing that program at a blistering pace, so much so that by March 1, 1985, some 10 *Skorost* missiles had already been produced, and an initial flight test conducted. The test was a failure—a manufacturing error caused a nozzle failure after launch. But the problem was easily fixed, and Nadiradze was confident he would have the program back on track in no time. As soon as Gorbachev was briefed on the missile and its purpose, however, he ordered all work stopped; the nine remaining *Skorost* missiles and all launcher prototypes were put into storage.

But the biggest change came from Gorbachev himself. Whereas under Ustinov the Politburo had been held hostage while Ustinov crafted policy options that were subsequently presented as a *fait accompli*, Gorbachev reversed the tables, coordinating ahead of time with the new Defense Minister, Sergei Sokolov, and the new Foreign Minister, Eduard Shevardnadze, to develop an agreed policy, and then transmitting this decision to Zaikov to develop the means of implementing this decision bureaucratically.

It quickly became clear that the old Soviet arms control negotiating position and the vision of arms control being espoused by Gorbachev were incompatible. Gorbachev was publicly espousing a policy of separating the INF negotiations from the others and simplifying START by going straight to a 50% reduction in strategic delivery systems. Not only was what Gorbachev proposing disruptive of what had been an agreed upon Soviet negotiating position, it was also threatening existing major weapons contracts.

To curb Gorbachev's enthusiasm, Sergei Sokolov proposed that the Soviet Union offer complete nuclear disarmament within 15 years, believing that the impracticalities of such a position would slow down the feverish pace of disarmament Gorbachev seemed to be pushing. Much to Sokolov's surprise, Gorbachev embraced the idea, unveiling this new policy to the world in a speech on January 15, 1986, where he proposed "complete nuclear disarmament" by the end of the millennium. Moreover, by embracing Sokolov's attempted poison pill, Gorbachev undermined any objections the Ministry of Defense and the military might raise to the Soviets swallowing the American version of the same pill—the "Zero Option."

The stage was now set for Gorbachev's famous meeting with Ronald Reagan in Reykjavik, Iceland, on October 11–12, 1986. While the summit produced no tangible results, it did allow Gorbachev the chance to articulate major policy initiatives that would serve as the foundation for a future INF and START treaty. In quick succession, Gorbachev challenged the US, first by proposing the elimination of all INF weapons in Europe, allowing for a force of 100 warheads each to be based east of the Urals (for the Soviets) and on US soil (for the Americans). Most surprising, the Soviets acceded to stringent verification procedures incorporating on-site inspection. After a tepid American reply, Gorbachev, in March 1987, upped the ante by proposing a "Global Zero" regarding INF weapons—a universal ban.

The Soviet military was outraged, having been excluded from the deliberations leading up to the decision to advance "Global Zero" as Soviet policy. They became even more so when, in response to the "Global Zero" proposal, the US upped in turn but one-sidedly, insisting that the ban include a short-range missile, the SS-23 (also produced at the Votkinsk factory) as part of the list of weapons systems being eliminated. In a meeting with US officials in Washington, DC in September 1987, Eduard Shevardnadze acceded to the US demands, and then returned to Moscow to get Gorbachev's concurrence. The road toward the successful conclusion of an INF Treaty had been paved—it was just a matter of the Soviets and the Americans agreeing to journey down the path together.

For Vladimir Sadovnikov, the arrival of Mikhail Gorbachev on the Soviet political scene was a breath of fresh air. Sadovnikov had been elected as a deputy to the 27th Congress of the Communist Party of the Soviet Union, held from February 25 through March 6, 1986 in Moscow. This was Gorbachev's first major event since becoming General Secretary, and Sadovnikov was infatuated. "He is a second Lenin!" Sadovnikov told his colleagues upon his return from the conference. Sadovnikov was comfortable with the Votkinsk factory's ability to rise to the new challenges presented by Gorbachev's call for reform. They had, after all, built the SS-20 in record time, coming in ahead of schedule with a product of the highest quality. He felt that adapting to the emerging realities of a new Soviet economy was but a new challenge that would be ably met by the workers and managers of his factory.

The view from inside an SS-20 missile assembly hall inside the Votkinsk Final Assembly Plant, mid-1980s. Photo credit: Votkinsk Production Association.

Missiles were still the largest money maker for the factory. Following an extensive flight test program involving 17 test launches (only four of which were failures), the first SS-25 missiles had been delivered to the Strategic Rocket Forces in July 1985. SS-20 missiles continued to roll off the assembly line, and while Gorbachev had killed the Chukhota deployment scheme, work on the follow-on *Pioneer-3* design continued, and was close to entering the flight test stage. The Nadiradze bureau likewise was conducting successful tests of the rocket engines to be used on the *Kourier* system at a special artillery range in the Moscow region of Krasnoarmeysk.

In September 1987 Sadovnikov was informed that Gorbachev was planning on signing a treaty with the US that would eliminate not only the SS-20 missile, but also the SS-23. This was devastating news for the factory director. Inside the walls of his factory were components for some 36 SS-20 missiles that would never be delivered to their customer. Worse, bad news arrived from Moscow—Sadovnikov's long-time partner, Alexander Nadiradze, had died of a heart attack shortly after he had been briefed about the demise of the SS-20 due to the requirements of the planned INF treaty.

While Nadiradze's death had little practical impact on the work of the Votkinsk factory (the engineering work in support of the SS-20/SS-25 missiles had been taken over years earlier by Nadiradze's deputy, Lev Solomonov, and Nadiradze's deputy, B. N. Lagutin, had likewise taken over as the Chief Designer for the design bureau), the emotional impact of losing the man who had been the father of some of the Soviet Union's most advanced weapons, and a mentor and friend to Sadovnikov and the other engineers and designers who had been involved in supporting Nadiradze's various projects since the mid-1960s, was devastating. At Nadiradze's funeral, Sadovnikov commiserated with his fellow factory directors, whose frustration at the pending INF treaty and the detrimental impact it would have on their livelihood was palpable.

In November 1987 Sadovnikov was presented with more bad news. Soviet negotiators had realized late in the process that the first stage of the SS-20 was virtually identical to the first stage of the SS-25, creating a verification problem that could only be addressed by the stationing of a full-time presence of American weapons inspectors outside the gates of the Votkinsk final assembly plant. The INF treaty was expected to be signed during Gorbachev's scheduled visit to Washington, DC in December 1987, which meant the treaty would come into force some six months later, following ratification. Sadovnikov now had to prepare for this unprecedented intrusion of inspectors from "enemy number one" into the city and factory he built.

The INF Treaty was signed on December 8, 1987. Immediately afterwards, Viktor Protasov, the director of the Central Research Institute for Special Machinery who manufactured the launch cannisters for the SS-20 and SS-25 missiles, resigned in protest. Sadovnikov had considered a similar protest, but pride and a sense of duty and responsibility to his workers compelled him to stay on.

In February 1988 Vladimir Sadovnikov travelled to the United States for a two-day visit at the Hercules Plant in Magna, Utah, where the Pershing II missile had been produced. Under the terms of the INF Treaty, Soviet inspectors would be permitted to monitor the Magna Plant in a similar fashion to the inspections that would be carried out by their American counterparts in Votkinsk. Sadovnikov was invited to Magna to understand the reciprocal nature of the treaty, in hopes that it would help him better prepare for the arrival of the Americans.

Sadovnikov himself was facing a challenge of a different sort. The robust 57-year-old factory manager had always been the epitome of good health. But tremors that had recently appeared in his hands were getting worse. Eventually he agreed to check himself into a Moscow sanitorium, where the doctors delivered the bad news—he had Parkinson's disease. For Sadovnikov, this diagnosis represented yet another challenge. He believed he could overcome it, despite the doctors' caution that his symptoms would only get worse.

Preparation was something Sadovnikov understood. In preparing to cope with the effects of his disease, Vladimir Sadovnikov had sought to condition his body to fight back. He ran every morning, weather permitting, jogging along the embankment he had constructed along the Votkinsk *Prud*. He practiced yoga, watched his diet, sought the advice of the practitioners of modern medicine and folk treatments alike, and read voraciously about the disease that was ravaging his body. He refused to surrender without a fight.

Dealing with the impact of the INF Treaty on his factory, and lives of the workers he had grown to love as his own children, presented Sadovnikov with a completely different problem, but one he was prepared to fight, nonetheless. Defense conversion was the order of the day, but the time he had thought would be available to prepare for this challenge never materialized, and the patience he had hoped for among the citizens had long since evaporated. While Sadovnikov struggled to find adequate work for those who had previously supported the now-discontinued SS-20 and SS-23 manufacturing processes, he was inundated with letters from angry workers who blamed him for all their woes. Perestroika—the rebuilding of the Soviet economy—was all the rage, and yet no one seemed to know what exactly it was, or how it was supposed to be achieved.

The First Secretary of the Regional Communist Party Committee, an ally of Gorbachev's, had lashed out at what he termed "the old guard"—those managers who had held their positions since the time of Brezhnev, demanding their replacement by younger cadres. Sadovnikov had been mentioned by name as one of those who needed to go. The Minister of Defense Industry, Pavel Finogenov, personally intervened on Sadovnikov's behalf, letting the Party know in no uncertain terms that defense matters were none of its affair. The criticism, however, had shaken Sadovnikov, causing him to question all that he had accomplished in his life. He had always viewed himself as part of the solution, leading the fight to build a modern socialist paradise. Now those on whose behalf he had labored were openly questioning his life's work.

Vladimir Sadovnikov returned from his visit to Magna, Utah a broken man. America, he told his friends and family, was a "fairy tale country." Left unsaid was the realization on Sadovnikov's part that "enemy number one" seemed to have accomplished that which he had worked toward his entire life, and yet failed—a worker's paradise, filled with everything and more a citizen could ever hope for.

Sadovnikov resigned from his position as factory director shortly after his return. Whether it was the realization that his life's work had not achieved its intent, or that his failing health would hamper him in his effort to help the Votkinsk factory through the difficult times ahead—or both—his time as Votkinsk's leading man had come to an end. His retirement was formally accepted in early September. The city and factory he had nurtured and directed for the past 22 years would have to face the presence of the American inspectors, and the changes portended by their presence, without him to guide them.

A Child of the Cold War

I GREW UP as a child of the Cold War, the byproduct of a military family raised during the decades of the 60s and 70s. Among my earliest memories are waiting on a military runway in 1964 while my father disembarked from a transport aircraft that brought him home from a six-month deployment to Izmir, Turkey. There he had served as an aircraft maintenance officer for F-100 fighter-bombers as they stood "strip alert," the jets fully fueled and loaded with nuclear bombs, the pilots sitting in the cockpit, waiting for a signal that would send them off on a mission to attack targets in the Soviet Union. This was a year after the Cuban missile crisis, where John F. Kennedy cut a not-so-secret deal with Nikita Khrushchev to pull Jupiter-class nuclear-armed missiles out of Turkey in exchange for the Soviets withdrawing their nuclear-tipped SS-4 and SS-5 medium- and intermediate-range missiles out of Cuba. The deployment of the F-100s to Ciğle Air Base, outside the coastal city of Izmir, was part of the American effort to replace the nuclear strike capability lost when the Jupiter missiles (also based at Ciğle) were dismantled.

I was not cognizant of either the geopolitical or military realities associated with my father's deployment—I picked these up later, overhearing snippets of conversations he had with my mother and other officers. All I knew was that he was gone—a lot. A year later he was deployed again, this time for 12 months, part of the 10th Fighter-Commando Squadron (the "Skoshi Tigers") which were responsible for introducing the new F-5C fighter-bomber into the Vietnamese conflict. I did not know much about Vietnam, or the reasons why my father had to go over there, but I did like the colorful squadron patch, with its roaring tiger's head, and the de-militarized 20mm cannon rounds my father brought as gifts for me.

When he returned home, my father was assigned to the 94th Fighter-Interceptor Squadron (FIS), the "Hat in the Ring" unit made famous by Eddie

Rickenbacker, America's most prolific ace during World War I. We were stationed at a variety of Air Bases affiliated with the North American Air Defense Command (NORAD), first in Paine Field, in Everett, Washington (at the site of the current Boeing test runway), and then Selfridge Air Force Base, outside of Detroit, Michigan. The 94th flew F-106 "Delta Dart" supersonic interceptors, armed with "Genie" nuclear air-to-air missiles. Operating from alert air strips in Alaska, the F-106 fighters regularly intercepted Soviet bombers flying over the Bering Sea. In time of war they would have been called upon to shoot the Soviet aircraft down with their nuclear-tipped missiles before they could reach their targets in the United States.

In June 1969 my father deployed with the 94th FIS to Osan, Korea as part of a build-up of American military power in the region in response to the capture of the *USS Pueblo* and subsequent downing of a US Navy reconnaissance aircraft by the North Koreans. He was gone for six months this time, a fact seared into my mind when I was compelled to watch Neil Armstrong land on the moon without him (a big deal for an eight-year-old boy infatuated with the US Space program). When he returned home, we moved again, this time to Wurtsmith Air Force Base, the new home of the 94th FIS.

I have distinct memories of my room at the time. Two framed posters decorated my walls, one with the words of Article One of the US Code of Conduct spelled out ("I am an American, fighting in the forces which guard my country and our way of life. I am prepared to give my life in their defense"), the other a silhouette of John F. Kennedy, with the words "Ask not what your country can do for you—ask what you can do for your country" emblazoned over it. My parents were not trying to brainwash me—this was the life we led, the reality of an Air Force brat at that time. I was becoming more aware of the world I lived in—on my desk I had a map of the world, with North Korea circled in red. Another red circle was around Alaska, where my father would frequently deploy with the alert aircraft. And Vietnam was circled, too, because in 1970 my Uncle Rick was sent there as a soldier in the US Army, where he participated in the invasion of Cambodia.

In 1971 we again moved, this time to Hawaii. For the first time, I was confronted by the reality of the extent of the opposition to the war in Vietnam, as throngs of anti-war protestors would gather outside the main gates of the various military facilities on the island of Oahu, chanting their slogans and jeering at the military personnel and their families as they drove on and off the base. The contrast between the actions of these protestors and the service of men like my father was, in my young mind, stark. Then, suddenly, the war was over; "Peace with Honor" was declared, and the protests stopped.

We lived on Hickam Air Force Base, in World War 2-era housing located in what was known as "Area 19," adjacent to the main airstrip. Being this close to an active runway, I was always alert to the arrival of new and strange aircraft. Whether it was an SR-71 "Blackbird," a U-2 spy plane, or a British Vulcan bomber, I would chart their arrival and, without fail, ride my bike to the remote parking areas, where I would sneak in close to take photographs with my Kodak instamatic. Then, in early 1973, some new aircraft started arriving. The war was over, and the American prisoners of war were coming home. I had emulated one of my heroes, John Wayne, by wearing a bracelet with the name of a captured US pilot inscribed on it. The POWs were flown in batches from Hanoi, in North Vietnam to American bases in the Philippines, where they were evaluated before being sent back to the United States. Their first stop on American soil was Hickam Air Force Base. My mother made a point of greeting every single planeload of returning POWs, and always brought me with her in hopes that I would get to meet "my" POW (I did, and was able to give him "his" bracelet back). It was a sobering reality to ponder the fact that some of these men had been separated from their families for years. The verbiage of the Code of Conduct resonated even more after that experience.

After the POWs came home, so did the aircraft—hundreds of them. Squadron after squadron of fighters, fighter-bombers and bombers filled the skies over Hickam Air Force Base, landing for a few days before taking off for the flight back to the mainland. It was an awesome thing to behold—the physical manifestation of American military might. I was too young to ponder the notion that these mighty weapons of war were returning from a conflict we had not won. That reality did not sink in until later. During this time, my father would often deploy to Vietnam, helping oversee the "Vietnamization" of the war.

But in 1975 all his efforts, and those of the US government, were undone when the North Vietnamese Army overran Saigon and defeated the South. The images on television of American pilots punching panicked South Vietnamese, and of helicopters being pushed from a US Aircraft carrier, its deck packed with refugees, took on an even more personal aspect when, in June 1975, my family brought in a South Vietnamese family to live with us for a few weeks, part of a church-sponsored program to assist refugees in their resettlement efforts. A month later the South Vietnamese family had moved on to their new home in Houston, Texas.

In October 1975, my father received orders to deploy to the Joint United States Military Mission for Aid to Turkey (JUSMMAT), which at the time functioned as the largest military assistance and advisory group in the US Department of Defense. Turkey was an important American ally, having fought side-by-side with US forces during the Korean War and, since joining the North Atlantic Treaty Organization (NATO) in 1952, had secured the southern flank of the transatlantic alliance from the perception of a Soviet threat. JUSMMAT was in Ankara, the capital of Turkey. There was no base housing, so we rented an apartment in the middle of the city.

If my childhood in Hawaii exposed me to some of the reality of the Cold War in Southeast Asia, my experience in Turkey opened my eyes to aspects of that conflict in Europe. While Vietnam had gone "hot," consuming American lives and treasure at prodigious rates, in the grand scheme of things it was but a side show. The main event between the US and the Soviet Union was in Europe, where millions of men backed by the largest concentrations of modern military equipment in the history of the world faced off along a long front stretching from the Arctic Circle in the north to the Anatolian peninsula in the south. Turkey anchored the southern flank of this line of confrontation.

By the time my family arrived in Ankara, relations between the US and its Turkish ally were frayed. Following a military coup by Greek officers in July 1974, the intent of which was to unite Cyprus with Greece, the Turkish military launched an amphibious invasion, the ostensible purpose of which was to safeguard the Turkish population of Cyprus. By August 1974, the Turkish Army had occupied around 40% of the island. In December 1974, the US Congress implemented an arms embargo which banned the sale of US military equipment and other military aid to Turkey, which went into effect in January 1975.

We lived on "the economy," (i.e., not on base) in a rented apartment in the posh neighborhood of Kavaklidere, an old wine-making district that was opened for development in 1925 for two-story residential homes intended for an expanding civil servant class. We rented the ground floor of one such apartment, with our landlords (the owners) living on the top floor. The rest of the American community lived like us, scattered across the city in rented properties. We all learned rudimentary Turkish (some better than others—I took two years of high school Turkish and qualified as an "interpreter" for the local Boy Scout troop), and frequented Turkish shops and restaurants.

The "heart" of the American community, however, was in Balgat Air Station, a US Air Force installation on the outskirts of Ankara that housed a commissary (where we could purchase a limited quantity of US canned goods and meats), a theater where we could view Hollywood movies about six months after they were released in the States, and a Department of Defense school that taught grades 1–12. There was also a hunt and saddle club, complete with stabled horses, a youth association where kids could congregate after school, and a variety of sporting fields that were used by kids and adults alike. The base was served by two "bus lines" (basically a Blue Air Force school bus) that operated two routes through the city on a scheduled basis.

Balgat was also home to the headquarters of an organization known as TUSLOG, or Turkish-US Logistics, a cover designation for a wide-range of unrelated military detachments, or "Dets," scattered across Turkey, some of which were based out of Balgat. As military brats, we were all familiar with the work done by everyone else's parents, and as such the missions of these various Dets were well-known to a tight-knit American community where nothing was secret—even the secrets. For example, Det 4-1 was the Aviation and Liaison Section which supported Det 4, a top-secret electronic intercept station which operated near the Black Sea coastal city of Sinop which monitored Soviet signals and communications, including telephone calls and the occasional space launch. Personnel from Det 4-1 would rotate in and out of Sinop on a regular basis. Another TUSLOG detachment, Det 18, operated the Belbaşı Seismic Research Station, located outside Ankara. Here US technicians would monitor Soviet underground nuclear tests conducted at the Semipalatinsk Test Site, the primary testing venue for the Soviet Union's nuclear weapons located on the steppe of northeast Kazakhstan.

And then there was Det 183, an Air Force nuclear munitions security and support unit which operated out of the Murted Turkish Air Force base. At Murted the US stored hundreds of nuclear bombs that were earmarked for delivery against Soviet targets by specially designated Turkish Air Force aircraft. There were a dozen other TUSLOG detachments headquartered out of Balgat, some involved in more mundane work, others in highly classified activities, but all part and parcel of a massive US-Turkish military cooperation program which, with the imposition of the arms embargo, had come to a screeching halt.

The arms embargo impacted my father's work at JUSMMAT as well. In June 1974, one month prior to Turkish invasion of Cyprus, the United States began delivering advanced F-4E Phantom II fighter aircraft to the Turkish Air Force as part of a NATO-wide modernization program intended to replace the ageing F-100 Super Sabre fighters as Turkey's prime nuclear weapons delivery platform. Some 40 aircraft were ordered, most of which had been delivered by the time the embargo went into effect in January 1975. Spare parts and critical aircraft maintenance training, however, was frozen by the embargo, making my father's job of advising the Turkish Air Force on F-4E aircraft maintenance extremely difficult.

My father also advised the Turkish Air Force on their F-5 fighters, some of which had to be cannibalized to keep the others flying. Turkey had procured eight F-5s from Libya to keep the overall fleet operationally viable, an act that was, in and of itself, a violation of the embargo. My father had to be on the lookout for these Libyan aircraft, since he was prohibited by law from aiding in their maintenance or operation. This bit of skullduggery only further exacerbated relations between the US military and their Turkish hosts.

Ankara was not the only concentration of Americans on Turkish soil. The Department of Defense operated four separate schools in Turkey: in Ankara, Incirlik (Adana), Izmir and Karamursel. These schools had thriving sports programs that had a remarkably high rate of participation from a small student body desperate for something to do. Virtually every weekend during the school year found student-athletes boarding chartered buses which would drive them across the width and breadth of the Anatolian peninsula, where they would be hosted by their fellow Americans in preparation for inter-scholastic competitions.

In this way, we intermingled with the children of parents who operated a massive 500-foot-diameter AN/FLR-9 circular "Wullenweber" antenna array. Erected in Karamursel and appropriately nicknamed the "Elephant Cage," it spied on Soviet and Warsaw Pact communications. Comprised of an outer reflecting screen consisting of 1056 vertical steel wires supported by 96 120-foot towers. the "Elephant Cage" literally dominated the landscape of the base, looming over the student-athletes as they play football, soccer or ran cross country or track. There was no escaping it.

In Izmir we played against the progeny of US military personnel assigned to Allied Land Forces South-Eastern Europe, a major NATO command responsible for overseeing the operations of both the Turkish and Greek armed forces during time of war. And at Incirlik we faced off against the children of the myriad of military professionals one would expect to find on any major US Air Force installation housing fighters, tankers, and nuclear weapons. While we all strived to have as normal an experience as any American teenager, we were surrounded by the constant reminder of why we were there in the first place, and the role our parents played in confronting a Soviet enemy who lived—literally—just over the horizon.

After two adventurous years in Turkey, in November 1977 my father received new orders, this time to West Germany, where he was assigned to the 17th Air Force, stationed at Sembach Air Force Base. If Turkey provided a window into some of the more sensitive intelligence operations conducted by the US against the Soviet target, Germany represented the tip of the spear when it came to actual warfighting capability, the accoutrements of which were on display daily.

Sembach itself was located some two miles from a busy airfield from which the US Air Force operated a wide mix of aircraft, including light observation, ground attack, and electronic warfare fixed-wing aircraft and heavy-lift search and rescue helicopters. These aircraft joined thousands of others from the various US and allied squadrons based in West Germany and elsewhere that filled the German skies on a continuous basis, training for a war with the Soviet Union no one wanted, but everyone was prepared for.

Sembach was but one of a half-dozen US military facilities in the greater Kaiserslautern region of the West German State of Rheinland-Pfalz which were home to some 75,000 Americans. As was the case in Turkey, my family opted to live "on the economy," initially renting a single-family home in the small village of Schallodenbach, some 13 kilometers, or 8 miles, from the city of Kaiserslautern, where the American high school was located. Even as remote as our tiny German village was, the preparations for war were ever present. US military vehicles were constantly trafficking the roads, with trucks transporting men and armored vehicles to a never-ending series of military exercises, including some which found US tanks and armored personnel carriers maneuvering in the farm fields around Schallodenbach.

Not a day went by without one confronting one or more military convoys traversing the German roads and highways. In the fall, the tempo of military activity increased by an order of magnitude as the US Army undertook its annual REFORGER (Return of Forces to Germany) exercise, flying in tens of thousands of US troops from bases in the United States, who would then marry up with prepositioned military equipment in a rehearsal of their wartime mission of reinforcing NATO in the event of a Soviet attack.

The Soviet threat was very real. Every American dependent of a certain age who lived in West Germany in the late 1970s was familiar with the Fulda Gap, an area between the Hesse-Thuringian border and the West German city of Frankfurt-am-Main. Here, NATO military planners believed the Soviets would launch their main attack if war were to break out. The initial attack would be conducted by the four divisions of the 8th Guards Army, followed by another four divisions from the 1st Guards Tank Army, which would complete the drive to the Rhine River (it was estimated that the Soviets could reach the Rhine River in 72 hours).

Standing in their path was an armored cavalry regiment and two infantry divisions belonging to the US Army; the hills around Schallodenbach represented one of the last lines of defense for these American units. The mission of the US forces was to slow the Soviet advance long enough for reinforcements to be flown in from the United States (those REFORGER exercises, it turned out, were preparatory). It was always going to be a race against time, one most people who lived in West Germany at the time believed the US would lose unless it used tactical nuclear weapons to blunt the Soviet advance.

The issue of nuclear weapons became quite personal when, in the summer of 1978, my family moved from Schallodenbach to the village of Marnheim, some 21 miles or 34 kilometers east of Kaiserslautern. Marnheim was adjacent to the village of Weirhof, where my mother worked as a nurse in a military clinic located there. The Weirhof clinic serviced a US Army community affiliated with the nearby Kriegsfeld Special Weapons Depot, also known as North Point, where the bulk of the US Army's tactical nuclear weapons in Europe were stored. It was common knowledge that Kriegsfeld would be one of the highest priority targets for the Soviets if war were to break out. Those who lived and worked around Weirhof joked that their home was "ground zero" for a Soviet nuclear weapon assault.

For most American dependents living in West Germany, the Soviet threat was abstract, a hypothetical lacking in substance. We knew it existed but could not put a face to it. The closest most of us got to an actual confrontation was the "spy versus spy" fantasies we would imagine while taking our driver's license test. Posters were mounted on the wall of the testing facility depicting a bright yellow license plate emblazoned with a Soviet flag, and the words "If you see a license plate like this," followed by detailed reporting instructions. Any vehicle bearing such a license plate belonged to the Soviet Military Liaison Mission, consisting of Soviet military officers stationed in West Germany, who were permitted to drive around certain areas to monitoring the military forces of the other occupying powers (the US, France and Great Britain). Kaiserslautern was an area of particular interest to the Soviets, and there were, in fact, numerous sightings of Soviet mission vehicles by military dependents cruising the West German backroads.

There was another way to see the Soviet threat, up close and personal. Since the end of the Second World War, the former German capital city of Berlin was under occupation by the four major powers, each of whom controlled a "sector" of the city. The three "sectors" belonging to the allies (the US, France, and Great Britain) were jointly referred to as West Berlin, while the Soviet sector was called East Berlin. In 1961 the Soviets constructed a wall around the western sectors, cutting them off from East Berlin and East Germany. The only way in and out of West Berlin was along air or ground corridors approved by the Soviets.

I was able to travel to West Berlin twice during my time in West Germany, once by vehicle and once by train. On both occasions I was able to come face to face with Soviet soldiers as they processed my paperwork. They were very professional, maintaining strict discipline regarding their interactions with the Americans they encountered, including myself.

When one crossed the border between West and East Germany (Checkpoint Alpha) and East Germany and West Berlin (Checkpoint Bravo), it was like a scene out of a movie, with border fortifications, guard towers and barbed wire topped fences patrolled by armed soldiers accompanied by large German shepherd working dogs. Inside West Berlin, I visited Checkpoint Charlie (the crossing point between West and East Berlin) and toured the Berlin Wall. On the other side were guard towers manned by armed Soviet and East German soldiers, who stared back at me through their binoculars.

From the Halls of Montezuma...

GROWING UP in Turkey and West Germany helped drive home the perception, if not reality, of the Soviet threat, and solidified my goal of joining the military so I could take my place along the border as part of the American shield that protected Europe and the United States from the scourge of Soviet communism. Upon graduation from Kaiserslautern American High School in 1979, I enlisted in the US Army to do just that. I had originally applied to the US Military Academy at West Point but was turned down. The Army offered me the opportunity to attend the United States Military Academy Preparatory School (USAMAPS) located in Fort Monmouth, New Jersey, where I would spend the next year studying, with the understanding that if I did well academically, I would be given an appointment to the Academy.

While my test scores were good, it became clear to me that the Army and I were not going to mesh well. Rampant racism, flagrant drug use, and a somewhat lackadaisical approach toward military service were some of the things that turned me off. There was a Marine detachment on the base, and I recalled how impressed I was by their bearing and esprit. I made enquiries about transferring my commission to the Marine Corps upon graduation from West Point and, when told that this would be an impossibility, I opted to resign from USAMAPS, leave the Army and attend a civilian college, where I would then seek a commission in the Marine Corps.

When it came to what I was looking for in a college, a Russian Studies program was a prerequisite. I was planning on entering the Marines for the sole purpose of confronting the Soviet threat, and I was a firm believer in the adage "to know your enemy as you know yourself." The admissions material I reviewed indicated that one was available at Franklin & Marshall College in Lancaster, Pennsylvania. I applied, was accepted, but once I arrived on campus, I found that the Russian Studies program had been disbanded the year before I arrived. Undaunted, I petitioned the Academic Dean for permission to build my own Russian Studies program, cobbling together an academic program that roughly replicated what I was looking for. Weaving history, government and economics courses together and after a further petition, I got the college to reinstate a Russian language program in time for me to get two years of college-level language training under my belt. I ended up majoring in Russian history, graduating with Departmental Honors (my honors thesis explored the historical roots of Soviet military doctrine, tracing them back to Tsarist times).

I also followed through on my commitment to join the Marine Corps, signing up for the Platoon Leaders Course (PLC), a commissioning program which required participants to attended two six-week training courses, one in the summer between your sophomore and junior year (the "Junior Course"), and another between your junior and senior year (the "Senior Course"). Assuming your position on the yellow footprints on the asphalt parking lot at Camp Upshur in Quantico, Virginia, while being ushered off the bus by bellowing Sergeant Instructors, is something that anyone who has experienced it will never forget. The same holds true for running the Obstacle Course and the Endurance Course, which included the dreaded Quigley (an obstacle-filled ditch containing a liquid morass of unforgettable stench and equally unappealing consistency, which officer candidates like myself had to negotiate), and the Small Unit Leadership Exercises, which tested one's physical and mental capacity under extreme duress. When I graduated from each of my PLC sessions, I held my head high. I had earned the right to do so.

Upon graduation from F&M in May 1984 I was commissioned as a Second Lieutenant, and later that year was sent to The Basic School (TBS), a six-month finishing program in Quantico designed to turn all Marine officers, regardless of their eventual military occupational specialties, into leaders capable of commanding a platoon-sized force (30-plus Marines) in combat. In 1985, while I was attending TBS, I published an article on anti-Soviet resistance in Central Asia, drawn from some of the research I had done for my honors thesis, in *Soviet Studies*, a prestigious academic journal. It was on the strength of my academic degree, my performance at TBS, and this *Soviet Studies* article that I was able to petition Headquarters Marine Corps to waive the normal three-year combat arms service requirement for officers wanting to enter the field of intelligence.

I received orders to report to the Marine Corps Air Ground Combat Center in 29 Palms, California. My first assignment was to the G-2 Staff (intelligence) of the 7th Marine Amphibious Brigade (MAB), the Marine Corps component of the Rapid Deployment Force (RDF). I had yet to complete my formal intelligence training, and the G-2 staff had no clue about what to do with a freshly minted Lieutenant with zero practical experience. I was tasked with updating the primary contingency plan for 7th MAB deployment into the Middle East region. At that time, the two primary threats we were preparing for were the possibility of an Iranian offensive that broke through Iraqi lines and threatened Kuwait, as well as a Soviet invasion of Iran that sought to gain control of Iranian ports along the Persian Gulf. Based upon my work updating the contingency intelligence plans, I was subsequently tasked with tracking Soviet operations in Afghanistan and developments in the Iran-Iraq War.

In the summer of 1985, the 1st Marine Division, to whom the 7th MAB was subordinated, conducted its annual Command Post exercise (which focused on staff functioning, with no actual combat units being deployed), this time responding to a simulated Soviet invasion of Iran. I remember explicitly watching the battle unfold on the map from inside the command tent—the establishment of the Marine beachhead in Iran, the advance inland, and the initial contact with Soviet forces. I also recall how the Soviets eventually punched through our lines and observed the decision making that went into authorizing the release of tactical nuclear weapons by Marine artillery for the purpose of halting the Soviet advance. The exercise ended when the 8-inch tactical nuclear round was fired. When I asked what would happen next, I was told "Nothing. The War is over. The Soviets responded with a massive nuclear counterstrike, and we're all dead."

Shortly after that exercise, I was sent to Washington, DC to attend what was called "Soviet Military Power Week," a conference put on by the Defense Intelligence Agency (DIA) to familiarize military intelligence officers from all services with the Soviet threat. The conference coincided with the publication of the 1985 edition of *Soviet Military Power*, a glossy publication produced by the DIA that was filled with photographs, charts and illustrations depicting the Soviet armed forces in all their glory. I left the conference duly impressed with the power of the Soviet adversary and fully committed to the task of beating them on the field of battle.

After completing my formal training as an intelligence officer, I was reassigned to 5th Battalion, 11th Marines—the very unit which, during the Command Post exercise the previous summer, had been tasked with firing the nuclear artillery shell that initiated the simulated nuclear Armageddon. Upon checking in, I was challenged by the Commanding Officer, a hard-charging Lieutenant Colonel named Nick Carlucci, as to what I expected my role in the Battalion to be. I gave him the school-house solution: "Intelligence drives operations, Sir."

"Do you really believe that?" he asked.

"Yes, Sir," was my naïve reply. I left his office tasked with preparing an annual training plan built around a realistic intelligence-based threat.

"Your predecessor was relieved for failing to meet the Commander's high expectations," the Executive Officer, Major Kibler, told me. I was determined not to suffer the same fate.

Shoot, move, communicate—these are the core tasks of Marine artillery. We needed to do these tasks faster and more efficiently than our enemy or die. I studied Soviet artillery tactics and operations and trained the firing batteries on the standards they would have to meet in combat if they were to survive against such a threat. I brought in target acquisition radars and tracked outgoing artillery rounds fired by the 5/11 firing batteries back to their point of origin, plotting simulated counterbattery fires based upon that intelligence. If the firing battery was still in place when my simulated rounds impacted, they were considered *hors de combat*, a result the Battalion Commander frowned upon.

I travelled to the US Army's National Training Center (NTC) in Fort Irwin, where I rode along with the Opposing Forces (OPFOR), trained and organized to fight as a Soviet Motorized Infantry Regiment, as they engaged US Army units in large-scale force-on-force combat—and watched as the "Soviets" repeatedly defeated their American counterparts with overwhelming firepower and massed formations. Based upon these observations of the simulation, I knew that Marines could not stand toe-to-toe with the Soviets and expect to survive for long. So instead, I worked with the S-3 (operations) staff to construct training evolutions where we learned to fight a fluid battle, always moving, probing, retreating, attacking, and counterattacking to wear down and ultimately defeat the enemy.

I was stationed in 29 Palms, California, home to the Marine Corps Air Ground Combat Center, which specialized in combined arms training. 29 Palms had a huge training area which, if one planned carefully, could be used in its entirety to simulate the kind of distances we would be called upon to operate in, should we be called upon to fight in the Middle East. I would often coordinate with supporting infantry, armor, light armor, and air to turn a simple battalion live fire exercise into a regimental combined arms battle that would unfold for hundreds of miles, stressing realism at every level. I sharpened my skills in directing supporting arms by attending the Naval Aerial Observer course, where I learned to call in artillery, naval gunfire, and close air support while operating from the back seat of an OV-10 Bronco.

I knew that, as a nuclear-capable artillery battalion, we would be a prime target for Soviet special forces—Spetznaz—who were tasked with hunting us down and killing us before we could be employed in a nuclear role. To better prepare for this, I became qualified as an instructor in the use of the multiple integrated laser engagement system, or MILES, used by the Army at NTC to replicate live combat as realistically as possible, and then trained the battalion personnel on the use of this system. The MILES system allowed force-on-force engagements between ground forces using small arms and supporting weapons. The weapons would fire blanks, which would in turn activate a laser system attacked to the weapon, "firing" a beam toward the target. Each Marine was equipped with a sensor harness which detected incoming laser beams and, if it was determined that the laser beam had hit with lethal effect, would activate an alarm indicating the Marine in question was "dead."

I then organized my own Soviet OPFOR—in this case a platoon-sized *Spetnaz* force using Marines from Headquarters and Services Battery, Scouts from 3rd Tank battalion, and Scout-Snipers from 1st Battalion, 4th Marines— which would engage the firing batteries of the battalion in force-on-force laser-assisted combat. I did my best to replicate Soviet tactics, having vehicle-mounted patrols inserted into the rear area via helicopter, and then conducting aggressive patrolling and reconnaissance to locate, identify, close with, and destroy Marine artillery units before they could accomplish their nuclear mission. Through training such as this, I helped transition the West's largest self-propelled artillery battalion away from Vietnam-era tactics into the epitome of what a cutting-edge maneuver warfare-oriented fire support unit should look like. I will always be proud of what I accomplished there.

In the military, all tours eventually come to an end, and by the close of 1987 my time at 29 Palms was up. On my annual fitness report, where it asked for preferred assignment preference, I had put down "any FMF," for "Fleet Marine Force." I wanted to be on the frontlines of any future fight, and that could only happen if you were assigned to a frontline unit. In December 1987 I was informed that I was being assigned to the 11th Marine Amphibious Unit (Special Operations Capable), where I was to serve as the Assistant S-2. I was thrilled with these orders, as they would put me at the tip of the proverbial spear for any real-world contingency (i.e., combat) that might arise.

I was aware that my commanding officer had placed a call to my career monitor at Headquarters Marine Corps, telling him that my talents would be wasted in the fleet, and that I should be given an assignment of a more "national" character. At the time, there were no such billets available for a junior First Lieutenant, and it looked like my job as the 11th MAU S-2A was secure. I was wrong. On January 19, 1988, Headquarters Marine Corps signed off on Marine Corps component staffing for what was to become the On-Site Inspection Agency (OSIA). (This was a full week prior to OSIA being formally established.)

Two days later, on January 21, my orders to the 11th MAU were cancelled, replaced by a new set which had me travelling to Washington, DC, reporting to Headquarters, Marine Corps no later than February 7. All I was told at the time was that this assignment had something to do with the INF Treaty that had been recently signed by President Reagan and General Secretary Mikhail Gorbachev. The next day, January 22, my orders were amended, this time indicating that I was to report to the Defense Nuclear Agency for duty with OSIA as an Intelligence Analyst, and that I was further to report to the Commandant of the Coast Guard no later than February 4.

In between checking out of 5/11 and packing up my belongings, I spent time with my good friend, Paul Marx, who was the Intelligence Officer of 3rd Tank Battalion and, like myself, singularly focused on closing with and destroying the Soviet enemy. We read news reports about the INF Treaty and tried to piece together what kind of work I might be called upon to do. I did not know anything about ballistic missiles, and we both agreed my utility as an inspector would be minimal at best. The job description was for an "intelligence analyst," so the best we could come up with was that I would be responsible for keeping track of Soviet missile inventories. We both ruminated about the end of an era, noting that if the INF treaty worked as planned, the likelihood of a US-Soviet military confrontation would be greatly reduced. "Well," Paul joked, "if you can't shoot them, at least hug them to death."

For a while, it looked like I might be denied even that opportunity. When I arrived at the Defense Nuclear Agency, I was told that the position of Intelligence Analyst no longer existed. The receiving officer had no additional information, telling me that I would find out more about what my job would be when I checked in with OSIA at its temporary offices in the old Coast Guard Headquarters, in downtown Washington, DC. However, when I arrived at Buzzards Point (where the Coast Guard Headquarters was located), I was told that the On-Site Inspection Agency did not yet exist. "You're early," I was told. "You're not supposed to be here until Monday (February 8)."

I exited the Coast Guard Headquarters on that cold February morning, a Marine with no job, no parent organization, and no idea what he had just gotten himself into.

CHAPTER TWO

The Human Factor

The Technical On-Site Inspection (TOSI) Demonstration Facility,
Sandia National Laboratory, Albuquerque, New Mexico, April 1988.

> *"Then I heard the voice of the Lord saying,*
> *'Whom shall I send? And who will go for us?'*
> *And I said, 'Here I am. Send me!'"*

ISAIAH 6:8

The Verification Equation

IN SEPTEMBER 1987, a new member of the US INF Delegation in Geneva, a scientist named Stan Fraley, tabled a draft Inspection Protocol for the Soviets to consider. A little more than a year prior, Stan Fraley had been appointed as the liaison between Sandia National Laboratory (part of the Department of Energy's complex of nuclear weapons laboratories), and the Office of Verification Policy in the Department of Defense. His first task was to write a draft INF Inspection Protocol that considered the various arms control verification technologies then being developed at Sandia. This draft was appended to the draft INF Treaty presented by the US delegation in Geneva in March 1987, although the actual protocol was not shared with the Soviets due to concerns on the part of the US delegation that to do so would be a waste of time until the Soviets indicated they were serious about concluding a treaty.[1]

In September 1987 this threshold was reached. Fraley was dispatched to Geneva, where he served as the US Chair of the US/Soviet Working Group for the Inspection Protocol of the INF Treaty. Fraley shared his draft Inspection Protocol with the Soviets at this time (although, as he later acknowledged, it had been "rewritten by Committee before the Soviets saw it."[2])

Normally the Soviets would wait months before responding with their own counterproposal. This time, however, the Soviets responded within a week, stating that they would be willing to work off the US draft. A little more than two months later, the Inspection Protocol had been finished—eight pages of carefully crafted text, each word having been checked and double checked by the working group before being approved.

The key elements of the verification regime designed by Stan Fraley and introduced to the Soviets in September 1987 included:

- The requirement that all INF missiles and launchers be in agreed areas or in announced transit between such areas during the reductions period.
- A detailed exchange of data, updated as necessary, on the location of missile support facilities and missile operating bases, the number of missiles and launchers at those facilities and bases, and technical parameters of those missile systems.
- Notification of movement of missiles and launchers between declared facilities.
- A baseline on-site inspection to verify the number of missiles and launchers at declared missile support facilities and missile operating bases prior to elimination.
- On-site inspection to verify the destruction of missiles and launchers.
- Follow-on, short-notice inspection of declared facilities during the reductions period to verify residual levels, until all missiles are eliminated.
- Short-notice, mandatory challenge inspections of certain facilities in the United States and Soviet Union at which banned missile activity could be carried out.
- A separate "close out" inspection to ensure that, when a site is deactivated and removed from the list of declared facilities, it has indeed ended INF-associated activity.

Prior to being assigned to the Office of the Secretary of Defense, Fraley had served as the supervisor of Sandia National Laboratory's Verification Systems and Technology Division and was the program leader for what was known as the Technical On-Site Inspection (TOSI) demonstration facility. Fraley's division was involved in executing a contract with the Department of Defense to explore and develop potential verification methods for arms control treaties. Even though at the time the contract was let in 1983, the INF negotiation process was on hold. Fraley's efforts proved instrumental in creating confidence among US negotiators that the strict verification provisions envisioned for an INF treaty could be fulfilled, at least from a technical point of view.

Stan Fraley and the rest of the INF negotiators were prisoners to policy—if the policy makers in Washington, DC were inclined to be supportive of arms control, then the prospects for a successful treaty being negotiated were good; otherwise, the arms race would continue. Policymakers were not necessarily politicians, although they were heavily influenced by political trends. By the time Ronald Reagan was elected President, the political trend was drifting away from the notion of verifiable arms control, with the US arms control community soured by reports of Soviet non-compliance with the SALT I and SALT II agreements.

This negativity dominated the thinking of those policymakers to whom Stan Fraley reported, in particular the Director of Verification Policy within the Office of the Assistant Secretary of Defense for International Security Policy, Sally K. Horn, and her deputy, George W. Look. Sally Horn was a 1968 graduate of Pembroke College who began her government career in the Policy Plans Office of the Department of Defense's Office of International Security Affairs. A specialist in Russian affairs, Horn started out as an analyst, gradually working her way up to become a member of the Special Executive Service.

George Look was a former colleague of Fraley's. After receiving his PhD in high energy physics from Purdue University in 1977, Look joined Sandia, where he spent the next nine years involved in nuclear safety and security. He left Sandia in 1986 and spent a year as a private consultant on arms control verification, participating on a Defense Science Board panel that helped define the role of missile production as a verification focus, before taking his position as Horn's deputy in 1987.

Both Horn and Look lived in an esoteric, wonkish world dominated by science and math. Here, calculations such as the "verification equation" were used to evaluate the expected advantages that might motivate the Soviets to violate an arms control agreement.[3] In this equation, factors such as the "benefit perceived by the Soviets if they successfully evaded detection" (*BS*) and the "disadvantage to the Soviets if a violation was exposed" (*DS*) were viewed as quantifiable concepts. Both *BS* and *DS* incorporated military, economic and military benefits and risks. In the calculation, the probability that the United States would detect a violation was denoted by *P*, and *E* would denote the expected advantage of a successful violation of the agreement to the Soviets.

Accordingly, a "verification equation" could be symbolically written like this:

$$E = ((1 - P) \times BS) - (P \times DS).$$

Accordingly, verification would be a deterrent to cheating by the Soviets if

$$E < 0$$

or

$$P > 1/1 + (DS/BS)$$

In this equation, the "probability of detection" (P) was controlled by the United States, dependent as it would be on the quality of its verification technology and operational procedures.

BS and DS, however, were dependent upon the intentions and psychology of the Soviets—the greater the differentiation between BS and DS, the more likely verification is to succeed.

Prior to the INF treaty negotiations entering their final phase, the DS/BS ratio was considered insufficient to expect a verifiable arms control agreement from reaching fruition. The expected benefit for cheating on the part of the Soviets was too high (witness, by way of example, the Soviet decision regarding the SS-16 ICBM). But even if the disadvantages to cheating were increased through the improvement of relations between the Soviet Union and the United States, the United States still needed to be able to detect a potential violation in order for the equation to balance out.

Prior to Stan Fraley tabling his Inspection Protocol, P was a factor of National Technical Means (NTM)—America's fleet of spy satellites. The traditional standard used by American arms control negotiators when it came to treaty compliance verification was known as "adequate verification," meaning a situation where no cheating would be possible "that could change the military balance." From this perspective, National Technical Means (NTM) were considered "adequate." Since nuclear weapons were involved, this was a virtually meaningless standard.

In moving toward accepting an INF treaty with the Soviets, the Reagan administration adopted a new standard, known as "effectively verifiable," that took into account possibilities of cheating that had consequences of military significance, and involved detailed obligations on the part of the inspected parties as well as explicit mechanisms for enforcement.

To meet this "effective" standard, the NTM-only factors that went into P in the "verification equation" had to change. By incorporating on-site inspection into the equation, the value of P could be adjusted enough to meet the new standard.

Sally Horn and George Look were no fans of on-site inspection—the human factor was too volatile to be reliably captured mathematically so that it could be inserted into the "verification equation" in any meaningful sense. But while policymakers advised the decision makers, they did not make decisions—

the President and his Cabinet did. And by the summer of 1987, the decision had been made to go forward with finalizing the INF Treaty. Stan Fraley's Inspection Protocol would give Sally Horn and George Look, whether they liked it or not, the on-site inspection modifier that made the value of P able to meet the new "effectively verifiable" standard.

That was, until mid-November 1987, when the Soviets informed their US counterparts about the similarities between the first stage of the SS-20 and SS-25 missiles. This problem was raised in the aftermath of the meeting between Secretary of State George Shultz and Foreign Minister Eduard Shevardnadze in Geneva, Switzerland on November 22–24, 1987. The Soviet acknowledgement that the first stage of the SS-25 ICBM was "outwardly similar" to the first stage of the soon to be banned SS-20 intermediate range missile presented the INF treaty negotiators with a complex issue of verification that needed to be resolved prior to the Reagan-Gorbachev summit and treaty signing ceremony scheduled to take place in Washington, DC in two weeks' time. A fifth type of on-site inspection was now required—Perimeter Portal Monitoring, or PPM. Fortunately for the negotiators, Stan Fraley had a ready solution—the Technical On-Site Inspection (TOSI) demonstration facility.

The TOSI demonstration facility grew out of an Office of the Secretary of Defense initiative in the early 1980s to explore the technical requirements associated with arms control compliance verification. Given the deep freeze that existed between the US and the Soviets regarding arms control negotiations that had existed since 1983, the OSD-driven study was driven by theoretical requirements, as opposed to any user-driven directives. One of the concepts pursued was that of perimeter portal monitoring of missile production facilities. Beginning in 1986, the perimeter portal monitoring concept, centered as it was on the idea that one could "capture" a missile factory with technology which enabled the ability to monitor production with a high degree of verifiable certainty, was turned into a full-scale demonstration complex known as the Technical On-Site Inspection (TOSI) Project. The TOSI demonstration facility was completed on December 15, 1986, and incorporated hardware from several Sandia departments, including those involved in nuclear safeguards in support of the nonproliferation treaty.

In May 1986 a table-top model of the perimeter portal monitoring (PPM) facility was briefed to the Soviets in Geneva as representing the kind of detailed, intrusive verification inspections that would be required to monitor any residual force of SS-20s. The American objective wasn't to convince the Soviets to allow them to deploy PPM, but rather to get the Soviets to agree to "absolute zero," the total elimination of INF systems, including the SS-20, to eliminate the need for intrusive PPM inspections. As such, when the Soviets finally agreed to eliminate all SS-20 missiles, the US dropped its insistence on PPM. By banning the SS-20 altogether, the verification equation became simplified—NTM was considered effective enough to differentiate between an SS-20 and an SS-25. The fact that SS-25 missiles were being produced in Votkinsk simply did not factor into the INF compliance verification equation.

Then the Soviets announced the similarity between the SS-20 and SS-25 first stages.

Suddenly the monitoring of the ongoing manufacture of the SS-25 missile at the Votkinsk factory *was*, in fact, relevant to the INF treaty. Now, the Votkinsk Missile Final Assembly Plant needed to be "captured" by PPM inspectors who would monitor the exiting of all traffic, inspecting any vehicle or object large enough to transport the first stage of an SS-20 missile to ensure that the Soviets weren't using SS-25 production (permitted under the treaty) as a cover for the continued manufacture of a covert SS-20 force (banned by the treaty).

SS-20 missile (top), SS-25 missile (middle), and SS-25 launch cannister (bottom) as shipped from the Votkinsk Final Assembly Plant. Photo Credit: Soviet MoD

But the TOSI demonstration facility was intended to provide a technology test bed for the hypothetical perimeter portal monitoring of a *notional* missile production facility—*not* the Votkinsk Missile Final Assembly plant *specifically*. In defense of the INF treaty negotiators, they had less than three weeks to resolve the Votkinsk issue if the treaty was to be saved. Most of the technical issues were glossed over in the treaty text, with the negotiators opting to have them finalized through a series of technical talks to be held *after* the treaty was signed, but *before* it would be ratified, that would produce a Memorandum of Agreement that would be appended to the treaty.

The human factor had been inserted into the issue of INF compliance verification in a way that stolid verification policy experts such as Sally Horn and George Look would never have supported had the circumstances been different. But politics drives policy, and President Reagan had committed to the INF treaty. The question was no longer would on-site inspection be a part of any treaty compliance verification scheme, but rather just precisely how the human factor it encompassed would be managed.

The General

WHEN THE DECISION was made regarding which organization was going to take the lead for implementing the on-site inspection-based verification provisions of the INF Treaty, there was a recognition that this job had to be done correctly from the start, or else it would fail, and take years of arms control negotiations down with it.

Directing that an organization be formed for the purpose of carrying out the provisions of the newly signed INF treaty was the easy part. On January 15, 1988, President Reagan signed National Security Directive (NSD) 296, instructing the Secretary of Defense to create a new agency dedicated to overseeing the on-site inspection aspects of treaty implementation. On January 26, 1988—eleven days after the President signed the NSD directive—the Deputy Secretary of Defense, William H. Taft IV, established the On-Site Inspection Agency (OSIA) as a separate operating agency in the Department of Defense responsible for the implementation of the INF Treaty. The Director would report to the Under Secretary of Defense for Acquisition, and an executive committee consisting of the Chairman of the Joint Chiefs of Staff and the Under Secretaries of Defense for Acquisition and Policy would provide oversight and direction.

The decision to assign the responsibility for implementation of on-site inspections to the Department of Defense had not been a foregone conclusion. A ten-man task force, established in early December 1987 under the auspices of the Joint Chiefs of Staff (JCS), was responsible for not only defining the structure of what became the On-Site Inspection Agency, but also who would be responsible for running it. The choice came down to the Department of Defense or the Arms Control and Disarmament Agency (ACDA), part of the State Department.

The scope and scale of the operations anticipated under the INF Treaty meant that ACDA, with a staff of fewer than 190 persons, would be swamped by treaty implementation requirements necessitating several times that number of dedicated personnel. The new inspection organization would require Soviet area specialists, linguists and experts in the various INF weapons systems covered by the treaty, skill sets unique to the Department of Defense. ACDA was given a supporting role in the form of a Deputy Director position, but the Director of the new agency would be a military officer.

But the new inspection organization needed people, and unlike the lines and blocks of an organizational chart, these could not be conjured up with the simple stroke of a pen. "Weapons inspector" was not a job description that existed in the Department of Defense in early 1988. The American military was coming off a decades-long war in Vietnam, the consequences of which still resonated among those who had been enlisted or commissioned in the 1960s and early 1970s. The war in Southeast Asia was part and parcel of a larger project of containing the Soviet Union, commonly referred to as the Cold War, and a Cold War mentality, built around the premise that the Soviet Union must be confronted, permeated the ranks of the US military.

The Cold War had its ideological roots in George Kennan's famous "long telegram" of February 22, 1946, where he identified the Soviet Union as a long-term ideological adversary of the United States.[4] This approach was later solidified in Paul Nitze's 1950 National Security Council (NSC) Decision Paper 68, which articulated the Soviet threat in stark terms, and proposed a policy that rejected détente and containment in favor of actively rolling back Soviet influence around the world. (Somewhat ironically, Nitze went on to become the first Chief negotiator for the INF treaty. His famous 1981 "walk in the woods" with his Soviet counterpart, Yuli Kvitsinsky, underscored his commitment to find a solution to the problem of intermediate-range missiles in Europe).[5] The Korean War breathed life into NSC 68, and its policy formulations influenced the decision to intervene in Southeast Asia.

The American experience in Vietnam coincided with the massive expansion of the nuclear strategic capabilities of both the US and Soviet Union, as well as the decline of US conventional capabilities in Europe. As the US transitioned from a "hot" war in Southeast Asia to a "cold" war in Europe, it needed to rebuild a force possessing the kind of skill sets needed to confront the Soviet threat in the operational gray zone that existed between actively preparing for war, and war itself.

These Cold Warriors were unique in the history of the US military—men and women who prepared for the worst possible outcome while living in a world ignorant of the realities of their actions and the consequences of their ever having to pull the proverbial nuclear trigger.

Most were involved in the classic business of fighting wars—serving as infantry, or operating the tanks, artillery, armored vehicles, aircraft, and other accouterments of modern war that would be called upon to employ if the balloon ever went up. But there was another category of Cold Warrior whose job description was more hands-on when it came to the Soviet threat—the Foreign

Area Officer, or FAO. Theirs was a war conducted away from the conventional battlefield, collecting intelligence, and gathering, firsthand, insights about the Soviet Union and its capabilities that informed military and political decision makers at the highest levels in American government. It was from this crop of Cold Warriors that this new class of American servicemember—the "weapons inspector"—would be drawn.

To lead this new breed, the Department of Defense selected one of the greatest Cold Warriors of all time—Brigadier General Roland Lajoie. Lajoie entered the US Army not unlike most of his peers, receiving his commission in in 1958, following his graduation from the University of New Hampshire with a degree in Government. He was placed in the Intelligence Branch, specializing in Psychological Operations. Like most servicemembers of his generation, he saw service in Vietnam, doing two tours there as a company grade officer, during which he was awarded a Bronze Star medal for valor.

It was at this stage in his career that Lajoie began to separate from the pack. As a Captain, Lajoie was selected for Russian language training, and graduated from the Defense Language Institute (DLI) in 1968, before spending two years at the US Army Institute for Advanced Russian and East European Studies (USAIAREES), a unique finishing school for military officers from all branches who were training to be Soviet Foreign Area Officers.

The FAO program was, at the time, relatively new, growing out of what was known as the Foreign Area Specialist Training (FAST) program. When Lajoie attended DLI in 1968, he did so as part of the FAST program, in his status as a Psychological Warfare officer. (FAST also supported Attaché programs, Civil Affairs and Military Government). In 1969, FAST was revised, with the intelligence-oriented aspects of the program continuing under the FAST rubric, and a new Military Assistance Officer Program (MAOP) being formed to handle the regional political-military needs of supported commands. In 1973, these two programs were merged into the newly designated Foreign Area Officer program, which was designed to provide qualified officers to identified FAO billets worldwide.

Foreign Area Officers were usually selected as senior Captains/junior Majors who had achieved proficiency in their area of specialization appropriate to their rank (which generally meant having served in at least two Company-grade assignments and graduated from the Company-level professional development course). Qualified candidates would then attend a six-month FAO basic course before proceeding to a three-phased program involving language training, earning an advanced degree relating to a specific geographical region, and then obtaining overseas training in the country or region of specialization that would allow for cultural and linguistic immersion. Those FAOs who were selected to be Soviet specialists would normally spend a year at DLI taking the basic Russian language course, then spend another 1–2 years at a graduate school getting their master's degree in a relevant field. Many opted to attend the Naval Postgraduate School, which was co-located with DLI in Monterrey, California.

It was at this point their training would diverge from the other FAO specialties. Normally a FAO student would be assigned to the country of interest, where he/she would immerse themselves in the culture and language through travel and work. Given the poor state of relations between the US and the Soviet Union, this option was not available to the Soviet specialists. Instead, they were sent to the US Army Institute for Advanced Russian and East European Studies (USAIAREES), a unique program designed to replicate the cultural and linguistic immersion experience.

USAIAREES began its life in 1947 as Field Detachment "R," a War Department-sponsored program designed to provide Soviet specialist officers in the FAST program with immersive language and cultural experience prior to their posting to Moscow as an assistant attaché, or to Potsdam, East Germany as part of the Military Liaison Mission, a group of US military observers attached to the Soviet Group of Forces, Germany. The course made extensive use of Russian and Soviet defectors who, together with more conventional academics from the United States, taught courses and provided social interactions, all the while speaking Russian. In 1967 responsibility for Detachment "R" was turned over to Headquarters, US Army, Europe (USAEUR), and renamed the US Army Institute for Advanced Russian and East European Studies.[6]

Captain Lajoie was promoted to Major, graduated from USAIAREES, and went on to get his master's degree in History from the University of Colorado in 1971. He then attended the Army's Command & Staff College, graduating in 1973.

Lajoie's next assignment set the tone for the rest of his career—he was dispatched to Moscow, where he served as an Assistant US Army Attaché at the US Embassy. Lajoie's tour came on the heels of the legendary Samuel Vaughan Wilson, who as a Brigadier General served as the Defense Attaché in Moscow from 1971 to 1973. The standards put in place under Wilson carried over to Lajoie's tour, including his legacy as a near-native Russian linguist with a deep understanding and appreciation of Russian and Soviet history. Wilson was able to establish a solid rapport with senior officers in the Soviet military high command, and the insights he gained from these contacts were extremely valuable to US policy makers as they worked on improving US-Soviet ties and negotiated new arms control agreements. Wilson also simultaneously served as the CIA's Station Chief in Moscow, underscoring the hand-in-glove relationship between that agency and the military attaché system.

Major Lajoie served in Moscow from 1973 until 1976. Neither he nor any of his fellow attachés were expelled from the Soviet Union during this time, an indication of either good tradecraft on their part or restrictive reporting requirements from the US intelligence community (given the attention paid to the Soviet Union by US decision makers during this time, the latter is highly doubtful). Unlike their CIA counterparts, defense attachés were not usually tasked with covert intelligence collection (unless their status as a military attaché was itself a cover assignment for assignment as a covert CIA officer; Samuel Wilson's dual-hatted status as Defense Attaché and CIA Station Chief stands out).[7] When defense attachés got in trouble, it was usually for unauthorized photography, receiving unsolicited classified documents, or travelling in prohibited areas. For the most part, the job of a defense attaché was to keep their eyes and ears open hoping for serendipitous exposure to something of interest, or to engage their Soviet counterparts in conversation, hoping to elicit the same. Lajoie finished his tour in Moscow without incident, the sign of a successful tour.

Lajoie left Moscow as a newly promoted Lieutenant Colonel, heading to West Germany, where he took command of USAIAREES, the finishing school for Soviet Foreign Area Officers. The program Lajoie took over in 1976 was less than satisfactory. The primary problem was the linguistic qualifications of the students being sent from DLI, which were uniformly poor. Since the entire curriculum at USAIAREES was taught in Russian, this meant that valuable time had to be taken away from the rest of the institute's curriculum, and from the staff itself, to tutor individuals to the bare level of proficiency needed to graduate from the program. FAO students, practically assured of completing the program once in the training pipeline, had little motivation to push themselves to learn what was a difficult language. Working with the Department of the Army and DLI, Lajoie sought to create a minimum standard of linguistic competence that would need to be met for a FAO student to graduate from DLI, and later to graduate from USAIAREES—poor performance would no longer be tolerated. (Later, when he needed to draw upon the ranks of Soviet FAOs to fill his need for inspectors at OSIA, this tightening of linguistic standards would pay off.[8])

While he struggled to correct the language deficiencies inherent in the Soviet FAO program, Lajoie was also called upon to oversee the reorganization of USAIAREES, transferring responsibility away from USAEUR and to the US Army Intelligence Command (INSCOM). This reorganization was completed in October 1978, and USAIAREES was renamed the United States Army Russia Institute (USARI). With a new name came a new attitude; gone were the days of just getting by.[9]

A senior US Foreign Service Officer, Phillip Brown, who attended USARI in 1977–1978, recalled an incident when he and a few military officers were sent to Moscow on a familiarization visit. Upon returning, the officers complained about the quality of the hotel and food they had encountered. According to Brown, Lajoie blew his top. "I didn't send you there on a tourist trip," Lajoie informed the officers in question. "I sent you there to observe, and if everything was not comfortable, that's exactly what I wanted you to find out!"[10]

By the time Roland Lajoie finished his tour as Commandant, USARI, he had put an indelible imprint on the US military's premier Russian language training program, institutionalizing a standard of professionalism that would shape the Soviet FAO program for years to come.

Lieutenant Colonel Lajoie returned to the regular Army in 1979, taking command of the 1st Psychological Operations Battalion, located at Fort Bragg, North Carolina. His tour there was notable for the deployment of his unit in support of the Cuban refugee crisis, in 1980. From 1980 to 1981, Lajoie returned to academia, first as a research fellow at the United States Army War College, in Carlisle, Pennsylvania, and then at Harvard University, in Cambridge, Massachusetts. After finishing his stint at Harvard, Lajoie, by now promoted to the rank of Colonel, returned to Moscow in 1981 as the Army Attaché at the US Embassy.

When Roland Lajoie last set foot in Moscow, détente was in the air, and the two nations acted accordingly. By 1981, détente was dead, and the Cold War was raging as strong as ever. Moscow was the forward edge of the battle area of this conflict, the area where combatants engaged with their enemy in a game of intelligence and counterintelligence, spy versus spy. A shooting war was a real possibility, and the insights one could glean about enemy intent and capability in this battle in the shadows could very well provide the edge one side needed to overcome the other, when the real bullets started to fly.

The attaché business was a gentleman's game, played using a distinctive set of rules which had the participants shrouded in a veil of diplomatic immunity while they did their best to gain access to the secrets of the other side. If one was caught, the price was expulsion. And, because the rules of the game included strict reciprocity, sometimes even if you didn't get caught, you were expelled none the less.

It was often a rough game, with each side trying to set up the other for failure. Prior to Lajoie arriving in Moscow, two assistant Army attachés, Major James Holbrook and Lieutenant Colonel Thomas Spencer, had been dispatched to Ukraine to monitor Soviet military activity in the Carpathian Military District. The Defense Intelligence Agency, which ran the attaché program, had placed a high priority on tracking the Soviet response to the unfolding situation in Poland, where the Solidarity movement was taking hold. Holbrook and Spencer travelled to the city of Rovno, where they booked a room in a hotel. While eating a meal at the hotel restaurant, both Holbrook and Spencer were overcome by illness, believed to have been brought on by drugs injected into their food by the KGB for the purpose of incapacitating them. Holbrook and Spencer became separated, and later Holbrook was solicited in his room by prostitutes hired by the KGB to produce compromising photographs of him. A Soviet Colonel whom Holbrook knew from his previous work with the US Military Liaison Mission in Potsdam suddenly appeared and offered to help Holbrook out of the situation. Holbrook refused. He and Spencer were detained for several hours and denied access to communications as the KGB pressured the Americans to cooperate. The attachés were finally released and returned to Moscow, where they reported the incident. Both were subsequently sent back to the United States.[11]

It took a year for the Americans to hit back. In February 1982, Major General Vasily I. Chitov was declared *persona non grata* and expelled from the United States "for activities inconsistent with his diplomatic status." Chitov headed the Soviet Embassy's military attaché office. He had arranged to meet a civilian employee of a private company engaged in sensitive military contracting. The rendezvous was to take place in a shopping center in the metropolitan Washington, DC area. The employee turned out to be an informant working for the FBI, whose agents were on scene when Chitov took possession of what the FBI had termed "sensitive documents." After a high-speed car chase in which Chitov sought to evade the FBI, he was pulled over and arrested.[12]

Luck—both good and bad—often was a factor. In March 1983 Richard Osborne, the First Secretary of the US Embassy's Economic Section, went for a walk together with his family in a Moscow Park. He was carrying his briefcase with him. Hidden inside the briefcase was a miniaturized satellite communication set the CIA, Osborne's true employer, wanted to give to select Soviet agents so they could communicate directly with the CIA, bypassing the risky face-to-face meetings with CIA officers in Moscow. Osborne was testing the device, making sure it functioned as advertised, before handing it over to the agent. The KGB, however, had detected the signal during previous tests, and was following Osborne in case he was to try another. Osborne was caught red-handed, the satellite communications device seized, and the unlucky First Secretary expelled from the Soviet Union.[13]

What connected Osborne to Lajoie was the fact that the covert communications device that was being tested had earlier been dispatched to Moscow to be used by David Rolph, an assistant Army attaché working directly for Roland Lajoie. Rolph's attaché work, however, was a cover for his real job, as a case officer for the CIA. Rolf was running Adolf Tolkachev, one of the CIA's most important and productive spies. Communications with Tolkachev were tricky, and in 1982 CIA Headquarters wanted Rolph to train Tolkachev on the use of the new satellite communications system. But when Rolph took it out for the kind of test that got Osborne caught, the system failed, prompting Rolph to send it back to Langley to be fixed. Why the KGB caught Osborne, but failed to catch Rolph, is anyone's guess—luck, tradecraft, simple serendipity. Rolph worked for Lajoie, and had he been caught, there would have been hell to pay.[14]

If Moscow was tough, Colonel Lajoie's follow-on posting was even tougher. The United States Military Liaison Mission, or USMLM, was one of the most storied units in the history of American intelligence. In March 1947, Soviet and American authorities had instituted the Huebner-Malinin Agreement, which established the United States Military Liaison Mission. Based out of Potsdam, East Germany, the agreement accredited no more than 14 US military observers the right to travel throughout the Soviet zone of occupation in East Germany without escort, except in areas designated as "places of disposition of military units."

Travelling in teams of two or three personnel, known in vernacular of the Mission as "tours," the officers (trained Soviet FAOs all) and enlisted (hand-picked from the ranks of the Berlin Brigade—often from Special Forces units—for their skill in driving and coolness under pressure) would travel in souped-up sedans for the purpose of observing and photographing Soviet military activity. "The tours," Lajoie later commented, "were really nothing more than overt mobile observation platforms crisscrossing the [German Democratic Republic], seeking militarily useful information. The search, of course, was not entirely random."[15]

The USMLM was a national intelligence collection resource, and the tours would receive collection requirements from national intelligence agencies, as well as the various military intelligence commands located in Europe. Military equipment, order of battle, capabilities, and anything else of military value were fair game to these trained professionals. The Soviets had a similar team tasked with monitoring US forces in West Germany, so issues of reciprocity kept the opposing sides from closing the Missions.

But this did not mean that the Soviets made it easy for the members of the Mission to conduct their tours—far from it. "Getting clobbered" (the term used by the Mission members to describe being caught by the Soviets while operating in denied areas) could be very unpleasant. Teams had their vehicles rammed by Soviet trucks, ambushed by Soviet special forces who dragged them from their vehicles and beat them, and had been shot at. The death of one of the USMLM officers, an Army Major named Arthur Nicholson, at the hands of the Soviets proved to be the defining moment of Colonel Lajoie's tour as the commander of USMLM.

On March 24, 1985, Major Nicholson, together with his tour driver, an experienced Staff Sergeant named Jesse Schatz, were engaged in a routine tour of a Soviet tank training facility near Ludwigslust, East Germany. Nicholson had dismounted from his vehicle to investigate vehicle sheds affiliated with a Soviet Motorized Rifle Regiment. A Soviet sentry surprised Nicholson and shot him in the back as he tried to run back to his vehicle. Nicholson bled to death while the sentry held Jessie Schatz at gunpoint.[16]

Colonel Lajoie, accompanied by Marine Lieutenant Colonel Lawrence Kelley, his deputy and an experienced NCO driver, responded to the scene of the shooting, initiating what would be a month's long crisis between the US and the Soviets over what the Americans called a murder, and the Soviets an unfortunate, yet wholly justifiable, incident. Nicholson's death at the hands of a Soviet sentry thrust the work of the USMLM into the international spotlight, and in doing so made Roland Lajoie a household name. In the months that followed, Lajoie helped lead the US response to the shooting, meeting regularly with his Soviet counterparts to properly apportion blame, seek reparations for Nicholson's family, and ensure such never happened again.[17]

Despite the sense of tragic loss brought on by Major Nicholson's death, the members of the USMLM continued their tours—and continued to get "clobbered." This was a reality that even Colonel Lajoie experienced himself. On July 13, 1985, Lajoie was a passenger in a USMLM tour vehicle dispatched to observe the annual summer military exercises of the Soviet Group of Forces, Germany—*Soyuz* '85. The exercise began on July 6, and involved some 50,000 troops, complete with supporting armor, artillery, and air forces. Previous *Soyuz* exercises had operated from a premise that had Soviet forces "counterattacking" from prepared defensive positions. *Soyuz* '85 was different—for the first time, Soviet forces were starting the exercise on the offensive, which in the grand scheme of things could only mean one thing—they were training for an invasion of West Germany. From an intelligence standpoint, the *Soyuz* '85 exercise was of tremendous interest. USMLM tours were scouring East Germany, looking for anything that might provide insight into how the Soviets waged war. As the Commander of USMLM, Lajoie led from the front—which in this case meant going out on tour as well.

After he had observed aspects of the *Soyuz* '85 exercise, Lajoie's vehicle—clearly marked as belonging to USMLM, was passing a Soviet military convoy on a highway that was not restricted to USMLM traffic. A Soviet 5-ton Ural truck pulled out of the convoy and proceeded to follow Lajoie's vehicle at a high rate of speed. Concerned about safety, Lajoie ordered the USMLM tour vehicle, driven by Jesse Schatz, to pull onto the shoulder of the highway to let the Soviet truck pass. Instead, the Soviet truck skidded to a halt, slamming into the rear of Lajoie's vehicle. Lajoie was thrown about inside the USMLM vehicle, badly bruising his cheekbone and breaking his nose.[18]

The USMLM vehicle, spilling gasoline from a ruptured fuel tank, proceeded on to the Mission House in Potsdam, followed by the Soviet Army vehicle. Colonel Lajoie disembarked and, still bleeding from his nose and face, proceeded to engage the Soviet driver in a heated discussion over his skills as a vehicle operator. The Soviet command later apologized to Colonel Lajoie and took full responsibility for the accident—an unprecedented move. The incident underscored just how dangerous the USMLM mission was, as if those who bore witness to Major Nicholson's death needed any reminder.

Lajoie finished his tour at USMLM, was promoted to Brigadier General, and sent to Paris, France, where he was expected to serve out his career as the Defense Attaché—the apex of a career as a Foreign Area Officer. And then the phone rang, and one of America's most experienced military experts on the

Soviet Union found himself being called forward for one more tour on the front lines of the US-Soviet relationship, this time as the Director of the Department of Defense's newest organization, the On-Site Inspection Agency.

The Team Leaders

I ARRIVED AT Buzzards Point on the morning of February 8. I found a gaggle of about 40 officers from various branches of service milling about in a large, empty room. As a First Lieutenant, I was the junior officer present—and one of only four Marines. There were a handful of Captains, with the rest of the officers a mix of Majors, Lieutenant Colonels and Colonels. I snuck into a corner, kept my mouth shut, and waited.

Within minutes the room was called to attention, and Brigadier General Roland Lajoie made his entrance. He gave a brief welcoming address and then turned straight to business—we had a big job, he said, and but little time to get it done. This was the President's personal project, Lajoie said, and the eyes of the nation and the world were on us. Lajoie held up a copy of the INF Treaty text. "This is your Bible," he said. "You'll need to know this inside and out." Lajoie then ran through a list of things he wanted done, and I saw various officers taking notes. Near the end of his presentation, he gestured to an empty office. "This is where I will be working. We're running a world-wide operation. I'm going to need a map on the wall that shows our area of operations."

He then left for one of the innumerable high-level coordination meetings he had to attend during these early days. The other officers clustered together in groups (many clearly knew each other from prior assignments) and left for various offices they had already claimed for themselves. Soon the room was empty save for me. I had no idea what I was supposed to be doing. I looked over at the empty wall in what would become General Lajoie's office, and it hit me: I'll get him a map.

I found a directory and looked up the address of the Defense Mapping Agency. Within an hour I arrived at its main offices and asked to speak to someone involved in production. An Army Colonel arrived, and I briefed him on what I needed—a special product, showing all the Soviet Union and Europe, upon which each inspection site would be annotated. He was surprisingly supportive. When he asked me about who would be paying for this, I told him OSIA, and he didn't blink. I then asked him when this could be done, and he said it would take months. I asked him if he had any generic large-scale maps of the area of interest that I could use in the interim, and he brought me about a dozen rolled up air navigation charts. "You'll have to cut and paste them together," he said, "but these should do the trick until we get your special product up and ready."

By the time I got back to Buzzards Point, everyone had left for the day. I laid the maps out on the floor and began cutting and taping them together until I had one giant map, which I taped to Lajoie's wall. By the time I finished, it was close to midnight, so I found a spot on the floor, curled up and went to sleep. In the morning I was kicked awake by an Army Lieutenant Colonel named Tom Brock. "Did you sleep here?" he asked, incredulously. I told him yes and pointed to the map before he could ask why.

Right about that time General Lajoie walked into the area and entered his office. He took one look at the map on his wall, spun about, and entered the main room. "Who the hell put this up on my wall?" he asked, his voice raised. Tom Brock looked at me, a hint of a smile on his face, his eyebrow raised.

"I did, Sir." I stepped forward.

"Who told you to do that?" Lajoie snapped.

"You did, Sir."

"I gave no such instructions," he said.

I looked him in the eye. "Sir, where I come from if the commanding general says he wants a map on the wall, that's the only order he needs to give. You said you wanted a map of the area of operations. I got you a map."

Lajoie looked at me, then over at the map, and then back at me. "I guess I had better watch out what I say in front of the Marines." He returned to his office, leaving me standing there with Tom Brock, who was laughing. (Later, when the Defense Mapping Agency called asking about billing authority, someone had the foresight to cancel my original map production request).

"Who do you work for?" Brock asked me. I told him I had no clue—apparently, I wasn't on the new organizational chart. "Do you speak any Russian?" he asked.

I told him I had two years of college Russian, but that I was playing football and drinking beer at the time. Tom Brock laughed at that. "We can work around that. How would you like to be an inspector?"

"Yes, Sir," I said, without any hesitation. "I'd love that."

Another Army Lieutenant Colonel walked up to Tom Brock and I, and introduced himself as Paul Nelson. Tom recounted the story about the map, and Nelson laughed as well. "We could use that kind of motivation and initiative," he said. They sent me home to get showered and changed, with orders to report back to them later that day.

What I came to find out was that Tom Brock and Paul Nelson had been entrusted, together with a Marine Lieutenant Colonel named Lawrence Kelly, with developing the operational requirements for the conduct of on-site inspections. They had great flexibility when it came to selecting team members, and it looked like I was destined to be a member of either Team Brock or Team Nelson. This, I told myself, was exactly what I wanted to do.

I found the two Lieutenant Colonels later that afternoon, and reported in. The Defense Intelligence Agency (DIA) had been tasked with developing an inspector's course, and I was told to make my way over to Bolling Air Force

Base, where DIA Headquarters was located, and establish liaison with the people putting the course together. I had barely made my way down the hallway when I was ordered to halt by a Marine Lieutenant Colonel—Lawrence Kelly. "Are you Lieutenant Ritter?" he asked sharply.

I answered in the affirmative, after which he proceeded to speak to me in Russian, the words coming out of him in rapid order. I was not prepared for this, and it took me a few moments to even realize he was speaking Russian, let alone comprehend what he was saying. Kelly had a well-deserved reputation as the finest Russian linguist in the US military. He also spoke so fast that he acquired the nickname *pulemyot*, or "machinegun."

After about 30 seconds of listening, I interrupted, informing Kelly in my best second-year beer-infused college Russian that I did not understand him, and could he please repeat himself, and speak slower. His eyes flashed with genuine anger. "You don't speak Russian worth a damn, do you?"

"I never said I did, Sir," I answered.

"We can't have you embarrassing the United States and the Marine Corps," Kelly snapped. "You're not qualified as a linguist, and as such you're not qualified to be on an inspection team. And as long as I'm here, you will not step foot in the Soviet Union as a member of this organization."

I returned to where Tom and Paul were and informed them what had happened. Lieutenant Colonel Nelson chuckled. "Well, Colonel Kelly oversees language qualifications, and we can't go around his back. The treaty is going to be around for a while. Get your language skills up to speed, and we'll find a way to get you on a team."

And like that, I was back to being unemployed.

Lieutenant Colonel Kelly was correct; based upon the standards that had been defined by General Lajoie, I was not qualified. The Team Leaders would be carved from the mold of Lajoie himself—Soviet Foreign Area Officers, with formal linguistic training, advanced degrees in a relevant field, graduates of USARI in Garmisch, and at least one utilization tour under their belts, preferably at the USMLM in Potsdam or as an assistant attaché in Moscow. As Lawrence Kelly later noted, "The team chiefs would be, to use an analogy, the independent patrol leaders, with whom you'd have precious little contact once they deployed, and on whom you had to rely implicitly. You had to train them up as far as you could, give them adequate guidance, fill them full of treaty specifics, provide them with the kind of surrogate wisdom that they might not otherwise have at the outset, give them 'what if' situations to death, force them to do all of the homework that this required, and them count on them to apply the tools of their trade to get the job done."

Both Paul Nelson and Tom Brock were Soviet FAOs, with Tom graduating USARI in 1974, and Paul in 1983. Tom was older, an infantry officer who served a tour in Vietnam with the Studies and Operations Group (SOG), a highly classified special operations unit that conducted clandestine missions in Laos and Cambodia. He came to OSIA from the staff of the Assistant Chief of Staff for Intelligence of the Army, where he planned and administered the officially hosted visits of foreign dignitaries to the United States.

Paul Nelson was a West Point graduate, who served in the Adjutant Corps until becoming a Soviet FAO. Paul's initial utilization tour was with the USMLM, where he served under General Lajoie and developed a reputation for aggressive intelligence collection. After leaving USMLM, Paul was transferred to the Soviet desk in the Defense Intelligence Agency, where he oversaw collection efforts against the Soviet 40th Army in Afghanistan. Both Tom and Paul were handpicked by General Lajoie to be the core inspection team leaders for OSIA.

There were other team leaders—some 20 in all—selected for the initial baseline inspection period. Ten were envisioned to be full-time staff, while ten others were "reserve" team leaders who would be used full-time during the baseline period, and then periodically called up later to assist as needed. These were extremely competent men, like Lieutenant Colonel Thomas Wyckoff, a USARI graduate and USMLM veteran who served with Lajoie in Potsdam, and Lieutenant Colonel John Lohmann, a 1981 graduate of USARI.

And then there was Lieutenant Colonel Lawrence Kelly—aka the "machinegun." I had hard feelings toward the man in the weeks following my "firing" at his hands. All I saw was what I wanted to see—a pilot and a martinet, whose skill set extended to defying gravity at taxpayer expense, speaking Russian, and not much else. I couldn't have been more wrong.

Larry Kelley was intelligent—he graduated from Princeton University with a degree in Russian studies after spending a semester studying at Leningrad State University. He was brave, taking his commission in the Marine Corps before going on to become a naval aviator, flying A-4 Skyhawk aircraft on ground-attack missions in Vietnam. He was no slouch at flying, later qualifying as a flight instructor. Larry Kelley was also not one to shirk the ground side of the Marine Corps, serving as a forward air controller and battalion air liaison officer with Marine infantry units in combat.

As a young Captain, Larry Kelley was selected as a Soviet FAO, and did the requisite training at DLI and USARI, before getting his master's degree in Russian Studies at Georgetown University. His FAO utilization tour was as the Presidential translator on the Washington-Moscow Hot Line. In 1983 then-Major Kelley was transferred to the USMLM on short notice, taking the place of a Marine Captain who had the misfortune of riding along a Mission tour that ran over and killed a Soviet officer, resulting in his expulsion from the Mission.

Promoted to Lieutenant Colonel while at Potsdam, Kelley developed an outstanding reputation as a tour officer, where he was unmatched as a linguist. "We were not cowboys," Larry Kelley later recalled about his experiences with

USMLM, "but we did tour aggressively." That aggression came with a price. Kelley served as Colonel Lajoie's deputy and was in that position when he and Lajoie had responded to the shooting of Major Nicholson. After Colonel Lajoie and Larry Kelley spent hours in a tense standoff with Soviet authorities, Lajoie returned to West Berlin with Staff Sergeant Schatz, Major Nicholson's driver. Lieutenant Colonel Kelley was left to spend the night alone in a morgue, standing watch over Major Nicholson's body, all the while fending off Soviet efforts to conduct an autopsy.[19]

The next morning, when a US military ambulance arrived, Kelley accompanied the fallen officer's remains as they were transported back to West Berlin, where Nicholson's family and colleagues were waiting. On the Glienicke Bridge between Potsdam and West Berlin (better known as the "Bridge of Spies" for its role in Cold War spy exchanges), Kelley stopped the ambulance and replaced the blanket covering Nicholson's body with an American flag.

Once I learned the true character of this Marine Officer, I never again doubted his decision to remove me from Team Nelson/Brock—the fact of the matter was that I *wasn't* qualified, and I had to accept that reality. With men such as Larry Kelley leading the way, I had all the confidence in the world that OSIA would be able to accomplish its mission during the difficult baseline inspection period and beyond. My opinion, however, mattered for nothing. General Lajoie's did, which is why Larry Kelley was his selection to lead the first OSIA Baseline Inspection team into the Soviet Union on July 1, 1988.

The Monitors

MY EVENTUAL service in the Soviet Union as an inspector was, ironically enough, born from my unceremonious relief as a weapon inspector by Lieutenant Colonel Kelley. After being "fired," I was bounced around OSIA for a period of several weeks as the organization tried to find an appropriate place to put me. There were two major obstacles that had to be overcome, at least in from the perspective of the OSIA hierarchy. First, I was far too junior; a First Lieutenant just did not have any clout, anywhere. Second, I literally had no experience that made me useful in the highly charged political arena that was Washington, DC, especially when it came to joint staffing and project management.

General Lajoie tried bringing me on to his personal staff as a special projects officer, but quickly realized that my rank got in the way of accomplishing anything meaningful—I'd have to be accompanied by a Major or Lieutenant Colonel to get anyone to listen, and so why not hire a Major or Lieutenant Colonel to begin with? I was handed off to Major Paul Trahan, a holdover from the JCS Task Force, who was busy briefing Congress on OSIA's mission and organization in anticipation of Senate ratification hearings. I learned a lot by attending briefings and meetings with the various Senate staffers. My lack of experience, however, again got in the way, as I was incapable of answering questions about OSIA with any authority. I was little more than a glorified slide holder, and there was some talk of returning me to the Marine Corps for reassignment.

In early April I was called into General Lajoie's office, where I was introduced to Colonel Donald MacNicoll, a US Air Force counterintelligence officer from the Office of Special Investigations (OSI). The OSIA organization called for a Deputy Director for Counterintelligence, who would be provided by the Federal Bureau of Investigation (FBI). Ed Curran, a senior FBI special agent with extensive experience working the Soviet target, had been picked for this position, but he was not available for another month or so. Colonel MacNicoll had been assigned as Curran's deputy, but he had to return to West Germany to finalize his move to Washington, DC. I was given the job of filling in for Colonel MacNicoll while he was away—in short, I was put in charge of counterintelligence for OSIA.

To be fair, I don't think anyone saw it that way when I was given the job. I was supposed to be a place filler, a desk officer who answered phones and took messages until the big boys came home. However, while I may have been junior, and I may have lacked relevant Washington, DC experience, I was an Officer of the Marines, which meant that if a mission presented itself, it would be accomplished, no matter what.

The phone rang. And rang. And rang. The entire world, it seemed, had questions about the fact that a bunch of Soviets were about to appear on American soil—sensitive American soil—and the callers wanted to know what they were expected to do about it. The US Army Intelligence and Security Command (INSCOM) was calling; the National Security Agency (NSA) was calling; the Defense Investigative Service (DIS) was calling. They all expected me to have the answers, and I literally had no one to turn to for help—I was truly on my own.

My time with Paul Trahan served me well. Having sat through a number of Senate briefings, I had been immersed in the minutia of OSIA organization and mission facts, upon which I was able to draw to begin framing answers to the questions being posed. I started attending meetings, not as a hanger-on, but as the OSIA principal, which exposed me more to the reality of the world that OSIA was expected to operate in. I attended a meeting at the State Department with the Federal Aviation Agency (FAA), where the procedures for having Soviet aircraft enter US airspace expeditiously and without interference were hammered out. I conducted Counterintelligence surveys of sensitive manufacturing facilities in San Diego, where the impact of Soviet inspectors on their work was discussed with plant directors and their military program officers. I helped draft plans to deal with the issues anticipated to arise when the Soviet inspectors finally arrived. I met with officials from the FBI and NSA to create protocols for screening

Soviet inspection equipment that would be brought in by Soviet inspectors, and I wrote the first draft of the counterintelligence essential elements of information (EEIs) that would be used nation-wide regarding the Soviet inspections under the INF treaty. It was heady stuff for a First Lieutenant straight from the Fleet Marine Force.

The game changer was my meeting with the Defense Intelligence Service. The INF Treaty allowed for no more than 30 inspectors to be present to conduct the perimeter portal monitoring (PPM) inspections in Votkinsk. Of these, five were planned to be drawn from the OSIA military staff or other government personnel. The remaining 25 would be civilian contractors. These contractors were essential for the operation of the Portal Monitoring Facility, but by late April the contract for this task had not yet been assigned. We were running out of time to get enough qualified personnel recruited, trained, and cleared through security if we were going to be able to meet the demanding timeline set by the treaty for implementation. With the Treaty expected to enter into force on July 1, 1988, it was clear that OSIA would need to draw upon the 10-man baseline inspection teams, on a rotational basis, to meet the manpower requirements for the initial portal monitoring inspections. This was acceptable during the early days of the inspection process. But once the specialized equipment envisioned for the permanent operation of the site started arriving, the temporary inspectors would need to be replaced by the trained civilian technical personnel.

The US had never confronted a counterintelligence problem like this—30 Americans, involved in sensitive arms control compliance verification work, living, and working in the middle of the Soviet Union (an acknowledged hostile intelligence threat) more than 700 miles from the nearest US Embassy. The DIS agent impressed upon me the need for a comprehensive pre-employment screening process, inclusive of a counterintelligence-scope polygraph, for all civilian contract employees expected to be deployed to Votkinsk. The normal timeframe for a screening process such as the one envisioned was months. I needed it done in weeks. Together we worked through the details needed to fast-track this effort.

My meetings with DIS left me wondering what was being done regarding the US military personnel who would be assigned to Votkinsk. If anything, these personnel were at greater risk than the civilians, given their sensitive backgrounds. I scheduled meetings with senior counterintelligence agents from NSA and INSCOM to discuss the issue. Their recommendation was that I set up a parallel screening process for all military and government personnel assigned to Votkinsk, inclusive of a counterintelligence scope polygraph.

The first obstacle I faced was security—I had to keep the existence of such a program secret, on the theory that if the Soviets knew about it, they could find ways to defeat it. I set up meetings in the Pentagon at the Assistant Deputy Undersecretary of Defense level to create what was known as a Special

Access Program, or SAP, for my yet-to-be defined Votkinsk counterintelligence support plan. I impressed upon the Pentagon the need for urgency, and the SAP was approved in less than a week—an unprecedented accomplishment at the time. Then, working with NSA and INSCOM polygraph experts, I designed a polygraph support plan that required all personnel being deployed to Votkinsk to undergo a pre-deployment polygraph, as well as post-deployment polygraphs and random polygraphs. This plan was likewise approved, under the SAP.

The last part of my counterintelligence support plan was to meet with the Assistant Deputy Undersecretary of Defense for Acquisition, who oversaw the work of OSIA, and ask that the Defense Department allocate an additional three full-time positions within OSIA for dedicated counterintelligence officers to be assigned, under cover, to OSIA to support the Votkinsk mission, with at least one of these officers deployed to Votkinsk at all times—again, all to be accomplished within restrictive confines of the SAP. This, too, was approved.

Colonel MacNicoll returned to Washington, DC in mid-May, followed in short order by Ed Curran. I proceeded to brief both men on what I had accomplished in their absence, and they were simultaneously impressed and distressed.

"Who else knows about this?" Ed Curran asked me.

"Besides the people at the Pentagon who approved it, and you two? No one," I replied.

"Not even General Lajoie?"

My answer in the negative floored them. "Well," Curran said, "he is going to have to be briefed."

The decision was made—to save me from summary courts-martial—that Lajoie would first be briefed by Curran and MacNicoll, and then I would be brought in to answer any questions. But there was one more person that had to be briefed: Doug Englund, one of the co-Directors of the Portal Monitoring Directorate. Doug had just returned from a second round of Technical Talks in Vienna, Austria, where issues pertaining to Portal Monitoring were still being ironed out between the US and Soviets. The other Portal Monitoring Colonel, George Connell, was busy following up on issues raised during these talks, and as such unavailable.

I wasn't present when Curran briefed Lajoie and Englund, but I was later told that the briefing did not go over well. Englund wanted me fired, and my entire counterintelligence plan unceremoniously flushed down the toilet. Curran, however, was able to point out that I had done OSIA a favor my adding three additional manpower slots to an organization chart everyone was beginning to realize was critically understaffed for the mission the agency was about to undertake. Lajoie made a command decision—since the polygraph program had been approved by the Assistant Deputy Undersecretary of Defense for Acquisition, who was technically his boss, it couldn't be ignored. He, Englund and Connell would each take the polygraph, after which Ed Curran would quietly make the program go away.

I was then invited into Lajoie's office. Lajoie was cordial enough, but Doug was still seething—not something a First Lieutenant wants to experience.

"I've been told I have you to thank for getting me three additional bodies for Portal Monitoring," Doug snapped.

I replied in the affirmative.

"Fine," he replied. "I'll take them, but on one condition. You will fill one of these positions. You will work for me. And I will know everything you are up to."

Lajoie and Curran concurred, and just like that, I was the Directorate of Portal Monitoring's newest officer.

Portal Monitoring, it turned out, was the red headed stepchild of OSIA. As he had done with the Team Leaders who would carry out the baseline, elimination, closeout, and short-notice inspections in support of the INF treaty, General Lajoie turned to those officers he knew and trusted to lead it. Given the anticipated full-time presence of American inspectors in Votkinsk, Portal Monitoring was manned according to Navy submarine standards, with a "Blue" and "Gold" team concept that had one team in Votkinsk, and the other back in Washington, DC. These teams would swap out every six weeks on a rotational basis. Lajoie needed two experienced Colonels for the job, and he had just the right men in mind.

Doug Englund had graduated from the University of Minnesota in 1962 with a degree in International Relations. Commissioned as an Artillery officer, Doug served two tours of duty in Vietnam, before being selected to become a Soviet FAO. After graduating from the DLI Russian course, Doug got his master's degree in Russian Studies from the Center for Russian, East European and Eurasian Studies at Kansas University, in 1973. Doug's next stop was Garmisch, West Germany, where he spent two years perfecting his language and cultural skills at the US Army Institute for Advanced Russian and East European Studies, graduating in 1975.

From 1976 to 1979, Doug served in Moscow as an assistant Army attaché. It was here that he met Roland Lajoie for the first time (Lajoie's final year in Moscow overlapped with Doug's first). Englund and Lajoie hit it off immediately, especially after Doug cursed in perfect colloquial Russian at a recalcitrant Soviet bookseller who refused to sell the Americans an encyclopedia they wanted. Doug and Roland walked out of the bookstore with the encyclopedia in hand, and relations with the bookseller secure.

Doug's Moscow tour consisted of the standard adventures experienced by most defense attachés, with visits to the far reaches of the Soviet Union punctuated by social gatherings at the US Embassy. But it was the events of August 26, 1977, that came to define Doug's Moscow experience. That evening, a fire broke out on the 8th floor of the US Embassy, home to the economic section. The Marine Guards were aggressively fighting the fire, but the age of the building, combined with haphazard construction modifications which produced hidden compartments and gaps in the ceiling and walls, allowed the fire to rapidly spread. Soon the sixth, seventh and ninth floors were engulfed in flames as well. Soviet firefighters were called in, and soon began driving the fire back on the lower floors.

As the fire began to encroach on the tenth floor, where the Defense Attaché and CIA offices were, the US Ambassador refused to allow the Soviets access. "Let it burn," he said, aware of the sensitive papers and equipment that were contained there. But several Americans, including the CIA Station Chief and personnel from the Defense Attaché office, refused to evacuate, remaining behind to safeguard the classified material until it could be properly destroyed.[20]

One of these men was Doug Englund, who helped organize the Marine Guards initially fighting the fire. Later, when the US Ambassador acceded to Soviet requests to send firefighters in to battle the blazes on the upper floors, Doug escorted newly arrived firefighters as they gained access to the most sensitive spaces of the US Embassy.

This second wave of firefighters, while competent, were interspersed with officers from the KGB (easily discernable in their brand-new firefighting gear), who combined firefighting with a search for classified material. Through the heroic and exhaustive efforts of Doug and the other Defense Attaché staff, the fire was eventually extinguished, and the Embassy's secrets secured.

At some point during the fire, Doug sat down to rest in what turned out to be a pool of acid from melted batteries, suffering a painful burn to his buttocks. This injury, combined with efforts to fight the blaze and safeguard classified material, earned Doug the Soldier's Medal, the Army's highest award for heroism in a non-combat incident.

After Moscow, Doug completed Army Command and Staff College, and had begun training for an assignment as the Army Attaché in Hungary when he got caught up in a massive wave of tit-for-tat expulsions of diplomatic personnel between the Soviet Union and the US. While technically not designated as *persona non grata*, Doug was denied entry into Hungary, and was unable to take up his post. When the INF Treaty was signed, Doug was serving as the head of foreign intelligence on the Army Staff at the Pentagon. When General Lajoie offered him the job of co-Director of Portal Monitoring in February 1988, Doug jumped at the chance.

Joining Doug as co-Director for Portal Monitoring was Marine Corps Colonel George Murdoch Connell. George was younger than Doug by a year, graduating from St. Bonaventure University, in Olean, New York in 1963. By 1965 George was in Vietnam, serving as a platoon commander with Charlie Company, 1st Battalion, 9th Marines—the famous "Walking Dead," so named because of the large numbers of casualties sustained fighting in Vietnam (747 Marines and attached Navy Corpsmen died while fighting with 1/9, the highest number for any unit serving in Vietnam). George completed his year-long tour, and then volunteered for an extension so he could command a company in combat.

It was during this extended tour that Connell earned a Silver Star, the nation's third highest award for heroism, leading a combined infantry-armor attack to rescue a squad of Marines that had been cut off and surrounded by the North Vietnamese. The accompanying tanks were halted by terrain and enemy fire, leaving Connell, who had been wounded in the arms and shoulder, to press home the attack using just the infantry he commanded. After ordering his Marines to "fix bayonets," Connell led the charge, personally killing six of the enemy before driving them from the battlefield and rescuing the beleaguered squad.

After his Vietnam service, Connell went on to command other Marines before getting his master's degree from the University of North Carolina and training as a Soviet FAO. Connell attended USARI in Garmisch from 1977 to 1979 (a rare two-year assignment for a Marine), spending his first year there under the command of Roland Lajoie. After Garmisch Connell moved to Moscow, where from 1980 to 1982 he served as the assistant Naval attaché. Roland Lajoie arrived in Moscow as the Army Attaché in 1981, and for one year was able to watch George Connell in action.

An attaché can spend an entire tour collecting information and writing intelligence reports that have little or no impact on the consumer; the information provided either duplicates data received from different, often better, sources of information, or is simply so trivial as to be of no interest to anyone but the most dedicated analyst, for whom no detail is too small. Attachés are a known quantity, meaning they operate overtly, and the KGB had them under surveillance at all times. This made it virtually impossible for an attaché to gain access to the kind of sensitive areas where the information of most interest resided. It took a clever mind coupled with aggressive instincts—with more than a little luck thrown in for good measure—for an attaché to get an opportunity to collect information of great value. George Connell had all of these attributes.

In early 1981 George and a British naval attaché were able to take detailed photographs of a Soviet Alfa-class submarine in the final stages of production. The Soviet Alfa class nuclear attack submarine was a game changer. Possessing a titanium hull and powered by a compact lead-cooled nuclear reactor, the Alfa could move faster and dive deeper than any submarine in the US inventory, forcing the US and Royal navies to spend millions of dollars developing sensors and weapons to defeat the new threat.

The Alfa submarine was produced at the Sudomekh 196 shipyard, located in the west-central part of the city of Leningrad, on the south bank of the

Neva River. Security screens constructed by the Soviets frustrated American photographic interpreters, as they prevented overhead satellites from getting a clear picture of what was happening inside the construction building. George and his British counterpart were able to evade their KGB surveillance, sneak aboard a commuter ferry whose route took it past the Sudomekh 196 facility, climb up the funnel of the ship, and peer over the security screen as the ferry sailed past, taking multiple rolls of close-up pictures of the Alfa submarine.

The film, accompanied by a report prepared by the two attachés, was dispatched to their respective intelligence services via diplomatic courier. The pictures produced were invaluable, providing US and British naval intelligence with close-up images which enabled them to design improved sensors capable of tracking the Alfa submarines, and high-speed torpedoes capable of destroying them. In the Cold War then raging between the two nations, the intelligence Connell and his British colleague collected against the Alfa submarine literally altered the balance of power in favor of the US and NATO. Not too many attachés get to make such a claim.

Connell left Moscow in 1982 and attended the National War College. Later, after being promoted to Colonel, Connell was assigned to the Naval Criminal Investigative Service (NCIS), where he served as the deputy director. Connell headed up the investigation of Marine Sergeant Clayton Lonetree, a Marine Security Guard at the US Embassy in Moscow accused of providing classified documents to the KGB after being blackmailed for having an illicit romantic relationship with a Russian female who was controlled by the Soviets. One of his last actions at NCIS was assisting the prosecution in securing Lonetree's conviction at trial. Like Doug Englund before him, when General Lajoie called and offered him the job of co-Director of Portal Monitoring, George didn't hesitate to accept.

Working for Connell and Englund was an exercise in contradictions. The two men were opposites when it came to leadership styles and approaches to problem solving. George moved quick, to the point of seeming frenetic (he was not); Doug was more methodical, to the point of seeming lethargic (he was not). For someone like myself, caught in the middle between these two differing personalities, things could get very interesting, very fast.

Fortunately for me, Doug's initial animosity toward me was offset by George's immediate affinity. Perhaps Colonel Connell saw something of himself in the young Lieutenant he had under his charge, or perhaps it was just one Marine looking out for another. Maybe it was a little of both. The fact is George Connell became my mentor from the first day we met, taking the time to make sure I was informed on what was happening, and affording me the opportunity to learn by failing if I didn't make the same mistake twice.

Doug and George spent most of their time preparing for technical talks with the Soviets, where the specific technologies and inspection methodologies associated with Portal Monitoring were being worked out. Back at Buzzard's Point, a staff of experienced Foreign Area Officers was assembled to backstop the Colonels and transform theory into reality. One of the first of these FAOs to come aboard was Navy Lieutenant Commander Charles (Chuck) Myers.

Commander Myers was commissioned in 1972, after receiving a degree in Russian Area Studies from Eckerd College. Chuck specialized in submarine electronic warfare which, given his Russian language skills, meant he was involved in some of the Navy's most highly classified submarine-based intelligence collection operations carried out during the early-to mid-1970s, most of which remains secret to this day. Chuck attended the Naval Post Graduate School, where he graduated with distinction in 1982. He followed this up in 1985 with a master's degree in Russian area studies from Georgetown University. With his engineer's mind, and a submariner's dogged perseverance, Chuck quickly immersed himself in the complexities of the portal monitoring system that was going to be installed at Votkinsk.

Chuck was joined by Air Force Major Mark Dues, who had previously served as an instructor on the History faculty of the US Air Force Academy, and Army Majors Charles (Barrett) Haver and Richard Kurasiewicz. Both Haver (Class of '75) and Kurasiewicz (Class of '74) were West Point graduates; Rich became an artillery officer, while Barrett joined the infantry, where he qualified and served as an airborne ranger (an accomplishment that speaks volumes in and of itself). Both men entered the FAO program at the same time, graduating from DLI before getting their master's degree (Rich from the Naval Post Graduate School, Barrett from John's Hopkins). They were classmates at USARI, graduating in 1985 before both being assigned to the 6th Psychological Warfare Battalion (Airborne), based out of Fort Bragg, North Carolina.

The mission of the 6th Psyops Battalion was the dissemination of propaganda by radio broadcast and leaflet. Insofar as Europe was included in its area of operations, for Soviet FAOs like Rich and Barrett it became their focus of effort. American intelligence staffs in Europe at that time were focused on assessing the reliability and resistance potential of the Warsaw Pact forces, especially with regard to Poland and Czechoslovakia. Assessments were produced on a quarterly and annual basis.

The expertise of both Rich and Barrett would have been valuable in support of this effort, which is why the Army assigned qualified Soviet FAOs to the unit. But both men had yearned for the plum assignments out of USARI—the assistant Army attaché positions at the US Embassy in Moscow, or an assignment to the USMLM. When the Army was tasked with providing two Majors to support Portal Monitoring operations in the Soviet Union, both Rich and Barrett were tapped for the position. Both gladly accepted.

When compared to the preparations underway by the Team Leaders in the Inspection Directorate, which focused on learning the technical details of the Soviet INF systems set to be eliminated by the treaty and conducting mock inspections to sharpen their operational skills, the work being done in Portal Monitoring seemed mundane—logistics and civil engineering are not normally associated with high adventure.

The inspectors preparing for Baseline Inspections knew exactly what they were getting into—every detail was spelled out in the treaty text. Their counterparts in Portal Monitoring, on the other hand, were operating in an environment where very little was known about the specifics of what they would be doing in Votkinsk. This leap into the unknown would end up testing their skills as Soviet FAOs like no other job in OSIA.

Company Grade

THE ORGANIZATION CHART for the Directorate of Portal Monitoring called for two Colonels, and four field grade officers (Majors and Lieutenant Colonels). This number was later expanded to five. The officers were expected to be fully qualified Soviet FAOs, with all the formal education, linguistic training and operational experience that entailed. There was no mention of company grade officers (Lieutenants and Captains) on the organization chart simply because it was assumed that personnel that junior would not have the requisite training and experience to meet the FAO standard.

Given that one could not even be accepted into the FAO training pipeline until at least a senior Captain, this assumption was well founded. What the chart failed to recognize was the reality that, during the Cold War, there was another category of Soviet specialist—the front-line operator and intelligence professional—who populated the enlisted and junior officer ranks. For these, preparing for war entailed becoming just as intimate with the Soviet threat—and in some cases, more—as many of the field grade FAOs.

The Directorate for Portal Monitoring was unique in OSIA in that it became populated with a diverse mix of company grade officers whose presence proved to be instrumental in the success of the Portal Monitoring mission. This wasn't, however, due to prescient planning by a manpower specialist, but rather the kind of serendipitous luck that often befalls organizations during times of turmoil and transition.

Within the Directorate for Portal Monitoring, I was very much a fish out of water. The field grade officers assigned there—Barrett Haver, Rich Kurasceiwicz, Chuck Myers and Mark Dues—were knee-deep in preparing for portal monitoring operations from the moment they joined OSIA. While I had a superficial understanding of what portal monitoring entailed from my time with Paul Trahan, the enormity of the task and the incredible detail which was involved only became apparent when I entered their workspace. The four field grade officers were friendly enough, but they literally had no time to spare to read me into what they were doing. I sat down at my assigned desk and tried my best to be useful.

Less than six months prior, I had been a Battalion Intelligence Officer with a General Support Artillery Battalion in the Fleet Marine Force. Prior to that, I had served on the Intelligence Staff of a Marine Expeditionary Brigade. I knew nothing about arms control, ballistic missiles or joint staff planning. My job had been to facilitate the Marine Corps mission of closing with and destroying the enemy—in this case the Soviet Army—through firepower and maneuver. My sole focus for more than two years had been killing the Soviet enemy. Now I was tasked with helping to implement a new treaty designed to reduce tensions and promote peace with that same Soviet enemy—not as an intelligence officer, a specialty in which I was qualified, but rather as a counterintelligence officer, for which I lacked any formal training or relevant experience. It was a strange new world.

Shortly after I arrived, I was joined in Portal Monitoring by another fish out of water—US Air Force First Lieutenant Stu O'Neill. Stu had been recruited by Colonel MacNicoll during his last trip to West Germany. At the time Stu was assigned to Ramstein Air Force Base, where he performed mundane tasks as part of the assigned Office of Special Investigations detachment there. MacNicoll was looking for experienced field grade officers or senior Captains in the counterintelligence field who spoke Russian and would want to work for him back at OSIA. He came up short, and was about to return to Washington, DC empty handed when he ran into Stu. Like me, Stu had studied Russian history in college (in his case, the University of Arizona), along with a smattering of college level Russian. For Colonel MacNicoll, this was good enough, and Stu was soon issued orders to join OSIA.

When I was informed that Stu would be joining Portal Monitoring as one of the three counterintelligence officers, I don't know what I expected to see. It certainly wasn't the man who introduced himself to me. My father had been a career Air Force officer, so I knew the ins and outs of what an Air Force uniform should look like. Foreign jump wings and a Soldier's Medal (the highest award for heroism not involving direct combat issued by the US Army) were not on the list of what an Air Force First Lieutenant should be wearing; neither were a Joint Service Commendation Medal and an Army Commendation Medal. They were on Stu's.

Stu's resume was, for an Air Force OSI special agent, as spectacular as it was bizarre. Although assigned to a counterintelligence position with OSIA, Stu's background was with the US Army Special Forces. But not just any Special Forces unit—Stu had been assigned to one of the most classified units in the history of the US Army—the 39th Special Forces Detachment, or Detachment "A," Berlin Brigade.[21]

Det "A," as the unit was commonly known to those select few who were aware it existed, was one of the most unique organizations of the Cold War era. Based in the American sector of occupied Berlin, the mission of Det "A" was to function as a "stay behind" urban guerilla warfare unit in the event the Soviets ever rolled in and occupied the city. The men selected for Det "A" were experts in guerilla warfare (espionage, assassination, sabotage, propaganda and small-unit combat), unconventional warfare (building and operating a resistance movement or insurgency in a denied area), counterterrorism (neutralizing terrorists and their networks), direct action (short-duration precision offensive actions designed to achieve a specific objective), and special reconnaissance (clandestine or covert intelligence gathering using non-standard methodology in a hostile environment). The members of Det "A" operated under cover as non-US nationals, wore civilian clothing, and used non-US weapons and equipment.

The members of Det "A" were considered the subject-matter experts in their field—their close quarters combat training was later adapted by Delta Force as its standard, and the Central Intelligence Agency and British Special Intelligence Service (MI6) drew upon the unit's expertise in covert infiltration/exfiltration and agent handling techniques when devising their own operations. Even the Military Liaison Mission in Potsdam drew upon the experience of Det "A" personnel, employing them as drivers during their intelligence collection tours in East Germany. As Lieutenant Colonel Tom Wycoff, an USMLM veteran and OSIA team chief, noted, "If there was a downside to getting NCOs from the Special Forces, it was that they had no fear. Being chased or shot at by a single, upset Soviet soldier or vehicle was nothing in comparison with many of the things they had experienced. On the upside, they were really cool in the tensest of situations."[22]

Stu was the epitome of cool.

Trained as a combat engineer before transitioning into Special Forces, at Det "A" Stu was assigned to Team Six, where he delved into the complex and diverse missions he was tasked with performing. A contemporary photograph shows a man with a huge head of unruly red hair, equally bushy mustache, and lamb-chop sideburns. While Stu spoke and understood a smattering of German, his Irish background pointed to an operational cover of a different nature. Passports were obtained and reworked to match the covert identity, as well as the appropriate German identification cards and supporting documentation. Stu became an expert at infiltrating into East Germany and operating covertly in the shadows of the Soviet military. As an engineer, he would have been tasked with the various demolition assignments associated with unconventional warfare—blowing up a wide range of targets designed to make life difficult for the Soviet occupiers.

Stu was also an accomplished operator in the field of counterterrorism, skilled in the deadly art of close quarter combat and hostage rescue. It was this skill set that got Stu assigned to participate in the Iran hostage rescue mission in April 1980. The story of how Iranian student activists seized the US Embassy and took its occupants hostage is well known; the role played by Det "A" in attempting to rescue these hostages is not. From the very onset of the Iran hostage crisis, a potential rescue mission was plagued by the lack of actionable operational intelligence. Det "A" was able to provide a pair of skilled intelligence collectors who were trained to operate under civilian cover and who knew what information would be vital to a rescue mission, and how to collect it. These men flew into Tehran, spent several days casing the Iranian capital and the targets of interest, before leaving with invaluable intelligence that made a rescue mission viable.

As of April 1980, there were 52 Americans being held hostage in Tehran, 49 of whom were sequestered at the US Embassy compound. The task of rescuing these hostages fell to the US Army's elite special mission unit, the 1st Special Forces Operational Detachment-Delta, better known as Delta Force. But there were three other American diplomats being held in a separate facility—the Iranian Ministry of Foreign Affairs (MFA). Delta Force lacked the manpower to carry out simultaneous rescues at both locations, and so the Pentagon looked to Det "A" to provide a team capable of accomplishing the MFA mission. Stu was selected to be a member of this elite group.

After extensive training, Stu and the other members of the Det "A" team flew to Egypt, where they joined up with Delta Force and other American special operations personnel participating in the operation. The tragedy that subsequently unfolded at Desert One—the aborting of the rescue mission due to too many helicopters suffering mechanical failures suffered when flying through a massive sandstorm, and the collision of one of these helicopters with a C-130 transport on the ground, causing an explosion and fire that killed eight of the rescuers—is etched in history.

To Stu and the other soldiers watching the disaster in real time, it quickly became clear that not everyone had made it off the stricken aircraft. One of the C-130 crewmembers had been trapped by the burning flames and was screaming for help. A Delta Force operator ran back inside the burning aircraft to rescue the airman, but both were overcome by the fire. Seeing this, Stu ran into what was, by this time, a fully involved conflagration, and dragged both men to safety, badly burning himself in the process. For this action, Stu was awarded the Soldier's Medal. (Stu and the other participants in the rescue attempt were awarded Joint Service Commendation Medals and Humanitarian Service Medals for their efforts; Stu always joked that the latter should come with a combat "V").

Stu later left the Army to attend college. He remained in the Army reserves during his studies, serving with a reserve Special Forces unit. He suffered a serious shoulder injury during training, which precluded his returning to the Special Forces after graduation. Instead, Stu took a commission in the Air Force, and then trained to be a special agent in the Office of Special Investigations, and was given orders to Ramstein, Germany, where Colonel MacNicoll found him.

Colonel Englund now was faced with a quandary. He had two of the three company-grade counterintelligence billets now filled, which on paper ostensibly helped with the manning shortfalls in the Portal Monitoring Directorate. The problem was that neither Stu nor I were sufficiently proficient in the Russian language to be of much service in Votkinsk. While Stu at least could credibly perform the tasks of a counterintelligence officer (unlike myself, who had zero training or qualifications in the field), the last thing Doug Englund wanted—or needed—in Votkinsk was a counterintelligence officer. He needed people seeped in the Russian language and culture, able to rapidly assimilate complicated treaty-mandated tasks and turn them into reality on the ground at a remote location in the middle of the Soviet Union, a task that would require extensive interaction with Soviet personnel on the ground using the Russian language. Neither Stu nor I fit that description.

The third counterintelligence position was to be filled by the Army. Rather than wait for the Army personnel system to send him a clone of Stu and myself, Doug opted to become personally involved in the selection process, making several phone calls to track down someone who at least possessed some of the skills he was looking for as a Deputy Site Commander in Votkinsk.

In mid-July 1988, following my return from my initial deployment to Votkinsk, Doug asked me to conduct a telephone interview with a candidate for the third counterintelligence position. On the other end of the line was US Army First Lieutenant John Sartorius, who at the time was finishing up his formal training as an intelligence officer in Fort Huachuca, Arizona.

I gave it my best Marine Corps effort. "Are you a counterintelligence officer?," I asked. There was a slight hesitation on the other end before a reply. "I am trained in counterintelligence."

Check.

"Do you speak Russian?" The voice on the other end exploded into a stream of complex Slavic-sounding noises my brain told me was, in fact, the Russian language.

Check.

"Do you have any relevant experience?" Again, a slight hesitation on the other end. "I was prior enlisted and served in West Germany."

"What kind of work did you do?" I asked, probing deeper.

"I can't tell you over this line" he said. "But it involved the Russian language." Secret squirrel stuff; must be good.

Check.

My detailed pre-employment screening interview complete, I asked John when he could start.

"Colonel Englund is in contact with my branch monitor to get orders cut as soon as I graduate from my school."

It became clear that Doug had already made up his mind, and I was just there to tick the "counterintelligence" block.

Check.

My initial face-to-face meeting with John was the exact opposite, impression-wise, of my meeting with Stu. I had deployed back to Votkinsk in late July, and was wrapping up a six-week tour, when John arrived for his initial Votkinsk rotation. I was preparing to go on a 3-mile run, and John asked if he could join me. "Can you keep up?" I asked, as only a Marine Corps officer contemptuous of all other non-Marine life can. John said yes. I looked him up and down and concluded that he could not.

I was right about the run—I pulled away from the start, and he never caught up. But it wasn't for a lack of trying. That impressed me—there was no quit in this guy. And it soon became apparent that John wasn't sent to Votkinsk to engage in physical fitness activity in any event. He also wasn't sent to perform the role of a counterintelligence officer—the only training he had in counterintelligence was the introductory courses he had received at Fort Huachuca (in John's defense, he *had* told the truth during our interview—somewhat).

What John possessed was a combination of linguistic skill, historical and cultural awareness and raw analytical talent that made him the perfect inspector. He wasn't a natural born combat leader—but that wasn't the job he was brought in to do. What he *did* do was lead by example, setting forth a standard for excellence and attention to detail that left mere mortals such as myself blinking on the sideline in amazement. John could read a treaty-related text, and immediately discern what parts were relevant, which parts contained ambiguities, and come up with a range of options on how to resolve the ambiguities, all of which would be viable. This talent had been honed by a past that, like all of us, had been shaped by the realities of the Cold War.

After graduating High School in 1977, John had enlisted in the Army, where he was trained as a Russian language intercept operator. After graduating from the Defense Language Institute, John was stationed in West Germany, assigned to Field Station Augsburg, a top-secret communications intercept facility run by the NSA, but manned by Army intelligence personnel.

Field Station Augsburg operated a giant circular "Wullenweber" antenna array known as the AN/FLR-9, part of a global network of similar radars known as "Iron Horse" responsible for locating and intercepting high frequency communications. As a Russian linguist, John's job was to listen in on Soviet communications across the border in Czechoslovakia and East Germany, trying to glean intelligence that would be useful to military decision makers—some of the most highly classified work done by military intelligence at that time. John was stationed in Augsburg during the late 1970s and early 1980s, where he performed his duties with distinction.

Near the end of his enlistment in 1983, John convinced the Army to give him an ROTC scholarship, which he used to finish his final two years of college at the University of California Berkeley. Majoring in Russian Language and Literature, John took advantage of a semester-long study abroad program in Leningrad, where he further immersed himself in Soviet culture and the Russian language. Upon graduation in 1985, John delayed taking his commission in favor of getting an advanced degree. John moved to the Washington, DC area, where he earned a master's degree in Russian Area Studies at Georgetown while working full-time for the Center for Naval Analyses (CNA), a private think-tank that specialized in studying current trends in Soviet naval developments. Eventually the Army caught up with John, ordering him to active duty. That's where Doug Englund found him, mid-way through his basic intelligence officer course.

What made the presence of Company Grade officers like me, Stu, and John in Votkinsk noteworthy was the fact that we were not supposed to be there. We simply did not fit the model envisioned by General Lajoie when he used the Soviet Foreign Area Officer as the standard for an OSIA inspector. Portal Monitoring inspections, however, were unlike any other aspect of OSIA's mission. For those preparing to deploy to Votkinsk, the assignment seemed very much like a disconcerting journey down the rabbit hole, into the kind of unstructured fantasyland that most military officers disdain. There was a major role for the Soviet FAO to play in Votkinsk, if for no other reason than to impose structure and discipline on a situation that, left to its own devices, could easily have spun out of control. But there was also a role for those junior officers who, because we were young enough and brash enough not to know any better, embraced the chaos as the new normal, and thrived.

Program Managers, Civilians and Contractors

THE PROVISIONS of the INF Treaty were clear—no more than 30 portal monitoring inspectors would be allowed in Votkinsk at any given time. The military officers assigned to the Directorate for Portal Monitoring were the official face of the On-Site Inspection Agency, and as such responsible for all matters pertaining to treaty implementation. They were, however, a distinct minority when it came to the overall manning of the Portal Monitoring Facility. The JCS Task Force recognized early on that the specialized nature of the work involved in the installation, operation and maintenance of the Votkinsk portal involved a skill set not readily replicated in the range of military specializations available. If the portal was going to be manned by a purely military contingent, then new military specialization codes would need to be created, along with the training and education required to sustain them on a career basis. This was not an option that was ever seriously considered. Instead, the JCS Task Force opted for a cadre of military officers who would oversee the work of civilian contractors.

Because the TOSI demonstration facility was operated based on an Air Force contract managed by the Electronic Systems Division (ESD), the decision was made by the JCS Task Force that ESD would manage the contract for civilian personnel to install, operate and maintain the Votkinsk portal, at least until it was up and running, at which time contract management responsibility would transfer to OSIA. Because the TOSI demonstration facility was, for all intents and purposes, going to be uprooted from Sandia and relocated in Votkinsk, Sandia was expected to play a key role in the overall process, including supporting OSIA with the initial installation and operation of TOSI equipment and training the civilian contractors on the TOSI demonstration facility once the contract was assigned.

The ESD and Sandia personnel involved in this work were not weapons inspectors. They were not Russian area specialists. They were technicians, scientists, logisticians, and managers who populated the arcane world of defense department contracting and program management. And yet, due to the compressed timelines involved in treaty implementation (the Votkinsk contract was not awarded until June 16, 1988—two weeks prior to the July 1 initiation of inspection activity), these non-inspectors would find themselves deployed to Votkinsk, where they would double as technical experts and portal monitors. Their role was unintended, their contribution undeniable.

In July 1988, following my initial rotation to Votkinsk, I accompanied Colonel Connell on a trip to Long Beach, California. The purpose of our visit was to meet with the management and personnel of Hughes Technical Services Company (HTSC). HTSC had been awarded the contract for the installation, operation and maintenance of the Votkinsk Portal Monitoring Facility, and Colonel Connell and I were tasked with helping create a sense of the need for haste at HTSC—OSIA had planned for three rotations of short-notice inspection teams into Votkinsk to man the portal until which time the civilian contractors arrived in mid-August. By the time Colonel Connell and I visited, we were a month away from that deadline.

I was given the task of briefing the HTSC personnel assigned to Votkinsk about the reality of life inside the Soviet Union. A total of 34 persons had been hired for the Votkinsk project, of whom no more than 25 would be in-country at any given time. They would work nine-week rotations, after which they would have a three-week break before returning to Votkinsk. HTSC operated as a subsidiary of Hughes Aircraft Company's Support Systems Division, and the initial cadre of personnel picked for the Votkinsk mission were drawn from the ranks of Support Systems. Jim Saunders was appointed as the overall manager of what was being called the "Technical On-Site Inspection (TOSI) program." Jerry Porter, an employee of HTSC, was picked to be the TOSI site manager.

Porter was responsible for picking his team. When HTSC was selected for the Votkinsk portal project, more than 300 employees from within the Hughes system submitted resumes. Porter was looking for "patient, reasonable" candidates, and placed "a lot of emphasis on the personality of the people" he would ultimately select.[23] The human factor took precedence over technical expertise.

I had the opportunity to meet several members of Porter's team while in Long Beach—Hal Longley, Gary Teetsell, Scott Yoder, Jim Luscher, Jim Stewart, Jerry Ildefonso, Hien Trang, Tim Kubik, Mark Romanchuk, Angelo Mavrorasakis, Joe O'Hare, Zoi Haloulakos, Bill McClellan, Jim Hull, Sam Israelit, Anne Mortenson, and others. Porter had done well—they were all very personable and highly professional. But they were software programmers, engineers, technicians, communications specialists, equipment operators, managers, and linguists. They were not Foreign Area Officers, intelligence specialists or any other professional category that I had come to associate with the term "OSIA inspector" over the course of the previous five months. Moreover, after I briefed them, it was clear to me that they had no real idea about what they were about to become involved in.

And yet, they were, to a person, anxious to get involved. "They all have a sense of being part of history," Jerry Porter said of his team. "They are willing to sacrifice."

Over the course of the months and years to come, they would be called upon to make great sacrifices in the cause of implementing the INF Treaty.

And, in doing so, they made history.

CHAPTER THREE

Trust, but Verify

*The first US Portal Monitoring team, together with their Soviet factory escorts,
outside the Joint Temporary Inspection Building, July 2, 1988.*

*"When a man's ways please the Lord, he makes
even his enemies to be at peace with him."*

PROVERBS 16:7

The Low-Tech Solution

"THE IMPORTANCE of this treaty transcends numbers," President Ronald
Reagan declared in comments made together with General Secretary Mikhail
Gorbachev immediately after signing the INF Treaty on December 8, 1987.
"We have listened to the wisdom in an old Russian maxim. And I'm sure you're
familiar with it, Mr. General Secretary, though my pronunciation may give you
difficulty. The maxim is: *Doveryai no proveryai*—trust but verify."

Gorbachev looked at Reagan and smiled. "You repeat that at every
meeting," he said.

"I like it," Reagan responded, also smiling, before he continued with his
prepared remarks.

"This agreement contains the most stringent verification regime in history, including provisions for inspection teams actually residing in each other's territory and several other forms of onsite inspection, as well."[1]

Slightly less than seven months later, on July 1, 1988, the inspectors of the On-Site Inspection Agency were ready to turn theory into reality.

Unknown to most who were following the progress of the new agency at the time was the fact that a small advance team of five specialists—they were not yet inspectors—had deployed to Votkinsk to carry out site surveys and conduct advance coordination with the Soviet factory personnel who would be helping facilitate the implementation of perimeter portal monitoring (PPM) inspections there. Led by Navy Lieutenant Commander Chuck Myers, the Votkinsk Advance Party included Army Major Richard Kurasiewicz, another OSIA portal Monitoring officer, Major Timothy Parker, an engineer from the US Air Force's Electric Systems Division (ESD), Margaret Gomes, a civil engineer with MITRE Corporation working with ESD—and me, a Marine with no apparent qualifications who stuck out from the others like a sore thumb (so much for maintaining "operational cover"—the Soviets had me pegged as an intelligence officer from day one).

We were billeted, together with an accompanying Soviet delegation from Moscow, in the Dacha of the deceased Minister of Defense, Dmitri Ustinov, in accommodations that were as comfortable as they were pleasant. For the next two weeks we hammered out the details associated with the pending deployment of up to 30 American inspectors to a remote part of the Soviet Union that did not normally see foreign visitors.

While the four experts labored over the technical details associated with the looming inspections, I was given the job of addressing ancillary non-technical tasks, such as sorting out the medical support infrastructure available in Votkinsk for inspectors. While this entailed a tour of the local hospital and meetings with the staff, I also had to come to grips with the reality that the area around Votkinsk was infested with ticks that carried a deadly strain of tick-borne encephalitis. Scores of locals were infected every year, it seemed, including several who died. Vaccines would have to acquired and dispensed to inspectors. I was also the lead person for ensuring that the temporary housing facility for the inspectors—a hotel being constructed on the ironically-named Dzerzhinsky Street (after the founder of the Soviet KGB, Felix Dzerzhinsky)—would be ready in time. It was.

But for the most part I just watched and listened, trying to learn as much as I could about the people who would come to dominate my life for the next two years, and the place they called home. Three individuals stood out in particular: Anatoli Tomilov, the quiet, bespectacled Director of what the Soviets called Department 162, the Department of Cooperation with the US Inspection Team, and his two deputies—Aleksander Merzlyakov, a diminutive fellow full of nervous energy who was responsible for the social life of the inspectors, and

Vyacheslav Lopatin, a taciturn bear of a man who was responsible for overseeing the installation of inspection equipment at the Votkinsk factory.

As we labored in Votkinsk, the rest of OSIA prepared to execute what was going to be the most intensive phase of on-site inspections in support of implementation of the INF Treaty—the baseline inspection period. Baseline Inspections were but one of five types of on-site inspection specified in the Inspection Protocol of the INF Treaty. For a period of 60 days, inspectors would be dispatched to every inspectable site listed in the treaty text, seeking to verify the numbers of treaty-limited items located there, as well as their technical characteristics. These inspections were critical for establishing a foundation of data (the "baseline") upon which all other inspections would be based.

The next type of inspection was the Elimination Inspection, where inspectors monitored the host nation's efforts to destroy treaty-limited items in a manner that made their use impossible. Six distinct Soviet missile systems were mandated for destruction under the treaty: the SS-20, SS-12, SS-4, SS-5, and the SSC-X-4 cruise missile.

The third type of inspection was the Close-Out Inspection, conducted within a 60-day window that opened once a site was declared free of all treaty-limited-items. The purpose of the Close-Out Inspection was to confirm this.

After the 60-day window that served as the trigger for Close-Out Inspections, if an inspecting party wished to re-visit a designated site for whatever reason, but usually related to concerns over a treaty violation, then it could conduct a fourth type of inspection, what was known as a "Short-Notice Inspection," which operated on a strict quota system.

The fifth and final inspection type specified in the Inspection Protocol was Perimeter Portal Monitoring inspections—what we were preparing to conduct in Votkinsk.

For the 200 OSIA weapons inspectors, organized into 20 teams of ten inspectors each, the Inspection Protocol was their bible. They had trained using its provisions as their standard and were constrained by the four corners of these provisions. The work they did was challenging, stressful and important, but there was no room for interpretation or deviation—what was written down on paper was the law, from inspection equipment to inspection procedures.

The first INF Baseline Inspection was carried out by Team Kelley, named after its Team Leader, Lieutenant Colonel Lawrence Kelley. General Lajoie accompanied this team. The object of their inspection was the SS-20 missile operating base at Rechitsa, in Byelorussia. The inspection was carried out in strict accordance with the Inspection Protocol, and Kelley's team was back in Rhein Main Air Force Base, West Germany, within two days, preparing for a new assignment. The other Baseline Inspection teams carried out operations at a similar tempo.

Yet another type of Baseline Inspection was the "special inspection," whose purpose was to verify the technical characteristics of each INF weapons system. Navy Commander John C. Williams, a Navy FAO who had served with General Lajoie in Moscow as a Naval Attaché, was designated as the leader of this effort. Over the course of the summer of 1987 he visited the various sites used by the Soviets to eliminate the various missiles and launchers banned by the INF treaty, measuring a randomly designated missile, launcher and associated piece of equipment, which was then subjected to detailed measurements that became the standard which all other inspections would work from.

Commander Williams led the first Elimination Inspection team to Kapustin Yar on July 22, 1988, where he conducted the required technical measurements of an SS-20 missile and launch canister before monitoring its destruction. Other similar Elimination Inspections soon followed.

On August 9, 1988, the Soviets eliminated the first SS-20 launcher at a missile base at Sarny in the Ukraine under the watchful eyes of Team Williams, which once again carried out the measurements required of his special inspection team.

The INF treaty allowed the Soviets to conduct a special kind of elimination event known as "launch to destruct." No telemetry was permitted during these events, and the launch canisters were to be crushed under OSIA monitoring immediately after the launch occurred. The first Soviet SS-20 missiles were eliminated by launching at the Chita and Kansk missile sites in Siberia on 25 August 1988. Seventy-two SS-20 missiles would be destroyed in this fashion during the first six months of the treaty.

Little by little, missile by missile, launcher by launcher, the threat once posed by the SS-20 missile was eliminated in accordance with the provisions of the INF Treaty. Other missile systems were eliminated as well, but none had altered the international security landscape as had the SS-20. The INF Treaty had done its job—the threat to Europe and NATO had been removed.

Almost.

The Temporary Portal

THE FINAL—and most important—inspection required to verify that the SS-20 missile would never again threaten European peace and security was the Perimeter Portal Monitoring (PPM) Inspection, or PPM had not yet been undertaken. Here, OSIA inspectors were to ensure that banned SS-20 missiles were not being covertly manufactured and shipped out of the Votkinsk Missile Final Assembly Plant disguised as permitted SS-25 ICBMs.

But here Stan Fraley's Inspection Protocol, so carefully crafted by committee and through negotiation, faltered. PPM was never supposed to happen—it had been just a demonstration model, a theory designed as a negotiating ploy to get the Soviets to "zero." Only when the issue of similarity between the first stages of the SS-20 and SS-25 missile arose during the final stages of the negotiation of a treaty both parties very much wanted, was PPM reintroduced as a solution to the problem. In the rush to get the INF Treaty signed, the technical details concerning implementation of PPM inspections at Votkinsk had been left out, as the treaty negotiators had been looking to a series of technical talks that would be conducted prior to the treaty entering into force as a mechanism for finalizing the inspection procedures.

By the end of the third session, in May 1988, it was clear that there were many details that still needed to be worked out. It was determined that these issues would be settled by the Special Verification Commission, or SVC, a special body created by the INF Treaty to resolve any disputes that might arise during treaty implementation. Unlike their counterparts serving on Baseline Inspection teams, whose every action was detailed in the Inspection Protocol, the Portal Monitors would be operating off a virtual clean slate, trying to implement inspection provisions in parallel with the negotiations that were defining them. This lack of definition led to one of the most interesting and challenging experiences in the history of arms control implementation—the establishment of the Votkinsk Portal Monitoring Facility.

On July 1, 1988, the Votkinsk Advance Party transitioned into the advance contingent of the Votkinsk portal monitoring inspection team. We had sorted out living arrangements for the team, organized temporary inspection facilities at the Votkinsk factory, conducted a preliminary site survey in preparation for the permanent portal monitoring facility, and established initial protocols for perimeter patrolling and initial inspection operations. And now, at the stroke of midnight on June 30, we became the first American INF inspectors on Soviet soil. While General Lajoie, Colonel Englund, Lieutenant Colonel Kelley and the other inspectors and portal monitors prepared to board the aircraft that would fly them from West Germany to Moscow, the Advance Party was moving out of the Ustinov Dacha into the temporary inspection quarters and finalizing preparations to meet the rest of the team upon their arrival later in the day. It was an auspicious start.

We had six months from entry into force to get the portal monitoring facility up and running—until the stroke of midnight on December 1, 1988. Virtually the entire portal system, however, was being held hostage to the ongoing SVC discussions in Geneva. There were certain inspection items that were not restricted, including the reliable tape measure, a clipboard, paper and pen, and a motivated set of eyes belonging to a trained inspector. These we had, in spades, and we planned on putting them straight to work.

According to the Soviets, there were only two types of railcars that exited the Votkinsk missile assembly plant that could carry a treaty-limited item. The first was a six-axle temperature-controlled railroad car used to carry SS-20 and SS-25 missiles, and possibly other "containerized" objects produced by the factory (an admission made by the Soviets during the May 1988 technical talks in Vienna). The other was a four-axle railroad car for the transport of system components. There was only a single rail line out of the missile final assembly plant. The Soviets had installed a joint temporary inspection building, consisting of prefabricated Czech-made construction trailers, which sat adjacent to this rail line just outside the factory gate. So long as we had inspectors stationed there, nothing was exiting without our inspecting it, if the circumstances warranted.

The initial party of portal monitors, led by Colonel Englund (who served as the Site Commander), and including Mark Dues and Stu O'Neill (the OSIA Duty Officers), two Sandia representatives (Frank Martin and Ken Ystesund) and a 10-person INF Baseline Inspection Team (Team Guiler, led by Lieutenant Colonel Douglas Guiler), arrived in Votkinsk around 11 PM on July 1, after a long day's journey from Rhein Main Air Force Base to Moscow via a US Air Force C-141 Starlifter. After landing in Moscow's Sheremyetovo Airport, the inspectors transferred to an Aeroflot Tu-152 airliner for the flight into Izhevsk, before proceeding by bus to Votkinsk and their new temporary accommodations at 20 Dzerzhinsky Street.

The temporary monitoring system (traffic lights, outdoor lighting, and portable road scales) didn't catch up with the inspectors until July 3, but the factory security personnel indicated that even then, the equipment would not be released to the inspectors until it was thoroughly examined by Soviet customs personnel who would be flying in from Moscow. In the meantime, the new inspectors improvised, placing a hand-lettered 18"x36" cardboard sign labeled "Stop" in both English and Russian outside the main factory gate. They began setting up shop in the Czech shelters that served as a joint interim portal monitoring facility until which time more permanent structures were completed. (The Soviets were in the process of constructing a building that would house their escorts, while the US facility, known as the Data Collection Center, or DCC, was being prepared in Sandia for transport to Votkinsk.[2])

Team Guiler soon settled into a schedule, with sub-teams of three inspectors working in shifts—two 12-hour nights, two 12-hour days, followed by two days off. The OSIA duty officers worked 12 hours on, 24 off, manpower permitting—otherwise the shift lasted if it needed to, sometimes extending to 24–36 hours. And even when off shift, the work requirement continued—there were innumerable "taskers" associated with getting the inspection regime up and running, which consumed every waking hour not spent on shift. There were no complaints—every person present in Votkinsk was a volunteer, carefully selected for the position he or she was filling. A team photograph, taken by a Soviet escort using the inspector's Polaroid camera, shows a band of smiling inspectors intermingled with their Soviet counterparts assembled outside the entrance to the temporary portal shelter.

The most exciting part of the early days of portal monitoring were the perimeter patrols, which were undertaken twice a day at random intervals. The Soviets had requested a 90-minute notice so that they could put together an escort team and notify the Internal Security troops who guarded the perimeter of the factory that the Americans would be walking around outside the factory walls. This was something the inspectors readily agreed to—we did not want a trigger-happy guard taking pot shots at us. There was no established walking path around the factory. What passed for a path provided less than 20 centimeters of visible trail at best, and at worst, just tall grass and bushes that were infested with ticks.

The wild vegetation concealed numerous potholes, which presented an ever-present hazard (indeed, one of the inspectors from Team Guiler badly twisted his ankle by stepping into one). The Soviet practice of throwing construction debris over the wall also led to an assortment of poles, wires and concrete blocks being scattered about. Over 50% of the perimeter path transited through what was best described as swamp, and other areas had large fallen trees, ditches and steep slopes that led down to deep ravines.

From an inspection standpoint, the perimeter patrol was an exercise in futility—it was painfully obvious to all who walked it that there would be no treaty-limited items escaping over the perimeter wall. Indeed, the early baseline inspection teams which supplemented the Portal Monitoring team were unanimous in recommending that this treaty requirement be scrubbed as superfluous. But there could be no "perimeter portal monitoring" without the "perimeter," so it remained, if only to appease the political sensibilities of the arms control experts back in Washington, DC.

Railcars were exiting the factory, including a few of the 4-axle "system component" versions. The railcar was typically pulled by a single locomotive, connected to a smaller "buffer" car attached to the larger 23.5 meter 4-axle railcar. The Soviets would declare the exit of this railcar as being long enough to carry a treaty-limited item, but empty. The train would stop upon exiting the factory, the inspectors would measure the length and width of the railcar using a hand-held tape measure, and then ask the Soviets to open the railcar up so they could look inside and confirm that it was, indeed, not carrying an item that was 14 meters in length or greater.

The most excitement generated by these early inspections came on July 9, when one of the Team Guiler inspectors, Dianna DiCarlo, was stopped by a senior Soviet factory escort, Vyacheslav Lopatin, who was focused on the small personal dosimeter, used to record radiation exposure levels, that Ms. DiCarlo was wearing. The dosimeters had been issued to Team Guiler by the Treaty

*US Portal Monitors inspect a Soviet 4-axle railcar outside the temporary
joint interim portal monitoring facility, September 1988.*

Monitoring Management Office (TMMO) in Rhein Main prior to their departure
on July 1.

While it was an acceptable item for baseline inspections, the dosimeter
was not approved for portal monitoring, so Mr. Lopatin asked that Ms. DiCarlo
remove it prior to entering the railcar. She did so, and the dosimeter was returned
to her once she left. However, the story grew in the retelling, and soon rumors
abounded about how Mr. Lopatin had forcefully seized the dosimeter from Ms.
DiCarlo, leading to a formal investigation which, once the facts were gathered
and assessed, quickly quashed the tall tale. (It also led to the baseline teams
leaving their dosimeters behind when travelling to Votkinsk.)

Team Guiler departed after a two-week tour, to be replaced by Team
Gothreau (led by US Army Colonel Andrew Gothreau, who was on loan to
OSIA from the US Army War College). No sooner had Team Gothreau arrived
than they were thrown into the fire, so to speak—on July 15, the first 6-axle
temperature-controlled railcar carrying an SS-25 missile exited the factory. The
OSIA duty officer for this auspicious event was Stu O'Neill who, along with the
members of Team Gothreau, promptly christened the missile "Pittsburgh." Ten
days later, a second missile exited the factory, which Team Gothreau nicknamed
"Des Moines." (Barrett Haver was the OSIA duty officer for this inspection).

The inspection procedure for a six-axle railcar was the same in terms of
measuring the dimensions of the 4-axle railcar. However, the six-axle railcar

contained a missile inside a launch canister, which filled the interior of the railcar with little room to spare. It was agreed that two inspectors, accompanied by three Soviets (two factory escorts and an interpreter) would conduct the interior inspection, which included taking measurements of the missile canister. The lead inspector would squeeze his or her way down the side of the missile canister, holding onto the rolled tape measure, while the second inspector remained at the rear of the missile, holding onto the "zero" end of the tape measure. "The Soviet escorts," Barrett Haver reported after the July 25 inspection, "held straight edges in place on the missile at each end...both ends of the missile were flat, without obstructions, making the process very straightforward." The inspectors were satisfied that the measurement was accurate.

Measuring the diameter of the canister was more of a challenge, both in terms of the tight conditions at the rear of the railcar, where the missile's front end was located, as well as the geometry of the launch canister itself, which made getting an accurate measurement difficult. "The problem," Barrett Haver noted, "is the distorting effect on the straight edges" created by the existence of a support ring on the canister's front, which caused the straight edges used for measurement to angle out, adding about 2 centimeters to the diameter of the canister. The Soviets were non-plussed by this effect, and so the numbers were reported as measured. In making these measurements, however, the inspectors and their Soviet escorts quickly found that there wasn't enough room at the inner end of the railcar to accommodate five persons. The solution was for the Soviet interpreter to follow last, resulting in a situation where he could not see what was happening, but could hear the others speak and be heard if his services were needed.

The claustrophobic effect of being inside a missile-filled railcar was real. Once an inspector entered the railcar through the side personal access door at the rear of the car, he or she turned right through a small passageway, then came face to face with the boost-assist device of the launch canister. The interior of the railcar was dimly lit, and the air smelled of grease and fresh paint. The Soviets did not want the inspectors to touch the launch canister, so they had to work their way down the railcar by leaning back onto the side of the railcar and shuffling over the missile dolly which carried the launch canister (the wheeled dolly was winched onto the railcar using a set of rails installed on the floor of the railcar). This was not a task where one wore their Sunday finest—inspectors would often emerge from a missile inspection with grease stains and torn clothes. But it was the job they were sent to do, and no one who was offered an opportunity to inspect a missile turned it down.

If inspecting a road-mobile ICBM that might eventually target an American city weren't adventure enough, the Soviets found a way to make inspections even more so. "A curious incident took place on the night of August 2," Chuck Myers reported back to OSIA Headquarters. "We were notified in advance that at 21:30 a four-axle long-enough railcar would exit the plant without a missile.

*Interior of a Soviet 6-axle railcar with an SS-25 missile cannister,
from the perspective of a US inspector.*

When the inspectors looked inside the railcar, they were amazed (as were their escorts) to see an apparent SS-25 launch canister (presumably empty). After some confusion, the escorts stated that the car was coming out simply in order to turn around at the railyard and go directly back into the factory. This is in fact what was done (with two US inspectors on the train the entire time it was out of the factory)."

Later, in discussions with Mr. Anatoli Tomilov, the head of Department 162, Chuck Myers was provided with an explanation about how and why this event transpired. "The 4-axle and 6-axle railcars should be taken into the plant in a specific direction," Tomilov said, "but it is all the same to the railroad men, and sometimes they are taken in facing the wrong way."

The process for loading a missile into the launch canister, and then loading the launch canister onto a 6-axle railcar, was a miniature ballet conducted in several shops throughout the plant, all connected by rail. The 4-axle railcar would enter with an empty launch canister, which would then be removed from the railcar and prepared for insertion of the missile. If the 4-axle railcar entered facing the wrong way, this process couldn't take place, so the railcar would have to be taken to the turn-around area outside the plant, where it would be brought back facing the right direction. At that time, the canister would be loaded with a missile, then placed onto a special dolly, and then loaded onto the 6-axle railcar.

However, if the 6-axle railcar had been brought in facing the wrong direction, it would likewise need to be turned around before the canister and dolly could be loaded. As such, there could in fact be two turn-around operations required for a single missile—a rare, but not unheard of, occurrence.

The Soviets were very concerned that the US inspectors would treat this as a treaty violation and report it through diplomatic channels. Chuck Myers, together with Colonel Connell, indicated that while the event would need to be reported as it occurred, the inspection report would be corrected, and no "treaty ambiguity" (the most serious charge that could be leveled by inspectors on site) declared. In the end, procedures were established for the conduct of turnaround operations, where the Soviets would declare the need to turn a railcar around and exit the factory. Inspectors would then climb aboard the buffer car and accompany the locomotive and railcar in question as it proceeded down to the turnaround area, conducted the required maneuver, and returned to the factory gate, where the train would stop, and the inspectors disembark. Utilizing these procedures, there would be no need to inspect the contents of the railcar, since from an inspection standpoint, the item wasn't actually departing the factory.

What made the experience even more interesting is the fact that the Soviet Railroad Troops who escorted the missile shipments also rode on the buffer car, so the inspectors got to stand side-by-side with an armed soldier who, while ordered not to talk, would often share a smile. And, of course, the inevitable did occur: "[D]uring a turnaround," one weekly report wryly noted, "the returning train did not stop to let the inspectors off; they and their escorts were carried into the plant. The train then pulled out again to discharge the bemused Americans and their apprehensive escorts."

There was one more variation of this theme—the rejected launch canister. Based upon the August 2 experience, it was apparent that the SS-25 launch canister was shipped to the final assembly plant with its lid attached. But on October 25, a 4-axle railcar exited with the plant with an open and empty launch canister, its lid laying on the floor of the railcar. This was not a turnaround—the launch canister had apparently failed a pre-assembly inspection and was being returned to its manufacturer. Because there was no missile, the Soviets forgot to declare that the railcar contained an object large enough to contain a treaty-limited item.

At first the Soviets did not want the inspectors to measure the length and width of the canister, since it was obviously empty. But after being reminded that an SS-20 launch canister was, empty or otherwise, a treaty-limited item, the empty launch canister would have to be measured to confirm that it was an SS-25 launch canister (permitted) and not an SS-20 launch canister (banned). Inspection procedures were adjusted to meet this new situation.

During the technical talks in Vienna in May 1988, the Soviets indicated that Votkinsk also produced "other canisterized items that could be confused for treaty accountable items."[3] The treaty allowed inspectors to inspect anything equal to or greater than an SS-20 without its front end, which was agreed to be 14 meters. What the inspectors didn't know was that the Soviets were going forward with the production and testing of the *Kourier* small ICBM, which was shipped from the final assembly plant in a standard 6-axle temperature-controlled railcar. To the inspectors, an object was either a non-treaty-limited item, which was none of their business, or a treaty-limited item, which was.

On July 27, a *Kourier* missile, in its launch canister, was shipped from Votkinsk in a 6-axle temperature-controlled railcar. It was declared as an item less than 14 meters, which meant the inspectors could not inspect its contents. However, to confirm this, the inspectors needed to measure the actual canister. The *Kourier* canister had a greater diameter that the SS-25 canister, which precluded the inspectors from making their way down the interior of the railcar to make a measurement.

Colonel Connell implemented a solution which had inspectors subtracting the empty interior space (10.5 meters) from the exterior length of the railcar (23.5 meters), which provided for a maximum length of the item in question of 13 meters, which was less than the threshold for inspections set by the treaty. The inspectors believed that, through this procedure, they had met the requirements set forth in the INF treaty regarding the determination, "by visual observation or dimensional measurement" that there was no treaty-limited items onboard the railcar.

However, the policymakers in Washington, DC demanded that the canister must be measured, creating a quandary for the inspectors and the Soviets. It was clear that the canister in question was not 14 meters in length. The problem was that, once the inspectors observed the canister, there was a perceived need to confirm, through direct measurement, that it was indeed less than 14 meters. This would entail the Soviets removing the canister from the railcar, an unsafe and totally unnecessary measure.

On August 30–31, a five-person delegation of American verification policy experts, led by George Look, who had by this time been appointed as the Secretary of Defense's representative to the Special Verification Commission (SVC), visited Votkinsk. While their stated purpose was to learn more about the specific construction materials used in the railcar as they related to the proposed CargoScan radiographic imaging device then under discussion at the SVC, it also allowed Mr. Look, who had led the objection to the procedure put in place by Colonel Connell regarding the *Kourier* missile canister inspection on July 27, to investigate the procedure more thoroughly based upon a first-person examination of the railcar in question.

Eventually a solution was reached which had the Soviets install a canvas shroud separating the launch canister from the rest of the railcar. With the shroud in place, there was, in effect, no canister that needed to be measured, since none could be observed. The inspectors then simply repeated the measuring technique that had previously been used. "We inspected the first partitioned railcars this week [November 16]," Colonel Englund reported back to OSIA Headquarters, "and have adopted procedures for handling these inspections. The railcars are partitioned off by a canvas screen that completely closes off the screened portion of the railcar—side to side and floor to ceiling." A special worksheet was used to record the measurements and calculations done by the inspectors. "The partitioned-off space must be unambiguously less than 14 meters," Englund noted. "Given our accuracy in measuring seems to be within 2 centimeters, I would judge that any space closed-off from inspection that calculates to 13.80 meters or less can be judged to be unambiguously less than 14 meters."

Sticks and Mirrors

THE U.S. INSPECTORS at Votkinsk had ably demonstrated their ability to effectively implement the treaty requirement for monitoring the exit from the Votkinsk factory of items large enough to contain a treaty-limited item. One of the numerous treaty implementation issues confronting the inspectors, however, was how to fulfil the treaty provisions to conduct measurements of an SS-25 missile inside its launch canister "so as to ascertain that the missile or missile stage is not an intermediate-range GLBM [Ground Launched Ballistic Missile] of the inspected Party, or the longest stage of such a GLBM, and that the missile has no more than one stage which is outwardly similar to a stage of an existing type of intermediate-range GLBM."

When the issue of compliance verification at the Votkinsk factory was first discussed in Geneva, after the Soviet declaration concerning the similarity between the first stages of the SS-20 and SS-25 missile, the Soviets initially proposed that the inspectors simply open of one out of every 30 missiles to exit Votkinsk, where the interior of the launch canister could be visually observed, as a sufficient measure. The US side rejected this, noting that the frequency of missile canister openings would have to be increased to twelve a year (a compromise was reached on the number eight), and that a procedure for measuring the stages of the missiles devised to confirm that the second stage of an SS-25 was not the same dimensions of the second stage of an SS-20.

The Soviets, however, complicated this solution by insisting that a missile, once inserted into the launch canister, could not be removed for measuring, noting that the SS-25 "system" (i.e., a missile loaded into a canister) was treated like a sealed round of ammunition. The Soviets initially proposed that the measurement could be done by inserting a "stick" into an opened canister, but then withdrew that notion once their technical experts noted that this could damage the missile. The US countered with a proposal that had the inspectors using laser range finding equipment that would be set up outside the opened canister and as such provide a "hands off" method of measuring. This, too, was rejected by the Soviets. Both sides agreed that the specifics of how the stages would be measured would be left for technical talks that would occur after the treaty was signed.

Following the signing of the treaty, the Soviets tasked the Chief Designer of the SS-25 missile, Lev Solomonov, to come up with a solution to the requirement to measure the second stage of the SS-25 missile. Solomonov constructed a stage measuring device, designed to be inserted inside a missile canister containing an SS-25 missile, which could then be used to obtain the desired measurements. It was agreed that the Soviets would provide the Americans with a model of the stage measuring device, along with a mockup to be used to calibrate the device. These would be sent to Sandia National Laboratory, located on Kirtland Air Force base, outside of Albuquerque, New Mexico, where scientists and technicians would evaluate its utility.

The Soviets shipped the stage measuring device to the US in early June 1988, loading it aboard a commercial airliner bound for New York City's JFK Airport, where it was to be transferred to a US Air Force C-141 Starlifter, which would deliver it to the awaiting Sandia engineers. The crate was sealed and considered diplomatically inviolable. However, there had been no prior coordination with US Customs, whose agents promptly seized the crate and refused to allow it to be forwarded until the crate was opened, and its contents thoroughly examined.

Colonel Connell and General Lajoie were engaged in a heated discussion on how to handle this situation when I arrived at the temporary OSIA offices located in the Coast Guard Headquarters at Buzzards Point and was making my way to the PM office spaces. Colonel Connell spotted me and executed a classic Marine Corps knife-hand in my direction. "Lieutenant Ritter!" Connell shouted. "Stay right there! Do not move!" I complied with my instructions, while the two men disappeared into General Lajoie's office.

A few minutes later, Colonel Connell came striding down the corridor. "Go to National Airport," he said. "Catch the shuttle to JFK. When you arrive, go to the cargo receiving area for United Airlines. Call me from a payphone. I'll give you further instructions at that time."

These orders were simple enough. I drove myself to National Airport, only to find the parking lot full. Circling the terminal, I spotted an empty spot in front of the main terminal building. The only problem was that it was marked "Reserved for Supreme Court Justice." I parked there anyway and found a local police officer. "I'm on official business critical to the national security of the United States," I said. "I'm parking here. Do not tow my vehicle." I was wearing the Marine Charlie uniform—khaki shirt over green dress trousers—and was using knife hand gestures, a Marine Corps trait, to make my point. "No problem," the cop said.

I jogged over to the Pan Am Shuttle desk. "I need to get on the next shuttle to JFK," I told the clerk behind the desk. She looked down the terminal, toward the gate. "They just closed the gate on our current flight," she said. "The next flight will be in an hour."

"I'm on national security business. I need to be on that flight," I said, pointing to the now-closed gate, using a knife-hand as emphasis.

There must have been something about my stare, the tone of my voice, and the continued use of knife hands that impressed her. She picked up the phone, spoke into the receiver, and hung up, taking my OSIA-issued credit card, and issuing me a ticket. "They're bringing the plane back to the gate for you. Good luck!"

I ran down to the gate to find the door to the gateway opened and a bewildered flight attendant peering out. I showed her my ticket, and she stepped aside to let me board the aircraft. Any pretense of discretion was lost as the pilot, co-pilot and several dozen passengers all stared at me as I took my seat.

Upon arrival at JFK, I exited the Pan Am terminal and made my way toward the United Airlines cargo receiving terminal, where I found a payphone and called Colonel Connell. "I'm here, Sir," I said. "What next?"

Connell's instructions were concise. "There's a wooden crate at the United cargo terminal. It contains diplomatically inviolable material. It has been seized by US Customs agents. You are to retrieve this crate. Under no circumstances can it be opened and inspected by Customs. There is an Air Force C-141 on the tarmac outside the United cargo terminal. You are to get this crate loaded onto the C-141 and get that aircraft on its way to its destination. Do you understand?"

I did and said as much. "Then execute your mission."

I walked into the Customs area at the United cargo terminal, where I found a Customs agent sitting behind a desk. I introduced myself, and said I was here about a crate that had been seized. "I don't care if they send in the entire goddamned Marine Corps," the Customs officer exclaimed. "I'm not releasing that crate until it has been inspected."

My instructions provided zero latitude for negotiations. "I don't think you understand the seriousness of the situation," I said.

"Oh, I do. I don't think you understand how customs inspections work," the Customs officer replied.

He was correct—I did not have a clue. All I knew was that he could not inspect the contents of that crate. Calling Colonel Connell only to report what he obviously already knew was not an option, either. It was put up or shut up time. I reached for my wallet and pulled out a business card from a Colonel O'Neil, whom Colonel Connell had introduced me to a few days prior. Colonel O'Neil worked as a Scientific Advisor in the Office of the President, and his business card was clearly marked "The White House."

I laid the card down on the table so that the Customs agent could read what was written on it. "We can do this the easy way," I said, "or the hard way. You see, the contents of that crate relate to the Intermediate Nuclear Forces Treaty. This Treaty is President Ronald Reagan's personal baby. By seizing this crate and threatening to open it, you are putting the treaty at risk. The easy way," I said, "is that you release the crate to me as it is, and I get on with my business."

I picked up the phone on his desk. "The hard way is that I call the White House, give them your name, and explain to them how you are personally trying to screw up the INF Treaty. The White House will then call the head of Customs, who will then call you, and you will have to explain yourself to your boss. I don't know what kind of career trajectory you envision yourself having, but I don't think that's a phone call you really want to be having."

I was not bluffing about making the call. However, I did not know if Colonel O'Neil would take my call, and if he did, if any of the actions I had just laid out would transpire. My mouth was, more than likely, writing checks I would not be able to cash.

The Customs officer did not say a word, so I began dialing the phone, my heart in my throat, trying to figure out what I would say if Colonel O'Neil answered. The Customs officer reached out and put his finger on the cradle, terminating the call. "Look, there might be a way out of this," he said. "Are you willing to take full responsibility for the contents of that crate?"

I indicated I was. The Customs officer searched the drawers of his desk and extracted a document. He filled out the appropriate portions detailing with the item in question, and then turned it over to me, pointing out where I should print my name, the date, and affix my signature. Once completed, the Customs officer handed me a copy of the document, and gestured toward the crate. "It's all yours," he said. "Get it out of here."

The C-141 was parked outside the hanger, so I walked over to it and waived up to the cockpit. Soon the pilot and the crew chief came out and joined me in the hanger. I pointed at the crate. "That's your cargo," I said. "You need to get it to your destination." The crew chief handed me some more forms to sign, turning the cargo over to their control and vouching for the safety of its contents. I still had no idea what was contained in the crate. Once completed, the crew brought out a forklift, and I watched as the crate was loaded onto the aircraft. I then returned to the warehouse, where I would wait until the C-141 was off the ground and on its way.

About five minutes later, the crew chief approached me. "We've got a problem," he said. "The traffic pattern is full, and we won't be able to depart for several hours." I asked if I could speak to the pilot, and the crew chief took me out to where the aircraft was parked and handed me a headset and microphone that was connected to the aircraft via an umbilical cord.

Back in April, before I had been loaned out to Counterintelligence, I had accompanied Major Trahan, the man responsible for briefing Congress and US agencies on INF Treaty implementation issues, to a meeting at the State Department with the Federal Aviation Administration (FAA) regarding treaty-related flights. I recalled that to ensure that all treaty-related aircraft were not subjected to unnecessary delays, given the constraints imposed on time by treaty mandate, a special call sign had been established for treaty-related aircraft—INFO 001. Any aircraft thus designated would be given priority over all other aircraft.

"I need you to re-designate your aircraft with the call sign INFO 001," I said.

"On whose authority?" the pilot asked.

"Mine," I responded, giving him my name and title.

Within a minute, the pilot came back to me. "I don't know what kind of black magic you just pulled, but we're cleared for immediate take off!"

I handed the headset back to the crew chief, who boarded the C-141. Within minutes it was taxiing out to the runway. I watched as, all around, aircraft aborted landings, and other aircraft froze in place on the taxiways. Planes were stacked in the skies over JFK, and all up and down the east coast aircraft went into holding patterns, their flight plans suddenly disrupted. Thus, unencumbered by competition, the C-141 took to the air, and made is way toward Kirtland Air Force Base. My mission was complete.

I made my way to the payphone outside the United cargo terminal and called Colonel Connell. "The crate has been loaded onto the C-141. It was not inspected by Customs. The C-141 is in the air," I reported. Connell was pleased. "Listen, Sir," I continued, "there might be a few ruffled feathers…"

"Don't worry about anything," Connell said, cutting me off. "You got the job done. General Lajoie will be pleased. Come on home."

I did so, taking the Pan Am shuttle back to National Airport, and finding my car where I left it, no parking ticket in sight. I drove back to Buzzards Point and made my way to the PM office. I was intercepted in the hall by Lieutenant Commander Myers. "Report to Colonel Connell directly," he said.

It turned out that in the time it took for me to fly from New York City to Washington, DC, all hell had broken loose. The White House had called, asking why a Lieutenant was invoking its authority. The FAA had likewise called, demanding to know why some Lieutenant was re-designating military aircraft with treaty callsigns before the treaty had entered into force. Colonel Connell relayed all of this to me while I was standing at attention in front of his desk. I was struggling to find words that could explain why I did what I had done, recalling General Lajoie's earlier admonition that "when you're explaining, you're losing."

I did not have a chance to speak. "General Lajoie was pretty pissed off," Connell said. "He wanted your head on a platter. I reminded him that he was the one who authorized you to go to New York, and that he set the conditions of your task. All you did was obey orders and accomplish the mission. Bravo Zulu. Now go home. Things will be calmed down by tomorrow."

I turned to exit his office. "Oh, by the way," Connell added. "You owe Colonel O'Neil a beer. I would not advise you using that trick again. Once was more than enough."

It was only later that I found out that the crate I had rescued contained a Soviet manufactured stage measuring device. If the crate had been opened by Customs, it would have had to have been returned to the Soviet Union, and a new one shipped, setting back US inspection capabilities by several months. Connell was personally invested in the stage measuring device, and my intervention in getting it cleared through Customs and expeditiously transported to Sandia helped keep what was, at that time, a critical piece of verification technology on track for use by inspectors in Votkinsk.[4]

By July 1988, however, the American inspectors were in Votkinsk, but the stage measuring device, which was still being worked on at Sandia, was not. But even if we had had a stage measuring device on hand, there were still obstacles that needed to be addressed before a missile could be inspected. During discussions with Votkinsk factory officials conducted by the advance party, in June, we were informed that the SS-25 missile required specific temperature and humidity conditions to exist before a launch canister could be opened for inspection. Moreover, the weight of the canister lid (80 kilograms) required special equipment to be removed safely. Likewise, the unwieldy nature of the stage measuring device mandated the presence of a stable platform for its use. These conditions, the factory officials noted, would only be met when a purpose-built inspection building was constructed at the inspection site. However, this building was not expected to be finished until on or about December 1, 1988.

The Soviets asked if the Americans would be willing to forego canister openings until the building was completed or, if the US inspectors would accept a visual inspection without the stage measuring device, then arrangements could probably be made to accommodate this. We reported this conversation back to OSIA Headquarters, which forwarded it on the Special Verification Commission, which had convened in Geneva to address the numerous technical issues relating to Portal Monitoring inspections that remained unresolved.

During the inspections of the SS-25 missiles nicknamed "Pittsburgh" and "Des Moines," on July 15 and 25, respectively, the required measurements were taken, allowing the inspectors to ascertain that the launch canister was large enough to contain an SS-25 missile. However, void of the ability to either visually inspect the inside of the canister and measure the missile it contained, or conduct radiographic imaging of the missile, inspectors had no way of determining whether the canister contained a permissible SS-25, or the banned SS-20.

Both the Americans and the Soviets understood the inadequacy of the current arrangement. During the inspection of the "Des Moines" missile on July 25, the Soviets indicated that they would be prepared to begin opening SS-25 launch canisters for interior inspection beginning August 9 and inquired if the US would be prepared to use the stage measuring device at that time. The acting Site Commander, Chuck Myers, informed the Soviets that he had no information on the status of the stage measuring device, but echoed the Soviet position put forward during the advance party's visit that the inspectors could simply conduct a visual inspection without it, which would count against the eight annual openings permitted under the treaty.

On August 10, the US Embassy in Moscow forwarded to the Soviets the results of the Sandia technical evaluation of the stage measuring device. The Sandia technicians, after evaluating the device, carried out physical modifications which they believed would better facilitate its treaty mandated functions. The Soviets, after considering the American proposals, objected to these modifications, noting that they allowed for measurements beyond that required under the treaty to distinguish the second stage of an SS-25 missile from that of an SS-20 missile. The Soviets proposed that a demonstration of an unmodified stage measuring device, which was at the Votkinsk factory, be conducted during one of the eight annual canister opening inspections permitted under the treaty. Concurrently, the Soviets had prepared interim procedures for the opening of a missile canister for visual inspection—without the use of a stage measuring device. These procedures were presented to the US inspectors on August 16.

That same day, a US Air Force C-5 Galaxy landed at Moscow's Sheremetye-vo airport. Onboard were 28 pallets of technical inspection equipment, weighing some 160,000 pounds—and the Sandia-modified stage measuring device. The equipment, including the stage measuring device, was transferred to four Soviet Il-76 aircraft, which flew on to Izhevsk airport on August 18–19. There, the pallets were transported by truck to an agricultural warehouse near the Votkinsk factory, where they were inspected by a team of ten Soviet Customs officials between 20–23 August.

On August 24, the Soviets shipped an SS-25 missile from the Votkinsk Factory. The inspectors declared that they would be requesting that the Soviets open the canister for inspection. While the Site Commander, Doug Englund, had hoped to prevail upon the Soviets to use the modified stage measuring device— which Englund referred to as "sticks and mirrors"—in the first missile opening, the technical documentation accompanying the modified stage measuring device had yet to be translated into Russian, and the modifications themselves would need to be approved by Lev Solomonov, the SS-25 Chief Designer, before the device could be used.

The Soviets had converted a railcar shed located on a rail spur off the main track leading into the factory to serve as an interim inspection building until the permanent one, then under construction, was finished. Following the inspection and measurement of the canister, which took place outside the factory gates, the Soviets moved the railcar carrying the missile canister to the interim inspection building. Two inspectors rode with the missile on the train, while the rest of the team, along with the factory officials, were driven to the rail shed in a Soviet bus. After removing the canister cover, the Soviets allowed the inspectors, led by Doug Englund and the ubiquitous Stu O'Neill, to approach within four meters of the opened canister to make their observations.

"The missile," Colonel Englund noted in his report, "appeared to have three stages, with a front section attached to the third stage. The missile, with front section, was flush with the end of the canister with lid removed." The ease in which the inspection unfolded, including the degree to which the inspectors could see into the canister, together with the accommodating approach taken by the Soviets, was apparent to all. From a verification standpoint, visual observation was sufficient to ascertain that the missile inside the launch canister was a three-stage SS-25, and not a two-stage SS-20.

The issue of treaty-mandated measurements was an outstanding issue, however, that required resolution. The Americans were pressing for use of the Sandia-modified device, while the Soviets believed the original design by Solomonov was adequate for the task. In cases of technical differences such as this, the treaty called for the intervention of the Special Verification Commission. As such, the matter of the stage measuring device was forwarded to Geneva and placed in the hands of the diplomats, who by early October had decided that the best way forward was to conduct an "experiment" in Votkinsk, using an actual SS-25 missile under inspection conditions.

The SVC delegation arrived in Votkinsk on October 11 and conducted their "experiment" the next day, October 12. After a series of discussions over the practicalities associated with the conduct of the experiment, the delegation waited on the sidelines as the formalities of a treaty-mandated inspection unfolded. The Soviets declared to the American inspectors their intent to exit a railcar carrying a missile, after which the railcar departed the factory and both the railcar and missile canister it contained were measured by the inspectors on duty. Only after the inspection was complete did the SVC delegation take over, and the railcar was moved to the temporary inspection building where the factory personnel prepared it for the stage measuring device experiment.

The "experiment" did not go well, despite the best efforts of all involved. There was an opening moment of levity, when Colonel Connell, one of two Portal Monitoring inspectors on the American delegation (the other was Jim Stewart, a Hughes employee) asked what he could see while peering inside the open canister, replied, dead pan, "C-h-i-c-a-g-o." After this, the exercise devolved into a series of unfulfilled expectations.

The American delegation had been led to believe that there would be a shiny metal band around the junction between the two stages, which could be used as a point of reference in determining length. Instead, the band had been painted over, eliminating the expected visual cue and making it difficult for the team to orient itself onto the missile. Moreover, while both sides agreed that the stage measuring device performed consistently, the Americans wanted to make several measurements at five-centimeter intervals along the entire length of the stage to confirm its diameter, while the Soviets preferred a single measurement regarding the gap between the missile and the canister.

"We are a bit concerned," Colonel Connell wrote in the OSIA Weekly Report, "that the accuracy requirements will demand additional equipment and elaborate procedures that will make internal inspections hideously complicated and difficult to replicate exactly. This process has to be kept user-friendly."

In the end both sides agreed that the stage measuring device, as currently designed, was insufficient for the task of repeatably measuring stage length on missiles stored in a launch canister. The Soviets indicated that the identified shortfalls could be resolved by using a second device that Lev Solomonov was prepared to produce. It was agreed that the stage measuring device issue would be returned to Geneva, where discussions would continue to find a mutually acceptable resolution.

At the suggestion of Colonel Connell, the inspection report contained the following comments: "Length and diameter not recorded because canister opening was not an inspection. Canister opening and measurements were to determine the effectiveness of the device for measuring the second stage of the SS-25 missile. This experiment was at the request of Special Verification Commission in Geneva. This experiment is not included in the agreed number of eight canister openings per year."

On October 24, the Votkinsk factory asked the American inspectors about the status of the stage measuring device, since it impacted the ongoing construction of the permanent inspection building. A "stable platform" would need to be constructed to use the device, but the exact dimensions of such a platform depended on how the device was going to be used, and if there was going to be a second device involved. The Americans responded that they knew nothing more than that there were problems with the device, which had been sent back to Sandia for re-evaluation.

On November 1, members of the Soviet SVC delegation, led by Ambassador Strel'tsov, visited Votkinsk, where they met with representatives from both the inspection team and the factory on what Colonel Englund, the senior American present, called an "information gathering" trip. Among other topics, Ambassador

Strel'tsov lamented that the issue of the stage measuring device had not been satisfactorily resolved before the conclusion of the second session of the SVC.

A resolution to the device's technical viability as a means of verification would have to wait for the new year.

The saga of "sticks and mirrors" had, for the time being, come to an end.

The Temporary Portal

WITHIN THE FIRST four months of their arrival, the portal monitoring inspectors, working in concert with their Soviet counterparts in Department 162, had demonstrated a level of professionalism and creativity in confronting inspection scenarios that had not been considered when the INF treaty had been signed. The reality was that these inspectors, armed with little more than a clipboard and measuring tape, were able to exercise good faith and outstanding judgement in the execution of their duties—which in the case of the Votkinsk operation, was to ensure that no banned SS-20 missiles exited disguised as permitted SS-25's.

Had the INF negotiators simply agreed that every SS-25 launch canister exiting the portal would be opened for visual inspection, the issue of treaty compliance verification would have terminated at this juncture. This was not to be the case. Instead, the OSIA inspectors were given the task of installing and implementing a TOSI design that was inherently incompatible with the actual operations at Votkinsk, something that had become glaringly obvious to the inspectors as they prepared to implement the treaty.

The Soviets had declared that only railcars were used to transport objects large enough to contain treaty-limited items. "It may be the case," a Portal Monitoring point paper, prepared in April 1988, noted, "that any railcar long enough to contain a [treaty-limited item] will also be heavy enough to contain a [treaty-limited item], and thus will invariably be subject to visual inspection of the interior." Acceptance of this reality would have precluded the need to install infrared measuring devices and rail scales.

But even the issue of weighing a missile canister was fraught with impracticalities from the start. "Although the Treaty allows us to weigh the missile canister," the Portal Monitoring staff observed in their point paper, "it is unclear whether this is possible in view of the Soviet explanation of their missile loading procedures." The Soviets were asked during the technical talks how they planned on facilitating the weighing of a missile canister. No answer had been provided by the time the Portal Monitors began to deploy to the Soviet Union in July.

The CargoScan x-ray likewise remained an open issue. "We need to determine how the x-ray will be used to adequately measure parameters of a declared missile and which parameters will be measured," the point paper stated. "The Soviets have proposed their own version of non-damaging equipment which does not afford penetration of the missile and thus appears to be spoofable."

The civilian contract personnel from HTSC who were tasked with the installation, operation and maintenance of the Votkinsk Portal Monitoring Facility would not be prepared to deploy to the Soviet Union until sometime in August 1988 (indeed, at the time the point paper was written, the contract had not even been awarded). Rather than wait until the contactors were recruited and trained, OSIA determined that it would implement a temporary monitoring operation to "demonstrate the US determination to exercise its treaty rights" and "enable us to examine our monitoring procedures and provide invaluable information to the contractor to assist him in preparing for the installation of permanent monitoring equipment and in creating detailed and standardized operating procedures."

It was recognized that "initial and interim operations will be significantly limited since the more sophisticated measurement and imaging devices planned for the permanent site will not be available at the outset." The initial team of inspectors would bring with them a suite of temporary sensors which would be installed at the Votkinsk factory to enable remote monitoring of an exit that was located about 300 meters from the main factory gates, despite the fact that the Soviets had notified the Americans that the exit was for emergency use only, and that the "average vehicular traffic through the exit on a monthly basis is zero." Rather than install equipment that was clearly not needed, a decision was made between the inspectors and Soviet factory personnel to simply block off the secondary exit, leaving the Votkinsk Final Assembly Plant with only one exit—the main gate.

The inspectors would also bring temporary traffic lights and CCTV cameras that would be installed at the main gate until which time the full complement of portal monitoring equipment, including infra-red profiling equipment, weight scales, induction loops, traffic control systems and integrated CCTV monitoring system, together with sufficient lighting to enable 24-hour operations, could be delivered, together with a Data Collection Center (DCC) which would serve as the nerve center of portal monitoring operations. The delivery of these materials was envisioned in phases, with the interim monitoring equipment brought in on day one, followed by Phase One materials (the portal monitoring equipment minus the DCC), then Phase II (the DCC), followed by Phase III (the CargoScan X-ray facility).

Even on paper the plan looked overly ambitious. "No plan," the old military axiom goes, "survives initial contact with the enemy." As far as deploying the Votkinsk Portal Monitoring Facility went, this applied with full force. Installing the interim monitoring equipment turned out to be far more difficult than imagined. The Soviets were very sensitive about equipment being installed outside the gates of a secret military industrial facility. Integrating inspection theory with Soviet reality was also a problem.

On July 20 the head Soviet technical escort for the factory, Vyacheslav Lopatin, gave Frank Martin, the Sandia representative responsible for installing the temporary monitoring system, permission to place the traffic lights in the desired location. This was done.

"The rail inspector arrived later," Martin noted, "to say that at least two meters of clearance was needed from the rail to the nearest part of the light... [we] moved light 18 millimeters south." But placing the lights only increased the inspector's woes. "Later in the day a car exited the facility but didn't stop," Martin reported. "The Soviet escort complained the reason the car didn't stop was because the traffic lights didn't work. Of course they don't work—power installation won't be until tomorrow. Back to the cardboard sign!"

The power was connected to the traffic lights on July 22. It wasn't until July 29, however, that power was provided to the towers mounting the CCTV cameras and lighting. Even here, Soviet distrust abounded. Lopatin watched as power was turned on to the video monitor connected to the CCTV camera. The lightning protector on the tower would not allow the signal to be passed. Frank Martin removed the lightning protector, and the signal came through fine. "If that really was a lightning protector," Lopatin observed, "it would have worked."[5]

The TOSI demonstration facility had been designed for autonomous use, with the sensors being transmitted back to a remote facility, where human monitors would activate lights and gates from a data control center hundreds if not thousands of miles removed from the actual factory being monitored. In Votkinsk, with the portal monitors working directly on-site able to conduct manual measurements, the integrated system—vehicle presence detectors (induction loops), traffic lights and semaphore gates, together with vehicle dimensional measuring equipment (the road and rail infra-red profilers) and a surveillance system consisting of fixed position, downward looking video cameras and lighting—was not only overly complicated, but for the most part superfluous.

Richard Trembley, a logistics officer assigned to the US Air Force's Electronics Systems Division (ESD) who was responsible for shipping the portal monitoring system from the TOSI demonstration facility to Votkinsk, noted in a paper he wrote for the Air Force Institute of Technology that the TOSI planners had assumed "that there would be very few American inspectors allowed to be continuously based at the site. Therefore, the monitoring system had to be fairly automated. The development work proceeded in the absence of specific user requirements. When the treaty was signed and ratified, both sides had approximately six months to establish monitoring facilities. The short lead time drove the decision to deploy the system at Sandia, even though it was developmental. That decision complicated logistics planning because there was very little work done in developing bills of material, drawings and technical data needed for establishing logistics support of the system."[6]

Trembley had interviewed Mike Embree, a Hughes logistician based in Albuquerque who was responsible for receiving the TOSI equipment from Sandia and integrating it into the Hughes logistical management system in preparation for deployment to Votkinsk (Hughes had taken over the contracting responsibilities at the Votkinsk portal monitoring facility in mid-August; delays created by issues regarding the issuance of Soviet visas kept most of the Hughes inspectors out of country until the end of August). As Embree observed, "[Sandia] integrated a lot of parts to make an end item. And it was turned over to us very quickly to meet the shipment schedule. They would give us items and say, 'This is called' whatever the nomenclature was used. We took it and put it down on paper as receiving it, just for accountability records, and it went to Votkinsk immediately—but with no documentation to support what it really was."

The Phase One portal monitoring equipment was delivered to Izhevsk on 18–19 August onboard four Aeroflot Il-76 aircraft. It was taken to a locale warehouse that had been rented by the Votkinsk factory for that purpose, where it was inspected by Soviet customs officials before being turned over to the inspectors.

"Problem!" Colonel Englund reported back to OSIA Headquarters on August 22, in a statement that would be repeated in the weeks and months ahead. "We do not have a complete set of the absolute latest site drawings!" Without the drawings, the Soviets at the site, with Lopatin taking the lead, challenged every placement decision regarding lights and cameras, which in turn delayed the digging of trenches and the laying of power cables.

The Soviets were also worried about the complexity of the monitoring system. So, too, were the OSIA Site Commanders. "The idea of simplification has apparently taken root," Colonel Connell noted in a report back to OSIA Headquarters. By September 4, Colonel Englund recommended that OSIA do away with the rail profiler, noting that "It will not decrease our inspection work load (but will increase our maintenance work load), and [i]t will not be nearly as reliable and accurate as are the manual measurements we are now making." In short, Englund observed, "the rail profiler will be considerably more expensive, complex and difficult to maintain than the manual systems we are now using, but at the same time will be less accurate and much less reliable."

The policymakers in Washington, DC overrode his concerns—the rail profiler would be installed as designed. So, too, would the road profiler, which had to be relocated from its original location when it was pointed out by the Soviets that it would interfere with the construction of their permanent escort operations building.

Rail Scales

WHILE THE INSPECTORS struggled with the issue of sorting out and installing the Phase One portal monitoring system, they simultaneously wrestled with the issue of weighing the railcars. The language of the INF treaty text was quite specific: "the right to weigh." The trouble was not in the verbiage, but rather in the method of execution. It turned out that weighing a railcar loaded with a missile at a working missile assembly plant was virtually an impossible task.

The drafters of the treaty apparently failed to coordinate with the factory workers of the Votkinsk Machine Building Plant when they crafted the treaty text calling for the weighing of railcars. This point was made quite clear by the technical experts from the factory during the first round of technical talks, who noted that the missile canister was secured to a dolly, which was in turn rolled onto the rail car using rails built into the carriage. The only way to access the canister was from the open end of the car, which made weighing the missile canister impossible. If the missile was to be weighed, the Soviets noted, it would have to be done while loaded into a launch canister that in turn was loaded into a rail car. This point was reinforced to Colonels Connell and Englund during the May visit to Votkinsk, when the Soviets gave them a tour of the factory rail holding yard and the rail scales installed there.

During the advanced party mission in June 1988, the Votkinsk factory technicians proposed that only the special railcars designed to carry missile containers be counted as being "heavy enough" to carry a treaty-limited item, since they were the only ones large enough to do so. They also proposed that the method used for determining the weight of a missile container be obtained by first weighing an empty railcar, and then weighing it after it had been loaded with a missile canister. The Soviets proposed using Soviet rail scales of the type shown to Connell and Englund during their May visit, suggesting that these scales be installed on a rail spur that would be constructed in support of a permanent inspection building intended to be used to visually inspect missiles. Chuck Myers, the head of the advance party, was noncommittal to these suggestions, waiting instead for a formal US position to be developed during the Special Verification Commission talks ongoing in Geneva. The issue of where the rail scales would be located, and which scales would be used, was still outstanding by the time the inspectors arrived in Votkinsk in July.

To the surprise of the inspectors, the Soviets were proceeding with preparations regarding the installation of rail scales—theirs. As early as July 18, Colonel Connell noted that the foundations the Soviets had begun to install "may not be sufficient if non-Soviet rail scales are to be used." The Soviet rail scales, Connell observed, "have already been purchased and are at site. Both sides are waiting for a decision from the US side." Perhaps most importantly, Connell reported, was the Soviet promise that "they would not let a railcar that could hold a [treaty-limited item] out of the plant if Soviet-manufactured scales break down…if US-manufactured scales are to be used and they break, this is the US problem and railcars will continue to leave the plant." Connell, hearing nothing back from OSIA Headquarters, pressed the issue in a report dated July 29: "I hope you all decide to use the Soviet scales if the statement here concerning breakdowns that we previously reported is an official Soviet position."

For his part, Colonel Englund had soured on the use of rail scales. "In my view the question of whose scales to use is not nearly important as is the issue of *how* these scales are to be used," Englund wrote back to OSIA Headquarters on August 12. "Agreed weighing procedures have not yet been developed, however, and may not be for some time. For this and other reasons, I continue to believe that the best solution to the weighing problem is to avoid it altogether by opening all railcars that are large enough. After nearly a month and a half of inspections of many railcars that clearly do not contain an item large enough to be an SS-20, the Soviets should have noticed that our inspections have been relatively nonintrusive."

The issue of rail scales remained in limbo throughout the remainder of the summer and into early fall. The Soviets continued construction of the concrete foundation where the scales would be installed—inside the Environmentally Protected Building (EPB) that was to be used for missile inspections. This created an issue of access to the scales by the inspectors, as well as the calibration of the scales (the inspectors would lose control of the scales when a missile-carrying railcar was taken into the EPB and the lid removed from the launch canister). Like all other rail scale-related problems, this one was forwarded to Geneva for resolution by the SVC.

And then, without warning, the issue of rail scales was over. On November 1, during a visit by members of the Soviet SVC delegation, the head of the delegation, Ambassador Strel'tsov, notified Colonel Englund that the SVC in Geneva had decided to do away with all scales, road and rail. It seemed the SVC had been listening after all.

The Data Control Center (DCC)

THE NEXT CHALLENGE facing the inspectors was the installation of the Data Control Center—the DCC. The problem of trying to rapidly deploy the TOSI development facility and simultaneously convert it to the Votkinsk Portal Monitoring Facility without first adequately documenting everything would haunt the inspectors. "The lack of documentation is still a problem," Colonel Englund noted in mid-November. "As expected, none of the hoped-for technical material for the Data Collection Center came in on the 3 November rotation. The Soviets are saying they cannot properly inspect the DCC until after they have thoroughly studied these detailed materials and that if they are not received shortly the technical inspections will have to be delayed accordingly."

Jerry Porter, the Hughes Site Manager, further lamented on November 19 that "All necessary cable information drawings not yet received from [Sandia]."

Even when the documentation did arrive, there was the problem of transferring the material to the Soviets. "A problem," Mark Soo Hoo noted, "has come up in that we don't have a formal procedure for transferring drawings to the Soviets." Bill Langemeier, a Hughes inspector responsible for tracking documentation in Votkinsk, came up with an interim form to document such transfers. The issue was discussed with Colonel Englund on November 16. "With Colonel Englund's agreement," Mr. Soo Hoo noted, "it's been decided to transfer what drawings are in the Hughes files, using the transfer form and procedure that Bill Langemeier has developed."

But even this procedure proved insufficient. "The key to convincing Mr. Lopatin that our equipment should be approved for installation is DOCUMENTATION," Rob Sederman, the on-site ESD representative, noted in a status report dated November 21. "That is still the major holdup with construction."

Sederman emphasized the importance of documentation when it came to the installation of the DCC. "If detailed documentation (i.e., wiring schematics) on the DCC does not get here until the Phase II shipment arrives," Sederman stated, "the Soviets have indicated that there will be delays."

But the documents did not arrive on the expected rotation of inspectors. "A telephone call to Ron Moya [a Sandia engineer] reveals that the drawings were in fact turned over to Al Gloe of Hughes (in Albuquerque)," Mark Soo Hoo reported. "I understand in talking with Chuck Biasotti (the Hughes cook!), who came in on the rotation, that he was to have been given the drawings, but never received them."

The situation regarding documents was reaching a crisis point. "Both Colonel Englund and I are beginning to find the insatiable Soviet demands for ever more documentation wearisome," Colonel Connell noted in a December 14 Memorandum to General Lajoie. "I recommend that you hammer home the point that [in accordance with the draft Memorandum of Agreement], technical inspections of our monitoring equipment precede the signing of the joint inventory and once that inventory has been signed, we 'have the right to begin installing and using the equipment...' After signature of the joint inventory, the burden of proof is then on the Soviets to establish that there is something unacceptable about a particular piece of equipment. This is a fundamental logjam that we need to break."

To accomplish just that, on December 16 Connell met with Mr. Tomilov, the head of Department 162 and Vyacheslav Lopatin's immediate boss. While sympathetic to Connell's concerns, Tomilov was adamant in insisting on adequate documentation. "The Soviet side must be convinced that equipment installation conforms to documentation," Tomilov said, "and although the American side has given the Soviets many drawings of separate elements of the system, it has not provided an overall functional description." Tomilov stated that the Soviets must have a general functional description of the system to determine which drawings are missing so that they can request them.

The Soviet side, Tomilov noted, was meeting the American side halfway, despite the absence of accompanying documentation. The DCC shelters, which were held up in Moscow pending inspection, could have been inspected at Votkinsk "had they been accompanied by complete documentation." Tomilov concluded by reminding Connell that "the documentation for the monitoring system at the permanent inspection facility in Votkinsk has still not been received."

Colonel Connell told Tomilov that he believed that the inspectors had provided a copy of the "Functional Description of TOSI Equipment" on November 21, and that this document should provide the Soviets with an understanding of the general function of the TOSI system. Tomilov promised to investigate whether this document had indeed been provided and apologized in advance for any misunderstanding.

As it turned out, the fault was not on the Soviet side. In a comment for the record on the December 16 memorandum documenting the meeting with Tomilov, the OSIA Duty Officer noted that "[e]ven though the system overview 'Functional Description of TOSI Equipment' appears on the list of documents already given to the Soviets, they may, in fact, have never received it. In a US caucus that followed the meeting with the Soviets, Mr. Kubic, the [Hughes] inspector in charge of document control, stated that he actually never gave the paper to the Soviets, but thought that Colonel Englund did. A telephone call to Colonel Englund revealed that he had not provided the paper to the Soviets. They now have a copy and we await their reaction."

As Tomilov had noted, the DCC shelters had been stuck in Moscow, awaiting documentation that would permit inspection. This was finally accomplished on December 6, and by December 7 the Soviets were prepared to deliver the shelters to Izhevsk for onward transportation to Votkinsk.

The original DCC shelters had been designed by Sandia for demonstration purposes only. When the TOSI demonstration facility was selected to be deployed to Votkinsk, the US Air Force's Electronic Systems Division (ESD) took over responsibility for managing the acquisition and deployment of the six ISO shelters that comprised the DCC. However, in configuring the shelters for use as part of the DCC, the new design precluded using the four top corner secure points to lift the containers, meaning that they could only be moved by using a device called a spreader bar, which allowed the shelter to be picked up from the bottom corner attach points. The spreader bar, however, was incompatible with the crane system used by Aeroflot, and as such, ESD borrowed six M1022 Mobilizers from the 101st Airborne Division in Fort Campbell, Kentucky. These Mobilizers were designed to be attached to ISO shelters so they could be towed like a trailer, and as such were perfect for getting the DCC to and from the Soviet aircraft.

On December 7 two inspectors met the initial two DCC ISO shelters (the Exit Shelter and the mudroom) as they arrived in Izhevsk aboard a Soviet Il-76. According to an account provided to OSIA by one of them, Captain Patrick Rizzuto, a transportation specialist with ESD, the effort to move the DCC from Moscow to Izhevsk was nearly a disaster. It almost killed an inspector as well as damaged or destroyed the DCC shelters involved.

The Soviet crew, Rizzuto observed, "was in a great hurry, constantly trying to speed us along." The Soviets wanted the inspectors to lift the first shelter without either securing it or levelling the aircraft. The inspectors refused, noting that this would have allowed the shelter to roll free and "probably would have resulted in the destruction of the shelter." Only after the Soviet aircrew levelled the aircraft did the inspectors raise the shelter. But the Soviets, still in a hurry, started guiding the Mobilizer off the aircraft without American supervision, and wedged it into the ground. "The Mobilizer was finally freed," Rizzuto noted, "but only after we attached a chain and used a truck to swing the Mobilizer's wheels around. This could have damaged the Mobilizer and was only done as a last resort."

After inflating the air shocks on the second Mobilizer, the Soviets neglected to remove the slack from the winch cable being used to ease the shelter off the aircraft. Before either inspector knew what was happening, "the Mobilizer/shelter was rolling freely towards the end of the aircraft, rapidly accelerating approximately 10–15 feet before the winch cable abruptly stopped it." The Mobilizer/shelter combination, Rizzuto pointed out, weighed more than 14,000 pounds, and had it not stopped it would have "continued out of control off the end of the aircraft and onto the tarmac, causing significant damage to the rear of the aircraft's cargo area, and quite likely damaging the shelter and the attached Mobilizer beyond repair."

Jim Hull, a Hughes employee, was standing with a Soviet aircrewman between the Mobilizer and the side of the aircraft. Hull, according to Rizzuto, "sacrificed his personal safety to assist the Soviet away from the oncoming shelter…[w]ith no exaggeration, I maintain that if the winch cable has even six more inches of slack in it, Mr. Hull would have been seriously injured, and possibly even killed."

It took five hours to transport the Mobilizer/shelter combination to Votkinsk, driving slowly to avoid loss of control on the hilly, icy slick roads. Every hour the convoy pulled over to the side of the road for safety checks on all the equipment, before finally arriving safely at the Votkinsk portal.

US inspectors work to disconnect a DCC module from an M-1022 Mobilizer,
December 1988.

Four days later, Rizzuto, this time joined by two Hughes inspectors, returned to Izhevsk to receive the remaining four ISO shelters comprising the DCC complex. Upon his arrival, Rizzuto noted that the first two shelters were already on the tarmac, the Soviets having arrived and off-loaded them without waiting for the Americans.

"The Soviet aircrew," Rizzuto reported, "without US consent, guidance, or formal instruction, had improperly operated the Mobilizers by not having an air compressor to inflate the air shocks to provide the necessary clearance between the aircraft cargo deck and the shelter bottom. After the shelters were downloaded, the Soviet ground crew then improperly towed one Mobilizer and shelter behind the other using an attachment point which is only to be used when the Mobilizers are not carrying a load. (The attachment point is not designed to support the shelter's additional 10,000 pounds.)" Rizzuto inspected both the shelters and the Mobilizers. "There had been relatively minor damage to one shelter and to one Mobilizer," Rizzuto noted. Ultimately, he decided "that it would be safe to transport them back to Votkinsk."

The final two ISO shelters arrived later that day and were offloaded without incident. All four were subsequently transported to the Votkinsk portal without incident.

The four modules comprising the DCC were installed on December 16. By December 30, the installation of cables, racks, and computer flooring in the DCC was nearing completion. The critical electronic components had been bench tested in the inspector warehouse and were ready to be installed once power was connected to the DCC. But the delays in shipping and installation had proven fatal to the time schedule; the DCC would not be ready for occupation and work until the spring, when the weather improved, and final installation could be performed.

The installation of the CargoScan x-ray facility was likewise a problem. The entire CargoScan issue was held up in Geneva, where the SVC continued to wrestle with the issue of operational and technical parameters of the system. Held hostage to the diplomats, there was little either the inspectors or their Soviet counterparts in Votkinsk could do. Colonel Englund had been advising against OSIA shipping any CargoScan-related equipment until site preparations were completed to receive it. The inspectors seemed to have a complete set of site preparation plans for CargoScan as of mid-November. However, Englund was not certain that the plans for the foundation had been finalized, so he was withholding releasing the documents to the Soviets until he could confirm that this was, in fact, done.

He did, however, initiate a preliminary discussion with the Soviets on the issue of construction. "The Soviets," Englund noted, "had indicated that they will be ready to start by the first of the year." But, Englund reported, "I have already been stumped by their first question—how many cubic meters of concrete will be required. Also, in looking for this information I found a note that says, 'All concrete shall be class c2 in accordance with specification 19757-C-005'; we do not seem to have this specification."

There were even more fundamental problems regarding CargoScan. Sam Israelit, the Hughes engineer responsible for CargoScan installation and operation, gave Colonel Connell a heads up in mid-December that all was not well with the preparations for getting CargoScan to Votkinsk. The first issue was maintenance training. CargoScan, Israelit emphasized, was not a "turn-key" system. "It may be possible to train someone in a few hours to properly operate the system and take an x-ray of an object," he explained in a note to Colonel Connell, "but this does not qualify him to provide care and maintenance for the system in an isolated portion of the Soviet Union."

Israelit had been told that prior to the CargoScan system being shipped to Votkinsk, he and the other critical Hughes employees would attend a special two-week training course that would enable the person being trained to handle "80 to 90 percent of the problems that may arise." Because of schedule changes and political pressure being placed on Sandia to deploy CargoScan, the specialist training course had been cancelled. "Without this course," Israelit noted, "reliable maintenance of the system cannot be guaranteed...we are introducing a potential maintenance nightmare into the portal monitoring system."

The other problem was with documentation for CargoScan—the vendors, according to Israelit, appeared "unwilling to provide any documentation, formal or informal, concerning the real-time radiography portion of the system." Sandia was telling Hughes that "the documentation being provided was sufficient," but having just experienced the documentation fiasco with the DCC, Israelit was not so sure.

There was no doubt that OSIA had failed to meet its treaty-mandated requirement of having a functioning portal monitoring facility up and running in Votkinsk by December 1, 1988. In retrospect, this goal was always a bridge too far, especially given the fact that the US was attempting to convert what was little more than a demonstration concept into an operational reality that involved deploying intrusive, unproven technologies to a secret military industrial facility located in one of the most remote areas of the Soviet Union. That the Portal Monitoring inspectors, working together with their Soviet counterparts, had achieved as much as they had in such a short time was a tribute to their joint dedication to the spirit, if not the letter, of the INF treaty.

There were legitimate reasons for the delays being experienced in Votkinsk, almost all of them outside OSIA's control. Despite all our hard work since the treaty came into force, the fact was, as 1988 transitioned into 1989, the inspectors in Votkinsk appeared to be losing their fight to effectively implement the provisions of the INF Treaty.

The Photograph

THE RUSSIAN WEATHER, it turned out, was one of the greatest threats facing US inspectors in Votkinsk. When we first arrived in Votkinsk, in the summer of 1988, we were greeted by a mixture of heat and humidity, and our biggest worries were ticks and the purity of our drinking water. The month of July had been marked by the combination of heat and rain. The geology at the Votkinsk Portal was not conducive to effective drainage, resulting in swamp-like conditions around the perimeter of the factory that threatened to collapse the concrete wall that secured the grounds of the factory, and made for uncertain footing for inspectors who patrolled the factory perimeter twice a day—every day. Flies, mosquitos and ticks thrived in this environment; inspectors did not. As July transitioned into August, there were fewer sunny days to offset the rain, and Votkinsk—like all of Russia—found itself in the grip of the dreaded *Rasputitsa*, or mud season. The rich soil around Votkinsk transformed into a heavy, sticky morass, which was as all-pervasive as it was all-encompassing.

"This week's rain and mud have absolutely convinced me that we need to add another section to the permanent portal monitoring building," Colonel Connell wrote in the weekly report back to OSIA Headquarters on August 6, 1988. "We've had mud everywhere and have had to sweep and swab the floors four or five times a day…without it I think we'll trash the rest of the building fairly quickly."

The rain kept falling, and the mud only got worse. Movement was a struggle. The mud followed the inspectors everywhere, to the point that we imagined we could even taste it in the food we ate. "The present asphalt road in place is so caked with several inches of mud that there is no evidence the road is even paved," Mark Soo Hoo, an engineer from Sandia, observed.

Then the weather changed: the first snow flurries arrived on September 22, and by the next day the pools of water that had accumulated throughout the site were frozen over. The inspectors were informed that, because of issues related to software, the DCC would not be shipped until mid-December. Jerry Porter tried to spell out the reality of that decision back to his bosses in California: "The temporary facility has no heat, the roof leaks, a beam is starting to punch through the hallway floor, the hot water heater doesn't work and a big bucket sits underneath it to catch the leaks, and the toilet is so cold the crew hates to use it."

The first frosts of late September, however, did bring much welcomed relief from the mud. But the temperature kept falling. By October 21, snow already covered the ground. Frost heaving, according to Mark Soo Hoo, was readily apparent. "Telephone poles and fence poles," he observed, "are as much as 15 degrees off vertical."

We had all seen the grainy photographs taken by Raymond F. Smith, the acting deputy chief of mission at the US Embassy in Moscow at the time, during his visit to Votkinsk on February 4 and 5, 1988 (Smith went on to become the first Deputy Director for International Negotiations at OSIA); snow and warmly dressed people was a common theme throughout. But looking at an image was one thing, experiencing the cold firsthand, another. The American inspectors started donning their winter clothing in order to better cope. Their Soviet counterparts at the factory laughed at them. "You have nice fall clothing," they said. "But it's not real winter clothing. You'll see."

As October faded away into November, and November became December, the truth of the Soviets' words was revealed. "The weather in Votkinsk at this time of year," Fred Campbell, a representative from ESD, wrote in a report back his headquarters, "is so cold as to be dangerous. If ESD sends another representative to replace me, that person should be equipped to face cold as he or she has never expected."

By early December, the frigid cold prompted David Pearson, a Physician Assistant from Hughes, to put in a request for "a video tape on hypothermia, frostbite and other cold climate medical problems so that I can use them in a training effort for health awareness on these subjects."

The task of installing a technologically advanced inspection facility in a remote foreign location was daunting enough. The addition of extreme winter conditions made it even more so. At the Votkinsk factory, the conditions were brutal. Inspectors worked abbreviated shifts installing various equipment used in the inspection process, before retreating into a heated structure to thaw out. One of them got a slight case of frostbite on his fingertips, despite the efforts of David Pearson. The Soviets were reduced to using a hydraulic-powered jackhammer to break through the frozen soil so holes could be dug so the concrete footings for the lights and cameras could be poured. The power and copper cables that were being manually pulled through underground conduit were not rated for such extreme temperatures; neither were the transformers used with the DCC, which failed almost immediately after being powered up.

The inspectors' feet were the first to feel the effects of the cold. The winter temperature in Votkinsk averaged minus 30 degrees Fahrenheit. The Sorrel boots issued by HTSC stopped providing thermal protection at around minus 20 degrees Fahrenheit; the "Mickey Mouse" government-issued vapor barrier boots provided to the military personnel from OSIA were even less effective. "It is difficult to stay outside for more than an hour," Connell observed.

Some inspectors—including myself—took to acquiring Russian hand-made felt boots known as *valenki*, which could be purchased from vendors in the city of Votkinsk. "Lieutenant Ritter and Jerry Porter (the Hughes Site Manager) wear their *valenki* most of the time," Colonel Connell noted in his weekly report back to OSIA Headquarters in mid-December, "and claim to have the warmest toes in town." Recognizing a good thing when he saw it, Connell requested that he be granted the authority to buy a pair of *valenki* for each OSIA duty officer as an issued uniform item.

"Hats," Connell continued, "are another matter. Everyone here is now wearing his or her own version of a warm hat; the result is distinctly nonuniform and sometimes bizarre." Colonel Connell wore a Soviet Army fur hat procured during his tour in Moscow as an attaché; I wore a Soviet Naval Infantry fur hat purchased at the Soviet military store in Moscow. Jim Stewart, a Hughes employee, had us both beat—he wore a Soviet thermal insulation cover procured from the Soviet military construction unit helping build the Portal facility. Connell made a plea for uniformity through adaptation to local norms. "Not only is there some wisdom in wearing what the Soviets themselves have found to be the best and warmest solution," Connell noted, "but we would also look less like creatures from outer space."

And so it was that on a cold December afternoon, with the daylight fading, a gaggle of "distinctly nonuniform" American inspectors, wearing a "bizarre" assortment of hats to ward off the cold, gathered in knee-deep snow outside the

US inspectors pose with a US flag outside the Votkinsk Final Assembly Plant, December 1988.

Votkinsk Machine Building Plant to take a group photograph that defined their spirit and dedication to a mission few Americans knew about, and the importance of which even fewer could ever begin to comprehend.

Colonel Connell, the organizer of this expedition, handed the group a large American flag which had last flown over the US Capitol, a gift from Jack Kemp, the Secretary of Housing and Urban Development in the Reagan administration. The inspectors unfurled the flag, proudly displaying the Stars and Stripes before them, its bright red and blue colors contrasting sharply with the brilliant white of the Russian winter. A Soviet factory worker, bemused at the spectacle unfolding before him, snapped a photograph, making a permanent record of the moment.

The photo opportunity was part and parcel of a shared experience radically at odds with anything the gathered inspectors had ever done before, or thought they'd ever be doing. The 21 inspectors in the photograph were a diverse group, drawn from different walks of life, but united in their shared experience in that first winter in Votkinsk. For the vast majority of those present, their paths would never have crossed with the others if it weren't for the INF Treaty and its unique portal monitoring inspection requirements. Their resumes listed various skill sets: linguists, engineers, physician assistants, paramedic, technicians, managers, cooks, and military officers.

They were, however, much more than just a collection of past experiences—they were human beings with names which in turn were attached to faces which exuded the unique personality and character of those engaged that permeated throughout the Portal Monitoring effort at that time and place in history: Zoi Haloulakos, Rick Martin, Ruth Berger, Dave Pearson, Fred Coy, Chuck Biasotti, Jerry Porter, Mary Jordan, Roy Peterson, Chuck Myers, Dave Langemeier, Barrett Haver, Hal Longley, Mark Romanchuk, Greg Robinson, Jim Hull, Jerry Ildefonso, Scott Yoder, Jim Stewart, Sam Israelit, George Connell—and myself. We worked alongside dozens of other inspectors who rotated in and out of the Votkinsk Portal, a site that we were all building from scratch.

My fellow inspectors and I were gathered in Votkinsk at a unique time not only in the history of the Votkinsk Portal Monitoring Facility, but also that of the United States and the Soviet Union. Despite the bitter cold that existed on that December day in 1988, the reality was that the Cold War that had defined US-Soviet relations for the previous 43 years was thawing out. Symbolic of this new relationship was the very location where we were building amid a frigid Russian winter.

The inspection provisions of the INF Treaty were scheduled to last 13 years—until July 1, 2001. The facility we were constructing was intended to be in operation during the entire life of the inspection phase of the INF Treaty and, if the thaw in relations continued, to extend into a new Strategic Arms Reduction Treaty (START). We were pioneers in what was to be the new frontier of superpower arms control—on-site inspection—that would define compliance verification for future treaties and agreements to come. Our work represented the standard upon which all future on-site inspections would be based and judged.

The permanence of our legacy, however, masked the transience of the moment captured by the photograph. The "distinctly nonuniform" character on display was reflective of a frontier-like reality that would—indeed, could—only exist once. The Votkinsk Portal, circa December 1988, was the wild, wild *East* of arms control, a place where the inspectors and inspected alike were writing the rules of the game as it played out before them. It was a time of transition for both sides—the inspectors were slowly being drawn into the kind of structured normalcy that always followed on the heels of all trailblazers, and the citizens and workers of Votkinsk were adjusting to the new policies of perestroika (restructuring) and glasnost (openness) being pushed by Mikhail Gorbachev which helped produce not only the INF Treaty that brought the American inspectors into their midst, but also manifested in the change in the social, political and economic realities that defined their lives.

The photograph of the inspectors holding the flag in the snow captured the imagination of all who saw it—and marked the beginning of the end of the sartorial free-for-all that defined the inspectors at that time. Alarmed by the fact that inspectors, visually speaking, were slowly morphing into Soviet clones,

OSIA Headquarters rejected Connell's request to purchase local boots, hats and coats, and instead undertook to procure clothing adequate to the task, ensuring that in the future all inspectors would be both warm *and* uniformly attired *and* look like Americans.

Votkinsk, like the rest of the Soviet Union, was undergoing a transition of its own. It was a one-factory town, built on the back of the Votkinsk Machine Building Plant and the missiles it produced. The SS-20 missile had, for more than a decade, been the lifeblood of the factory and, by extension, the city itself. The INF Treaty had done away with the SS-20 missile, and in doing so, tore out the economic heart of Votkinsk. Even as the inspection process solidified into a defined routine, the city which hosted the inspectors was adrift in the chaos of a nation-wide socio-economic transition that had not been anticipated, and for which it was ill prepared to address.

CHAPTER FOUR

Perestroika
in the Hinterland

*Mikhail Gorbachev convenes the 19th All-Union Party Conference
in Moscow, June 28, 1988. Photo Credit: Itar-TASS*

*"Start with the belief that your life can indeed be changed,
and that you have the power to change it."*

GEORGE BERNARD SHAW

Launching Perestroika

AT THE TIME of its opening on October 17, 1961, the Kremlin Palace of
Congresses was intended to host state meetings of great importance, such as
Congresses of the Communist Party of the Soviet Union (CPSU), as well as
other official gatherings, ceremonial meetings, and theatrical performances. The
team responsible for the design and construction of this grand project, led by
Moscow's Chief Architect, Mikhail V. Posokhin, was awarded the Lenin Prize
in 1962 for its efforts. With an exterior faced with white marble, and an interior

combining a mix of red granite, marble, figured tuff and precious woods, the palace was as beautiful as it was functional. Comprising some 40,000 cubic meters of space, the palace contained an auditorium capable of seating 6,000, along with a banquet hall that could hold upwards of 4,500 people. Lest anyone attending a function forget the egalitarian roots of the Soviet Union, the curtain of the meeting hall consisted of a chased panel containing the portrait of Vladimir Lenin.[1]

The opening of the palace was timed to coincide with the convening of the Twenty-second Congress of the CPSU; every congress convened afterward, including the Twenty-seventh, in 1987—Mikhail Gorbachev's first as General Secretary—was held at the palace. The palace also served as a second home to the world-famous Bolshoi Theater. For years Spartacus himself, Vladimir Vasiliev, graced the stage of the palace together with his wife, the world-famous ballerina, Ekaterina Maximova. In 1988 the famous pair, along with other famous soloist dancers, split from the Bolshoi over creative differences.[2] This divorce set the stage for an even greater shakeup as Mikhail Gorbachev, concerned about the situation in the Soviet Union, convened the Nineteenth All-Union Conference of the CPSU from June 28–July 1, 1988, to be held at the Palace of Congresses.

The convening of a party conferences was not a common occurrence. Indeed, the last one had been held in February 1941, on the eve of what was at that time an anticipated war with Nazi Germany. Conferences are the equal to congresses in every way in terms of representation and function. The normal work of the CPSU, however, is conducted through the vehicle of the congress, which since 1961 had been mandated by party rules to be convened once every five years. An all-Union conference, however, can be convened if a need to do so arises, such as pressing questions of implementing party policy, as determined by the Central Committee of the CPSU.

As General Secretary of the CPSU, Mikhail Gorbachev possessed tremendous influence over the Central Committee, and as such was positioned to put forward the idea of a conference to it. The problem facing Gorbachev, however, was that his goal was not to strengthen the CPSU, but rather to use the conference to push forward a restructuring plan that would greatly weaken the party Secretariat, which Gorbachev rightly deemed to be obstructing his overall policy of Perestroika reforms. In this light, Gorbachev set his sights on limiting the power of the Second Secretary, Yegor Ligachev, who chaired the Secretariat during its weekly meetings and in doing so, held his finger on the pulse of Soviet governance.

The power of the Secretariat at that time cannot be overstated. While its official mandate was quite narrow—"to direct current work, chiefly in the selection of cadres and the verification of the fulfillment of party decisions"—in practice the Secretariat assumed broad executive responsibilities, including the formulation of policy recommendations to the Politburo, the ability to decide which issues were put before the Politburo for a final decision, supervision of policy execution through the work of the various departments, and control via the party *nomenklatura* of the selection of personnel to serve in critical positions. If there was one body responsible for holding back Perestroika, it was the Secretariat. And the person who led this effort was Yegor Ligachev.[3]

Gorbachev first raised the "possibility" of a party conference during the January 1987 CPSU Plenum, citing a need to review the implementation of the decisions of the 27th Congress of the CPSU and to "discuss questions of further democratizing the life of the party and society as a whole." In his speech before the plenum, Gorbachev noted that Perestroika was possible "only through democracy and due to democracy," declaring that the democratization of Soviet society was, as such, an "urgent task" requiring the attention of the party.[4]

While the Politburo expressed its support of Gorbachev's proposal, the Central Committee was silent, indicative of the overall lack of support that existed within its membership for Gorbachev's reforms. Despite this reticence, however, the Central Committee agreed to convene the 19th All-Union CPSU Conference in June 1988 to discuss the matters that had been outlined by Gorbachev.

This concurrence on the part of the Central Committee did not signal support for Gorbachev's reforms among its members. If anything, the converse was true. Gorbachev hinted at this obstructionism in a speech delivered at the Smolny Institute in Leningrad on October 13, 1987 in which he warned his political opponents that they needed to "get out of the way" if they couldn't support his reforms. The symbolism of the location of Gorbachev's address was unmistakable: the Smolny Institute was where Vladimir Lenin had proclaimed Soviet power on November 7, 1917. Gorbachev, in proclaiming the power of perestroika, targeted not only the active opponents but, more critically, the "passive leaders" who had become "passive observers" with a "wait and see" attitude. Here he clearly had Ligachev in mind.[5]

Gorbachev wasn't the only person frustrated with the slow pace of reforms. Shortly after assuming his position of General Secretary in 1985, Gorbachev began recruiting like-minded individuals into his inner circle to help him implement his reform agenda. One of these people was a former construction boss turned First Secretary of the CPSU for the Sverdlovsk Oblast, Boris Yeltsin. Gorbachev appointed Yeltsin as the head of construction in the CPSU Central Committee, and then later as the First Secretary of the CPSU Moscow City Committee—making him, in effect, the "mayor" of Moscow—followed by an appointment as a non-voting member of the Politburo.

This rapid rise to political power seemed to suit Yeltsin, who quickly made a reputation for himself by firing corrupt Moscow city officials. Yeltsin's popularity was not appreciated by everyone, especially the old-school Communists of the

Central Committee, led by Yegor Ligachev. After Yeltsin impoliticly suggested substantive changes to a draft speech to be delivered by Gorbachev on the occasion of the 70th Anniversary of the October Revolution (Yeltsin believed the speech did not go far enough in pushing for Gorbachev's reforms), he found himself singled out by Ligachev for criticism regarding his conduct as the CPSU overseer of Moscow. Stung by these criticisms and Gorbachev's seeming indifference, Yeltsin took the unprecedented step of resigning from the Politburo. Gorbachev, taken aback, asked Yeltsin to reconsider his resignation or, in the alternative, to withhold it until after the October Revolution celebratory observances.

Instead, Yeltsin made his resignation public during the CPSU Plenum on October 21, 1987, taking to the floor to deliver a speech which heavily criticized the role played by Yegor Ligachev in holding back Gorbachev's reform agenda in general, and his own efforts to reform Moscow in particular, actions which predicated his resignation. Gorbachev, who chaired the proceedings, then turned the floor over to Ligachev, who denied Yeltsin's allegations, and instead labeled Yeltsin as a failure when it came to the oversight of the affairs of Moscow. Over the course of a three-hour period, Yeltsin had to endure the wrath of the totality of the Central Committee leadership, whose 22 members took turns politically eviscerating the erstwhile "Mayor of Moscow."

Given an opportunity to reply, Yeltsin refused to back down, instead continuing his attack on Ligachev, and demanding that the people of the Soviet Union be told the truth about the reality of perestroika so as to eradicate what Yeltsin termed "false optimism." Gorbachev then took the floor, and asked Yeltsin to rescind his resignation. Yeltsin refused. Gorbachev then proceeded to join the other members of the Central Committee in attacking Yeltsin. Yeltsin, Gorbachev declared, was quick to criticize, and yet offered no solutions of his own. Accusing Yeltsin of "personal ambition" and "political adventurism," Gorbachev decried Yeltsin's actions, which he likened to putting self before country and party.[6]

Yeltsin's actions were indeed unprecedented in modern Soviet history. Not since the time of Trotsky had a member of the Communist Party inner circle dared to challenge those in power in such a public manner. It took the Central Committee a few weeks to decide on how to handle Yeltsin's outburst. When they did so, it was decisive.

On November 11, 1987, the CPSU held a Plenum in which Yeltsin's outburst of October 21 was addressed. After a lengthy condemnation by the collective body, including Gorbachev, who labeled Yeltsin's outburst as "politically immature" and "erroneous," Yeltsin was stripped of his position as the First Secretary of the CPSU Moscow Central Committee.[7] He was then appointed to the position of First Deputy Chairman of the USSR Committee of

Construction, with the rank of Minister. At the CPSU Central Committee Plenum held on February 18, 1988, Yeltsin was officially released from the Politburo.[8] On May 24, Yegor Ligachev appeared to drive the last nail into Yeltsin's political coffin, announcing that Yeltsin had been stripped of his membership in the USSR Supreme Soviet Presidium.[9]

But Yeltsin wasn't yet finished. From May 29 through June 3, Gorbachev hosted US President Ronald Reagan in Moscow. The goal of this Moscow Summit was to strengthen US-Soviet relations, thereby adding substance to Gorbachev's calls for reforms on foreign and national security policy. On May 30, Yeltsin stole the show by giving an interview with the BBC in which he resumed his attack on Yegor Ligachev, whom Yeltsin singularly blamed for the failure of any meaningful reforms being implemented in the Soviet Union. When asked if Ligachev should be removed from office, Yeltsin answered, "Yes." Gorbachev was compelled to take a break from the Summit to publicly state that there was no question of Ligachev being removed, noting that the issue was "nonexistent."[10] Nonexistent or not, Ligachev felt obliged to comment on Yeltsin's accusations, declaring in a speech delivered on June 4 that he was "deeply loyal to restructuring."

Yeltsin's criticisms hit closer to home that he could have known at the time. When in mid-May 1988 it became clear to Gorbachev that there would be no major breakthroughs in Soviet-American relations—such as the conclusion of a strategic arms reduction treaty—the Moscow Summit became a simple matter of political theater, with Gorbachev turning his policy advisors onto the trickier problem of the upcoming 19th All-Union Party Conference. The two leaders did ratify the INF Treaty at a signing ceremony on June 1st, but this was a mere formality. From Gorbachev's perspective, the failure of the Americans to endorse his "new thinking" on security policy and specifically, their rejection of his plan to deemphasize the use of "military means" to solve problems, not only harmed his efforts to restructure Soviet foreign policy, but hindered his efforts to reform Soviet domestic policy as well.

The fact of the matter was that there existed real opposition to Gorbachev's proposals for real reform of the Soviet system. Gorbachev's admonitions aside, none of the holdouts from the Brezhnev period of political and economic stagnation, who still populated the upper ranks of the CPSU, were willing to simply "get out of the way." Gorbachev's initiatives were being stifled through official inaction. Simply bringing this reality to the attention of those perpetrating it would not affect the desired change.

If the 19th All-Union Party Conference was to have any chance of promoting the changes Gorbachev desired, he would need to populate the conference with delegates who were inclined to support his policies of change. One of the problems Gorbachev faced was convincing the mainstream CPSU membership, who were uniformly behind Gorbachev's efforts to reform the flagging Soviet economy, that there was a direct connection between economic and political reform, and you could not have one without the other.

Ligachev orchestrated a behind-the-scenes attack on Gorbachev's efforts at political reform. Perhaps his most public manifestation of this effort came in the form of a letter criticizing Gorbachev's reforms that was published in *Sovetskaya Rossiya*, the official press organ of the Supreme Soviet and Council of Ministers of the Russian SFSR. This letter, written by Nina Alexandrovna Andreeva, a lecturer at the Lensoviet Leningrad Technological Institute, and entitled "I cannot give up my principles," was a play on Gorbachev's exhortation in the February 1988 Plenary of the Central Committee that "we should not give up principles under any circumstances." In her letter, Andreeva launched a blistering attack on both glasnost and perestroika, likening those who promoted these policies to the "pretenders" of the past who interfered with the work of truly historical figures. (Andreeva's letter constituted a staunch defense of Stalin and Stalinism, answering the question as to just whom Gorbachev was operating against in pretense.) In order to be approved for publication, Andreeva's letter was subjected to several revisions put forward by the Central Committee of the CPSU, whose efforts were personally overseen by none other than Yegor Ligachev.[11]

The Andreeva letter was, by design, intended to mobilize the party faithful in opposition to the reform agenda being promulgated by Gorbachev. Elections to determine who would represent the party at the 19th All-Union Party Conference were approaching, and Ligachev, by using a respected Communist Party newspaper such as *Sovetskaya Rossiya* as a platform to criticize Gorbachev's reforms, was sending a clear message to the party faithful about where the party should stand on these matters.

If Andreeva's letter was designed to undermine Gorbachev, it failed. While the author gained a certain acclaim among hardliners, its publication, and its underlying message, was condemned by Gorbachev in successive meetings of the Politburo, where he chastised Ligachev for his actions. The official newspaper of the CPSU, *Pravda*, was given the task of condemning the Andreeva letter in a frontpage article published on April 5, 1988. The intervention couldn't have come too soon; in the three weeks between the publication in *Sovetskaya Rossia* and the article in *Pravda*, Ligachev had succeeded in throwing doubt on the notion of guaranteeing the irreversibility of perestroika.[12]

In meetings leading up to the convening of the 19th All-Union Party Conference, Gorbachev made it clear that the conference represented a critical border in the history of perestroika. The conference, Gorbachev declared, must be seen as representing the moment when "we are finally cutting the umbilical cord from the command-administrative system and from all the inheritance of

Stalinism. It is especially important," Gorbachev noted, "to say this considering 'Ninochka' [Andreeva]. She and others like her need to hear it from the tribune. The word 'irreversible' is becoming obsolete. The baby—perestroika—has already been born. The prenatal period is over. His further development will depend on the cleanliness of the swaddling clothes and the novelty of his toys."[13]

Based upon the strength of the *Pravda* rebuttal, Gorbachev's positions on glasnost and perestroika became mainstream just in time to influence the election of the delegates to the 19th All-Union Party Conference. Some 5,000 delegates were selected to participate in the conference, including the First Deputy Chairman of the USSR Committee of Construction. Boris Yeltsin, the disgraced former non-voting member of the Presidium, had been elected as a delegate by the Karelian CPSU. His battles with Gorbachev and Ligachev over the slow pace of reform were not yet finished.

Gorbachev Presents His Plan

FOLLOWING THE DEATH of Joseph Stalin in 1953, Georgy Malenkov assumed the position of Chairman of the Council of Ministers of the Soviet Union. The new Soviet Premier quickly moved to exploit the perks of leadership by ordering the construction of an estate in the Odinstsovsky District of Moscow, to be built on the foundation of a 19th century villa. Known as Novo-Ogaryovo, the estate was still under construction when Malenkov was removed from power by Nikita Khrushchev in 1955.

Construction, however, continued, and once completed, Novo-Ogaryovo, was taken over by the state to be used as a *gosdacha*, or "state dacha," for use by state guests as well as a workplace for various government committees. In June 1988 Novo-Ogaryovo was occupied by a gaggle of close advisors to Mikhail Gorbachev for the purpose of finalizing the agenda for the 19th All-Union Party Conference, as well as Gorbachev's opening address, which would set the tone for the policy of perestroika going forward.

The occupants of Novo-Ogaryovo were a "who's who" of Soviet insiders—Anatoly Chernaev, Gorbachev's principle foreign policy advisor; Aleksandr Yakovlev, a noted historian and advisor to Gorbachev; Vadim Medvedev, a leading party ideologist and economist; Anatoly Lukyanov, a classmate of Gorbachev from law school and early political ally; Georgy Shakhnazarov, a member of the Central Committee's International Department selected by Gorbachev to be a full-time adviser; and Ivan Frolov and Valery Boldin, two of Gorbachev's three personal secretaries. In the days and weeks leading up to the 19th All-Union Party Conference, they put in 12 to 13-hour days, starting at 10 am with the arrival of Mikhail Gorbachev on the premises. Together they produced hundreds of pages of reports on Gorbachev's proposed reforms of the Soviet political system, which were then forwarded to the Politburo for review and comment. Out of this process emerged the basis for the speech Gorbachev was to make at the conference—one of the most important of his political career and in the history of the Soviet Union.[14]

Before there could be a speech, there were bureaucratic processes to be carried out by many of the same functionaries Gorbachev was seeking to supplant. Gorbachev opened the conference at 10 am sharp, reporting that 4,991 of the 5,000 delegates were present, and then presiding over the election of a 112-man conference Presidium. Gorbachev then turned the floor over to Yegor Ligachev, who carried out the remainder of the bureaucratic housekeeping— additional conference organs were elected, and the conference agenda and procedures to be followed were voted on and approved by the delegates. Once these tasks were completed, Gorbachev returned to the dais.

With the members of the Central Committee seated behind them, and the visage of Lenin staring down on him from the stage, Gorbachev faced the newly elected conference delegates. "We are facing many intricate questions," he began. "But which one of them is the crucial one? As the Central Committee of the Communist Party of the Soviet Union sees it, the crucial one is that of reforming our political system."[15]

Of course, there was no such agreement on the part of the Central Committee, only the words of its General Secretary, who had crafted his speech in the secretive solitude of the Novo-Ogaryovo dacha.

"The Central Committee," Gorbachev continued, "has expounded its platform in the theses for the conference. We did not intend to give ready-made answers to all matters. We figured that new ideas and proposals would arise in the course of the discussion, and that the conference would take them into account. Its decisions then would really be a collective achievement of the whole party and people."

The "*we*" in this passage was in actuality "*he*," singular. This was Gorbachev's make or break moment. He would either rise or fall on the strength of this speech.

"It follows that the political objective of our conference is to examine the period after the April 1985 Central Committee plenum and the 27th congress of the Communist Party of the Soviet Union comprehensively and critically, to enrich the strategy and specify the tactics of our changes, and define the ways, means and methods that would assure the steady advancement and irreversibility of our perestroika, and to do so in the spirit of Lenin's traditions and with reference to available experience."

Gorbachev then moved on to discuss the matters which were first and foremost on the minds of most Soviet citizens—the improvement of the supply of food. "Experience shows," Gorbachev noted, "that the shortest and most dependable way of achieving the desired output of food is broad introduction everywhere of lease arrangements and other effective forms of organizing and stimulating labor. That is the key element of the current agrarian policy.

> The results achieved by collectives that have lease or contractual arrangements have proved that crop yields and animal productivity can be raised in a relatively short time, that labor productivity can be substantially heightened, that losses can be reduced, and that farm products can be of good quality. Precisely this experience, comrades, yields the answer to the main question, that of how soon the country can resolve the food problem. Everything depends on how quickly we can arouse people's interests and promote the work of contractual and lease collectives, on how broadly we enlist farmers in this process and make them true masters on the farm.

Next the General Secretary addressed the issue of changes in the management of the economy. Here he wasn't so complementary. "We are running into undisguised attempts at perverting the essence of the reform, at filling the new managerial forms with old content. All too often, ministries and departments depart from the letter and spirit of the law on enterprises, with the result, as many economists admit, that it is not being fully carried out."

Through the implementation of the Law on State Enterprises, which came into effect in January 1988, Gorbachev and his advisors hoped to create financial incentives for enterprises and to encourage them to show more initiative and independence in their economic activity. The law's central idea was to enable each state enterprise, regardless of size, to independently dispose of its share of budget allocation, void of instructions from Moscow. If factories were free to administer their own budget and to set the prices for the products they produced, Gorbachev believed, then there would be greater incentives to improve overall performance and profitability. Putting theory into practice, however, was proving difficult.

According to Gorbachev, the plans of enterprises for the current year were little more than re-worked variations of the previous year's activity, "with the previous system of obligatory production quotas being, in effect, sustained under the guise of state orders. This is," Gorbachev observed, "nothing but abuse on the part of the ministries in the absence of requisite control, or in some cases the result of condonement, by the state planning committee and standing organs of the USSR Council of Ministers."

Gorbachev condemned enterprise managers' desire to attain so-called "gross output" targets by "means of state orders to manufacture goods that are not in demand." This practice, Gorbachev declared, "is wholly contrary to the sense of the reform, that it amounts to conservation of managerial methods that have driven our economy into a dead-end."

Gorbachev next turned his sights onto foreign policy, which he acknowledged had not been spared by the old command models of administration. "It sometimes happened," Gorbachev declared, "that even decisions of vital importance were taken by a narrow circle of people without collective, comprehensive examination or analysis, on occasion without properly consulting friends either." What Gorbachev said next should have made every member of the Soviet military and military industry sit up and listen.

> In response to the nuclear challenge to us and to the entire socialist world it was necessary to achieve strategic parity with the United States of America, and this was accomplished. But, while concentrating enormous funds and attention on the military aspect of countering imperialism, we did not always make use of the political opportunities opened up by the fundamental changes in the world in our efforts to assure the security of our state, to scale down tensions, and promote mutual understanding between nations. As a result, we allowed ourselves to be drawn into an arms race, which could not but affect the country's socioeconomic development and its international standing.

> As the arms race approached a critical point, our traditional political and social activities for peace and disarmament began, on this background, to lose their power of conviction. To put it even more bluntly, without overturning the logic of this course, we could actually have found ourselves on the brink of a military confrontation.

What was needed, Gorbachev concluded, "was not just a refinement of foreign policy, but its determined reshaping."

What these the three topics discussed by Gorbachev—the supply of food, economic management, and formulation of foreign policy—all had in common was that they were the byproduct of a political system in decay. The radical reformation of this system, therefore, became the top priority of the conference. The conference attendees, Gorbachev observed, were compelled to admit

> that at a certain stage the political system established as a result of the October revolution underwent serious deformations. This made possible the omnipotence of Stalin and his entourage, and the wave of repressive measures and lawlessness. The command methods of administration that arose in those years had a dire effect on various

aspects of the development of our society. Rooted in that system are many of the difficulties that we experience to this day.

This commentary was a direct stab at the effort by Yegor Ligachev, through the article published in *Sovetskaya Rossiya* and attributed to Nina Andreeva in March 1988, to breathe life back into the cult of Stalin. Gorbachev was having none of it.

The existing political system proved incapable of protecting us from the growth of stagnation phenomena in economic and social life in the latter decades, and doomed the reforms undertaken at the time of failure. While functions of economic management became increasingly concentrated in the hands of the party-political leadership, the role of the executive apparatus at the same time increased out of all proportion.

This apparatus, Gorbachev declared, "began practically to dictate its will in both the economic and the political field. It was these agencies and other administrative structures that handled the execution of the decisions taken, and that by their action or inaction determined what would be and what would not be…[i]t became a universal rule that the body taking the decisions bore no economic responsibility for the implications of its actions."

The result, Gorbachev noted, was "the excessive governmentalization of public life." While conceding that the functions of the state were great under socialism, Gorbachev emphasized that, "as conceived by the founders of Marxism-Leninism, management functions should be expanded not by strengthening power resting upon high-handed administration and compulsion, but above all increasing the role of the democratic factor and involving broad sections of the people in administration."

To accomplish this objective, Gorbachev outlined seven specific tasks designed to ascertain which qualities of the current political system have stood the test of time, and which needed to be replaced.

First, everything must be done to include millions upon millions of people in administering the country in deed, not in word.

Second, the maximum scope must be given to the processes of the self-regulation and self-government of society, and the conditions must be created for the full development of the initiative of citizens, representative bodies of government, party and civic organizations, and work collectives.

Third, it is necessary to adjust the mechanism of the unhindered formation and expression of the interests and will of all classes and social groups, their coordination and realization in the domestic and foreign policies of the Soviet state.

Fourth, the conditions must be created for the further free development of every nation and nationality, for the strengthening of their friendship and equitable cooperation on the principles of internationalism.

Fifth, socialist legality, law and order, must be radically strengthened so as to rule out any possibility of power being usurped or abused, so as effectively to counter bureaucracy and formalism, and reliably guarantee the protection of citizens' constitutional rights and freedoms, and also the execution of their duties with respect to society and the state.

Sixth, there must be a strict demarcation of the functions of party and state bodies, in conformity with Lenin's conception of the Communist Party as a political vanguard of society and the role of the Soviet state as an instrument of government by the people.

Finally, seventh, an effective mechanism must be established to assure the timely self-rejuvenation of the political system with due consideration for changing international and external conditions, a system capable of increasingly vigorous development and of introducing the principles of socialist democracy and self-government into all spheres of life.

These were not trivial tasks, and their accomplishment would require a deep commitment on the part of everyone involved to see them through to fruition. Gorbachev recognized the need for the average citizen to identify with the mission, to see not only the potential for gain from the enaction of the needed reform, but more importantly to recognize their duty as citizens to play an active role in their implementation.

"Just now," Gorbachev declared, "it is often being said and written by people in various localities that perestroika has not reached them; they ask when this will happen. *But perestroika is not manna from the skies - instead of waiting for it to be brought in from somewhere, it has to be brought about by the people themselves in their town or village, in their work collective.* What are needed today more than ever are deeds, actions, not talk about perestroika. Much here depends on our personnel, on leaders at the district, town, region, republic and all-union level.

> But it is not leaders alone who are to blame for the fact that we still have plenty of places where perestroika is riding at anchor. Pointing an accusing finger at the people in charge is known to be the easiest thing to do and it is a very widespread thing with us. This habit could be somehow understood when the social atmosphere in the country, and the activities of party and state bodies, were not creating the proper groundwork for people to take an active civic stand. But now, comrades, everything is changing radically, and many people have joined energetically in all the processes of perestroika. Therefore, we must put a blunt question to people who persist in complaining and pointing a finger at those in charge, at the "higher-ups": what have you yourself done for perestroika?

This was Gorbachev's equivalent of John F. Kennedy's Inaugural Address, delivered on January 20, 1961, where he had famously said, "Ask not what your country can do for you; ask what you can do for your country." It was a moment of individual empowerment, aimed at the 4,991 delegates who sat in the auditorium of the Kremlin Palace of Congresses, who were staring back at Gorbachev and the members of the Central Committee seated behind him.

Empowering people to act as individuals in the cause of perestroika required the free exchange of ideas, without fear of punishment, Gorbachev believed.

> I would like to dwell particularly on the political freedoms that enable a person to express his opinion on any matter. The implementation of these freedoms is a real guarantee that any problem of public interest will be discussed from every angle, and all the pros and cons will be weighed, and that this will help to find optimal solutions with due consideration for all the diverse opinions and actual possibilities. In short, comrades, what we are talking about is a new role of public opinion in the country. And there is no need to fear the novel, unconventional character of some opinions, there is no need to overreact and lapse into extremes at every turn of the debates.

In this light, Gorbachev expounded on issues such as "freedom of conscience," a euphemism for freedom of religion. "All believers," Gorbachev declared, "irrespective of the religion they profess, are full-fledged citizens of the Soviet Union. The overwhelming majority of them take an active part in our industrial and civic life, in solving the problems of perestroika. The law on freedom of conscience now being drafted is based on Lenin's principles and takes into consideration all the realities of the present day."

Gorbachev spoke on the issue of personal rights, and the need for the Soviet legal system "to guarantee strict observance of the rights of citizens to the inviolability of their private life, home, the secrecy of telephone communication, postal and telegraph correspondence. The law," Gorbachev said, "must reliably protect a person's dignity."

There were limits to what could be tolerated, Gorbachev noted. Absolute respect for the law went hand in hand with the expansion of democracy and glasnost. "Democracy," Gorbachev said, "is incompatible either with wantonness, or with irresponsibility, or with permissiveness." And there were other red lines as well. "As you know," Gorbachev declared, "we have lately more than once encountered attempts to use democratic rights for undemocratic purposes. There are some who think that in this way any problems can be solved—from redrawing boundaries to setting up opposition parties. The Central Committee of the Communist Party of the Soviet Union considers that such abuses of democratization are fundamentally at variance with the aims of perestroika and run counter to the people's interests."

To accomplish this, Gorbachev said, the conference had the task of "restoring the full authority of the soviets of people's deputies." Half-measures wouldn't do, Gorbachev noted. "We've got to tackle the problem in an integral way and devise a cardinal solution" guided by the singular principle that "not a single question concerning the state, the economy or the social fabric can be decided if the soviets are bypassed. The party's economic, social and ethnic policy should be carried out above all via the soviets of people's deputies as the organs of popular government."

The creation of the soviets of people's deputies, often referred to as "Councils of People's Deputies," was envisioned as a prime mechanism for infusing new political blood into the stultified Soviet system. And to make sure that these new soviets did not fall into the trap of stagnation that had captured their predecessors, Gorbachev proposed limits on service. "We have witnessed many respectable and able leaders exhaust their potential after serving in the same office for decades," Gorbachev said, "and become a dead weight, a liability while still occupying a high-level position." To prevent this, Gorbachev proposed that all elected and appointed officials be limited to serving no more than two terms in office.

To accomplish these objectives, Gorbachev, in the name of the Central Committee of the Communist Party of the Soviet Union, submitted the following proposals for consideration by the conference:

- ☐   That representation of the working people in the top echelon of government be extended by providing for the participation of civic organizations already incorporated into the Soviet political system. As such, 1,500 deputies would be elected from the territorial and national districts, with another 750 deputies elected at the congresses or at plenary sessions of the governing bodies of party, trade union, cooperative, youth, women's, veterans,' academic, artistic, and other organizations. These deputies, elected for a five-year term, would comprise a new representative supreme government body known as the Congress of the Union of Soviet Socialist Republics People's Deputies. The Congress would be convened annually to decide on the country's more important constitutional, political and socio-economic issues.

☐   That the Congress of People's Deputies would elect from among its members a bicameral USSR Supreme Soviet body comprising some 500 members which would consider and decide all legislative, administrative, and monitoring questions and direct the activities of the bodies accountable to it and of the lower-level soviets. It would be a standing supreme government body reporting to the Congress of People's Deputies.

☐   That the post of President of the USSR Supreme Soviet would be established to enhance the role played by the supreme representative bodies and by the entire system of the soviets of people's deputies, strengthening the rule-of-law basis of government and improving the representation of the Soviet Union in world affairs. The President would be elected and recalled by secret ballot by, and be fully answerable and accountable to, the Congress of the USSR People's Deputies. The President of the USSR Supreme Soviet would be granted sufficiently broad state authority powers, including the ability to exercise overall guidance in the drafting of legislation and of major socio-economic programs, decide on the key issues of foreign policy, defense and national security, chair the defense council, submit proposals on nominating the Chairman of the USSR Council of Ministers, and discharge several other duties traditionally connected with the presidency.

☐   That there should be a Presidium of the USSR Supreme Soviet which would be guided in its work by the President of the Supreme Soviet. Serving on the presidium would be two senior vice presidents (one being the Chairman of the USSR People's Central Committee), 15 vice presidents (one from each union republic), and the chairmen of the chambers, standing commissions and committees of the Supreme Soviet.

Over the course of the next three days, the conference bore witness to a debate unprecedented in modern Soviet history. Some 261 delegates had applied to address the conference, but only 65 were chosen—by Gorbachev himself—to speak. The majority of those who addressed the conference spoke not only in praise and support of perestroika, but also harshly condemned the incompetence of the party and state. But even these supporters had a warning for Gorbachev— if genuine reforms didn't come soon, the patience of the people would wear out, and they would turn on him as well.

The Soviet press was also targeted. Many party officials, including those who vociferously supported perestroika, held deeply hostile views on the issue of glasnost as it applied to the press. Gorbachev himself delivered a lukewarm appraisal of the Soviet press, declaring "The local press is embarked more slowly on the course of restructuring and not yet fully unfurled the potential of glasnost and democracy."

Such setbacks aside, by the fourth and last day of the conference it looked as if Gorbachev was well on his way to securing the support of the assembled delegates for his program of reform. But then: after a final flurry of speeches, some of which attacked Boris Yeltsin by name, Gorbachev took to the rostrum and announced that the time for speeches was past. Apparently, Yeltsin had been told earlier that he would be allowed to address the conference in an effort to plead his case for rehabilitation, and Ligachev, in turn, was allowed to prepare a response. Gorbachev, recognizing that any exchange between Yeltsin and Ligachev would be negative in nature and as such a distraction from the goals of the conference, decided to nip the potential problem in the bud.

Yeltsin would have none of it. Clasping his prepared remarks in his hand, Yeltsin strode down the aisle of the auditorium, coming to a halt before the platform upon which Gorbachev stood, and loudly demanded that he be given an opportunity to address the conference. Gorbachev, joined by Ligachev, whispered amongst themselves, before yielding the platform to Yeltsin.

Yeltsin proceeded to lambast the conference for being, in essence, too little too late. The party had fallen behind in restructuring, Yeltsin argued, and nothing put forward by Gorbachev would be able to overcome this. Yeltsin singled out senior members of the Central Committee for their corruption and unwillingness to support reform. And he attacked those who had attacked him, noting that he had nothing to apologize for, and demanded his exoneration. Most of the delegates sat in stunned silence. Others murmured amongst themselves, while a few hissed at Yeltsin directly.

When Yeltsin finished, Ligachev took to the floor to respond. Much of his speech was spent attacking Yeltsin, but here Ligachev's actions backfired, if not for the content of his presentation, but rather the presentation itself—the sight of the number two man on the Central Committee lowering himself to engage in a bitter exchange with someone who, at the time of the conference, was but a minor party official.

"Dear comrades!" Ligachev declared. "We should not be silent because communist Yeltsin has chosen a wrong path. It turned out that the man does not have a creative, but a destructive force. His assessment of the perestroika process, the approach and the method of work have been declared untenable and erroneous in the party." Yeltsin's speech, Ligachev said, "indicates that you, Boris, have not drawn the correct political conclusions." Ligachev addressed the former Politburo member directly: "Boris, you are wrong!"[16]

Missing altogether from Ligachev's presentation was any words in support of Gorbachev or his program of reform. Instead, Ligachev made several veiled threats against the General Secretary, hinting that his record during the period of stagnation that preceded his rise to power was open to criticism, and suggesting that Gorbachev owed his current position to Ligachev himself, after Ligachev declared that the March 1985 Plenum of the Central Committee which selected Gorbachev as the next General Secretary could have ended in a different result if it weren't for Ligachev's actions, and those of several of the old party members whom Gorbachev was targeting through his reforms.

The Yeltsin-Ligachev feud forced Gorbachev to alter his closing speech to the conference. Instead of focusing on the accomplishments of the conference, Gorbachev instead attacked Yeltsin for his past and current actions and attitudes. There would be no exoneration, no forgiveness. As far as Gorbachev was concerned, Boris Yeltsin's days as a political force were over.

Gorbachev didn't come away with everything he wanted from the conference, but he did secure the one agenda item that, for the kind of political reform he was seeking, mattered most—his proposal for the creation of the Congress of People's Deputies was approved. The 19th All-Union Party Conference, in the end, provided both Gorbachev and the policies of perestroika he embodied a mandate to continue. It was a mandate he fully intended to implement.

In July 1988, Gorbachev again assembled his inner circle of advisors to the Novo-Ogaryovo guest dacha to prepare his next moves. Getting the approval from the 19th All-Union Party Conference to proceed with the idea of forming a Congress of People's Deputies was one thing, turning this approval into reality another. Standing in Gorbachev's way was Yegor Ligachev and a host of old-guard communists who populated the Secretariat of the Communist Party. As Second Secretary, Ligachev was positioned to use the party apparatus to slow or stop any reforms Gorbachev was able to push through the Politburo. Simply removing Ligachev would run counter to the spirit of perestroika and glasnost. Gorbachev needed to sideline the old communist.

To accomplish this, Gorbachev's advisers crafted a general restructuring of the Secretariat, creating six policy-oriented party commissions to replace, in form and function, the existing Central Committee and Central Auditing Commission members. The commissions, which correspond to the main foreign and domestic sectors of Soviet policy, had the effect of eliminating the power and influence of the party Secretariat. Because there were more Secretariat members than commissions, the proposed reorganization would require several senior party officials to enter mandatory retirement, while others would be compelled to accept lesser assignments. The net effect of this reorganization would be to neuter opposition to Gorbachev's planned program of reformation of the party.[17]

Gorbachev's reorganization was announced in the September 1988 Plenum of the CPSU, and subsequently adopted without change. One of the most crucial changes was the transfer of Ligachev to head the commission of agriculture, thereby denying him any role in general policy discussions. Thus liberated, Gorbachev proceeded to publish detailed proposals for the creation of the Congress of People's Deputies on October 2, 1988. Based upon these proposals, Gorbachev was able to gain approval during a meeting of the Supreme Soviet in late November 1988 for amendments to the 1977 Soviet Constitution authorizing the creation of the Congress of People's Deputies, from which a new law on electoral reform was enacted, setting the date for the election of deputies for this new Congress for March 26, 1989.

Glastnost Comes to Votkinsk

"IT IS ASTONISHING how quickly people adapt to anything new," Elvira Bykova wrote in the July 6, 1988 edition of *Leninski Put'*. "If in July 1987 anyone told us that in a year Votkinsk would become a place where American citizens would live and work, it would have been taken as an unsuccessful joke or a display of mindless fantasy." Bykova, the editor in chief of *Leninski Put'*, the official newspaper of the City Committee and Regional Committee of the Communist Party Central Committee, the City and Regional Soviets, and the People's Deputy of the Udmurt Autonomous Soviet Socialist Republic, had put pen to paper to write an article, "American Experts in Votkinsk," based on an interview she herself had conducted at the temporary inspection building outside the main gate of the Votkinsk Machine Building Plant. "Most of the shift gathered there," Bykova noted, led by Colonel Doug Englund, whose Russian language was, she observed, "quite good—and fluent!"

Leninski Put' ("Lenin's Path"), established in September 1930, was a relative latecomer to the field of information purveyance in Votkinsk. In the midst of the Russian Civil War, when Votkinsk was virtually levelled as a result of back and forth fighting between the Red and White armies, Nedezhda Krupskaya, the wife of Vladimir Lenin, had observed that the hapless city was "cut off from the rest of the world." Once the fighting ended, postal service was restored, followed by telegraph and telephone service. In 1924 Votkinsk acquired its first radio, which was situated in the V. I. Lenin Club. In 1927 a radio broadcast relay center was built in the city, and within a years' time there were some 200 radio receivers in operation.

Formed in the shadow of the great purges of the 1930s, *Leninski Put'* served as the primary means of dissemination of state propaganda. The fact that Votkinsk had evolved into a sensitive military region only intensified the need for the propagation of a press culture aware of its duty to the party and the need to safeguard state secrets. Mikhail Gorbachev, in addressing the controversy surrounding the publication of Nina Andreeva's letter in *Sovetskaya Rossiya*, had made reference to "the means of 1937" in confronting her message. The implied imagery of the State imposing iron-like discipline on the press was apparent to all who heard him; suppression of the press was something Gorbachev sought to avoid. The fact that so many of his contemporaries identified with press discipline as late as April 1988 underscored just how fragile the relationship was between the principles of glasnost (openness) being pursued by Gorbachev, and the reality of life in the Soviet hinterland.

Bykova's comments hinted at the existence of this history. *Leninski Put'* was more than a small-town local newspaper—it was the official organ of the local Communist Party. As such it had an important role to play in preparing the citizens of Votkinsk for the arrival of the American inspectors, and the changes that this "mindless fantasy"-come-true portended.

"We believed," Bykova wrote of the INF Treaty, "in its ratification and carried out preparations to receive representatives of the other side." These preparations included two working meetings on which *Leninski Put'* had already reported, including a detailed description of the inspector's accommodations at 20 Dzherzhinsky Street, where the Americans were provided with "everything for normal relaxation" and to "help foreigners adapt to unfamiliar conditions."

But Bykova spoke of an even greater mission. "It would probably be no exaggeration," she wrote, "to say that we, the citizens of Votkinsk, are in the best position to give [the Americans] their basic impression of our lifestyle, and show them what a great, kind, peace-loving and hospitable people we are. As everywhere, we have a few shortcomings, but we have most of all a feeling of national dignity and modesty, trust in human ideals and respect for the traditions of others, as well as openness and cordiality."

About the meeting with Americans, Bykova noted that "We still have much to learn about each other." To this end, she admonished both sides "to never forget that we are the representatives of two powers which are responsible for the fate of the world, who have been called upon to justify the hopes of other people."

No greater challenge could someone thrust upon their own shoulders— the responsibility of serving as an informational bridge designed to facilitate a common understanding between two former foes. Over the course of the next two years, Elvira Bykova and the staff of *Leninski Put'* proved themselves to be more than up to the task.

The curiosity over the American presence in Votkinsk continued unabated. On November 26, 1988, Elvira Bykova made a return visit to the Votkinsk Final Assembly Plant, accompanied by other journalists from *Sovetskaya Udmurtiya* and *Komsomolskaya Udmurtiya* (organs of the Udmurt Central Committee of the Communist Party and Young Communist League, respectively), and the Udmurt literary journal, *Molot*. Bykova and her colleagues were very interested in the Americans' impressions of Votkinsk and the Soviet Union. When asked what the Americans had learned from their Soviet counterparts, the inspectors replied that "we all sense that we are personally involved in solving global problems, because for the first time in human history reductions are being made in nuclear weapons, and we are participating."

The Soviet journalists probed the inspectors with questions about American politics, lifestyle, and culture, before asking about their impression of life in the Soviet Union. The last question was perhaps the most important: "Have you seen any signs of perestroika in the Soviet Union, and can you give us any specific examples?"

"Definitely," the inspectors replied. "The changes are very noticeable. First of all, glasnost is widespread, and issues that could not have been mentioned just four years ago are being discussed in the Soviet press."

Left unsaid in that answer was the fact that the American inspectors had become voracious readers of the Soviet press, especially *Leninski Put'*, Elvira Bykova's local Votkinsk paper. While the inspectors were actively interacting with the citizens of Votkinsk, meeting with students, teachers, and other civic groups, those meetings, while very pleasant, were extremely copacetic, the exchanges as vanilla as the softball questions lobbed at the inspectors by the Soviet reporters. But in the pages of *Leninski Put'* the inspectors were given a glimpse of the what life in Votkinsk was really like, the struggles associated with the new changes that brought the Americans to Votkinsk in the first place. As the Americans were discovering, the transformations brought about by perestroika and glasnost weren't all a bed of roses.

"In connection with the reduction of intermediate range missiles," the official newspaper of the Presidium of the Supreme Soviet, *Izhvestia*, observed in an article that was published in December 1988, "an enormous and more crucial reconstruction lies ahead. The assembly plant next to which the American inspection group is located is only one subdivision of the Votkinsk Plant Association. Why deceive ourselves? The valuable output of the plant determines both gross revenue and, traditionally, the level of labor production."

Back in January 1987, the author of that article, journalist Alyans Sabirov, had noted that there were 36 SS-20 missiles in various stages of assembly located in the Votkinsk assembly plant. "Now production has been halted." This was the new economic reality facing Votkinsk, one the Americans were only exposed to through the pages of the Soviet press. "How and with what is one to replace the lower figures? At what expense are we to correct the economic situation?"[18]

The Votkinsk Machine Building Plant, Sabirov wrote, "founded the city of Votkinsk. To this day, it remains the main source of the city's prosperity…in the 'ranks' of departments, well-qualified and, of course, highly paid cadres work… is it easy to anticipate the lowering of salaries? Will [the workers] be able to, as was written in one newspaper 'with gladness and a light heart' turn down real privilege?" The cessation of SS-20 production cut deep into the earning ability of the Votkinsk plant, Sabirov noted. "The wage fund has remained intact, but the volume of industrial output has dwindled. In general, the town is tens of millions of rubles behind the planned figures for development, and this figure is growing."

Sabirov quoted Yuri Chertkov, the head engineer at the Votkinsk plant, who was seeking solutions to the problem of converting the output of the factory from defense to civilian production. "We have experience organizing the output of civilian production," Chertkov said. "For example, highly accurate lathes with automated controls—a type of processing center. We are also producing equipment for the food industry." Chertkov then addressed the two civilian items the plant was best known for. "Over a short period of time, more than one million small, popular washing machines, the 'Feya,' have been introduced. Our baby carriages are also much in demand."

A year ago, such a statement by an official would have been printed without question. But this was the era of glasnost and perestroika. So Sabirov now asked the obvious question. "I don't know (this remains a secret) what one SS-20 missile cost the public," he wrote, "but to achieve equivalent value a legendary quantity of those carriages would be required." Sabirov continued: "Is it difficult to switch over from missiles to everyday goods which are needed for our stores? It is not so simple (if it is even possible) to adapt unique equipment; it is also difficult to retrain people."

Votkinsk, Sabirov observed, "is like a poor relative who has become accustomed to stretching out his hand before his rich relative. At this time, the city does not have an overall plan of development. A Department of Economic Development is missing from the City Planning Commission. The meat packing plant is in a sorry state…there are not enough kindergartens, schools, or hospitals…how can one dream, for example, about a concert hall?"

For the American inspectors, the issues raised by Sabirov would have been invisible if not for their access to the Soviet press. Glasnost was opening a door to the realities of perestroika, warts and all. The honeymoon was over, and reality was setting in. This phenomenon, the Americans would learn, cut both ways. "Here is a noteworthy fact," Sabirov concluded. "In order to guarantee normal living conditions for the American inspection group in Votkinsk, four new buildings have been constructed, while the foundation for the one and only building for Soviet specialists is not being hurried. Apparently, it is considered normal that our people, who have been given work no less important than the Americans, must manage for a long while without the basic necessities."

"Disarmament economics" was all the vogue, a by-product of the reform-minded thinking that was emerging in the aftermath of the 19th All-Union Party Conference. *Pravda* published an article on August 20, 1988 by the noted economist, Alexei Kireyev, which defined disarmament economics as "the study of the effects of a balanced and proportional reduction of military budgets, the implementation of the conversion of military production, the restriction and banning of the international arms trade, and the transfer of resources saved as a result of disarmament to the conversion process." Soviet party officials viewed the assets of the military-industrial complex as a vehicle for revitalizing a moribund civilian economy. Optimistic forecasts predicted some 60% of the defense industry's production capacity switching over to consumer goods by 1995.[19]

But the reality was that Soviet defense industry itself required systemic reform before any consideration could be made about it providing any positive impact on civilian economic performance. This was especially true in Votkinsk, a city where the economy was so totally linked to the performance of the Votkinsk Machine Building Plant. The Votkinsk plant employed some of the Soviet Union's most qualified workers and engineers operating the most technologically advanced equipment that made use of the highest quality raw materials. To offset the cost of producing expensive, technologically advanced missiles, the Votkinsk plant received extensive monetary subsidies from the central government, linked to the plant's ability to fulfil "the plan"—or, as Gorbachev noted in his opening remarks to the 19th All-Union Party Conference, the need to measure success by "gross output."

At the height of its missile productivity in 1987, the Votkinsk Machine Building Plant was producing some 157 advanced missiles per year (30 SS-23, 65 SS-20, and 62 SS-25). Additional contracts for the older SCUD missiles were likewise being fulfilled to the tune of several hundred missiles per year. Each SS-23 missile required approximately 6,820 man-hours to produce, with the time nearly evenly split between operations at the main plant in downtown Votkinsk, and operations at the final assembly plant, which was being monitored by the American inspectors. The numbers were higher for the SS-20 (7,000) and SS-25 (7,200). The total man-hours expended by the Votkinsk plant for missile production in 1987 was some 1,105,600 (204,600 for the SS-23, 455,000 for the SS-20, and 446,000 for the SS-25). With one stroke of the pen, Reagan and Gorbachev had eliminated some 659,600 man-hours of productivity, representing more than 60% of the Votkinsk plant's annual income generation.[20]

The sudden advent of the INF Treaty had taken everyone by surprise, especially the managers and directors of the Votkinsk plant. The nature of the secretive, highly specialized work required to manufacture and assemble ballistic missiles was such that the same work force was used to produce the SS-23, SS-20, and SS-25. These specialists would have to remain in place, given that the Votkinsk plant was still producing the SS-25 missile. Their status would not change, meaning they would still have their salaries subsidized by state funds. What was missing from this accounting, however, was the income generated by the quantity of missiles produced—the factory was paying a workforce the same amount of money for only 40% of the previous productivity.

While Alyans Sabirov didn't know how much it cost to produce a single SS-20 (it was, at the time, a state secret), the price per missile was around 165,000 rubles (around $217,000 in 1986 US dollars, or $516,000 in 2020 US dollars). The profit margin for the Votkinsk plant, when it came to missile production, was around 3.3:1—for every ruble spent, the factory brought in 3.3 in profit. The Votkinsk plant spent some 3,100,000 rubles per year on SS-20 production, taking in over 10,261,000 rubles in income, thereby realizing a profit of over 7,161,000 rubles. Similar profit figures existed for the SS-25 missiles, with SS-23 profits coming in slightly lower.

The concept of profit as utilized by the Votkinsk plant, however, bears little resemblance to concepts of profit as it applies to a genuine market economy. The price of a single missile produced at the Votkinsk plant was dictated by the command-administrative processes associated with the defense industry bureaucracy, which used a well-defined set of price-setting rules for military production. It was these rules, rather than the realities of market forces, that determined price levels.

These price levels in turn reflected end-use calculations as opposed to sector-of-origin; that is, the cost of a missile shipped to the Strategic Rocket Forces reflects only the cost of the product as sent to the point of final demand (end-use), rather than incorporating costs incurred throughout the missile's manufacturing cycle (sector-of-origin). While the pricing system used by the Soviets made an effort to compensate for this by adding to the end-use price of the missile the cost of components (which accounted for some 70% of a missile's total price), the price of components again reflected only their own end-use prices as shipped from their respective plants to Votkinsk.

The bottom line was that the price utilized by the Soviet defense industry bureaucracy was not representative of the actual cost of the missile, which was far higher than what was being charged. The prices set by the Ministry of Defense were fixed arbitrarily, without regard for actual costs. This could be done because of the free flow of subsidies defense industry plants like Votkinsk enjoyed. One of the largest of these subsidies came not from the suppression of the cost of the price of the product, but rather the suppression of the producer's inputs, which in the case of Votkinsk meant the cost of labor and materials. By providing, without charging a premium, a labor force of the highest quality to the Votkinsk Plant, the Defense Industry bureaucracy in effect lowered the cost of the labor inputs that were involved in missile production. As such, the price of a missile becomes virtually irrelevant, as it is the subsidies from the central bureaucracy, rather than the actual cost of the missile, that underwrite the cost of missile production.[21]

The factory managers tried their best to adapt to the new circumstances, but the challenges were daunting. To offset the loss of income from the closure of SS-23 and SS-20 production, the Votkinsk plant put in place a reorganization plan that forecast a 33% increase in the value of the non-military production at Votkinsk, which would off-set by 15% by the lost manpower labor inputs. But there were hard realities that had to be overcome—the workforce was split between two facilities (the main plant downtown and the final assembly plant), and given the specialized nature of the work done at the final assembly plant, only the downtown factories could be reorganized.

Even there, transitioning from missile-specific operations to civilian manufacturing required the factory to change and adjust technological processes and equipment and master new techniques. To accomplish this, approximately 5% of the workforce would have to be completely re-trained, a process that took 6 months to implement at a cost of over 500,000 rubles.

Even where the factory was thought to have possessed a potential advantage, such as in the production of VM-501 numerically controlled manufacturing units (advanced lathes), reality soon set in. The factory calculated that the labor inputs per unit to produce the VM-501 closely replicated that of the SS-23 missile (similar tasks which used 5,133 manhours for the VM-501 to the 6,820 manhours for the SS-23). However, the specific processes and operations were technologically dissimilar, involving the use of different materials and parts of different shapes. Workers who formerly worked on the missile production line had to be retrained to acquire new skill sets.[22]

The Votkinsk Plant invested heavily in the VM-501 conversion concept and planned to produce some 160 units in 1989 for export purposes. But when the Votkinsk Plant tried to market the VM-501 at international trade fairs, they found no interest on the part of foreign buyers—the VM-501's computer control system did not meet international standards. The VM-501 was not the most advanced lathe produced by the Votkinsk Factory—those were used in missile production, and as such were treated as State secrets. While the plant sought to design a more modern lathe, the VM-503 PMF4, for the export market, it was still in the design stage. Any hopes that the VM-501 would serve to anchor defense conversion at Votkinsk were dashed.

As the primary generator of profit-based income in the Votkinsk region, the Votkinsk Machine Building Plant had an outsized impact on the social development of the city and its surrounding environs. The "Law on the State Enterprise" mandated that the Votkinsk Plant create a Social Development Fund

which would be deducted from the Plant's profits. This fund was further split int
two categories—a wage fund, and a social activities fund.

The wage fund was used to pay the employees of the Votkinsk Plant
and was based on the "average wage" of 400 rubles per month. Increases in
individual wages were obtained based upon the position held and the level of
individual expertise and were likewise sourced from the wage fund. Workers
also received monetary stipends for working in the Ural Economic Zone, but
these were paid for by the state. In short, the average Votkinsk worker enjoyed
a 60% salary boost for working at the Votkinsk Plant. The collapse in the profits
of the Votkinsk Plant brought on by the cessation of SS-23 and SS-20 production
depleted the wage fund, forcing the central government to step in and guarantee
that government subsidies would continue through 1990, after which time the
plant would be responsible for 100% of an employee's salary.

The social activities fund was itself divided into three categories—a
production, science and technology fund, a social development fund and a material
incentives fund. The production, science and technology fund underwrote capital
investments in the factory, and as such played a critical role in any restructuring
efforts undertaken by the plant to meet the demands of defense conversion.

The social development and material incentives funds had the greatest
impact on the daily lives of the workers and their families. Housing construction,
childcare, and other communal services were paid for by this fund, as were the
costs associated with the vacations taken by workers and their families. The
material incentives fund provided loans to workers who needed them.

Because of the overall collapse of profits brought on by the implementation
of the INF Treaty, the wage fund rapidly became depleted. In order to be able
to keep paying its workers, the Votkinsk Plant drew on the social activities
fund, severely impacting the multitude of social improvement projects the plant
had undertaken. As a result, the infrastructure of the city of Votkinsk and the
region was negatively impacted. Roads were not repaired, development projects
shelved, and vacations cancelled.

The pain felt by the employees of the Votkinsk Machine Building Plant was
felt by every resident of the city and region, such was the influence the plant had
on the region. There were three other major economic powers in the Votkinsk
area—the Radio Technological Production Association (PO-RTO), the Oil-Gas
Exploration Administration (NGDU) and the Construction Bureau (KB). Like
the Votkinsk Plant, these three enterprises maintained social activities funds
which were used to develop those parts of the city for which they were assigned
responsibility. In years past, the disparity in profits on the part of the Votkinsk
Plant meant that it played a major role in the development of the city—indeed,
the dominant role. It wasn't known as "the city built by Sadovnikov" (the former
Director General of the Votkinsk Plant) for nothing. But Sadovnikov was retired,

and the Votkinsk Plant was now all but bankrupt. Votkinsk was in the midst of a socio-economic crisis which was rapidly becoming a political problem.

Politics in Votkinsk, like in the rest of the Soviet Union, revolved around the supremacy of a single political party—the Communist Party of the Soviet Union. In Votkinsk, the party exercised its governance through three entities—the City Party Committee (GorKom), the City Executive Committee (GorIsPolKom) and the Communist Youth League (Komsomol). The individuals holding office were drawn from the width and breadth of Votkinsk society, nominated by the communist party organs within the various factories, enterprises and organizations. The Votkinsk government was responsible for the day-to-day activities of the city and region and played no role in the business activities of its resident factories. As such, given its outsized economic presence, the Votkinsk Plant played an outsized role in the composition and functioning of the communist party and, by extension, the government of Votkinsk. It hadn't developed the reputation of being a factory town without reason

Now, in the aftermath of the economic collapse triggered by the implementation of the INF Treaty and struggling to meet the market demands imposed by the policies of *khozraschyot* (cost accounting) being furthered under perestroika, the Votkinsk Communist Party found itself under pressure from a population who, empowered by notions of democratization and openness, began to find their voice. More often than not, the vehicle for making their voice heard were the pages of Elvira Bykova's *Leninski Put'*, which, by the end of 1988 and early 1989, was starting to publish articles reflective of the economic reality confronting Votkinsk, and as such critical of the powers that be. When it was announced that there would be elections for the creation of a new Congress of People's Deputies, Bykova's *Leninski Put'* found itself in the eye of a political storm, with an unheard-of struggle for political power playing out on its pages for all the inhabitants of Votkinsk to read.

Among these inhabitants were the American inspectors, who since the time of their arrival had subscribed to *Leninski Put'* and other regional newspapers and magazines. The Soviet Union was undergoing unprecedented historical change, and the American inspectors were uniquely positioned to observe it unfold in real time.

Perestroika in the Hinterland

ON FEBRUARY 10, 1989, the local communist party organs, trade unions and Komsomol convened to discuss the implementation of the new Soviet election law regarding elections for the Congress of People's Deputies. For the purpose of this election, Votkinsk was classified as "Votkinsk National-Territorial Constituency Region #662." The gathered functionaries considered the candidacies of five individuals presented by the communist party for two positions on the ballot, from which one person would be selected by secret ballot. Two candidates were selected—Angelina Protopova, the chief agronomist of the Voskhod collective farm, and Grigorii Novikov, a department head in the Radio-Techological Organization. Both were steadfast communists, with solid credentials in their respective areas of expertise.

At the time, the American inspectors were still residing at their temporary accommodations at 20 Dzerzhinsky Street and commuting back and forth to the Portal Monitoring Facility for work. It was a very busy time for the inspectors, and long days made for little time left for leisure pursuits. Copies of *Leninski Put'* were piling up at the DCC, unread. It was only happenstance that one of the HTSC interpreters, Zoi Haloulakis, read the announcement about the selection of candidates, and brought it to my attention. As a student of Russian/Soviet history, I was struck by the opportunity that had presented itself—to bear witness to a true moment in history, the first contested elections in Soviet history.

My approach to this was, in typical fashion, haphazard. Zoi and I kept our eyes peeled for the weekly *Leninski Put'*, which would then be scanned for anything relevant. The paper published candidates' respective biographies, along with a synopsis of their platforms. Mobile agitation teams, provided by the communist party, would drive throughout the city streets in vans equipped with bullhorns, broadcasting the respective merits of each candidate. In my off-time I roamed the same streets, trying to catch the mobile propaganda units in action, with some success.

The election was scheduled for Sunday, March 26. Polls opened at 8 am and closed at 8 PM. *Leninski Put'* published details on the logistics of the election: polling stations were to be established at designated "agitation centers," or *agit punkt*, throughout the city. Each *agit punkt* covered one or more precincts, which like their American counterparts, were based upon street addresses. Precincts also existed in the local Kolkhoz (collective farms) and Sovkhoz (collective factories) surrounding the city. Each precinct was designated by a title, such as *Partizanskii*, *Uritskii* and *Leningradskii*, which corresponded with the name of a dominant workers settlement located inside its boundary (for instance, the "*Partizanskii* Workers Settlement," located near the American's living accommodations). Balloting for both the *Partizanskii* and *Uritskii* precincts was to be conducted at School #10, within walking distance.

On March 26, I worked a day shift, then ate dinner before heading back to the living quarters. It was a cold night, and no one wanted to go out. Undeterred, I put on my coat, my *valenki* and my Soviet military fur hat, and headed over to School #10 to observe the election in progress.

The citizens of Votkinsk were still arriving at the polling station, passports in hand (a required document to cast a vote) and reported to a troika of election officials from the communist party, who verified the document, confirmed that the individual was at the right precinct by finding his or her name on a central roster. If everything checked out, a ballot was issued, and the voter led to a private booth, where their vote was cast in secret. Once finished, the voter folded the ballot, exited the booth, and, under the watchful eyes of the troika, placed the ballot in a ballot box. The act completed, the voter's documents were stamped, and the voter issued a *byulleten*, or coupon, which could be exchanged for a bag of hard-to-get foodstuffs.

The issuing of *byulleten* was something I was not prepared for. In discussions with local voters, it became evident that this was a normal part of Soviet elections, a mechanism for trying to get the vote out. Some of the *byulleten* were double or triple value coupons, depending on if a husband and wife voted together, or were voting as part of an extended family. I wasn't the only one confused by the system; many voters were observed leaving the polling station without picking up their *byulleten*. When approached, some indicated they didn't realize they were being distributed, and others said the process insulted them, noting that it was, in effect, a bribe and, as such, beneath them.

The troika became uneasy with my hovering around but left me in peace until a group of clearly drunk voters arrived at the polling center. The police were summoned, and the alcohol-infused miscreants led away. The police returned shortly afterwards with a town official (who turned out to be the deputy mayor) who asked me to leave. Having observed enough of the proceedings to get a feel for what was happening, and not wanting to cause a scene, I complied. Before leaving, I asked the official if I could take one of the election posters, a stack of which were laying on the table next to where the troika sat. He picked one up and handed it to me with a smile.

I exited the same way other voters had, which took me past a classroom situated near the building exit. There I paused to take stock of what was in the "goody bag": numerous cans of crab meat, fish, beef and ham, canned vegetables, and candy. The *byulleten* also entitled the bearer to purchase, at a discount, high-quality sausage, and loaves of bread, none of which counted against normal ration limits. The discounted goods were purchased at the time the goody bag was picked up. The official, noticing that I was still hovering in the area, sent a police officer to politely ask me to move on.

Poster for the March 26, 1989, election of people's deputies for the Votkinsk National-Territorial Constituency Region No. 662.

Over the course of the next few days, I discussed the election with numerous citizens of Votkinsk. Perestroika. The advent of a free press had ignited a political spark in some, but by no means all. Most of the people I spoke with expressed a feeling of helplessness in the face of a new Soviet system of government which they neither trusted nor understood. Apathy about the elections was widespread, with almost everyone—including those who were excited about voting—not understanding what they were voting for.

Moreover, the role and function of the Congress of People's Deputies was not fully cognizable. Elvira Bykova and her colleagues at *Leninski Put'* were doing their level best to educate and inform, but the new openness, while instilling a vigorous desire for reform in some, seems to have demoralized many others by exposing them to a long history of lies and deception on the part of the Soviet leadership. Things hadn't totally deteriorated at this point; this was more about losing confidence in a system once believed by many to be infallible. It was hard to explain, but the Soviets in Votkinsk had an almost child-like faith that the Party would never betray them. Glasnost was putting the lie to that notion, and it hurt. The average Votkinsk citizen, it seemed, no longer trusted anyone, and believed nothing.

Even with this negativity, when the polls closed at 8 PM, some 84.4% of the qualified electorate had cast a vote—a rate of participation unheard of in American elections, who had had previous experience of the fruits of electoral democracy. Despite this, neither candidate received a plurality of the vote (voters were allowed to vote against both candidates, an option many apparently opted to do). New elections were scheduled for May 14. I was scheduled to rotate back home on April 6. It looked like the elections would proceed without a nosy American inspector to observe them.

On April 25, John Sartorius arrived in Votkinsk to begin his six-week tour of duty. John was an experienced analyst of Soviet affairs, having spent a period of time at the Center for Naval Analyses (CNA) doing just that. I had dropped off a copy of a report I had prepared based on my election day observations with the OSIA Field Office, Europe (FOE) on my way out. John took one look at it, and realized two things: one, it was a fascinating topic and, two, he could do a better job capturing the Soviet view. Upon his arrival, he teamed up with Anne Mortensen, another HTSC interpreter, and together they embarked on a project which used articles published in *Leninski Put'* as the basis of electoral analysis they titled *Perestroika in the Hinterlands*.

The first report generated by this collaboration, published on May 8, set the stage for the repeat election scheduled for May 14. There were four candidates in the running this time, but only two were deemed viable: G.F. Novikov, the RTO Department Head, and A.K. Rybakov, a Deputy General Director for economic issues at the Votkinsk Plant. Novikov ran on an aggressive policy of reform, seeking to "eliminate the State budget deficit within five to eight years by decreasing military expenditures." He also proposed a program designed to convert some military industry over to consumer goods.

Rybakov, who emerged from a "heated" nomination process within the Votkinsk Plant that saw him win out over five other candidates, including the newly appointed Director General, A. Pal'yanov, ran on a platform built around balancing the State budget, legal reforms, and a focus on the nationalities issue. He also proposed, John and Anne noted, "turning control of enterprises producing consumer goods over to local soviets, stating that 'only those industries which determine the technical development of the national economy as a whole' should be managed by central agencies." The Votkinsk Plant was, of course, one such industry, and as such Rybakov's proposal wouldn't change any aspect of its current economic model.

"Rybakov is something of an environmentalist," the authors noted, advocating recycling and the development of "ecologically pure industrial processes" as the best means of preventing pollution. This issue would come back to haunt him down the road.

Social development, women in the workforce, the strengthening of local and regional autonomy when it came to the issue of distribution of goods produced within the Udmurt Republic, and the allocation of funds received from the sale of these goods, were all shared themes. "The candidates promise," the authors wrote, "to seek authority to spend money on improving consumer services, local roads, and housing construction."

"Local authorities," the pair wrote, wrapping up their inaugural issue of *Perestroika in the Hinterlands*, "seem concerned that the populace be familiar not only with the candidates and their platforms, but with the mechanics of the repeat elections as well." *Leninski Put'* published articles explaining why repeat elections were necessary, as well as guidelines for voting and handling ballots.

The second issue of *Perestroika in the Hinterlands*, published on May 24, brought the issue of who would represent "Votkinsk National-Territorial Constituency Region #662" in the Congress of People's Deputies to a close. "The Votkinsk elections for the USSR Congress of People's Deputies are finally over," John and Anne wrote, "and candidate Grigorii Fedorovich Novikov has won."

But it wasn't an easy journey for Novikov. Voters, the authors noted, "had to make three separate trips to the polls to elect Novikov as their representative." The repeat election scheduled for May 14 failed to produce a majority winner. According to Article 60 of the new election law, a third round of voting was needed, and scheduled for May 21; Novikov won with 74.3% of the vote.

The fact that Novikov beat out an opposing candidate from the Votkinsk Machine Building Plant was a remarkable result, especially since he advocated defense conversion and, the authors of *Perestroika in the Hinterland* noted, "the only cushion he offers to those whose job may be affected is to provide state subsidies as a temporary measure 'to support the average worker's salary while retooling is going on.'"

One of the reasons for this upset was a growing apathy amongst the voters. Only 76.6% of the eligible voters participated in the May 21 election, and that number fell further to 72.2% during the third and final vote. "Newspaper editorials worried publicly that voter turnout for the May 21 repeat vote would be low," John and Anne wrote, "and pointed out that the city and district could ill afford to have the Congress of People's Deputies convene on May 25 without a local representative present."

While Elvira Bykova and her staff at *Leninski Put'* did their best to keep the campaign focused on the issues, in the end, John and Anne noted, "Novikov and Rybakov used the reputations of their organizations to help sway potential voters." It was a battle between the Votkinsk Machine Building Plant versus the Radio-Technical Organization—and the latter won. Rybakov's reputation as a "factory man" ended up hurting him. Both he and Novikov campaigned on an anti-pollution platform but, as John and Anne pointed out, "the credibility of Rybakov's pledges suffered because the Votkinsk Plant dumps petroleum products into the Votka River on a daily basis." Rybakov also ran on a platform that opposed price increases. But, as an article in *Leninski Put'* pointed out, "Rybakov, the Votkinsk Plant's Deputy Director for Economic Issues, has permitted the price of the Plant's baby carriages to increase from 37 to almost 80 rubles."

"The general perception amongst citizens of Votkinsk," the authors noted, "seemed to be that if push came to shove, the Votkinsk Plant's interests would outweigh any promises Rybakov had made to voters during the campaign. As one Votkinsk resident put it, 'All Pal'yanov [the General Director of the Votkinsk Plant] has to do is whistle, and Rybakov will come running.'"

The second issue of *Perestroika in the Hinterlands* finished up with this assessment:

> Novikov's overwhelming victory gives him a political mandate in the Votkinsk area, though the ability of individual People's Deputies (and of the Congress of People's Deputies as a whole, for that matter) to implement programs and force changes at the local level remains to be seen. If he hopes to be successful, Novikov will have to move quickly to repair relations with the Votkinsk Plant. Though its candidate was defeated at the polls, the Votkinsk Plant is still the most powerful political and economic force in the area, and Novikov will have to work with it to accomplish his goals. [Note: In a post-election interview, Novikov confirmed that relations between the Votkinsk Plant and RTO had deteriorated in the weeks leading up to the election.]

The two issues of *Perestroika in the Hinterlands* covering the elections for the Congress of People's Deputies provided by John and Anne's combined research and analysis was considered invaluable by diplomats in the US Embassy in Moscow, whose job it was to monitor the political pulse of the Soviet Union. Additional issues would, no doubt, have been similarly received, if for no other reason than that Elvira Bykova and the staff of *Leninski Put'* had found their voice, and were producing the kind of probing journalism that would have made any of their American counterparts envious.

John and Anne, like all of the inspectors, were soon caught up in the extreme complexity of trying to bring CargoScan online, making the writing of additional issues of *Perestroika in the Hinterlands* difficult. But the legacy of the *Perestroika in the Hinterlands* project lived on long after memory of the elections that motivated it faded away. The transformation of *Leninski Put'* from a pleasant but simple mouthpiece of the local communist party into an intelligent and probing vehicle from which the American inspectors could better see and understand the reality surrounding the people they lived among made it a hot commodity among inspectors and diplomats alike. Anne Mortensen, Zoi Haloulakis and the other HTSC translators made it a point to translate the more relevant articles from each week's issue, placing them in a special folder on the DCC computer so that interested inspectors could better inform themselves. Copies were made and provided to the US Embassy and other interested parties in the US Government. These articles became "must reading" for any serious observer of how perestroika was being implemented in the hinterlands of the Soviet Union.

I was one of those "interested inspectors." I returned to Votkinsk in late May, just in time to witness the May 21 runoff election. My request to visit the polling station, however, was denied. Prevented from witnessing Soviet democracy in person, I instead turned to John and Anne's informative *Perestroika in the Hinterlands* analysis, along with other articles from *Leninski Put'*, again courtesy of John and Anne, which covered the opening session of the Congress of People's Deputies. The information it contained was enlightening. Interviewed by *Leninski Put'* three days after the initial session of the Congress of People's Deputies convened, the newly elected Grigorii Novikov expressed his displeasure at how things had proceeded to date. "I am extremely dissatisfied," the Deputy from Votkinsk said, "that the Congress was essentially unprepared for work...the delegate's time is being wasted due to poor organization."

Novikov's disappointment, however, did not translate into a lack of confidence in the Congress—far from it. "I have reason to believe that concrete resolutions will definitely be adopted because the deputies demanded that the agenda be altered for the very purpose...after all, the main reason we are gathered is to justify the people's hopes."

If the citizens of Votkinsk were indifferent to the election that produced the Congress, they were not so regarding the work of the Congress itself. In letter after letter to *Leninski Put'*, the hope the people placed in the work of the deputies was put on display for all of Votkinsk to see. "Many people are putting off their personal affairs and following the direct broadcasts from the Kremlin Palace of Congresses," one writer said, adding, "It seems to me that the speeches of certain delegates were unexpected both for the audience and the nation's leadership." Another letter writer, a party committee secretary, noted that "We are all satisfied with the way this Congress of People's Deputies is being held. The live television and radio broadcasts and extensive exchange of opinions is widely supported by the population."

Another letter, from a pair of machinists writing on behalf of the "workers of sector 4, shop 5, Votkinsk Plant Production Association," declared that "We are following the Congress with interest. In our opinion, the deputies are actually working for the first time instead of just unanimously 'approving' prepared resolutions. People are speaking openly and arguing, and that is good." And yet another noted, "Very recently, it would have been impossible to imagine that a frank discussion about our society's most urgent problems would take place in the Kremlin Palace of Congresses. Or that unbiased speeches, some of them even aimed at party and government leaders, would be given from the tribune… if only this isn't stopped by someone powerful before it gives birth to truth."

"The national parliamentary forum has an open and democratic character," another letter writer observed.

> For the first time in many years, we are witnessing arguments and discussions. Because we are not accustomed to this, we view debates on procedural and other questions as artificial and useless. Therefore, it has been suggested that the live broadcasts from the Palace of Congresses be cancelled. Personally, I oppose this. Right now, you can't tear people away from the television screens, and I think this clearly demonstrates their consciousness and desire to participate in the significant and historical events taking place in the country.

From this chaos, order was eventually re-imposed.

Gorbachev had taken a calculated risk in pushing for the creation of the Congress of People's Deputies. The elections that took place on March 26 exposed the fragility of the Communist Party's hold on power, with its monopoly on power challenged and often, toppled. Even Communist Party candidates who ran unopposed failed to win enough votes to declare victory, unable to cross the 50% threshold.

Gorbachev's own attendance at the Congress was a virtual guarantee—he was selected as one of the 100 delegates allocated to the CPSU, and his election to head the Congress was likewise assured. Less so was the election of his hand-picked deputy—his law school classmate, Anatoly Lukyanov. But after a heated debate, this, too, came to pass. Everything was unfolding as planned...almost.

Boris Yeltsin had emerged from his confrontation with Yegor Ligachev at the 19th All-Union Party Conference with his reputation for confronting authority intact, but his future as a political figure in doubt. Gorbachev, for one, wanted Yeltsin out of politics for good. On March 26, however, Yeltsin was elected as the at-large representative from Moscow, garnering more than 6 million votes—some 92% of the total votes cast. However, despite his extensive lobbying efforts, it looked as if Yeltsin was going to be excluded from the principal policymaking body of the new Congress, the Supreme Soviet.

"I think Yeltsin is history," Anatoli Chernyaev, Gorbachev's foreign policy advisor, wrote in his diary for May 28. "It looks like in this case he did most of the work himself—his imbecility became more evident at the meetings and at the Congress. Possibly the people who were creating a myth and using his imbecility realized that they won't get very far with him once real work and responsibility become necessary."[23]

Not everyone shared Chernyaev's assessment. Grigorii Novikov, the Deputy from Votkinsk National-Territorial Constituency Region #662, told *Leninski Put'* "I voted for those whom I wanted to see in power, regardless of whom the presidium or those sitting around me supported. Specifically," he added, "I consistently supported Boris Nikolaevich Yeltsin for the Supreme Soviet."

But Yeltsin had been squeezed out by the old guard, denied a seat in the ultimate policy making body. In years gone by, such a result would have been final. But this was the age of perestroika, and the old rules no longer applied.

"There was one more event that occurred on May 29 and probably left no one indifferent," Novikov continued. "This was Deputy Kazannik's request to resign from the Soviet of Nationalities and elect Yeltsin to take his place. I think Kazannik's decision was correct. About six million people voted for Boris Nikolaevitch. Let Boris work."

Alexei Kazannik, a lawyer from Siberia, had been selected to serve on the Supreme Soviet. He was a reformer and, like Gregorii Novikov, a supporter of Yeltsin. When confronted with the reality that Yeltsin had been blocked from gaining a seat on the Supreme Soviet, Kazannik gave up his own. But Kazannik's gesture was almost in vain. When the Siberian lawmaker stood up and announced his decision before the assembled Congress, Mikhail Gorbachev, taken aback, suggested that Kazannik's gesture be referred to a legal commission for review. Hundreds of deputies erupted in boos and hisses, causing Gorbachev to back down.

Far from being removed from the political scene, Yeltsin took advantage of Gorbachev's own political power play against the communist old guard to re-empower himself. He was back, stronger than ever, and—thanks to Kazannik's intervention—well positioned to challenge Gorbachev going forward.

"Perestroika," Gorbachev had declared in his opening speech to the 19th All-Union Party Conference, "is not manna from the skies—instead of waiting for it to be brought in from somewhere, it has to be brought about by the people themselves in their town or village, in their work collective."

Whether it was Elvira Bykova and the staff of *Leninski Put'* documenting the winds of change in Votkinsk, or Boris Yeltsin charging from the gates in Moscow, the "people" were heeding Gorbachev's call. The question now was, having thrust this responsibility on the shoulders of others, would Gorbachev be content with the path they chose to follow?

For the American inspectors in Votkinsk, perched in the front row seats they had acquired thanks to the INF Treaty, the struggle for the future of perestroika in the hinterlands would be a part of their daily lives in the weeks and months ahead as Votkinsk, and the rest of the Soviet Union, came to grips with a new reality.

CHAPTER FIVE

The Year of Living Dangerously, Part One

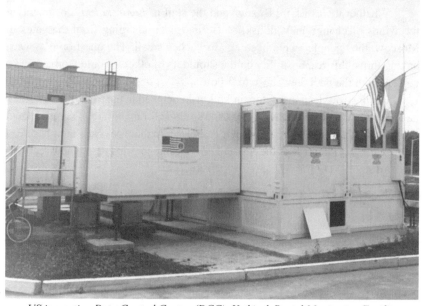

US inspection Data Control Center (DCC), Votkinsk Portal Monitoring Facility, June 1988.

"The secret of change is to focus all of your energy, not on fighting the old, but on building the new."

SOCRATES

New Year, Old Problems

VOTKINSK, DECEMBER 31, 1988—We gathered in the lobby on the ground floor of the US inspector's quarters, located at 20 Dzerzhinsky Street, in the Beryozovka neighborhood of Votkinsk. Purpose-built by the Votkinsk Factory to house some 30 Americans dispatched to Votkinsk to implement the INF treaty, the building's list of occupants had expanded since the Americans first took up quarters on July 1, 1988. Now, some six months later, several Soviet families called the building home—including a KGB officer from Moscow who monitored all Soviet interaction with the Americans who were residing in the formerly closed city of Votkinsk (the Soviets didn't know we knew this little fact, but we did). But the principal residents remained the 30 US inspectors who were responsible for installing and operating the perimeter portal monitoring inspection facility outside of a missile final assembly plant located some five miles north of the city proper.

The "lobby" consisted of little more than a foyer which connected the entrance with a set of stairs leading to the upper floors of the building. There was a wooden desk next to the stairs, behind which sat one of the so-called "social escorts"—young English-speaking university graduates recruited to assist the Votkinsk factory with managing the leisure activities of off-duty inspectors. These escorts reported to the Moscow KGB officer and were required to prepare "activity reports" about the activities of the inspectors. A second escort sat on a wooden chair next to the desk. Normally their job was to log the inspectors in and out of the building, and provide any other assistance, if needed, when it came to interacting with the local population.

However, this evening—December 31, New Year's Eve—was different. The inspectors had assembled to greet Father Frost and the Snow Princess (played by two Soviet factory personnel dressed for the occasion), who wished the inspectors a prosperous New Year while handing out twelve hand-written invitations for inspectors to bring in the New Year at the home of one of the factory escorts. I and three of the Hughes inspectors were handed an invitation from Igor Efremov, one of the shift leaders at the Votkinsk Final Assembly Plant.

I looked at the address on the invitation—1 Migurina Street. I looked at my watch—10.15 PM. The invitation said we were to arrive at 10.30 PM. I handed out the approved "representational" gifts purchased by the On-Site Inspection Agency for situations such as this, and then, accompanied by my charges, headed to the exit. We stepped outside and were immediately greeted by bone-chilling cold—the temperatures in Votkinsk this time of year averaged around 20–30 degrees below centigrade (between minus 4 and minus 22 degrees Fahrenheit).

I pulled out a dog-eared copy of "Votkinsk on 6 Rubles a Day," a xeroxed guide to the downtown section of the city prepared by Team Kirkpatrick during their two-week tour of duty back in August 1988, before the arrival of the Hughes inspectors. The guide was very detailed—so much so that a copy was seized by the KGB in Moscow as "evidence" of American spying. (It was later returned with apologies, once the Soviets realized what they had confiscated.)

"From the hotel," the guide noted, "three paths lead to Berezovka ('Birchville'): 1) the dam/bridge near the Pond; 2) the steampipe with a flattened sheet-metal walking surface (the closest and most challenging route under wet and muddy conditions); and May 1st Street (the muddiest and dustiest, depending on the season)."

I opted for route number 2—the steampipe. We navigated the sheet metal walking surfaces, crossing over the frozen pond, where stalks of bullrushes rose like skeletal arms through the ice, and immediately found ourselves along Migurina Street, a collection of brick apartment buildings bathed in snow and ice, which housed the families of hundreds of employees of the Votkinsk Factory.

The buildings also contained numerous shops and stores, with which we inspectors had become familiar over the course of the past few months. Number 9 Migurina was home to "a good bookstore, a library, and a post office." The bookstore personnel, the guide declared, were "quite friendly and helpful." Number 3 Migurina was home to "the best bread store with the best reputation among inspectors—banana bread has been found on occasion." Number three also contained a hardware and household goods store, the contents of which "will look very familiar."

Our destination was Number 1 Migurina, apartment 48. We had timed our journey just right, and at 10.30 sharp I knocked on the door. Igor Efremov opened it himself and invited us in. We were greeted by his wife, children, and a modest New Year's *Yolka*, or evergreen tree, decorated much as a Christmas tree would be in the United States.

I was the designated linguist for this grouping of US inspectors, which meant that most of the communication between our Soviet hosts and their American guests consisted of ghastly grammatically defective Russian, heavily punctuated by hand signs and carefully enunciated English, in the mistaken belief that if I spoke slowly, everyone would somehow understand.

Despite the obstacles presented by my deficient Russian, the evening was spent in warm camaraderie, with Igor and his wife proving to be the perfect hosts, plying us with sweets and holiday cheer, and presenting us each with a thoughtful gift. We congratulated one another when, at the stroke of midnight, the New Year began. It was a truly special occasion. One would have had a hard time reconciling the fact that Igor's guests were in Votkinsk to monitor missiles the Soviet shift leader had once produced, and which, when finished and delivered to their customers in the Soviet military, were to be targeted at American cities.

Punctuating the other-worldly nature of the gathering was the appearance on the television of both President Ronald Reagan and General Secretary Gorbachev, each reading a New Year's message to the people of a nation they once viewed as the enemy. "I am confident that relations between our two countries will continue on the positive course they have followed in the year just ending," Reagan declared, noting that "despite our disagreements, we have been able to find some common ground." The most prominent feature of this "common ground" was the INF treaty. Reagan pointed out that during his visit to Moscow in June, he and the Soviet General Secretary "signed the documents of ratification for the treaty eliminating an entire class of US and Soviet intermediate-range nuclear missiles, and the implementation of that historic treaty has proceeded smoothly." He went on to elaborate additional arms control measures that were being negotiated between the USA and the Soviet Union, adding that "while much has been accomplished in the area of arms control and reductions, we must continue efforts to ensure a lasting peace."[1]

No one in 1 Migurina, Apartment 48, disagreed.

General Secretary Gorbachev's New Year's address was no less remarkable, with the Soviet leader highlighting the fact that "1988 is memorable for all of us as a year when we began reducing the most terrifying nuclear weapons. That alone is enough for it to go down in history as a landmark, a great turning point in world affairs." I struggled to make sense of much of Gorbachev's speech, but I was able to make sense of one notable passage. "One cannot help thinking," the Soviet leader said, "that all people who live on this Earth, all of us, however different, are really one family. I am sure we will find enough wisdom and good will to establish together a true period of peace for all humankind."

At the conclusion of the televised addresses, I and the three Hughes inspectors joined the Efremov family for a traditional stroll down to the city center, where we stood underneath the large New Year's tree that had been erected for the occasion. After admiring the lights and exchanging well wishes with others who had gathered under the tree, we parted company, each heading home to our respective abodes.

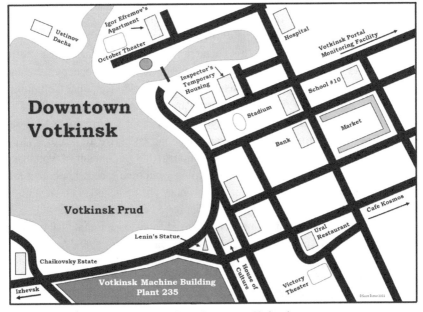

Figure Two: Downtown Votkinsk

Despite all the trials and tribulations of the first six months of treaty implementation, 1989 was getting off to a good start.

This, however, was not good enough for the detractors of arms control who resided in the US Senate. "During the ratification debate," the Republican Chair of the Senate Foreign Relations Committee, Jesse Helms, wrote in a letter to President Reagan, dated January 12, 1988, "the US inspection rights at the Votkinsk Factory Portal were correctly proclaimed by your Administration as the heart or keystone of the INF verification regime."

Helms pointed out in his letter that the CargoScan X-ray system had not been installed at Votkinsk "because the Soviets have made unacceptable demands for other procedures and provisions," and that "the Soviets have also failed to complete the construction of the necessary facilities for the X-ray equipment." Helms concluded that "the US has been totally unable to monitor effectively or verify whether the Soviets have continued to manufacture or deploy perhaps dozens of banned SS-20 missiles from the Votkinsk factory."

Despite the fact that these statements were patently false, Senator Helms, through written questions submitted to the Director of the Arms Control and Disarmament Agency, William Burns, continued his attack on the INF treaty implementation process. Helms characterized the non-installation of CargoScan as a "Soviet refusal to grant to the US its INF Treaty-mandated rights to X-ray." Helms also brought up the issue of inspection rights concerning the weighing of railcars exiting the Votkinsk factory. "Did the US somehow waive its weighing rights?" he asked. "Why were these US weighing rights waived? Under whose authority were these weighing rights waived?" Helms went on to label the "Soviet refusal" to allow INF Treaty mandated weighing and X-ray rights "the most serious Soviet violation so far of the INF Treaty."

Helms was wrong both in his characterization of what had transpired in Votkinsk, and why. Politics and reality, however, did not often occupy the same space. The concerns of the Chairman of the Senate Foreign Relations Committee became the concerns of the Reagan administration, prompting the Director of Verification for the Assistant Secretary of Defense for International Security Policy, Sally Horn, to ask OSIA for clarification. "What is the status," Horn wrote in a letter to OSIA, "of the installation of US equipment at Votkinsk? Please provide specific information concerning what monitoring equipment has been installed and is functioning and what remains to be installed and/or turned on. Also provide rationale for any delays that have been encountered."

The Director for Verification Policy closed by declaring that "[t]he above information is requested by opening of business, January 26, 1989."

Like anything in Washington, DC, the issue of CargoScan not only became political, but also public. On January 24, 1989, *The Washington Times* ran an article written by Bill Gertz, a staff writer with a long history of receiving classified leaks from David Sullivan to help shape stories that pushed the Helms agenda. Titled "US balks at giving Soviets high-tech INF software," the article touched on an issue that was an ongoing subject of discussion at the SVC in Geneva, but beyond the purview of the work being conducted by the inspectors on the ground at Votkinsk. According to Gertz, the Soviets were demanding "access to US high-technology computer software" used to digitally enhance images created during the CargoScan imaging process. According to Gertz, the software, which would allow the Soviets to improve the reliability of "high-tech devices with sensitive triggering mechanisms, such as nuclear warheads of chemical weapons," had been banned from export to the Soviet Union on the grounds that it would "contribute significantly to Moscow's weapons technology."[2]

The Soviet interest in the CargoScan software may have included some tertiary curiosity on the part of an obscure research and development team sequestered in a closed region of the Soviet expanse, hoping to transform access to US technology into a magic key that could unlock the secrets to nuclear and chemical weapons. The fact of the matter, however, was that the Soviets were world leaders in both nuclear warhead technology and chemical weapons, and it is highly doubtful they were holding up the implementation of the INF treaty over such a trivial pursuit.

The real concern on the part of the Soviets was from a counterintelligence standpoint. According to KGB Lieutenant General Nikolai Brusnitsin, the Deputy Chairman of the State Technical Commission of the USSR, US inspectors deployed to Votkinsk "brought with them excessive amounts (hundreds of tons) of portable sound-recording, x-ray, and other microelectronic equipment, which they use for covert recording of conversations with Soviet specialists, sample collecting, and studying the inspected facilities."[3]

As has already been noted, all INF inspectors were under strict orders not to engage in any activity that could be construed as either covert or overt intelligence collection; serendipitous observations were permitted, but only under the conditions of extreme discretion. The allegations expressed by Brusnitsin were inaccurate. They were not, however, misplaced.

In an interview with *Leninski Put,*' published on December 20, 1989, the head of the Votkinsk city department of the Udmurt ASSR KGB asserted that, from a counterintelligence perspective, "counteracting foreign technical reconnaissance has been and remains the most pressing problem for us. We can already say that the American secret services have already acquired important intelligence about the production activities of our republic's enterprises." Information of value, the KGB officer noted, "can be obtained by analyzing light, noise, and thermal effects, and speech and signals can be taken from various communications systems and computers and analyzed."

.

The KGB paranoia was well-grounded in the practical experience gained in recent years of uncovering a wide variety of so-called "technical intelligence collection" activities conducted by the US against the Soviet target. According to the KGB, such activities included "autonomous intelligence collection devices" discovered on an underwater cable in the Sea of Okhotsk, a container "literally crammed with espionage apparatus" transported by rail,[4] a device "disguised as a tree" that could detect "the slightest emission" which would then be "instantaneously transmitted via a satellite communications system to a special center on US territory," and the presence of viruses built into computers that would respond to commands transmitted by radio signals.[5]

When asked by *Leninski Put'* if the presence of the US inspectors affected the activities of the Votkinsk city KGB in any way, the chief responded "Yes, naturally. Along with other departments and organizations, the local KGB agency is participating in measures concomitant to the INF treaty. It is doing this within its competence and is guided by the higher goal of ensuring the full implementation of treaty provisions and the positive development of Soviet-American dialogue on disarmament." The local KGB chief also noted that "seven former members of the Votkinsk Plant Production Association" were working for his department.

The problem, it seemed, was not that the Soviets were deliberately holding up the work of the American inspectors, but rather that the Americans were seeking to install equipment next to a sensitive Soviet missile production plant at a time when the Soviets were extremely concerned about ongoing technical intelligence collection activities on the part of the CIA. Indeed, a senior member of the USSR KGB Collegium, Lieutenant General V. Sergeyev, cited a contemporaneous comment by Robert Gates, the deputy director of the CIA, that the US had no intention of cutting back on the scope and scale of technical intelligence collection targeting Soviet defense activities, when underscoring the importance of continued vigilance on the part of the Soviet KGB.[6] The Soviets did not want to block the US from implementing measures permitted under the INF treaty; they simply wanted to make sure that whatever it was the Americans were doing, it did not facilitate the collection of information not permitted under the treaty mandate.

The problem was that the Americans were not being forthcoming with the information needed by the Soviets to ascertain the threat, if any, posed by the equipment being installed by the US inspection team.

On January 26 (the same date that Sally Horn requested answers to her questions), Doug Englund met with Anatoli Tomilov and Anatoli Chernenko to discuss the start of construction related to CargoScan. The holdup wasn't any spy-versus-spy wrangling over computer source codes, but rather the specific construction drawings that would be used in support of the actual work.

Chernenko, a friendly, affable man in his mid-40s who headed the local Soviet construction group, was one of the most important persons the Americans dealt with regarding the installation of the US portal at the Votkinsk Missile Final Assembly Plant. A consummate professional who ably led his troops (the construction group tasked with the Votkinsk group was a military unit), Chernenko worked with the US inspectors and the Votkinsk factory personnel to find the most efficient solution to the myriad of problems involved in a task as complex as the one he had been given. And now, Chernenko informed Doug, he was blocked from any one-on-one meetings with the US side regarding CargoScan construction.

The reason for this new restriction was the fact that Chernenko had been bending over backwards to accommodate the numerous vacillations in requirements that were coming from the US side. He would agree to a set course of action, and begin construction, only to be informed of changes by the US inspectors, which Chernenko would then seek to accommodate. These changes, however, often required work to be redone, which meant that there was a significant amount of wastage regarding construction materials, to which Chernenko's superior took umbrage.

Back in November 1988, Doug Englund had transferred to Chernenko a set of blueprints regarding the construction of the CargoScan structure. At that time, Doug had been assured by both ESD and Sandia that the blueprints were "complete and final." As Chernenko quickly discovered, however, the blueprints were conceptual in nature, often providing several options for solving a given engineering question, all of which would result in significant adjustments to the physical size and character of the CargoScan structure.

In early January 1989 Chernenko returned the blueprints, which had been translated into Russian, to the US so that the Russian translation could be checked by ESD and Sandia before actual construction began. Around this time, the Bill Gertz story broke about the Soviet's delaying the construction of CargoScan. Almost immediately, the Soviets requested the January 26 meeting with Doug Englund, where they indicated their readiness to begin construction from the existing blueprints.

Soviet law required that any construction project undertaken by a Soviet construction group be done from Soviet drawings, which meant that Chernenko would have to have Soviet draftsmen copy the US drawings, a process which increased the probability of mistakes being made. Chernenko had earlier proposed to Englund that the Soviets simply copy the US plans, removing the Sandia/ESD/Bechtel identification, and replacing it with that of the construction bureau.

This compromise enabled the Soviets to begin digging the foundation for CargoScan on February 7, 1989. The Soviets were now insisting that the US review the Soviet blueprints because the Soviets had adapted the nebulous instructions contained in the US blueprints to Soviet construction techniques (for instance, adding columns to keep the concrete walls of the structure from falling). The Soviets were in the process of installing significant amounts of rebar in anticipation of the pouring of concrete. Given the uncertainties surrounding the blueprints and the actual construction needed, it was decided that Chernenko would not pour any concrete until which time both he and the Hughes construction manager had reviewed the proposed construction activity in relation to the specific blueprint, and had jointly signed off on a "pour card" for that event.

Moreover, because of the publicity that the Bill Gertz article received in the Soviet Union, the Soviet side made it clear that, from their perspective, the six-month clock regarding the installation of the Portal Monitoring Facility did not start until the Soviets had received approved drawings from the US side. A review of the Memorandum of Agreement by the US inspectors drove home the reality that, on this issue, the Soviets were correct.

Soviet military construction workers pour concrete
for the CargoScan facility, February 1989.

Complicating matters further was the fact that in early March 1989, ESD and Sandia, when confronted by the Soviet readiness to proceed with the modified blueprints, ordered a halt to all construction until the Soviet drawings had been thoroughly reviewed by their respective engineers. This last measure quickly drew the ire of Doug Englund. "The construction of the CargoScan site is rapidly becoming an embarrassment," Englund wrote in a Weekly Report to General Lajoie on March 4, 1989. About the new US demand that all CargoScan construction halt pending further review, Englund noted derisively, "I will pass this information on to the Soviets but am dismayed that we have set ourselves up as the cause for any construction delays—especially in view of the priority we have accorded this project."

The blueprints were not the only issue holding up construction. CargoScan, like the rest of the Portal Monitoring Facility, required a significant amount of underground conduit to be installed, through which thousands of feet of wiring and power cables would be fed (the CargoScan system called for 4,500 feet of conduit and 17,000 feet of wire, while the Portal Monitoring System called for 6,600 feet of conduit and 52,000 feet of wire). Back in August 1988 it had been determined that the Soviets would provide the actual conduit, and construction of the underground trenches had begun accordingly.

In January 1989, however, Sandia informed the Hughes personnel on-site that the Soviet 90-degree "elbows" being installed were not compatible with the cable expected to be pulled, which required "sweeping bends" to prevent crimping of the wires. Despite Herculean efforts on the part of Chernenko and his team to adapt the existing Soviet "elbows" to meet the US requirements, in the end it was decided that the Soviets would simply leave holes in the ground where the "elbows" were to be installed, awaiting the arrival of the US-manufactured "sweeping bend" devices.

"The conduit situation," Doug Englund lamented in his March 4, 1989, report, "should have been anticipated. We had ample opportunity to calculate correctly the amount of conduit required and could have procured it and sent it in on any of our cargo flights. At the very least, we should have surfaced the issue much sooner than we did."

Even if the US side had properly anticipated the requirement for conduit, the US would still have been unable to proceed; the lack of a viable "cable pulling plan" (which, according to Bill Langemeier, the Hughes Site Installation Manager, is "a document which translates the engineering documentation into a physical wiring installation plan in appropriate detail to accomplish the engineering intent") brought the finalization of the Portal Monitoring System to a standstill.

Bill Langemeier was the American equivalent of Anatoli Chernenko—an intelligent, hardworking, no-nonsense professional whose ability to sort the wheat from the chaff turned numerous potential disasters into success stories.

Langemeier had prepared a cable pulling plan back in October 1988, but this ran afoul of the reality accrued when trying to reverse engineer the TOSI demonstration site at Sandia and reassemble it thousands of miles away in Votkinsk.

The Soviets, ever suspicious of American technical equipment, demanded documents (as was their right) which Hughes, through Sandia, simply could not produce because, simply put, they never existed. Sufficient cable had been shipped to Votkinsk back in August to enable the Hughes personnel to lay down a physical wiring matrix that could be connected once the actual CargoScan modules arrived on site. The problem, however, was that the Soviets were not going to allow the Americans to lay cable outside a sensitive missile production plant without first explaining why these cables were necessary.

"The reels of cable that were shipped to this site," Ruth Berger, a Sandia engineer deployed to Votkinsk, said in a January 26, 1989, memorandum back to her bosses at the TOSI demonstration facility, "do not have the manufacturer's part number attached." This was a problem, Ruth said, because the cable pulling plan "is constructed with all the references to cable specifying only the manufacturer's part number."

"All installations," Langemeier wrote in another memorandum, "require Soviet approval to proceed with the work. This requires a disclosure, which is usually drawings." The problem, Langemeier said, was that "all the drawings required have not been received on-site regardless of reason."

"The most critical need at this juncture," Doug Englund wrote in a turnover memorandum to George Connell, "is for complete and accurate matrices correlating to the cable types present on site to the drawings held on site and specifying load distributions (which load connects to which power cable." Without this, Doug concluded, "we have a lot of very expensive and cold metal cluttering the Votkinsk landscape."

The US inspectors in Votkinsk were at the mercy of the engineers at Sandia and their ability to produce the documentation Doug Englund had highlighted as necessary for work to continue. There was, however, another option. Bill Langemeier told Doug that the Hughes personnel on-site could "complete our own load study and then choose our wire from our fixed available inventory. However," he cautioned, "this is a significant duplication of effort" which could be "beyond contract scope" and, in the end, represented a *de facto* reverse engineering of the existing cable pulling plan.

The inability of Sandia and Hughes to coordinate long distance on assembling the data necessary to finalize a cable pulling plan, and the fact that any reverse engineering of the document, per Langemeier's input, would not only be prohibitively time consuming, but also outside the scope of the existing contract defining the scope and scale of the work Hughes was allowed to perform on-site, meant that nearly a month went by with no progress being made. Doug

Englund's fears about the Portal Monitoring Facility turning into some sort of post-apocalyptic wasteland seemed to be coming to fruition.

To break the log jam, Bill Langemeier travelled to Sandia where, between February 15–16, 1989, he attended a series of meetings with TOSI representatives about finalizing a cable pulling plan for Votkinsk. Two issues emerged—first, that the actual CargoScan system was going to require its own cable pulling plan, separate from the one being put together by Langemeier for the Data Control Center (DCC) and the Portal Monitoring System. This new plan was being developed by Sam Israelit and Jim Luscher. The other was that whatever cable pulling plan they eventually came up with would, by necessity, be incomplete, since Sandia lacked the necessary drawings and would have to make them from scratch, a process that could take weeks.

Bill returned to Votkinsk in late February, only to discover that measures that he thought had been agreed to during his meetings in Albuquerque were being altered without consulting him or the other Hughes personnel on site.

In a memorandum to Doug Englund dated March 6, 1989, Bill Langemeier finally put his foot down. "Someone," he said, "doesn't understand what we are doing here." The inane nature of the actions on the part of Sandia and ESD, Langemeier noted, "confirms my suspicion that personnel in the US have not been clearly informed." It appeared that persons in the US were trying to pass the blame for the delays in finalizing the cable pulling plan on the Soviets. Langemeier would have none of it. The issue was a lack of information being provided to the site by Sandia, information without which the Soviets were unable to approve final installation. "I propose to write a description of what we intend," Langemeier told Englund. "Someone is not passing out clear and complete information."

In the end, Bill Langemeier was able to cobble together a "sufficiently complete" cable pulling plan that would allow the Hughes personnel "to begin wiring at any time." The solution was the option Langemeier had proposed back in January 1989—the reverse engineering of the old cable pulling plan by matching the available cable with the appropriate load requirement. Rather than go through the time-intensive process of preparing a full document before work could begin, Langemeier proposed that the Hughes personnel and the Soviets coordinate on a day-by-day basis during the actual installation and, in effect, prepare the required documentation at the time of installation. This option was, surprisingly, acceptable to the Soviets.

The delays accrued in putting this plan together, however, had created new obstacles. The weather prevented the cable trenches and conduits that were dug last fall, which had subsequently filled up with mud during the *Rasputitsa*, from being cleared. This would not happen until the ground thawed, which wouldn't occur until sometime in April or May.

The other issue concerned the availability of materials and equipment. Under the Soviet system, resources were allocated based upon an annual plan. The slippage in the construction timeline brought on by the US documentation problems had resulted in construction resources previously earmarked for CargoScan being redistributed to other projects. To rectify this, Chernenko recommended that the Americans meet with his General so that he could authorize a re-allocation of resources. This, of course, would mean that other construction projects would be impacted, creating a domestic political problem for the Soviets as promised city improvements were pushed back.

Ultimately, Langemeier's concept was put into action, and a seven-phase plan for pulling cable implemented. Additional ESD and Sandia personnel were rotated into Votkinsk to oversee this work, which represented a major deviation from the original contracted plan, and as such required the presence of contracting officers on-site to make spot changes as necessary. Within a period of a few weeks, the "cold metal cluttering the Votkinsk landscape" began to come to life, with power lines connected and the control panels coming to life inside the DCC.

But even now, at the final moment, the problems associated with the long-distance installation of equipment began to crop up with increasing frequency. "The system was shipped as a 'turn-key' system," Langemeier wrote to Doug Englund in early March 1989, "i.e., no problems or solutions are supposed to exist." The reality of installing a complex monitoring facility thousands of miles from a home base, however, trumped theory. Moreover, Langemeier said, "Communications with Sandia National Laboratory is restricted due to the sensitivity of the software."

"The interface between the Operator Interface Processor (OIP) and the Force computer's central processor has an unidentified problem with its interconnect link," Langemeier wrote. "No source code documentation exists on site. Problem definition and troubleshooting is being done by telephone and fax messages between [the on-site Sandia representative] and Sandia National Laboratory with restrictions due to the sensitivity of disclosing software."

Langemeier further noted that the "Data Review Station (DRS) doesn't work as intended." Once again, the primary obstacle to resolving this problem was a lack of documentation regarding the source codes used in this process. Without the source code, "our staff cannot determine where the data downloads to the hard disk."

The "solution path," Langemeier advised, "is to wait for Frank Martin (one of the original Sandia personnel dispatched to Votkinsk back in July 1988) to arrive on March 14 with a substitute hard disk and IBM Core Distribution diskette to see if one or the other corrects the problem." Other software issues existed as well. The Hughes personnel were not able to simply use one of the other disk drives on-site "due to specialized use of software on each." Once again, the solution was to wait for Frank Martin, who would carry in a newly configured disk drive.

Bill Gertz had singled out the problem of sharing the CargoScan software with the Soviets as one of the main issues holding back bringing the US Portal Monitoring Facility up to full operational capability as required by the treaty text. But the reality was that virtually every delay experienced by the American side, from the initiation of monitoring operations in July 1988 to the time of Gertz's article in January 1989, was self-induced, the product of a rushed installation of a facility designed for demonstration purposes and never truly meant to be made operational.

Despite all these problems, however, the inspectors, together with their Soviet counterparts, got the job done in as timely a fashion as possible. By early March 1989 the US inspectors were able to operate the DCC non-stop under full power. As Langemeier's cable pulling plan progressed and the DCC connected with the various elements of the Portal Monitoring System, the US was able to bring the DCC online, allowing the inspectors to move out of the Czech-built temporary operations trailers and into their new custom-built facility.

The Trouble with Ticks

MY INTRODUCTION to the threat posed to the inspectors by tick-borne encephalitis came early on in my Vokinsk experience, during the advance party in June 1988. In addition to ensuring that the incoming inspectors would have a roof over their head upon arrival, I was also tasked with making sure there was a plan in place to provide medical care in case of an emergency. While the other members of the advance party discussed the vagaries of the portal monitoring system with their Soviet counterparts, I was dispatched to the Votkinsk factory hospital, located in the northern suburbs of the city. There I met with the Chief Medical Officer, Vladimir Shvetsov, who gave me a tour of the facility and provided a briefing on the services that were available to the inspectors.

The hospital was a modern, well-equipped (mainly East German) facility with 600 beds and four major departments. While the hospital had a surgical department with six operating rooms, Shvetsov made it clear that in the case of a major emergency involving an American inspector, his job was to stabilize and transport the patient to one of the major hospitals in Izhevsk. He had ambulances available for this purpose and, if needed, could call in specially equipped helicopters from Izhevsk for air transport.

The major diseases treated by the hospital were isolated cases of hepatitis and tick-borne encephalitis. Other contagious diseases were not widespread and very rare. The biggest problem, Shvetsov emphasized repeatedly, were the ticks. The strain of encephalitis they carried was unique to the Soviet Union and concentrated in the Votkinsk region. The region was, literally, infested with them. ("They fall off the trees," according to the doctor.) May was the worst month, followed by June. After that the ticks were dormant, and by August they were gone.

While only a few of the ticks carried the disease, hundreds of people were infected each year, and several died, mainly children and the elderly. To combat the disease, the Votkinsk authorities undertook an annual immunization campaign, using a vaccine derived from the antibodies contained in the blood of infected people who survived the disease. The immunizations were not obligatory, but most of the population, familiar with the danger posed by the ticks, opted to get the shot. The immunization campaign began as early as January to ensure everyone who wanted a shot could get one. It took around 8–9 weeks for the immunity to kick in, so the latest the vaccine should be administered was the end of February.

Shvetsov gave me some pamphlets about the ticks and information about the vaccine and cautioned me to be careful when entering the woods or fields. "This is a very serious problem," he said. "Even if you survive, the disease can incapacitate you for life."

I took the doctor at his word, briefing the other members of the advance party about the tick threat and preparing a memorandum for headquarters, alerting them that this was a problem that would need to be addressed. The inspection procedures called for foot patrols around the factory perimeter several times a day, through terrain seemingly purpose-made for ticks. According to Shvetsov, tick season was winding down, and without a vaccine, there was little we inspectors could do except maintain situational awareness through an aggressive program of self-inspection anytime we took a walk in the woods.

I reported my findings about the dangers posed by ticks and tick-borne encephalitis to Chuck Myers, who immediately requested that the Soviets provide us with a sample of the vaccine used by the Votkinsk Factory to protect its employees from the risk of exposure. On July 22, 1988, during a meeting with Colonel Connell, Anatoli Tomilov turned over the promised vaccine sample, which was subsequently transported back to OSIA headquarters for further evaluation.

The problem of ticks, however, was diminishing. Although inspectors were pulling ticks off their clothing during perimeter patrols conducted in early July 1988, by August the ticks were gone. OSIA consulted with Doctor Ernest Takafuji, the Disease Control Consultant for the Preventative and Military Medicine Consultants Division of the US Army's Office of the Surgeon General, on how best to deal with the threat of tick-borne disease in Votkinsk.

After doing some cursory research, which showed that the Russian Spring-Summer Encephalitis virus was a close relative of the Central European strain of TBE, Colonel Takafuji was able to find a supply of an Austrian vaccine,

Fruhsommer-Meingoencphalitis (FSME-IMMUN), which although not approved by the US Food and Drug Administration (FDA) for use in the United States, was used by the US State Department to vaccinate personnel located in European regions where the Central European strain of TBE was considered endemic. A quantity of this vaccine was purchased and shipped to Votkinsk via the US Embassy in Moscow.

However, when the vaccine package was opened by Dr. Dan Knodel, one of the temporary inspectors assigned to Votkinsk, on July 28, 1988, he discovered that the vaccine had an expiration date of July 8, 1988. While expired, Dr. Knodel assessed that it would still have some degree of potency, and he requested further guidance form OSIA headquarters on how to proceed. Ultimately it was determined not to use the expired vaccine, if for no other reason than tick season was, for all intents and purpose, finished. Instead, OSIA turned to Colonel Takafuji for more guidance on how best to safeguard US inspection personnel from the threat of TBE come spring 1989.

Dr. Takafugi designated Dr. Kelly McKee of the Disease Assessment Division of the United States Army Medical Research Institute of Infectious Diseases (USAMRIID) as the lead for investigating the TBE vaccine issue. Major McKee in turn reached out to Dr. Alexis Sholokov from the Salk Institute, who in turn contacted Dr. M. F. Balayan, the Deputy Director at the Institute of Poliomyelitis and Viral Encephalitis, part of the Academy of Sciences in Moscow.

Together, these individuals, in consultation with others familiar with TBE vaccines, determined that while the Soviet Union had three different vaccines which were considered to possess a high degree of potency against the Russian Spring-Summer Encephalitis virus, the legal issues associated with using these vaccines on US citizens were too great to overcome in the time required.

The FSME-IMMUN vaccine, on the other hand, had already been thoroughly investigated by USAMRIID, to the extent that a draft protocol for use of the vaccine by US personnel had already been prepared. The vaccine, administered via two intramuscular injections 1–3 months apart, provided a protection range of 95%, with no serious adverse effects reported. Colonel Takafuji, in a memorandum prepared for OSIA on January 18, 1989, recommended that OSIA implement a voluntary vaccination program for all US inspection personnel assigned to Votkinsk based upon the informed consent of those being vaccinated. In support of this program, Dr. Takafuji stated that OSIA should implement a blood sampling program for all vaccinated personnel, as well as a questionnaire to be filled out by vaccinated personnel if any side effects were noted.

OSIA ordered 150 doses of the FSME-IMMUN vaccine, and a protocol was set up where the vaccine could be administered by Hughes in Frankfurt, or by the on-site Physicians' Assistant in Votkinsk. By April 22, 1989, at the start of tick season, 39 of 42 inspectors had received the first shot, and 9 out of 42 full-time inspectors had been given the second shot (including myself). Three inspectors had refused the vaccine, and the other 30 were scheduled to receive their second shot as they rotated back in to Votkinsk.

The tick story, however, had one more chapter. Back on March 8, 1989, Colonel Takafuji met with Colonel Connell and other interested parties about the preparations being made regarding facilitation of a TBE vaccination plan for the US inspectors assigned to Votkinsk. In an aside, Dr. Takafuji noted that it would be useful if a "tick specimen preserved in isopropyl alcohol" were sent out of the Soviet Union for "examination." Mark Dues made note of this request, and subsequently passed it on to me for implementation.

I rotated out of Votkinsk in early April 1989, when the weather was still far too cold for the ticks to be prowling the Votkinsk perimeter. By the time I rotated back in, in early May, the ticks were out in full force. "As expected," a July 8, 1989 article, "A Doctor's Advice: More about Tick-Borne Encephalitis" which had been published in *Leninski Put'* noted, "there have been a great many ticks carrying encephalitis this year. During tick monitoring surveys, several times more were caught than in previous years." With more ticks came a greater chance of exposure to the disease. "The number of individuals bitten by ticks has increased," the article declared. "Many people have contracted the disease or are suspected of having it." This fact was underpinned by the following statistic: "The number of children suffering from tick bites has also grown, from 184 in 1988 to 253 this year."

The tick problem in Votkinsk was very real.

I waited until the end of May to carry out my tick harvest. To accomplish my mission, I donned one of the white coveralls used to eliminate static electricity during missile cannister openings, in hopes that the white cloth would provide ample contrast to enable any ticks that might attach themselves to my person to be readily identified and subsequently removed. I then proceeded to walk around the perimeter, making sure to rub up against as many shrubs, bushes, and tall clumps of grass as possible. Upon my return, Joanne Polka, the Hughes Physician's Assistant on-site at the time, was waiting for me, a pair of tweezers and a glass vial filled with isopropyl alcohol in hand.

My mission had attracted the attention of the inspectors and Soviets alike, who watched in amazement as Joanne removed tick after tick from my coveralls—some 48 in total, so many that she had to get a second vial of alcohol just to hold them all. Later, when I retreated to the bathroom to conduct the requisite post-patrol self-inspection, I found a few stragglers who had pierced my defenses and were making themselves at home on my body. These were killed without mercy.

Joanne wrapped the tick-filled vials in bubble wrap, which she then put into a small, unmarked cardboard box that I carried out with me when I left Votkinsk in late-June. I kept the cardboard box in my coat pocket throughout the journey, landing in Frankfurt, and then on to Washington, DC. The morning after my return, I drove myself to Fort Detrick, home of USAMRIID, and presented myself to Dr. Kelly McKee.

Major McKee had not been present when Colonel Takafuji had made his comment about the desirability of acquiring actual tick specimens from Votkinsk and was aghast when I produced the two vials containing the 48 Votkinsk ticks. "How did you bring these in?" he asked, only to blanche further when told that they had been hand carried through international borders and customs (and agricultural) controls void of any declaration. "We can't accept these," he said. "You have violated any number of US and international laws by bringing these here. Why would you do something like this?" The Major was visibly upset.

"I was ordered to," I replied, still holding the vials out to the Major.

"By whom?" McKee asked.

"My understanding is that the order came from Colonel Takafuji himself."

Major McKee stared at me for a long minute, then reached out and took the vials. "This," he said, "never happened."

During the entire time US inspectors were present in Votkinsk, there was not a single instance of an inspector contracting TBE. The efficacy of the FSME-IMMUN vaccine, combined with self-inspection procedures set up by the inspectors, was the key factor behind this success story.

Our Votkinsk Home, Sweet Home

THE 12-KILOMETER (7.5 mile) drive from our quarters on 20 Dzerzhinsky Street to the Missile Final Assembly Plant took about 30 minutes to cover. The Soviets provided a Rafik van and a driver, who dutifully delivered the morning shift to the inspection site, and took the night shift home, with stops both ways at the Café Cosmos for breakfast. In the evening, he repeated the process, this time pausing at the Café Cosmos for dinner. The Rafik also shuttled inspectors to the restaurant for lunch, and for midnight meals. And so it went, day after day.

To get to the inspection site, the van would head north from the Beryozovka neighborhood towards the Oil and Gas Production Supply Base, and past a cemetery tucked away amongst a larger stand of trees. With its assortment of old Orthodox crosses and weathered headstones, it looked like a scene straight out of a Turgenev novel.

Past the Oil and Gas Production Supply Base, the road intersected with an east-west highway (little more than a two-lane strip of asphalt). Turn left, and you head into the hinterlands of the Udmurt Republic, toward the regional center of Sharkan. Our Rafik always turned right, toward the Kama River, Ural Mountains, and the city of Perm. On our left were stands of birch trees situated among fields of wildflowers, on our right a series of single-story brick buildings representing various industrial enterprises that supported the city of Votkinsk, including a meat packing plant whose smell was, during the height of summer, enough to turn the strongest of stomachs.

Soon the road turned into a traffic circle. Take the first exit, and one would return to the city of Votkinsk. Take the second, and you would soon find yourself crossing the Kama River and entering the city of Chaikovsky. The third exit was ours, through fields of rye and tall grass where a scattered herd of cattle grazed, watched over by herdsmen, mounted on horseback, who kept their bovine charges moving by worrying their backs with whips of braided leather.

The fields of rye dominated the scenery along this stretch of the road, whether the bright fresh green of the newly planted crop in May and June, the dull yellow green of the maturing stalks in July and August, or the brilliant amber of the fields prior to reaping in September. On breezy days when the wind, sun and shadow combined to create a sea of liquid motion out of the waves of grain, one would struggle not to become hypnotized by the sheer beauty and tranquility of the landscape.

Soon the grain gave way to fields of potatoes, which in turn yielded to the Siva River, on whose banks those locals lucky enough to own a car would often be seen parked, having a picnic with their family. The village of Gavrilovka was located here. It was a quaint village composed primarily of old wooden *Izba's*, or log houses. Its population was primarily employed by the nearby Kholkhoz *Mir*, or Peace.

After crossing the Siva River, the road turned east, with giant fields of rye stretching out on the right-hand side of the road, and a growing forest of birch and fir trees on the left. After a few kilometers, a railroad track crossed the highway, signaling our own left-hand turn onto a road that snaked through a forest of trees, before eventually yielding to a cleared area in which was located

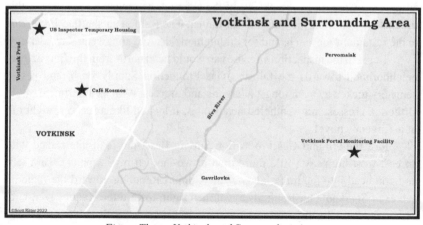

Figure Three: Votkinsk and Surrounding Area

the Votkinsk Final Assembly Plant, home of the Perimeter Portal Monitoring Facility.

We inspectors made this trip twice a day. During the spring and summer, the ride was magical. Come fall, the weather took a turn for the worse; the rains came, and with it the infamous *Rasputitsa,* or muddy season, which soon enough turned into the harshness of the Siberian winter. The landscape was turned a uniform white by snowfalls measuring several feet in depth, and the roads were covered by a permanent sheet of snow-covered ice, which often tested the studded tires and chains on the Rafik as the driver struggled not to slide off the road and into a ditch.

During heavy snowfall, the Rafik slowed to a crawl, the driver peering through the rapidly beating windshield wipers, trying to discern the road through the white-out of a blizzard. Such conditions produced numerous traffic accidents. Fortunately for the US inspectors none directly involved a vehicle they were riding in. One of these accidents, however, resulted in the Rafik being compelled to take an alternative route from the factory back to Votkinsk.

"This route," I wrote in a subsequent report, "entailed driving towards the emergency exit and diverting onto a makeshift snow road which was in existence across an adjacent farm field," noting that "this road coincided with a vehicle trail that that had existed in the same area during the summer and fall." The trail connected the Votkinsk Missile Final Assembly Plant with the Sovkov Votkinsk, some three kilometers away.

"The road was little more than a single lane consisting of a pair of ruts created by passing vehicles. The Rafik," I noted, "experienced considerable difficulty in making the transit, with snow build up in the center of the track often grounding the vehicle, slowing it down considerably and causing it to slew back and forth violently."

As difficult as the transit was, it did provide me an opportunity to assess the trafficability of the route that had been highlighted by the Pacific Sierra analysis warning of the possible use of tunnels and dirigibles for covertly removing SS-20 missiles from the factory. This experience put both of those theories to bed.

Come March the ground began to thaw, turning the frozen ground into a sea of mud, before firming up in May, and a return to the fairytale setting that had initially greeted us when we arrived in June 1988.

Almost immediately following the arrival of the US inspectors in July 1988, Anatoli Chernenko and his construction group began breaking ground for the construction of three housing units and one administrative building that would, once finished, become the inspectors' permanent home. Named after notable US Presidents of the past (Washington, Jefferson, and Lincoln were the housing units, while Roosevelt—Franklin, not Theodore—was the administrative building), these were substantial structures built to keep their occupants warm and dry in the most inclement weather.[7]

By late August 1988, the construction was far enough advanced that Doug Englund, accompanied by Jerry Porter and other Hughes personnel, was able to conduct a walk-through tour of the Washington dormitory. "This building is farthest along of the four," Doug wrote in an August 28 memorandum. "It has a roof, all windows have been installed, plumbing is roughed in, and the walls are being plastered."

The efforts of Chernenko and his men did not go unnoticed. "We were all quite favorably impressed with the quality of the work and by the amount of space we will have," Doug reported. According to the work schedule, the buildings were scheduled to be completed by mid-December 1988. Chernenko, however, believed that he would be done ahead of schedule. "Our experience with him," Doug noted favorably, "suggests he is likely to be correct."

The buildings, however, were empty. Before the American inspectors could occupy them, they would need to be furnished. While the Soviets had offered to provide top quality furniture domestically sourced, Doug Englund was in favor of Hughes purchasing the furniture from a European vendor and shipping it in to Votkinsk. "Our top priority here is clearly that of building a continuous monitoring site and carrying out the inspection mission," Doug wrote. "At the same time, however, we have to devote appropriate attention to those other activities which also carry deadlines. Consequently, I believe we need to focus more rapidly and more thoroughly on our furniture requirements."

Doug Englund's desire to use a European vendor, however, clashed with George Connell's vision of the American housing in Votkinsk serving in a representational role, allowing the inspectors the opportunity to present their country in as positive a light as possible to their Soviet counterparts. Instead of simply purchasing furniture off the European market, Connell sought out the services of an interior decorator, the Houghton Group, who put Connell in touch with a well-known high-end furniture manufacturing company located in North Carolina. When Doug objected to the complexity and cost of this venture, he was overridden by General Lajoie, who supported the representational rationale.

Over the course of the next few months, OSIA engaged in creative contracting, acquisitioning first-class furnishings inclusive of furniture, lighting, paintings, decorative plants, and carpeting. Once acquired, the furniture had to be broken down, packaged, and then transported to the Soviet Union, where it would be received by the inspectors, inspected by the Soviets, and then reassembled and placed in their respective locations. This was a tremendous administrative and logistical task that was ably handled by Barrett Haver and Richard Kurasiewicz. On site, Jerry Porter and Bill Langemeier juggled the ongoing installation drama involving the DCC, CargoScan, and cable pulling with the time-consuming demands of furnishing their future living and working spaces.

Unlike the DCC ISO shelters and the M-1022 mobilizers, which were flown into Izhevsk using Soviet Il-76 aircraft after transferring from US aircraft in Moscow, the furniture shipments were going to be flown directly from North Carolina, through Germany and on to Izhevsk using US Air Force C-141 aircraft. "The American side," Barrett Haver wrote in a memorandum to Anatoli Tomilov dated January 2, 1989, "recognizes that the shipment of this much cargo through an airport never before used by American airplanes will be a very complex task."

An initial C-141 was scheduled to land in Izhevsk on January 4, 1989 carrying a forklift and a K-loader, a specialized vehicle used in the handling of palletized cargo between the loading ramps and an aircraft. To assist the Soviets in better organizing to receive that aircraft and its cargo, I was dispatched to Izhevsk airport on January 2, 1989, to meet with the airport manager to arrange for the storage and security of the US cargo handling vehicles in heated conditions to prevent the freezing up of the oil and fuel. This meeting went well, and the initial C-141 flew in without incident.

The arrival of the C-141 in Izhevsk created quite a stir, with the local Soviet media noting the surprise among local citizens at the appearance of an "unusually squat, windowless plane, painted a strange dark green with black spots," whose tail section "was decorated with the stars and stripes of the American flag."[8] A total of 12 flights were planned, to take place in three waves of four flights each. While the Air Force provided personnel who oversaw the actual offloading of the aircraft, the breaking down of the pallets containing the boxes in which the disassembled furniture was packed was the responsibility of the on-site Hughes personnel, who assembled the aptly named "gorilla crew" for the task (some of the boxes were quite heavy).

By January 20, 1989, George Connell was able to report back to OSIA Headquarters that "all major items of furniture have been set in their designated places. All the plants have found a home (and really add a nice touch!)" The decision to use an interior decorator and to source the furniture and furnishings from a high-end US vender appeared to have been the right one. As Connell noted, "All the inspectors are delighted with their furniture and the Soviets are astounded at the quality."

There were some items of furniture that had been damaged in transit which needed to be shipped back and replaced, as well as some linen that was the wrong size, but these would be rectified in the last wave of flights scheduled for the end of February 1989. The Soviets had dispatched a "commission" of technical inspectors, led by Colonel Volkov, to Votkinsk for the purpose of ensuring that all the material sent was permitted for use by the inspectors under the terms of the INF treaty and its relevant annexes.

On January 30, 1989, the Soviets provided a memorandum to the US inspectors on the results of these inspections. "All equipment was physically inspected during the period – to 30 January 1989 by the Soviet side and was released to the US side in accordance with existing agreements, with the exception of television sets, for which use-in-principle at the portal living quarters has not been agreed." The television sets in question—three in total—were placed in a room under dual lock "until resolution of the issue of their use."

The document was signed by Vyacheslav K. Lopatin, the Deputy Chief for Technical Security, Department 162.

Lopatin had been a thorn in the side of the inspectors from the very first day of work. His interactions with Frank Martin during the installation of the temporary portal were legendary among the inspectors. Less so was his meticulous insistence on documentation, not so much because he was wrong in doing so, but because we hadn't prepared for this level of scrutiny, and compliance with Lopatin's demands were slowing down a construction timeline laboring under tremendous political pressure to be finished.

The inspectors had, over the course of the past seven months, developed a begrudging respect for Vyacheslav Lopatin and the role he performed. His insistence that everything we do conform to the absolute letter of the treaty was the proper approach, protecting the inspectors as much as it did his own side. Moreover, Lopatin was a genuinely nice person. He often was seen in the company of his son, on whom he doted.[9]

As the inspectors began to encroach upon the Votkinsk Final Assembly Plant, however, Lopatin's name increasingly became synonymous with trouble. The impounding of the television sets was but a symptom of a larger paranoia that existed among the Soviets in general, and Lopatin in particular, when it came to the true intent of the inspectors. This paranoia, the inspectors soon discovered, extended beyond the material that was brought into Votkinsk, to include the very living quarters the inspectors were preparing to move into.

The US had always planned to install phone lines connecting each room in the living quarters and administrative building to the DCC. This would allow for instant communication and accountability among the inspection team. The Soviets had, in principle, approved of this concept, and had cleared the phone-related equipment for installation in December 1988. And yet, when the US inspectors sought to install the phone lines from the second floor of each building down to the basement, and then back up through the floor to each room, they were blocked on order of Lopatin, who claimed that the basements were off limits to the inspectors.

In a meeting between George Connell and Anatoli Tomilov, Connell asked why, if the buildings in question were diplomatically inviolable, as stated in the treaty, was Lopatin preventing access to the basements? Tomilov responded that while the actual living and working spaces in the buildings being constructed by the Soviets for the Americans were, in fact, diplomatically inviolable, the basements and the territory surrounding these buildings were not. Tomilov pointed out that the relevant Geneva protocols governing the assignment of diplomatic inviolability, areas with diplomatic immunity must be bordered. The US side, he noted, had refused to allow a fence to be built around the quarters, and as such had foregone any claim to the basements and surrounding territory. Connell rejected the Soviet position out of hand.

The next day, January 12, 1989, Anatoli Tomilov presented George Connell with an *Akt*, or official document, transferring control of the Washington, Jefferson, Lincoln, and Roosevelt buildings to the US side. The *Akt* transferred the totality of the new structures "with the exception of the basements of these buildings," to the Americans.

Connell refused to sign the document, declaring that he would need to consult with his superiors in Washington, DC. The resulting controversy was to escalate into a significant diplomatic standoff, the result of which was that instead of being able to move into their new quarters, the US inspectors remained at 20 Dzerzhinsky Street, where they continued to undertake the long Rafik commute to and from the Portal Monitoring Facility twice a day.

The issue of the inviolability of the basements was soon escalated into a full-scale diplomatic incident, with the US Embassy in Moscow reaching out to the Soviet Foreign Ministry, and the US raising it as an issue at the Special Verification Committee on January 24. On January 26, Anatoli Tomilov, clearly embarrassed at the controversy surrounding this issue, reached out to George Connell with a compromise—the American inspectors could move into their new quarters, and the basements would be operated under the principle of joint access while the issue was resolved through diplomatic channels.

Before Connell could coordinate with OSIA Headquarters on Tomilov's proposal, however, the entire issue of the inviolability of the basements was taken out of the hands of the US inspectors and local Soviet authorities when the SVC officially became seized of the matter. On January 30, the US delegation to the SVC presented their Soviet counterparts with an official position paper which declared that the text of the INF treaty made clear that the living quarters of inspectors, including any basements, were to be accorded the inviolability and protection accorded the premises of Diplomatic agents pursuant to Article 30 of the Vienna Convention on Diplomatic Relations of April 18, 1961.

The US paper asserted that the issue of the inviolability of basements had been discussed during the May 1988 Technical Talks held in Vienna, Austria. Then, the Soviets agreed that their access to the basements would be at the invitation of the US inspectors only, similar in function to how Soviet firefighters were granted access to the US Embassy in Moscow. The US rejected the Soviet demands that the US sign an *Akt* that removed the inviolable status of the basements and requested that the Soviets permit the inspectors to occupy their new quarters immediately.

The Soviets, in their response, made some very telling observations, first and foremost of which was that Soviet building regulations restricted what activity could take place in basements, which contained "life-protecting communication lines." Moreover, the Soviets underscored the reality that "all life-protecting communication lines for the living quarters of the American inspectors are connected directly to the Votkinsk factory, which carries out the manufacture of means which do not fall under inspection according to the Treaty on medium- and short-range missiles. For the Soviet side, this raises serious concerns relative to the observance of appropriate operating procedures."

The Soviets withdrew their requirement for the Americans to sign an *Akt*, and instead proposed that access to the basements of the US living quarters be managed through a "dual-key" approach that would allow the Soviets to meet their legal requirement regarding maintenance while asserting a level of US control and access.

This response was agreeable to Doug Englund, who had replaced George Connell on January 31, 1989. Like George, Doug was struck by the need to move the inspectors out of their temporary quarters and into the new housing as soon as possible. Doug communicated his position to OSIA Headquarters repeatedly throughout the first three weeks of February, only to be met with silence.

During this letter writing campaign, Bill Gertz, using information provided by Senator Jesse Helms' staffer, David Sullivan, published an article in the February 24, 1989, edition of *The Washington Times* that threw a monkey wrench into the delicate negotiations then ongoing about the provenance of the basements. Titled "The Soviets want access to the inspector's basements," the article quoted an unidentified US official who stated that the US was challenging a Soviet demand to be allowed access to the basement of US quarters in Votkinsk. This official went on to declare that the primary issue was the security of the basements against "KGB electronic and acoustic eavesdropping." The article stated that the US inspectors assumed that their living quarters were not secure because "they were constructed by the Soviets." However, by allowing the Soviets access to the basements, the "KGB agents who accompany the US inspectors would have the ability to monitor closely all findings and decisions concerning Soviet compliance with the INF treaty."[10]

All hell broke loose. When the US Embassy faxed over the article, the US inspectors provided their Soviet counterparts with a copy as a matter of courtesy. The Soviets, however, mistook the article for an official US memorandum, and Anatoli Tomilov's boss, Aleksandr Sokolov, the Special Assistant for INF Treaty Issues to the General Director of the Votkinsk Factory, demanded an immediate audience with Doug Englund. After Doug explained that the fax was an article, not a document, and that it did not reflect the official position of the US government, Sokolov calmed down.

The same, however, could not be said about the Soviet Ministry of Foreign Affairs, which issued a non-paper to the US Embassy in Moscow on January 28, 1989, protesting the leaking of confidential information to the US media by US officials. In accordance with Section IX of the Memorandum of Agreement, all activities of the Special Verification Commission were to remain confidential. By leaking details of the basement controversy, which at that very moment had been taken up by the SVC, the US had violated its commitments.

Any hope of a timely resolution was further set back when, on March 1, 1989, General Lajoie, during testimony before the House Foreign Affairs subcommittee on Arms Control, International Security, and Science, stated that the US position on the issue of inspector housing in Votkinsk was that once the US took possession of the buildings, they would do so "from attic to cellar," with the entire structure enjoying inviolability. General Lajoie went on to state that the Soviet inspectors working at the Soviet Portal Monitoring Facility in Magna, Utah, would not be permitted to occupy their permanent quarters until this issue was resolved.

The basement crisis was rapidly growing out of control. Bill Gertz's article in *The Washington Times*, combined with General Lajoie's testimony before Congress, had injected an unwelcome element of politics which, if allowed to fester and grow, could derail the progress that was being made in getting the Portal Monitoring Facility in Votkinsk up and running. To break the impasse, the State Department, on March 7, 1990, presented the Soviet Ministry of Foreign Affairs with a new position paper which, while reiterating that the US "cannot accept any restriction to its treaty right to total inviolability of its permanent living quarters at Votkinsk," declared that the "US is prepared to permit immediate access" to the basements of the living quarters "whenever requested." The paper closed by urging "the Soviet Union to reconsider its position on this matter."

On March 10, the Soviet Ministry of Foreign Affairs sent its reply. Noting "the readiness of the American side to guarantee immediate access to the basements of the indicated quarters of Soviet technical service personnel for conducting routine examination and maintenance work on the water supply system, sewage, etc.," the Soviets declared that it would no longer "insist on organizing access to the basements on a 'dual-key' principle." As such, the Soviets proposed that the US occupy the living quarters in Votkinsk "at the earliest possible time."

This proposal was accepted by the US.

There remained, however, the issue of Soviet security. General Lajoie conducted a three-day visit to Votkinsk from March 14–16, 1989. In a meeting with Soviet officials on March 16, the issue of the US housing was again raised. General Medvedev, the Commander of the Soviet Nuclear Risk Reduction Center, the counterpart organization to OSIA, noted that the issue had been resolved to the satisfaction of all parties, and that the Votkinsk Factory would need some time—perhaps up to two weeks—to study the security implications of US access to basements that possess utilities that are supplied directly from the factory. In a move that appeared to provide cover for this work, Chernenko's boss toured the living quarters on March 11, and noted several "discrepancies" that he believed must be fixed prior to turning the buildings over to the Americans.

The implications of General Medvedev's comments became clear on the morning of March 17, 1989, when Doug Englund, accompanied by Stu O'Neill, arrived at the Portal Monitoring Facility, and tried to conduct an inspection of the housing area only to find, as Doug reported to General Lajoie in a memorandum, that "the entire housing area has been sealed off."

"The entrance to the area in front of the Washington building," Doug noted, "has been fenced, and the guard has been re-established at the main entrance. All other openings have been similarly sealed off."

Doug and Stu O'Neill, accompanied by Zoi Haloulakos, met later that morning with Vyacheslav Lopatin to discuss the situation. "Lopatin," Doug reported, "said he had inquired into the reasons for the closing and had been told that the 'special services' had arrived to do the required security work discussed during [the meeting between General Lajoie and General Medvedev], and that the housing area would be closed for an approximate three-week period." Department 162, Lopatin added, had been unaware that this was going to take place.

The Soviet paranoia was not baseless. When reviewing the US intelligence services' penchant for technical spying, the local office of the Votkinsk KGB was aware of the recent example of the CIA installing a device to "remove information from subterranean communications cables" that had been installed on a "defense enterprise telephone cable" like those that ran from the basements of the US living quarters into the Votkinsk Missile Final Assembly Plant. On the other hand, the spy-versus-spy fantasy of the KGB seeking to listen in on the conversations of US inspectors to uncover insights into the American approach to arms control verification was just that—fantasy.

The reality was that the Soviets were rightfully concerned about giving the Americans unrestricted access to the very types of communication cables the CIA had a history of trying to technically exploit. The work of the Soviet 'special services' appeared to focus on shielding the communication and power cables from any technical espionage on the part of an American team which was, at that time, bringing in literally tons of highly sophisticated electronics, much of which remained poorly documented in terms of purpose and capability.

To safeguard against elevating Soviet concerns that the US inspection team was seeking to hide anything regarding its activities on-site, instructions were given to all inspectors that they were under no circumstances to attempt to locate any listening devices or other technical surveillance measures that might have been installed by the Soviets. First and foremost, every inspector was briefed on the reality that everything he or she did or said while in the Soviet Union could be, and probably was, being collected by Soviet intelligence. Insofar as we assumed there was ongoing technical surveillance, there was, therefore, no need to look for it.

Most importantly, however, was the fact that the success of the INF treaty and other arms control agreements down the road depended on a modicum of trust on the part of each party that the other had entered the agreement in good faith. As such, we inspectors were prohibited from undertaking any actions that deviated from the letter and intent of the treaty. We were not spies, and therefore we should not act as such. If someone untrained in the art of conducting counter-technical surveillance were to start looking for Soviet "bugs," the Soviets would detect this, and have every reason to suspect that foul play was afoot.

Young, intellectually curious Americans that they were, however, some of the Hughes personnel disregarded these instructions and used a stud location device to "scan" the walls of the Lincoln basement, which was in the process of being converted into a poker room/unofficial sauna by one of the more enterprising inspectors from Hughes. Inevitably a "device" was discovered, and a hole dug into the wall to expose it for the purpose of being photographed. When the on-site counterintelligence personnel became aware of this activity, we immediately put a halt to it, while reporting the incident up the chain of command. While General Lajoie's initial proclivity was to immediately fire the persons involved, calmer heads prevailed, and each was let off with a sharp warning delivered by Colonel Connell in person.

The US inspection team left 20 Dzerzhinsky Street for the last time on April 4, 1989. The move into the new quarters was pulled off without a hitch, and soon the inspectors settled into the new routine of living outside a Soviet missile factory 24 hours a day, 7 days a week. Whereas prior to April 4, any inspector on-site was, by default, on duty, the Soviets had adopted a more relaxed posture when it came to inspector movement and to the wearing of inspector badges. Now, with the reality of a large body of Americans ostensibly off duty living next to a sensitive military industrial facility, the Soviets, led by none other than Vyacheslav Lopatin, sought to exert a modicum of control.

It was agreed that inspectors would begin wearing their badges, which contained a photograph and the name of the bearer, beginning June 1, 1989. The Soviets also insisted that while inspectors were free to travel to and from their housing units and the Roosevelt administrative building as they saw fit, any inspector entering the "technical zone" (i.e., the DCC, the warehouse, or any other part of the Portal Monitoring Facility) must first notify the Soviet side, which would either provide an escort or provide the inspector with permission to proceed unaccompanied. These procedures soon clashed with the American

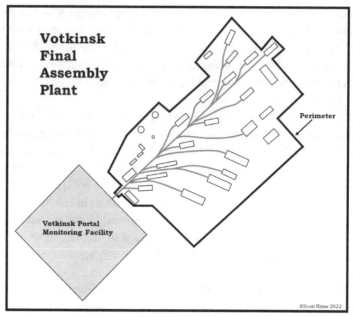

Figure Four: Votkinsk Final Assembly Plant

work ethic, which saw inspectors called from what was ostensibly their time off to respond to the needs of the Site Commander or Site Manager as they arose. The frustration of the Soviets was palpable, with inspectors being called to assist in installation activities assuming the work profile they had operated under for the past ten months and heading directly to the location where they were needed. Like anything new, the Soviet restrictions on movement took some getting used to, but by the end of April 1989 the number of daily infractions had fallen considerably (although they were not eliminated).

Another issue that manifested itself soon after the move to the new quarters was the condition of the perimeter trail around the Votkinsk Final Assembly Plant. The difficult traverse over swampy, uneven, and debris-filled grounds had been raised by the inspectors on several occasions during the summer and fall of 1988. The advent of winter, however, made the issue temporarily moot, and soon inspectors and their Soviet escorts were strapping on skis for what all agreed was a brisk, enjoyable cross-country skiing trek around the perimeter. With April, however, came the inevitable thawing, and the return of having to walk what was, under good conditions, a trying path and, under wet and muddy conditions, a trail that was downright dangerous.

The inevitable happened. One of the Hughes inspectors badly twisted an ankle while on perimeter patrol. When the inspection team raised this issue with their Soviet counterparts, their concerns were given short shrift, with Sokolov

The perimeter around the Votkinsk Final Assembly Plant consisted of difficult terrain which presented a hazard to the personnel required to patrol it twice daily.

noting that both sides faced the same hazards. To compel a Soviet response, the inspectors sought to include a protest in the Monthly Inspection Report, citing the unsafe conditions around the factory perimeter as a "treaty anomaly," or violation.

This tactic worked, and in exchange for the US side agreeing to drop the formal complaint, the Soviets agreed to receive a report from the inspectors listing the specific improvements sought.

I was given the task of conducting this survey. In my report to Doug Englund, I recommended that a walking path, approximately one meter wide, be constructed around much of the perimeter using gravel or an acceptable substitute. The purpose of the gravel base, I noted, was to "provide the US inspectors and their Soviet escorts with a walking surface that does not put them in contact with tick-bearing grass or shrubbery." In the swampier areas I recommended the construction of a raised walkway consisting of "wooden planks set flush together providing for a continuous walking surface of one meter width for its entire length." I also highlighted several areas where debris needed to be removed, and another where a railing should be installed to keep inspectors and escorts alike from falling down steep inclines.

The Soviets received the report and promised to make the requested improvements.

Diplomatic Breaches: My Toasts

DIPLOMACY IS a tricky business for those schooled in the art of negotiation, compromise, and non-commitment. Foreign Service Officers take years to develop this skill set. Foreign Area Officers receive enough formal training, backed up by some Embassy-based practical experience, to hold their own. Company-grade officers straight from the Fleet Marine Force, however, should never be entrusted with anything remotely requiring diplomatic finesse. I served as a living, breathing case in point.

In October 1988, General Lajoie made his first visit to the Votkinsk Portal Monitoring Facility. He was accompanied by his Soviet counterpart, Major General Medvedev, the commander of the Soviet Nuclear Risk Reduction Center. Near the end of his visit, the Soviets hosted a lunch in General Lajoie's honor at the Ustinov Dacha. I was a First Lieutenant, normally far too junior to be included in such a gathering, but because there were two other Marine Officers in Votkinsk at the time (Colonel Connell, the Site Commander, and Lieutenant Colonel Al Shively, General Lajoie's Chief of Staff), General Medvedev thought it would be a good idea to invite a third Marine—me.

The lunch was non-eventful, a very pleasant social gathering. I sat at my seat, silent, taking in what I deemed to be the rarified air of living diplomacy. The glasses were being charged, and toasts were being made by the participants in sequence, starting with the Generals, down through the order of precedence, until they finished with the lowest person on the totem pole—me.

My Russian was horrific, and I just assumed that they would pass me by, but General Medvedev insisted on hearing what "one of General Lajoie's Marines had to say about life in Votkinsk." I was, at that time, spending considerable time observing Anatoli Chernenko and his construction group as they carried out their various tasks on site. Chernenko was a natural leader of men, and every morning before work would start, he gathered his troops around him for a pep talk, which invariably concluded with a cheer along the lines of "*Raz, Dva, Tri...Zayabis!*"

I asked Chernenko what it meant, and he told me, "Strong work."

I started to tell the story of Chernenko's team, and how they were the living embodiment of the spirit of the treaty—working hard on behalf of the greater good. Across from me sat Chernenko himself, who had more than earned a spot at the table. As I started speaking, his face was locked in a smile, his head nodding as I said kind words about him and his men.

There was, however, a perceptible change in his demeanor as I mentioned his morning pep talk, which further transitioned into a look of abject horror as I finished my toast.

"So, in honor of the spirit of joint work that has marked the INF experience in Votkinsk so far," I said, rising to my feet, "I'd like to borrow a phrase Mr. Chernenko taught me while motivating his men every morning."

I looked at General Lajoie, then over to General Medvedev.

Chernenko's face was locked in a grimace, his eyes screwed shut.

"Gentlemen, *Zayabis!*"

The room was silent as I felt every Russian-speaking eye, American and Soviet alike, bore straight through me.

General Lajoie stared at me, his eyes narrowing, and then looked over toward Colonel Connell, whose mouth was agape.

I was saved by General Medvedev's booming laughter, which broke the ice, and soon all the Soviets were leaning back, guffawing to their hearts content. General Medvedev stood up, his eyes watering from laughing so hard, and raised his glass.

"I can drink to that," he said. "*Zayabis!*"

General Lajoie rose to his feet, along with everyone else, and pierced me with a gimlet-eyed stare while repeating, "*Zayabis.*"

The luncheon was over, and we headed out to the vehicles that would take us back to the Portal Monitoring Facility. General Medvedev shook my hand, still laughing. So did Chernenko and Lopatin. General Lajoie avoided me, and I was led to the waiting Rafik by Colonel Connell.

"Do you even know what you said?" he asked.

"Yes, Sir," I answered. "Chernenko told me it meant 'Strong work.'"

"Well," Connell replied, "I just want you to know that you're the first person I've ever seen toast a Soviet General by telling him to go get fucked."

That was the last official function I attended in the presence of General Lajoie.

Following the diplomatic wrestling match over the inviolability of the US quarters in Votkinsk, the issue of the Soviet quarters in Magna, Utah had become elevated as a reciprocal matter. Reciprocity drove much of the work at both locations, with each side sensitive to whether or not one side was being treated differently than the other. On April 18, 1989, the Soviets were scheduled to move into their new, purpose-built quarters in the Salt Lake City suburb of West Jordan.

Because of the attention the basement crisis had brought to the issue of inspector housing, a senior US delegation was dispatched to provide a presence at the ribbon cutting ceremony. Dave Pabst, a veteran Foreign Service Officer who took over from Ray Smith as the Deputy Director for International Negotiations, attended as the senior OSIA official. Colonel Connell was directed by General Lajoie to send an officer with experience in Vokinsk to accompany Mr. Pabst. As the only officer available, I was given the job. "No speeches," Connell told me before I left.

The ceremony went fine, and when it was time for people to make remarks, I disappeared into the background as ordered. We were then invited into the Soviet quarters for some refreshments. I found myself seated at a table with the head of the Soviet team, Colonel Lebedev, and a couple other Soviet inspectors. I was a frequent traveler to Magna, where I worked on issues pertaining to counterintelligence and reciprocity, and had come to know the Soviet inspectors well. They were curious about life in Votkinsk, and I started regaling them with war stories drawn from my experience on-site.

There were other people seated around the table, a mix of US personnel assigned to Magna, and outside dignitaries invited to the ribbon cutting ceremony. As I talked, one of these people, a small, middle-aged woman, was listening in, her face pinched. "I don't think you should be talking about that," she said at one point, as I discussed leisure activities in Votkinsk.

I didn't recognize the woman as anyone in my chain of command, and in any event thought she was joking, so I continued. Once again, she intervened. "You are discussing a policy matter," she said. "I think you should stop."

I looked at her, then looked around the table. I was dressed in my Alpha uniform, looking every inch the Marine Officer. "Excuse me, Ma'am, but I don't know you from Eve. This gentleman," I said, nodding toward Colonel Lebedev, "wanted to talk to someone about what life as an inspector in Votkinsk was like. As I look around the table, it seems that I'm the only person here who has served as an inspector in Votkinsk. As such, I am responding to his request. I would respectively request that you kindly keep your nose out of my business."

The woman, flustered, stood up and walked away. I continued with my narrative, to the delight of the Soviets.

Later, as I roamed the Soviet compound, Dave Pabst came up to me, a worried look on his face. "Did you tell Sally Horn to mind her own business?" he asked.

Sally Horn was the Director of Verification for the Assistant Secretary of Defense for International Security Policy, and one of OSIA's harshest critics. I had never met her before and said as much to Mr. Pabst.

"Well, you can't say that anymore." Dave looked embarrassed. "There's a car outside. It will take you back to your hotel. You're to catch the first plane back to Washington, DC. Ms. Horn doesn't want you to be a part of this delegation anymore."

I did as ordered. Upon arrival at the Portal Monitoring offices, Colonel Connell greeted me with a smile. "Well, you are *persona non grata* with Sally Horn," he told me. "That's not necessarily a bad thing," he said. "It means we can keep you in the field where you belong."

US Ambassador Jack Matlock Visits Votkinsk

I RETURNED to Votkinsk in early May 1989. My reputation as someone not to be trusted on the cocktail circuit was matched only by my reputation for accomplishing the most challenging of tasks. Thus, I was both taken aback and honored when Doug Englund, who was serving as the Site Commander at the time, handed me a binder, the cover of which was graced with the visage of the US Ambassador to the Soviet Union, Jack Matlock. "The Ambassador is coming to our Open House on June 10," he said, referring to our own "ribbon cutting" ceremony commemorating our move into the new inspector's quarters. "You're in charge of making it happen." He held onto the binder for a few seconds, staring at me, before he released to my control.

"Don't fuck it up."

One of the first lessons I learned was that a US Ambassador is a big deal. This was especially true of one posted to the Soviet Union during one of the most critical times in the relations of those two nations. Any movement by an ambassador inside his or her host country is likewise a very big deal, one that requires a tremendous amount of coordination and adherence to diplomatic protocol.

My initial draft plan calling for "Ambassador Matlock to deploy to Votkinsk on the morning of June 10" was quickly cast aside. An American Ambassador was coming to the Udmurt Republic—a previously closed area—for the first time. The idea that his visit was going to be limited to attending a simple open house ceremony at the Votkinsk Portal Monitoring Facility was mooted by the US Embassy from the start.

Fortunately, OSIA had a secret weapon in the form of the Arms Control Implementation Unit, or ACIU, which was permanently based out of the US Embassy in Moscow. Headed up by Ken Keating, an Army Lieutenant Colonel, the ACIU staff also included another Army officer, Major Steve Freeman, an Air Force officer, Captain Sandy Schmidt, as well as a State Department officer, Eileen Malloy. Ken Keating and his ACIU team had performed miracles in helping facilitate the transport of equipment and material through Moscow and onto Votkinsk and were always ready to assist inspectors during the weekly "mail runs" to Moscow. I quickly learned to lean on them as well when it came to helping coordinate the schedule for Ambassador Matlock during his scheduled two-day visit to the Udmurt Republic.

It became clear that Ambassador Matlock would be arriving in Izhevsk on July 9, one day prior to the open house. The reason for this was simple— diplomatic protocol required that the Ambassador meet with local dignitaries, of which it appeared there was no shortage. Ambassador Matlock would be greeted at the airport by a delegation which included the Chairman of the Presidium of the Supreme Soviet of the Udmurt Republic, the Chairman of the Council of

Ministers, along with various First and Second Deputies of the same. He would then be taken to the regional committee (OBKOM) of the Communist Party, where further introductions and ceremonies would transpire. The Ambassador's day would close with a series of meetings at Izhevsk University, followed by a dinner at the State Dacha in Izhevsk, where the Ambassador and his party would spend the night.

Most of this was *pro forma* scheduling handled by the US Embassy. My job was limited to getting the names of the principals involved on the Soviet side so that the Ambassador could be properly prepared when he met them. Fortunately, my counterpart on the Soviet side for this event, Aleksandr Sokolov, was going through a similar drill, and we were able to share notes, enabling me to keep him informed of the Ambassador's plans, which he passed up through his chain of command, with his helping me in return with the identities of the Soviet VIPs that would be meeting with Ambassador Matlock. All this information was passed on to the ACIU, which then coordinated with the Ambassador's scheduling team.

I was also tasked with assembling a guest list of local Soviets whom we inspectors would like to attend our open house. By June 1989 we had been in Votkinsk for nearly a year, during which time we had developed numerous friendships in the Votkinsk and Izhevsk communities. In early discussions with Doug Englund and Jerry Porter, we had agreed that 200 guests were probably the limit that could be handled responsibly. We also agreed that for many different reasons (including the fact that Votkinsk remained a closed zone) many of the people we invited would not be able to attend. Accordingly, we sent out invitations to around 250 people, both individual by-name invitations and so-called "block" invitations to various organizations and entities.

It turned out that everyone we invited accepted. And because many of the invitations to individuals also included spouses and children over five years of age, by the time I finished collating the acceptances, it turned out we were looking at more than 325 guests. This is where, as the person responsible for planning the Open House, things got interesting.

The biggest challenged we faced was, having issued the invitations, we could not now rescind them without a significant loss of face, a prospect no one on the US inspection team wanted to face. Moreover, any such embarrassment would be compounded by the high-profile visit of Ambassador Matlock, which would bring with it considerable press coverage. The press would undoubtably find out about the rescinded invitations and make that the story of the Ambassador's visit. One would be hard pressed to find a better way to generate the ire of an ambassador than to embarrass him or her on a high-profile diplomatic visit.

If we stuck with the expanded list of invitees, then we faced the equally difficult proposition of not being able to provide sufficient food and beverages at the function (very embarrassing) and losing control of the crowd (also embarrassing). As a Marine, I was confident I could put in place sufficient crowd control measures to avoid the site being overrun. When it came to food, however, we were limited with the supplies we had available, which as our resident Chef, Chuck Biasotti, repeatedly pointed out, was sufficient for 200 persons only.

Sufficient supplies, both in terms of quantity and quality, had been an issue since the arrival of the inspectors in July 1988. Initially, the Soviets contracted with a local establishment, the Café Cosmos, to serve meals to the inspectors until which time we could move into our compound at the Votkinsk Missile Final Assembly Plant, where we would have our own dining facility and full-time chef.

The staff of the Café Cosmos, led by a pair of gregarious cooks named Galina and Irina, served the inspectors three set meals per day (breakfast, lunch, and dinner) as well as a midnight meal for those inspectors standing night duty. The food was skillfully prepared and, when supplies were available, consisted of a delicious representation of Russian fare (I was particularly fond of the Beef Stroganoff and Chicken Kiev). Even when supplies ran low (as often happened), the ladies tried to make do. During one infamous stretch, when meat was scarce, Galina and Irina would prepare fish omelets, which sound precisely like they tasted. Having witnessed the disappointment on the faces of Galina and Irina when many of the inspectors sent their plates back, the omelets untouched, I went out of my way to order a second helping, which took all my Marine discipline to consume with abandon, a smile fixed on my face. They joy in the two cooks' eyes was worth the sacrifice.

Then the inevitable happened—the Café Cosmos received an order of meat, which the ladies immediately used to infuse their omelets with choice cuts. Every inspector who sat down was served a delicious meat omelet—except me. With great fanfare, Galina and Irina brought out a fish omelet, prepared especially for me, because I liked them so much. And when I finished the first, they brought out a second. I ate fish omelets for the next few months because I could never summon the courage to tell the two Soviet cooks the simple truth—they were awful.

The Café Cosmos, however, was always a temporary solution to the larger issue of how to feed the inspectors. With early estimates having the US inspectors occupy their permanent quarters sometime in mid-December 1988, finding a ready source of quality food in sufficient quantities that could be delivered, fresh, to Votkinsk became a challenge. After much negotiation, the inspectors were eventually able to come up with a delicate formula which had certain items (eggs, milk, and some vegetables) purchased locally, through the Votkinsk Factory, other supplies shipped in from Moscow on a contract basis with Vneshposyltorg (the Soviet entity which ran the diplomatic gastronome in Moscow), and the remaining items purchased by Hughes from the military commissary system in Frankfurt, West Germany, and flown in on rotation flights.

Given the complexity of this arrangement, menus had to be planned well in advance, and orders made accordingly. As Chuck Biosotti, the Hughes chef, pointed out repeatedly during the planning process for Ambassador Matlock's visit, the system was not designed to facilitate a last-second surge of some 320-plus mouths to feed in a single setting. It quickly became evident to Chuck and me that we had a major supply deficiency. After exhausting all possibilities, including the laying on of a commercial flight to fly food in from non-military European sources, it finally became clear that we were going to have to make do with what we had on hand. Fortunately, the site stocked a 30-day emergency food reserve in case of a critical supply disruption in one or more of our food sourcing options. It was agreed that to support the Open House, Hughes would be authorized to draw on these reserves to prepare food of sufficient quality and quantity to meet the needs of the Open House, contingent upon OSIA ensuring that these food reserves were replenished on the next available supply flight.

There still was the problem of how this food was going to be prepared. Chuck's primary mission was to provide three square meals a day to a team of some 30 hungry inspectors. This was, in and of itself, a full-time task. Even when we supplemented Chuck with the services of Tim Kubik, one of the Construction Managers, and three other Hughes personnel, there wasn't enough time available to simultaneously prepare for the Open House and continue to feed the inspectors three squares a day.

In a pinch, I turned to the Café Cosmos and the services of Galina and Irina for assistance. Perhaps my "love" for their fish omelets won them over. The two ladies agreed to help us out by resuming the three-a-day meal schedule we enjoyed when living at 20 Dzerzhinsky Street for a period of three days leading up to the Open House. Galina and Irina also agreed to help with the preparation of select items for the planned buffet, using their own supply of food supplemented by items provided by Chuck. Between the three of them, Chuck, Galina, and Irina made the food buffet at the Open House one of the best spreads ever served at Votkinsk.

While Chuck sorted out the culinary aspects of the Ambassador's visit, I turned to the issue of how I was going to choreograph this event. We had a sizeable delegation of Very Important Persons (VIPs) due to arrive on site and managing their visit would be challenge. But when you add an additional 300-plus regular guests, the potential for the Open House devolving into chaos was very real. The US inspection team, and by extension the United States, was going to be on full display to hundreds of people whose lives had, in one way or another, been directly impacted by the INF treaty experience. They could leave the Open House either impressed by our professionalism or dismayed at our incompetence.

I quickly realized that my best allies in this case were the Soviets themselves, especially the escorts from Department 162. They were being put under the spotlight every bit as much as we were, and as such it was in our mutual benefit for this event to come off seamlessly. I scheduled a series of meetings with Aleksandr Sokolov to discuss how we could best work together. This proved to be fortuitous. Sokolov was in contact with the Udmurt Communist Party officials about the needs and desires of their officials, and I was in contact with the ACIU about the same regarding Ambassador Matlock. But it appeared that the Udmurt Communists were not in contact with the US Embassy, and vice versa. So Sokolov and I served as an *ad hoc* communications conduit between the two entities, helping sync schedules with expectations.

I briefed Mr. Sokolov on some personal details about Ambassador Matlock—no preference when it came to food, but he did prefer Compari and soda over Vodka, and was a fancier of both red and white wines, as well as mineral water. I handed Sokolov a biographical handout prepared by the US Embassy in Moscow and highlighted the fact that the US Ambassador was an experienced expert on the Soviet Union, so much so that he considered Soviet Studies his "hobby." "All aspects of his trip to the Udmurt Republic will interest him," I told Sokolov. "You literally can't go wrong in setting up an agenda."

That was the easy part. Once Sokolov and I nailed down a specific agenda for the actual Open House, however, it became clear to both of us that the US inspectors did not have sufficient personnel available to manage the flow of people safely and efficiently while on-site. Moreover, given the need for effective communications, we needed people who were conversant in both the English and Russian languages. "We need the help of your translators," I told Sokolov.

"How many?" he asked.

"All of them."

He didn't blink.

Ambassador Matlock arrived in Izhevsk on June 9. He was met at the airport by Doug Englund and Barrett Haver. Chuck Myers remained at the Votkinsk Portal Monitoring Facility as the acting Site Commander. Stu O'Neill and I took turns standing watch as duty officer. But no missiles were going to be coming out of the factory that day, or the next. Instead, the US inspectors and their Soviet counterparts got busy turning the inspector's housing area into a large-scale reception area. We set up 21 tables (provided by the Soviet side), which served as drink stations. We unloaded another dozen or so barrels which did duty as trash receptacles. We laid out the site, setting up a speaker's platform, podium, and PA system, and roped off a designated area for the VIPs, both outdoors during the speeches and ribbon cutting ceremony, and indoors, once the buffet was open.

But the most important aspect of our preparation was the rehearsal of the tours. I had designated certain inspectors as tour guides. Each of them was paired with a Soviet translator. As the daytime duty officer, I would be responsible for conducting the VIP tour. Once that tour was complete, additional tours would be conducted every 30 minutes, with the first non-VIP tour starting at 4.30 PM, and

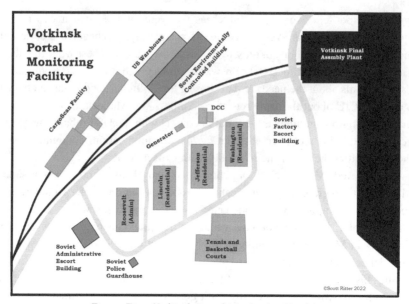

Figure Five: Votkinsk Portal Monitoring Facility

the last at 5.30 PM. In addition to the tours, we posted teams of inspectors and Soviet translators in the foyer of each of the housing units, and on the first and second floors of the administrative building, to help control the flow of people and answer any questions that might come up. We had two teams designated for this task, with a shift change scheduled to take place at the mid-way point in the tour. I walked everyone involved through their paces, emphasizing both the specifics of their respective tasks, and the timing.

I had to retrain myself in terms of leadership style. As a Marine, I was used to giving orders, and having them obeyed without hesitation. But I wasn't dealing with Marines here. The Hughes personnel, although subordinated to the OSIA chain of command when it came to inspection activities, did not work for me or any of the military officers assigned to Votkinsk. They took their orders from the Site Manager. Many of them were veterans of assignments in remote areas and took pride in their independence. Simply put, they were self-motivated individuals who did not respond well to being given direct orders. As for the Soviets, I was a guest in their country. Moreover, they were doing me a favor. The last thing they wanted was to be bossed around by some overbearing martinet.

I quickly found that being direct, not forceful, and having a good sense of humor was the formula for success. We had to get it right. But we also had to be able to work together. By the time we finished rehearsal, I think all involved agreed that we had found the right balance. None of the Hughes inspectors were threatening to punch me in the face, and the chemistry between the inspectors and their Soviet counterparts had never been better.

After so much preparation, the actual Open House seemed like a walk in the park, although it was not, by any stretch of the imagination. The Ambassador's party arrived at 1 PM sharp and was ushered to the designated VIP room on the second floor of the Roosevelt building. Chuck Myers and Stu O'Neill oversaw managing the VIPs. Barrett and Doug stayed with the Ambassador and his party (which, in addition to Steve Freeman, Kathy Schmidt, and Eileen Malloy of the ACIU, included the Embassy's resident State Department arms control guru, a Foreign Service Officer named Carrey Cavanaugh).

My job was to manage everything else. The plan called for the Soviet guests to begin arriving at 2 PM, and as such I had planned for the ushers to be in their positions by 1.50 PM. As things turned out, the first Soviet guests began arriving around 1.37 PM. Fortunately, the ushers were standing by, and quickly assumed their positions, ensuring that the traffic flow and crowd control assignments were carried out without a flaw. The Soviet VIPs arrived in a series of black sedans, with their passengers quickly led away to the VIP reception area. The regular guests arrived in buses, all of which seemed to arrive at once. Thanks to the hard work of the ushers, the site received this wave of humanity in an organized manner.

Over the course of the next five hours, speeches were given, performances made, and food and drinks served to a crowd that was broiling under a hot summer sun. There wasn't a cloud in the sky, allowing the guests to see the site in all its glory. We regaled the VIPs and normal guests alike with the technical wizardry of the DCC, explaining in minute detail the nature of our mission, and the way each piece of equipment supported that mission. In each of the four inspector buildings a painting of the building's namesake, and a brass plaque detailing aspects of their biography, was mounted on the wall in the entrance way, prompting numerous questions and discussions between the inspectors and their Soviet guests. (In retrospect, naming a building after Millard Fillmore would have been a PR disaster.) And, without exception, the Soviets were all impressed with the quality of the furnishings. George Connell's insistence on an interior decorator indeed paid a dividend.

Before we knew it, it was over. The Ambassador's party departed, followed by the Soviet VIPs, then the Soviet guests. We who remained behind, inspectors and Soviets alike, looked in wonder at the now empty spaces of the inspector's compound, which only an hour before had been filled with a crowd of more than 400—nearly 80 people beyond what we had planned for. But everyone had plenty of food to eat—no one went hungry. And there were sufficient refreshments for all. The event, we all agreed, had been a huge success.

After we finished cleaning up, I took a moment to collect myself in the dining hall, where the buffet had been set up. It was empty now—the crowd had finished off the last of Chuck, Galina, and Irina's spread. I had been so caught up in managing the event that I had not bothered to eat the entire day, and my stomach was growling. The door to the kitchen opened, and Chuck emerged, together with Galena and Irina, who had remained behind to help clean up (a Rafik was waiting outside to return them to the Café Cosmos). They were each carrying a plate of food. "We saved some for you," Chuck said, with a smile. "You earned it."

Chuck put down a plate with some cutlets and cold cuts. Galina set down a salad. Irina, who was last, put down a third plate, containing a fish omelet. I looked at Chuck, then at the two Soviet ladies, struggling to find words. Before I could speak, all three burst out laughing at my expense—Chuck had filled the ladies in on my secret. Playing along, I grabbed a fork, and scooped up a big chunk of the omelet into my mouth. "*Ochin vkusna,*" I said, rubbing my belly. "Very delicious."

And it was.

That night, sitting in the DCC as the night duty officer, I had time to reflect on the day's events. I had missed the various meetings with Ambassador Matlock (including the personal inspectors-only talk) but was present for the formal part of the ceremony, which Doug Englund kicked off with a welcoming speech. "When I first arrived in Votkinsk in May of last year," Doug observed, "this place was an empty field. Today, when much has been done by both sides, we are opening the beautifully built living complex and inspection workplace. The labor put into this, as you can see, is of the highest quality and reflects the serious attention of both sides towards fulfillment of the Treaty. But more importantly," Doug added, "we have built this together. From the very first day, we have worked in a spirit of cooperation." Doug mentioned that there had been some difficulties, which were resolved "without irritation." Doug then acknowledged the crowd. "The numbers of people in attendance here is also a sign that much has been accomplished and in various areas. We are thankful for the warmth and sincere friendship with which we were met here."[11]

Ambassador Matlock spoke next from prepared remarks. He thanked the Soviets for the quality of the living quarters. "The opening of the village," he said, "is important not only for American specialists and their Soviet colleagues. It shows everyone that a very serious treaty for the destruction of missiles is being carried out." Ambassador Matlock noted that the Open House had provided him with an opportunity to visit Udmurtia for the first time. "I am glad," he concluded, "that I am experiencing your kind hospitality. I can admire the beauty of the area and become better acquainted with the people of the Republic."

Other speeches followed, delivered by various Soviet officials as well as the Vice President of Hughes, Richard Mannheimer. The penultimate speech was delivered by General Medvedev, the Commander of the Soviet Nuclear Risk Reduction Center. "Two years ago," the General said, "few people on earth would have suggested that in Votkinsk or in Magna, near the gates of missile factories, groups of specialists would observe the exit of products. Less than

*US Ambassador to the Soviet Union, Jack Matlock, addresses
the crowd at the US Open House, June 10, 1989.*

that," he continued, "that the Ambassador himself would have ventured to be in Udmurtia, at the gates of such a factory. Nevertheless, today it is a reality."

But the best speech, in my opinion, was the last, delivered by Anatoli Chernenko's boss, A. M. Demidov. "We constructed these buildings with great pleasure," he said. "The necessity arose based on the successful political dialogue of our countries' leaders. In all phases of the construction, there was complete mutual understanding, which allowed us to get to know each other better. There are trees of friendship planted here last year with Mr. Jerry Porter. In these homes," he concluded, "may it be warm in the winter and cool in the summer."

The next night we invited the Soviet translators and escorts who had assisted us in the Open House to the Roosevelt building for a party in their honor. Chuck Biasotti put together some snacks, and we had buckets full of ice-cold soda and beer to wash them down. Someone brought a white kitten, named Vasya, who had been presented to the Americans during the Open House by the children of the Votkinsk Music School, a traditional Russian gesture to ensure that no misfortunes would befall us in our new homes. The kitten quickly found its way to the food, prompting a demand by Chuck that it be removed from the room.

Around 8 PM one of the Hughes inspectors hung a disco ball from the ceiling, and another assumed the role of DJ, playing music from an impromptu sound system. Furniture was cleared out of the center of the main room, and for the next few hours American and Soviets alike had a good, old fashioned dance party.

I spent most of the evening circulating, making sure to thank each and every one of the persons involved in making the Open House a success, American and Soviet alike. I then retreated to a far corner, and sat back, sipping a beer, and watching the festivities. Soon I noticed a presence nearby, and looking over, saw the hulking figure of Doug Englund, beer in hand, as he sat down next to me.

"Sally Horn wouldn't know what to think of this," he said, gesturing over to where young Soviet and American men and women were dancing, talking, and enjoying life.

"No one would," I replied.

Doug chuckled, took a sip of beer, and nodded. "No, I guess you're right," he said. "But that's their problem." He looked over at me and smiled. "*Zayabis!*"

I raised my beer in salute.

"*Zayabis!*"

CHAPTER SIX

The Year of Living Dangerously, Part Two

*A Soviet 6-axle railcar is positioned in the CargoScan facility
for tests of the X-Ray imaging system, December 1989.*

"Poverty comes from man's injustice to his fellow man"

LEO TOLSTOY

Perestroika's Long, Hot Summer

ON APRIL 29, 1989, Secretary of Defense Dick Cheney appeared on "Evans & Novak," a CNN news program, where he discussed the political situation in the Soviet Union, and in particular the difficulties faced by Mikhail Gorbachev in implementing his perestroika and glasnost initiatives. In the interview, which was recorded the previous day, Cheney said "My personal view is that the task that he [Gorbachev] set for himself of trying to fundamentally reform the Soviet system is incapable of occurring. If I had to guess today," Cheney continued, "I would guess that he would ultimately fail. That is to say that he will not be able to reform the Soviet economy to turn it into an efficient, modern society. And that when that happens, he's likely to be replaced by somebody who will be far more hostile than he's been in terms of his attitude towards the West."[1]

Cheney's comments put a public face on what the national security officials in the newly ensconced administration of President George H. W. Bush secretly thought but to which, in the interests of diplomacy, it had not given voice.[2] The Bush White House had been struggling to articulate an official stance on where it stood with Gorbachev and perestroika; Cheney's impolitic comments forced their hand. On May 1, at the advice of National Security Advisor Brent Scowcroft, President Bush publicly stated that his administration "wanted to see perestroika succeed."[3]

For Gorbachev and his inner circle, one of the most pressing challenges facing perestroika was the issue of economic reform, which in turn entailed the issue of bringing defense spending under control. In a meeting with the Central Committee plenum in 1989, Gorbachev highlighted the dangers of out-of-control defense spending, noting that while the 11th Five Year Plan, covering the years 1986–1990, called for a 40 percent increase in defense spending, the national income was only projected to grow some 22 percent.[4]

In a telling exchange between US Secretary of State James Baker and Soviet Foreign Minister Eduard Shevardnadze during Baker's trip to Moscow in early May 1989, the US Secretary of State urged his Soviet counterpart to "publish your defense budget, so that when you announce fourteen- or nineteen-percent reductions, we know what baseline you're working from."

"Well, you know, we'd like to know that information too," Shevardnadze replied. "And I think we're going to have to find it out and reveal it, because we're going to be required to say something on this subject to the Congress of People's Deputies."[5]

Implementing glasnost, it seemed, was a problem even for the most senior Soviet leadership.

Bringing defense spending under control was a top policy imperative for Mikhail Gorbachev. He had already set things in motion when, in an announcement before the United Nations General Assembly on December 8, 1988, he pledged to reduce the size of the Soviet military by 500,000, investing the money saved into the Soviet civilian economy.[6] This move was done in concert with the Soviet withdrawal from Afghanistan, which was completed in February 1989, ending a ten-year misadventure which had cost thousands of Soviet lives and billions of dollars.

The US treated the Soviet announcements as meaningless political gestures. Ronald Reagan's Secretary of State, George P. Shultz, responded to Gorbachev's UN announcement by noting that even after the reductions, the Soviets would retain superiority in important categories, and that "there will be a lot of negotiating to do" before the US and Soviet Union would reach an equitable military balance.[7] And when informed about the Soviet intention to withdraw from Afghanistan, deputy CIA director Robert Gates expressed his doubts, noting that "What the bear has eaten, he never spits out."[8]

Another area on which Gorbachev placed great emphasis when it came to reducing Soviet defense expenditures was arms control. The INF Treaty had paved the way for even greater cuts in the respective strategic nuclear arsenals of both the US and Soviet Union, but by the end of the Reagan administration, talks over a strategic arms reduction treaty (START) treaty had bogged down over accounting for air-launched cruise missiles. In an example of how glasnost was transforming Soviet decision making, the Soviet Research Institute for Aviation Systems sent a letter to the key defense decision makers making the case that the Soviets would be better off endorsing the US position. Moreover, the Soviet Foreign Ministry was asked to weigh in on the issue, and subsequently took the lead in preparing a new Soviet negotiating position which the Soviets were prepared to table once the START treaty negotiations resumed following the installation of the new Presidential administration of George H. W. Bush.[9]

The Soviets had been heartened when, during the initial meeting of Baker and Shevardnadze in Vienna, Austria in March 1989, Baker had informed his Soviet counterpart that the Bush administration's review of the START negotiations was progressing and could expect to be completed by the end of April.[10] But April came to a close, and all the Soviets got was Dick Cheney's dark prognosis, prompting Shevardnadze to complain to his aides, "Are the Americans willing to do *nothing* to help us? Are *we* the ones who have to make all the moves? We take these huge steps, and all we hear from Washington is '*More! More! You must do more!*'"[11]

Faced with zero evidence of any policy initiative coming out of Washington, Gorbachev took matters into his own hands. During his meeting with James Baker in Moscow in early May 1989, Gorbachev stated that he was preparing to announce the unilateral withdrawal of 500 Soviet short-range ballistic missiles from eastern Europe. For Baker, Gorbachev's announcement could not have been more unwelcome. The US was at that very moment embroiled in a policy dispute with its NATO allies over the future of the Lance nuclear-armed short-range missile system. The US was looking to upgrade the existing force of 88 missiles based in West Germany. Not only did the West German government adamantly oppose any Lance modernization on its soil, but it was also pushing for the elimination of the Lance altogether.[12]

Gorbachev told Baker that this initial disarmament should not be viewed by the US as being politically motivated, but rather as the first step in the elimination of all short-range nuclear forces from Europe, including the Lance missile. Baker, however, viewed Gorbachev's initiative as just that—politically motivated—a view that was shared by Brent Scowcroft and others in the Bush White House.[13]

The US Ambassador to the Soviet Union, Jack Matlock, pressed the new Bush administration to exploit the openings created by glasnost and perestroika by engaging in a summit with Gorbachev at the earliest possible opportunity. However, Baker, Scowcroft and other presidential advisors resisted, instead pushing the President to respond to Gorbachev's initiative with one of his own, in this case a proposal to implement the Open Skies initiative, first put forward during the administration of President Dwight Eisenhower in the late 1950s. The American initiative was met with dismay by the Soviets.[14]

Jack Matlock's visit to Votkinsk from June 9–10 had been a period of isolated calm in an otherwise stormy sea of US-Soviet relations. By the end of the month, the US Ambassador had been called back to Washington, DC for routine consultations. While he was troubled by the slow pace taken by the Bush administration in getting a Soviet policy in place and ready for implementation, Matlock was even more disturbed by what he viewed as the growing vulnerability of Mikhail Gorbachev to the very forces of instability that had been unleashed through his policies of glasnost and perestroika. On the plane ride back to the US, Matlock wrote down six key questions that needed to be answered in this regard.

First, Matlock addressed the election of the Congress of People's Deputies. Gorbachev called these elections a turning point. "Is he right?" Matlock asked. It was too early to tell, he noted. But the elections had unlocked forces which, if not given a proper platform, could rise and challenge the supreme Soviet authority. Gorbachev needed to be careful.

Second, how threatening is what Matlock called the "negative tendencies"— the bare shelves in stores, budget deficits, and ethnic and national unrest? From the Ambassador's point of view, these were very threatening indeed, especially if they could coalesce into a singular source of anger and frustration. Again, Gorbachev would need to tread carefully.

Third, Matlock questioned the viability of Gorbachev as the Soviet leader over the course of the next five years. And if Gorbachev was ousted, what forces would topple him? The Ambassador believed that the election of the Supreme Soviet, and Gorbachev's installation at the head of the entity, all but guaranteed that he would survive his five-year term. The worst threat would come from the Congress of People's Deputies itself, and its ability to oust Gorbachev in the next elections.

Fourth, what would be the consequences of Gorbachev being removed from power? A tragedy for the Soviet people, Matlock believed, but not for the United States.

Fifth, is there an organized opposition to perestroika? From a local and regional perspective, Matlock noted, there was some pushback. But on a national level, perestroika was still received with open arms. This could change, however, if conditions did not improve.

And, finally, point six—will the Communist Party apparatchiks acquiesce in their own demise? Not willingly, Matlock concluded, noting that they may not be given a choice.

Reflecting on his six points as he left the plane in Washington, DC, Jack Matlock observed that "it had dawned on me that the [Soviet] empire's reinforcing rods might soon disintegrate."[15]

The US Ambassador's concerns were echoed by some in attendance at the Congress of People's Deputies. When the decision was made to limit the number of speeches that could be delivered, lest the proceedings become paralyzed by rhetoric, several of the deputies took offense. One of these, T. Kh. Gdlyan, the representative from the Moscow 25th Territorial District, sought to have his speech published so that his voice would not be silenced. Gdlyan's speech was published in the August 3, 1989 issue of *Radiotechnolog*. (Soviet authorities later agreed to publish the texts of all the speeches that were not allowed to be given. *Radiotechnolog*'s decision to put Gdlyan's speech to print was made prior to the decision, and as such represented a moment of journalistic integrity and courage typical of the time of perestroika.)

"An analysis of the status of today's affairs," Gdlyan wrote, "brings us to the conclusion that the country finds itself not in a pre-crisis state, about which we often hear at the official party-state level, but rather in the deepest crisis in the area of economics, politics, ideology, legality, and morality."

> Society is in a fever; it is approaching the verge of breakdown and destruction. A certain situation arises when the "upper echelons" manifest indecisiveness and inconsistency on finding a way out of the blind-alley they created, and the "lower echelons" do not want to accept the existing, clearly abnormal, situation. Such instability and social tension cannot hold out for long and should be settled, by our estimation, in the course of one—maximum two—years. If we representatives of the people do not know how to change the prevailing destructive tendencies in the social-political sphere, then we will inevitably come to the establishment of a regime of individual power—that is, to a dictatorship or even to chaos and anarchy.

The social tension described by Deputy Gdlyan may have manifested itself among his constituents in Moscow, but in Votkinsk the "fever" Gdlyan described had not yet taken hold. There was, however, a general malaise that had overcome the citizenry. According to an article, "At the CPSU city committee," published by *Leninski Put'* on July 28, 1989, when the Votkinsk City Communist Party met that month to discuss the results of the first six months of "new management conditions" imposed by perestroika on overall economic productivity, the results were decidedly mixed. While 104% of the sales plan was achieved, and 105% of the planned capital invested made, these numbers were achieved more from labor productivity, which was 126% higher than in the preceding year, rather than efficient managerial operations.

The numbers were deceiving. Many industrial establishments had failed to meet their plans, and as a result, there were shortfalls in the provision of paid services to the population of Votkinsk. Construction projects lagged, with only four of ten planned projects having been completed. Moreover, the impressive sales figures were achieved almost solely on the back of increased alcoholic beverage sales. As the City Party Committee noted, "the public continues to experience difficulties in obtaining many goods. There are many deficiencies in the way consumer and community services are provided to Votkinsk residents."

Another *Leninski Put'* article, published on August 1, 1989, and entitled "We and Perestroika," noted that in the city's downtown area, the Votkinsk Production Association had installed a large structure designed to display propaganda supportive of the policies of perestroika. According to a member of a committee sent out to evaluate the effectiveness of communist party propaganda on the city populace, the propaganda stand "is composed of about twenty panels that proclaim Soviet power up, down, to the right, and to the left."

However, the committee member noted, "the content of the propaganda clearly does not correspond to what one sees in the area or even the panels themselves. 'My factory is my pride!' announces one of them, oblivious to the fact that it has holes in it. 'The party's policy is our policy!' pronounces another, and the words are underlined, but the sign is rusty. 'Quality is the guarantee of progress' asserts a third, but it is overgrown with weeds. The entire structure," the committee member observed, "looks very much like a fairy tale giant, fair and mighty, except that its legs are caught in the weeds, and it cannot move ahead to the place the 'progress' poster is calling him."

Here, in the words of a local reporter, was the living manifestation of Jack Matlock's "negative tendencies," a precursor to the very "breakdown and destruction" Deputy Gdlyan was warning about. Secretary of Defense Dick Cheney had predicted the inability of Mikhail Gorbachev to successfully implement his perestroika initiatives. In Votkinsk, the accuracy of this prediction was being played out before the US inspectors who intermingled with the city's populace daily. This intimacy, and the insights into the difficulties faced by Soviet authority in fulfilling the lofty goals perestroika promoted, were becoming an embarrassment to the local Soviet officials.

Perestroika Increases the Inspectors' Leisure Pursuits

"AN INSPECTOR is not a tourist," General Lajoie once told a Soviet reporter. Even so, the life of an OSIA inspector working in the Soviet Union was not all work, no play. In that same interview, Lajoie noted that the inspection team that he was on, its work finished, was scheduled to attend a concert at a local cathedral. Other inspection teams took in the sights at the various locations they were travelling to, time and circumstances permitting.

But at the end of the day, an inspector was not a tourist.

A portal monitor, on the other hand, was different. According to the Inspection Protocol of the INF Treaty, "Inspectors carrying out inspection activities pursuant to paragraph 6 of Article XI of the treaty (i.e., portal monitoring inspections) shall be allowed to travel within 50 kilometers from the inspection site with the permission of the in-country escort, and as considered necessary by the inspected party, shall be accompanied by the in-country escort. Such travel shall be taken solely as a leisure activity."

It seems that, in accordance with the provisions of the INF treaty, portal monitors were, in fact, tourists.

Even though leisure activity was a treaty right, from the very start the US inspectors ran afoul of the reality that they had been plopped down in a remote corner of the Soviet Union which, prior to their arrival, had been closed to all foreigners. The region was neither prepared to receive 30 American inspectors, nor equipped to provide anything more than incidental tourism of the most rudimentary nature. During the initial talks between Generals Lajoie and Medvedev about leisure activities in Votkinsk held in May 1988, even the Soviet side was hindered by both the lack of adequate maps (even the Soviet General only had access to a tourist map) and authority—Votkinsk was the sole purview of the Ministry of Defense Industry.

The US advanced party, which was in Votkinsk from June 19–July 1, 1988, was to get a better feel for what could be expected by the inspectors, who would be living in temporary accommodations in downtown Votkinsk. The Soviet escorts from the Votkinsk factory delineated an "escort-free" zone in the downtown area where the inspectors were free to roam on their own, and where personal photography could be undertaken without restrictions other than the blanket prohibition against filming military or military-industrial objects and locations. The Votkinsk Factory's downtown plant was located to the east of the "escort-free" zone, and readily visible to inspectors. Inspectors taking personal photographs were instructed to position themselves so that the factory was not in the background of any images.

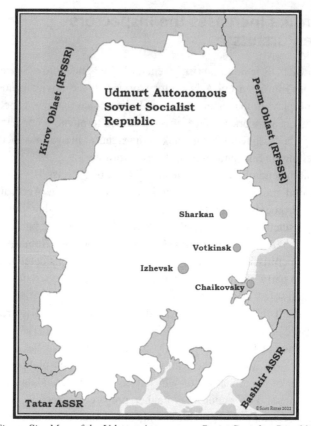

Figure Six: Map of the Udmurt Autonomous Soviet Socialist Republic

The first few weeks found the inspectors taking full advantage of the access they had been granted to Votkinsk. This all changed on the morning of July 18, when the Soviets informed the inspectors that due to a "Civil Defense Exercise," the Americans could not leave their quarters without an escort, and that all photography was prohibited. The restrictions were tightened further on July 19, when the Soviets informed the inspectors that they would require 24 advanced notice for an inspector to walk around Votkinsk, in effect terminating the "escort-free" zone.

The crux of the problem appeared to be information that the Soviets had received about the treatment of Soviet inspectors by the US in-country escorts in Magna, Utah. Colonel Englund investigated the issue, and indeed found that the Soviet inspectors were being subjected to an overly restrictive escort regime, with no fewer than eight US in-country escorts following each Soviet group that travelled inside their 50-kilometer leisure zone. There was also a total restriction on personal photography. Colonel Englund immediately pressed for the US escorts to alter their procedures. This took time to implement, given the US

The Year of Living Dangerously, Part Two*   227

government's own concerns about national security and the need to coordinate with various agencies when it came to altering security arrangements.

On 28 July, while I was on duty at the temporary portal facility, I spoke with Colonel Englund about the situation in Magna. Upon hearing that the Soviet inspectors were very pleased with their arrangements regarding leisure activities, I called Vyacheslav Lopatin over. Lopatin had taken the lead on imposing the restrictions on leisure travel in Votkinsk. I placed a call to Magna, Utah, and put Lopatin in direct contact with the head of the Soviet inspection team. When he hung up, Lopatin expressed his satisfaction with the US treatment of Soviet inspectors in Magna and told me he would endeavor to ensure that the treatment of US inspectors in Votkinsk would be approached by the Soviets in the same spirit.

On July 29, all restrictions were lifted, and conditions returned to the way they were when the US inspectors first arrived in Votkinsk. The issue of reciprocity was to be a sensitive one going forward, with both sides sensitive to any restrictions on the treaty right of leisure activity for their respective inspection teams. Indeed, one of my standing tasks upon rotating back to the US was to travel to Magna, Utah to get a feel for the US escort procedures there, with an eye to making sure nothing was being imposed on the Soviets that could create a backlash on the US inspectors in Votkinsk.

The day prior to the restrictions being lifted, Colonel Connell, accompanied by Barrett Haver and two inspectors from Team Gothreau (one of the 10-man inspection teams that helped man the portal monitoring facility until the Hughes inspectors could be brought on board) met with the City Executive Committee of Votkinsk. The meeting was at the invitation of the Soviets, who were genuinely interested in finding ways to get the US inspectors better acquainted with the citizens of Votkinsk. Up until that time, other than incidental contact, all interactions between the US inspectors and the Soviets had been conducted on an official basis. The City Executive Committee was keen on ending that, on providing the inspectors with a green light to interact with the residents of Votkinsk on a much less restrictive basis. The City Executive Committee made numerous recommendations to the inspectors about which organizations would be receptive to meeting with the Americans.

The meeting between the inspectors and the City Executive Committee opened the doors of Votkinsk to the Americans. The inspectors quickly established close relations with the American and English clubs of several local schools, including the local Musical Pedagogical Institute. Inspectors gathered mushrooms in the local forest under the watchful eyes of their escorts, who steered them away from the less desirable variants. Inspectors attended movies and theatrical presentations, and in early September began showing up at a weekly outdoor dance held at the Palace of Culture, which they attended until mid-October, when the cold weather brought an end to the festivities.

Inspectors attended services at the local Orthodox church and, in a sign that the times were, indeed, "a changing," attended a rock concert and a newly released film, both of which contained nudity, a deviation from the norm for conservative Soviet society. As the temperature dropped, the Soviets turned the sports stadium in downtown Votkinsk into an open-air skating rink. Many inspectors purchased skates from the local stores and joined the citizens of Votkinsk in either leisurely skating on surprisingly smooth ice or trying their hand at pick-up hockey games with the local youth.

The Americans also began their relationship with the Club of International Friendship from School #10. After a meet and greet event where a delicious buffet was prepared by the Soviet hosts, the teachers and some of the older students invited the inspectors to a game of basketball, setting off a rivalry of sorts (the Soviets won) and motivating the Americans to organize a basketball team capable of representing the United States with honor. Eventually the US basketball team gained enough renown (after thrashing the School #10 team 168-72) to be challenged to a game with the Votkinsk city champions. The inspectors were defeated before a standing-room only crowd by a score of 73–45. The inspectors, however, noted that most of their regular squad were not present, and asked for a rematch, which was granted. Later, with the full squad on hand, and before a capacity crowd, the inspectors put on a much more respectable showing, losing 97–91 in overtime.

In mid-October, in a change of policy that reflected the improved relations between the US inspectors and their Soviet hosts, the city of Izhevsk was opened to the inspectors for sightseeing and social events. Ostensibly outside the 50-kilometer leisure zone, the city of Izhevsk offered a greater range of activities than Votkinsk. We were quick to report this change of heart to the US escorts in Magna, who were encouraged to find appropriate venues for the Soviet inspectors that fell outside the 50-kilometer zone. In their inaugural visit, US inspectors were taken on a tour of the Izhevsk Factory Museum, where they visited the *Okhota* (Hunting) outlet and shown hand-crafted shotguns which were, according to the Soviets, available for purchase by the US inspectors at prices ranging between 500–1,000 Rubles. Several inspectors expressed an interest in buying a shotgun, creating a whole new "tasker" for personnel back in the US, as procedures had to be worked out with the State Department and the ATF for importing firearms from the Soviet Union.

In a clear sign that the inspectors were winning over the population of Votkinsk, on November 7, 1988, the Soviets invited a US delegation to attend the parade in honor of the October Revolution of 1917 that brought the Bolsheviks into power (the revolution took place on October 25 according to the "old" calendar). The inspectors were afforded a position near the official reviewing tribunal, located next to the Lenin monument in downtown Votkinsk. The one-factory-town nature of Votkinsk was amply demonstrated by the fact that it took more than an hour for the various departments of the Votkinsk Machine Building Plant to march on past. The intimacy enjoyed by the inspectors and townsfolk played out in public as many people—parents of the school children we had befriended, new friends, and casual acquaintances—spontaneously stepped out of the ranks of the marchers to present the American inspectors with flowers and balloons.

But the moment that cemented the relationship between the US inspectors and the citizens of Votkinsk was the participation by a team of inspectors in a talent competition sponsored by the "Club of Jolly and Inventive People." The opposing side was a combined team drawn from the Young Communist League (Komsomol) of the City Trade and Consumer Services organizations. The invitation was extended on November 12, giving the Americans a scant week to prepare for the competition, which was scheduled for the night of November 19.

John Sartorius took the lead in organizing the team, which included Mary Jordan (a Hughes linguist, who was elected team captain), fellow Hughes inspectors Tim Kubik, Gary Teetsell, Fred Coy, Jim Stewart, and Anne Mortenson, joined by Mark Dues, and Rob Sederman from OSIA/ESD. Because the event was to be conducted entirely in the Russian language, the Americans asked for help from the Soviets, who provided three English-speaking escorts— Marina Khatiashvili, Mikhail Ivanov, and Boris Nevzorov. Doug Englund was invited to serve on a five person "jury" which would be judging the event.

The event was held at the *Pobeda* ("Victory") theater, which had seating for 500 persons. For this event, it was filled to standing room only capacity with a crowd estimated in excess of 800 persons packed into the viewing area, with hundreds more left standing outside, unable to gain entry.

The Soviet team was clearly composed of experienced veterans of past competitions, and they excelled at the improvisational aspects of the competition, where the team captains and their representatives were called upon to spontaneously respond to situations presented to them by the event moderator. Even in the formal portion of the competition, the Soviets performed well, bringing down the house with skits that made fun of Soviets and Americans alike. For example, one Soviet "sight riddle" had three men dressed as Spanish explorers striking a resolute pose looking at the horizon. The US side was unable to get the answer, which was "Builders getting ready to begin construction of the Votkinsk Park of Rest and Culture."

Another Soviet skit portrayed an American inspector, named "*Polkovnik* (Colonel) Englund," wandering the streets of Votkinsk under heavy guard, "inspecting" everything, but clearly oblivious to everything going on around him, including black marketeers and prostitutes.

The American side responded with skits of their own, including an inspector attempting to learn the Russian language. ("I escaped from an insane asylum," "very yes" and "you are beautiful like a fire truck" were among the phrases the poor student, portrayed by Fred Coy, managed to utter to the crowd's delight.) The US also brought down the house with their renditions of inspectors trying to operate a Feya washing machine (a local Votkinsk product), Soviets smuggling baby carriages filled with babies out of the factory under the watchful eyes of inspectors (again, a reference to a local Votkinsk product), and inspectors, stripped to their shorts, in a Russian *banya* (bath), beating each other with heavy Russian brooms, causing obvious pain, while Mark Dues moaned "Are you sure you're doing this right?" (Russian *banyas* were known for their practice of lightly brushing the backs of the participants with birch branches to stimulate blood flow.)

The final US number, in the words of Doug Englund, "was a killer—a rendition of the Beatles' 'Yesterday' which had much of the audience joining in, followed by a stirring version of *Podvotkinskiye Vechera* (Votkinsk Nights—a take on the traditional Russian folk song, Moscow Nights) which spoke of being recruited in California where there was only 'sand, sun, and beaches,' and coming to Votkinsk, where there was only 'cold and snow, only snow, yes snow.'"

There wasn't a dry eye in the house.

"The Soviet team," Doug wrote back in a report on the evening's events to General Lajoie, "had a clear edge in their level of artistic achievement." Nevertheless, the US team won, by a score of 334–328, based upon what Doug described as "sheer energy and crowd reaction." But, Doug noted, "this was truly an event in which there were only winners: the friendly relations we have enjoyed with the other team both before and after the event; the talent and assistance provided by the participating Soviet escorts; and the heartfelt and spontaneous warmth demonstrated by the Soviet audience are all testimony to the fact that what came out of this event is immeasurably more than what went into it. Both sides have every right to take pride in something that was done very, very well."

Less than a week later, the US inspectors hosted 85 Soviets, consisting of colleagues from the Votkinsk factory and their families, and various members of the Votkinsk city government and community with whom the inspectors had grown close during their first few months in the Soviet Union, to what was billed as "First Annual Votkinsk Thanksgiving Celebration" in the main dining room of the Café Cosmos. The Hughes chef, Chuck Biasotti, worked with the staff of the Café Cosmos, to prepare a delicious spread of Russian *zavkuski* (hors d'oeuvres) along with a traditional American Turkey Day fare. The event was a great success.

As November turned into December, relations between the US inspectors, their counterparts at the Votkinsk Factory, and the citizens of Votkinsk only improved. Media attention grew, and the inspectors and their work in Votkinsk became a story line the Soviet press couldn't get enough of. The intensive social schedule, combined with the close working relationship exemplified by the participation of the Soviet linguists in the comedy competition, brought the inspectors and their social escorts even closer. The inspectors began inviting the escorts to attend "video nights" in the common room of their temporary quarters, where *Dr. Zhivago, Gone with the Wind,* and *Platoon* were shown at the request of the Soviets. (An American-selected film, *Doctor Strangelove,* was less well received by the Soviets, who couldn't comprehend how a story of nuclear war between the US and Soviet Union could be treated as a comedy.)

Unlike the factory workers-turned-treaty escorts who worked at the Portal Monitoring Facility, the Soviet social escorts were almost all from places other than Votkinsk. They were primarily recent college graduates who studied the English language and who were serving their two years of compulsory service in repayment of a free education. While most were recruited from Moscow, some came from Izhevsk as well as other regional university systems. Many had been drawn in by the prospect of working closely with Americans (some had believed they would be travelling to the United States as part of their work). None expected to be sent to Votkinsk, and life in such a remote location was as much a shock to them as to the US inspectors. While both sides were initially somewhat reticent about working in close proximity with people they were trained to view as potentially hostile (the Soviets had to report their interactions with the Americans to the First Directorate [Security] of the Votkinsk Factory, which was operating under the supervision of the local KGB, while the Americans were briefed to treat the Soviet social escorts—almost exclusively attractive young women—as probable sexual entrapment agents known as "Swallows"), eventually common sense took over and, to the extent permitted under the anti-fraternization rules strictly enforced by both the US and Soviet sides, relations between the US inspectors and the Soviet social escorts became friendly, if not quite friendships.

On December 7 the Soviet Republic of Armenia was struck by an earthquake that killed between 30–50,000 people and injured another 130,000. Hundreds of thousands were made homeless, and refugees were sent to communities throughout the Soviet Union, where temporary shelter was provided. As part of the effort to aid the Armenian refugees who had been sent to Votkinsk, the local authorities organized a *subotnik,* or working holiday, on December 17. Off duty US inspectors donated their time and labor to this effort, in addition to raising more than 700 Rubles (around $1,120 in US dollars) in voluntary contributions. The goodwill generated by this gesture was enormous.

Lieutenant Colonel Roy Peterson made his first trip to Votkinsk a memorable one by organizing an inspector choir which spent the days and weeks leading up to the Christmas holiday regaling various Soviet audiences with traditional Christmas carols. Appearances were made before the City Trade Council, various schools and on Christmas Eve, at the open-air market, where

Votkinsk residents politely watched as the inspectors worked their way through a repertoire of holiday classics.

On December 26 the Soviets from Department 162 hosted the US inspectors at a combined Christmas/New Year's celebration at the Café Cosmos, which was attended by more than 100 people. The Soviets provided their American guests with a wonderful dinner, and then entertained them with games, song, and dance. *Dedi Moroz* ("Father Frost," the Soviet Santa Claus, played by one of the Soviet factory workers) made an appearance to drop off gifts for the inspectors before being driven to the Portal Facility, where he visited with the US personnel on duty (as the duty officer that night, I can attest to how welcome this visit was).

As was the case in the United States, Christmas was a magical time for the Soviet citizens of Votkinsk. In every school, an elaborate Christmas pageant was staged for the children (the inspectors were invited to attend a few of these). On December 30, the Votkinsk City Council unveiled the "Fairy Tale City," a small village of ice sculptures erected especially for the Children on the main square in downtown Votkinsk. A dozen inspectors, including myself, attended this opening, and found our inner child liberated as we played with the kids among the elaborately carved statues. And on New Year's Eve, the Soviets opened their homes to the inspectors to bring in the new year with a spirit of friendship no one could have imagined when the treaty was signed a little more than a year past.

The Big Chill

AS GEOFFREY CHAUCER, the English poet, noted in his work *Troilus and Criseyde*, "There is an end to everything, to good things as well." This timeless aphorism applied with full force to the halcyon period of US-Soviet relations in Votkinsk that lasted from August through December 1988. On January 2, 1989, the pause button was hit on US leisure activities as the US inspectors undertook an "all hands" approach when it came to receiving the furniture shipments for the permanent US quarters then nearing completion outside the Votkinsk Missile Final Assembly Plant. When, a month and a half later, things returned to normal on the work front, the Soviets of Department 162 were perceptively less receptive to US requests for leisure activity.

The "no escort" zone in downtown Votkinsk continued to exist as advertised. However, the Soviets made clear that once the US inspectors left their temporary accommodations and moved into the permanent housing adjacent to the Portal Monitoring Facility, access to the City of Votkinsk would be granted on an "as requested" basis, and a Soviet escort would be required.

Requests for leisure activities outside the "no escort" zone, known as *zayafki*, were made in writing at least 24 hours prior to the Soviets, who would then arrange transportation and escorts, as required. The Soviets had assembled a list of regular activities, such as swimming, gym access, haircuts, and shopping, and US requests for these were almost always granted (the exceptions were when the establishments were closed).

Zayafki for other destinations, such as the city of Chaikovsky (within the 50-kilometer radius for permitted leisure travel, but located in the Perm *Oblast*, as opposed to the Udmurt Republic, and as such requiring additional coordination) required 48 hours or more notice but were almost always granted.

The first clue that there was a problem was when a routine request for a group of inspectors to eat a meal at the Ivrus Grotto Bar was denied. The Ivrus, a restaurant/club that had opened in September 1988, had become a regular destination for the inspectors (indeed, several dinner parties were hosted by the inspectors at the Ivrus in honor of the various short-term inspection teams that had supplemented on-site manpower in September–October 1988). The construction of the Ivrus was sponsored in part by the Votkinsk Factory Association, and was located in the Pervyi Posyolok neighborhood, home to several dormitories used by unmarried workers of the Votkinsk Factory, including all of the social escorts, from which the Ivrus hoped to draw a regular clientele.

Modelled after a similar establishment in the city of Kazan, the Ivrus was a modernistic restaurant whose walls were constructed to look like the interior of a cave. With a capacity of around 40 people, the Ivrus offered a relatively intimate dining experience comprised of ethnic Armenian dishes, such as shashlik (skewered chunks of lamb and/or chicken), lyulya kebab (minced meat served on skewers), and khashlama (Armenian lamb stew). The food was expensive when compared to other establishments but was of high quality and impeccably prepared and presented.

The Ivrus had a well-kept bar, where customers could purchase drinks, and a separate room for dancing. The dance floor could be converted into a video room, where customers could eat a meal while watching the latest releases. While the inspectors were attracted to the menu, of even greater interest was the fact that the Ivrus always had a vibrant crowd of locals who gave it a charm that made it an attractive destination for inspectors looking for a change from their routine. By mid-February 1989, with the furniture shipment and installation issues under control, several inspectors submitted a *zayafka* to eat dinner at the Ivrus. The *zayafka* was turned down. When pressed as to the reason behind the rejection, the Soviets responded with one word: "hooliganism."

The local authorities had been tracking an increase in the crime rate and attributed it to gangs of idle youths who liked to congregate in so-called "video halls" where, in the guise of watching movies, would engage in so-called "anti-social behavior"—drinking, smoking, and doing drugs, which led to petty theft, burglary, and assault. To combat this behavior, the Soviet authorities closed the "video halls" which, by extension, meant denying the Ivrus one of its most profitable activities. With the videos gone, the Ivrus began to attract a harder crowd composed of disenchanted young men and women who would get drunk at the bar and disrupt the affairs of other customers. The Ivrus, in the minds of the Soviet authorities, had gone from being a first-rate destination to the front line of a modern crime spree. Accordingly, the Soviet authorities placed it off limits to the inspectors.

Concerns about hooliganism drove the Soviets to curtail the freedom of access the inspectors had previously enjoyed throughout Votkinsk to more controlled and contained encounters. The inspectors, naturally, balked at these new restrictions, and tracking the number of rejected *zayafki* became a task for the OSIA duty officers. The issue of rejected *zayafki* even took on a personal aspect—after I had been denied permission to observe the election polling on May 21, I reported the incident to Colonel Englund, who opted to escalate the matter, formally requesting an explanation from the Soviets as to why my request had been denied. The Soviets appeared to take umbrage at the complaint, and I found myself on the receiving end of several personally requested *zayafki*, including to an appointment I had made with a local dressmaker who was going to make a dress for my wife. A truce was called as both sides prepared for the Open House and Ambassador Matlock's visit. But the issue of rejected *zayafki* continued to simmer, waiting only for the opportune time to rear its ugly head.

A Matter of the Heart

THERE IS A RUSSIAN SAYING, "You don't know where you'll find it, where you'll lose it" (*Nye znayesh, gdye naidyosh, gdye poteryesh*), that best captures the role fate plays in the greater scheme of things. This holds true when it comes to the leisure experiences of the US inspectors in Votkinsk. In January 1989, Richard McGibbon, a verification technology specialist employed by Sandia National Laboratory, was in Votkinsk helping with the installation of the Portal Monitoring Facility. Richard, along with other inspectors, was interviewed by a Soviet journalist, who quoted Richard as commenting on Votkinsk's "sea of snow," an observation that touched on what Richard said was a very positive experience in the Soviet Union.

On March 11, 1989, Richard experienced severe chest pain while performing his duties at the Portal Monitoring Facility. Dave Pearson, the Hughes Physician's Assistant on duty, determined that Richard's condition was serious enough to ask the Soviets to evacuate him via ambulance to the Votkinsk Factory Hospital in downtown Votkinsk. There, the Soviet doctors quickly assessed that Richard needed specialist care that could only be provided at the Izhevsk Cardiology Center. Dave Pearson, accompanied by Zoi Haloulakos, travelled with Richard in the Soviet ambulance as he was transported to Izhevsk, and remained with him while he was evaluated by a staff of experienced cardiologists.

It was quickly determined that Richard would need to be medically evacuated to a US military facility in Landstuhl, Germany for treatment. While the details of his transportation were being worked out, Richard remained under the close care of the Izhevsk cardiologists, who provided a life-saving non-surgical intervention to stabilize Richard so that he could be transported to Germany. By March 15, 1989, Richard's condition had improved to the point that he could travel under medical observation. A US Air Force C-9 Nightingale Medivac aircraft based out of Rhein-Main Air Base in West Germany flew direct to Izhevsk Airport, where Dave Pearson and the Izhevsk cardiologists handed Richard over to the care of the US Air Force onboard medical team. Richard was flown to Ramstein Air Base, where he was met by Mike Wilking, the local Hughes representative based out of FOE, Frankfurt, who accompanied Richard to the Landstuhl military hospital. Richard later fully recovered, although he was never to return to Votkinsk.

Richard McGibbon's heart attack brought the US inspectors in contact with an entire group of people which we otherwise would never have had the opportunity to meet—the doctors and nurses of the Izhevsk Cardiology Center. Given the nature of Richard's work, we needed to always maintain a constant watch over him, which meant we had two US inspectors at the Izhevsk Cardiology Center on a full-time basis, working 12-hour shifts. Richard was under sedation most of this time, so we had little to do but wait by his bedside as he was cared for by the Soviet medical professionals. We got to know the doctors and nurses by name, but because they were consummate professionals and we could never leave Richard's side, there was no opportunity for the kind of expanded conversations that would normally occur when people are put in proximity with one another.

With Richard safely loaded onto the C-9 MedEvac and headed home, we inspectors returned to our normal work schedules. We did take the time to single out the work of one of the Soviet escorts, Alla Zotova, who had provided stellar linguistic support throughout Richard's time in Izhevsk. The US inspection team was normally quite reticent about praising the work of our Soviet counterparts to their leadership, out of concern that this might bring unwanted attention from the Soviet security services, who might read malign intent behind our praise. But the work of Alla during this time was truly exceptional, so much so that we violated our own policies by writing a formal letter of appreciation for the support she provided to US inspectors and Soviet cardiologists alike.

The letter signed and delivered, we moved to put the McGibbon affair behind us. However, within a week of Richard's departure from Izhevsk, we received an invitation from Dr. Yevgeny Odiyankov, the Chief Cardiologist of the Izhevsk Cardiology Center, to attend a reception "to get to better know one another." I brought the invitation to the attention of Doug Englund, who thought it might be a good idea to attend. We submitted a *zayakfa* to Department 162, which was approved.

Doug Englund led a group of six inspectors to Izhevsk, where Dr. Odiyankov and his staff were waiting for us in the lobby of the Center. It was a very polite, somber affair—uncomfortably so. We exchanged pleasantries. We sat in silence. Dr. Odiyankov, sensing the mood, leaned over to Doug Englund. "Our leader, Mr. Gorbachev, has declared a war on alcohol. As good communists, we must support our leader. Will you join us in this struggle?"

Doug and I had talked before arriving about the alcohol policy then in effect with OSIA. As the resident counterintelligence guy, he looked to me for an adequate interpretation. "Diplomatic toasts only" was my reply.

After Dr. Odiyankov spoke, Doug looked at me. "Looks like we're in the clear." I nodded. Doug turned to Dr. Odiyankov and announced his pleasure in supporting abstinence.

The smile on Dr. Odiyankov's face stretched ear to ear. "Yes, in due course. But first there is the struggle. As a soldier you understand this." Dr. Odiyankov signaled to his staff, who produced several cases full of Vodka bottles. "We have many enemies to kill!"

The night went downhill from there—I recall being led to a hall, where a band was playing rock music and the staff, including many lovely female doctors and nurses, were waiting to dance. The other inspectors, including two female interpreters, were similarly ambushed. From a diplomatic standpoint, the affair was a great success. From a counterintelligence perspective, especially considering the rampant violations of the OSIA alcohol policy taking place, the meeting with the cardiologists was a disaster.

When we received a second invitation a few weeks later to join Dr. Odiyankov and his staff for a ride on the Cardiology Center's boat on the Kama River, Doug looked at the invitation with trepidation. We both agreed that we would be on our guard for any repeat of the Vodka ambush that we had walked into at the Cardiology Center. After Doug and I, accompanied by four other inspectors, were settled in our seats, and the vessel underway, Dr. Odiyankov confronted us with the following question: "We Soviets are proud of the product of our labor. Here, Armenian cognac is the very best. But in the West, Hennessy is the favored brand."

Dr. Odiyankov proceeded to produced two bottles, one of Armenian cognac, the other Hennessy. "We respect your judgement and ask that you help us resolve this question." Doug looked at me. It was just a single toast. What harm could befall us? I nodded.

Glasses were filled. We drained our respective drinks and announced our readiness to pronounce judgment. "Not so fast," Dr. Odiyankov said. "Issues of this magnitude require intense research. Final judgment must await the emptying of the bottles!"

The glasses were recharged two more times, at which point, our heads spinning, Doug and I issued our unanimous verdict—the Armenian cognac was far superior.

Cue Dr. Odiyankov's smile. "Perfect! Because we just happen to have a case of it which, in honor of the recognition of this Soviet victory over the West, must be consumed!"

My memory blurred after that point...I recall a village, shashlik, a *banya*, and being beaten half to death by birch branches. I remember a headache.

Thus, from Richard McGibbon's misfortune, was born an enduring friendship between the US inspectors and the men and women of the Izhevsk cardiology center. The inspectors made regular trips to Izhevsk to socialize with the doctors and nurses, albeit it in a much more civilized and constrained fashion than the first wild encounter. We also would regularly sail up and down the Kama River onboard their boat, swimming, fishing, and enjoying an outdoor picnic among great company.

Independence Day

ON JUNE 14, 1989, Doug Englund sat down with Alexandr Sokolov and Anatoli Tomilov to discuss what a resulting memorandum for the record described as "a variety of outstanding issues." It was the first substantive meeting between the US and Soviet sides since the Open House and Ambassador Matlock's visit. One of Doug's goals in this meeting was to take the temperature regarding the current state of US-Soviet relations in Votkinsk. Despite the success of the Open House and the forays with the doctors and nurses, otherwise relations between inspector and inspected seemed to be stuck at the same tepid levels that had existed prior to that event. If this was indeed the case, Doug hoped to find out why.

The first issue raised by Doug was that of tests regarding the quality of the water used by inspectors at the Votkinsk Portal Monitoring Facility. Doug presented this as an issue of increasing political sensitivity—Soviet press had questioned the American inspectors about their use of imported water during the Open House. But the reality was that inspectors had a legitimate health concern when it came to the water supplied to them at the portal by the Missile Final Assembly Plant.

The US inspectors had been concerned about water quality from the moment they arrived in Votkinsk in July 1988. As a precautionary measure, inspectors were instructed to boil all water prior to consumption pending the outcome of tests performed on water samples that had been collected at the temporary housing facility, the portal area, and a spring near the temporary housing facility used by inspectors as a water source. These initial samples were taken out with Dr. Ryan, who served as the on-site medical officer in Votkinsk from July 2–15, 1988, as part of Team Guiler. Dr. Ryan had the samples tested by medical authorities at Rhein-Main Air Base in West Germany, which found that in all three instances, the water was contaminated with numerous "non-specific cultures" which could be eliminated by boiling the water.

Colonel Connell, the on-site commander at the time, was displeased with the methodology used in the taking and evaluation of the samples, and ordered a second sampling, which was taken out of Votkinsk by Dr. Knodel, who had replaced Dr. Ryan when Team Gothreau took over from Team Guiler in mid-July 1988. These samples were evaluated by the US Air Force Environmental Health Laboratory, at Lindsay Air Station, West Germany, which likewise found the water to be contaminated with cultures that could be eliminated through boiling.

While the second water sample had been shipped out of Votkinsk in August 1988, OSIA did not receive the results until mid-December 1988. The delay prompted the dispatch of a third water sample, taken from water taps used by US inspectors at the portal facility in early December. Hughes assumed responsibility for this test, which was contracted to the Battelle Europe Company for analysis. Unlike the findings for the previous two samples, the Battelle sample found dangerously high concentrations of polychlorinated biphenyls, or PCBs, a manmade chemical whose resistance to extreme temperature and pressure made it popular for use in electrical equipment like capacitors and transformers, and as hydraulic fluid and lubricants. PCBs were banned in the United States in 1979 due to the danger they posed to both human and environmental health. However, the Soviet Union continued to make wide use of the chemical, which explained the presence of PCBs in the Battelle water sample at a level of 85.5 parts per billion, well above the 1 part per billion standard in effect at the time in the Department of Defense for ground water (this standard has since been revised to .5 part per billion).

Because PCBs could not be removed from water by boiling, the US inspectors were immediately placed on notice to cease consuming water sourced from the portal. Measures were implemented to dispatch enough bottled water and soft drinks to Votkinsk to provide each inspector with two liters of water and two cans of soda per day, until which time a water filtration system could be installed at the Portal Monitoring Facility.

To design a water filtration system for the specific water conditions at the portal, Battelle requested that a specific water test kit be used to collect samples that would then be used by their personnel to fine tune the specific filtration requirements. After consulting with Anatoli Tomilov, Colonel Connell determined that all future water sampling would be done jointly with the Soviets, and directed that two test kits be brought in, one which would be returned to Battelle for evaluation, and the other which would be turned over to the Soviets for their own independent analysis. The sampling was done under the observation of factory personnel, and the US sample dispatched with the outbound rotation in April 1989. This sample, however, was seized by Soviet authorities in Moscow, who declared the samples to have been collected in violation of the treaty, despite having been jointly collected with factory personnel in Votkinsk.

When the US inspectors protested this seizure to the Soviet officers from the Nuclear Risk Reduction Center, they were informed that the issue of Votkinsk water samples fell under the purview of the Ministry of Defense Industry, and not the Ministry of Defense. When the inspectors pointed out that the water samples had been taken in the presence, and with the permission of, personnel from the Votkinsk Factory—a Ministry of Military Industry-affiliated entity— they were told to bring the issue up with the factory leadership. The head of Department 162, Anatoli Tomilov, was apprised of the situation, and expressed surprise. However, once he contacted his superiors in Moscow, he went silent on the issue, saying only that the matter would be decided by his superiors. (Apparently there was concern on the part of the KGB that the water samples could reveal secrets regarding the production processes used at the Missile Final Assembly Plant, some of which used PCBs. The Soviet sample was seized by authorities for follow-on evaluation.[16])

Now, some two months later, Doug Englund was pressing Tomilov and Sokolov for an answer. The issue of Ministry of Industry approval to export the seized water samples was now moot, since the samples, which had been collected using specialized kits requiring refrigeration, had long since spoiled. Even if new kits were brought in and new samples taken, however, the US required Ministry of Defense Industry approval to proceed. At first Sokolov denied any knowledge of a water sample in possession of the Soviets; he later modified his position, noting that the local Soviet laboratory could not test for the presence of PCBs. Tomilov promised that he would investigate this matter when he visited Moscow in the coming week. In the meantime, Doug informed the Soviets that the inspection team would begin preliminary preparations to install a water purification system in the Roosevelt kitchen—the Hughes chef needed potable water in plentiful supply in order to support the site with fresh-cooked meals.

Colonel Englund then went on to iterate additional areas where recent Soviet cooperation had been less than satisfactory. Food was one such instance—the Votkinsk Factory had stopped providing the promised food shipments, forcing the inspectors to do their own shopping at markets in the town. Another was safety—back in April, the Soviets had been provided with a list of recommendations regarding improvements to the perimeter path around the Missile Final Assembly Plant.

At first, Sokolov denied ever having received such a list (although I had personally handed it to him). When prompted, Tomilov acknowledged that the Soviets had received the list, but noted that there was little they could do, as most of the recommendations required expenditures of resources that had not been planned for. Tomilov then snidely noted that if the American side wasn't pleased with this answer, they should raise the issue at the SVC, or else carry out their previous threat to cite Soviet noncompliance as a treaty anomaly in the next monthly inspection report.

Sensing Doug's growing ire, Sokolov intervened, and suggested that the US and Soviet sides carry out a joint, expanded perimeter inspection the next day, June 15, where specific possible improvements could be discussed. I was tasked with leading this inspection, in which the same recommendations that had been put forward in April were made. This time, with Soviet factory personnel present to witness the concerns of the inspectors, the message seemed to get through. Once again, the recommendations for improving the perimeter path were written up and shared with the Soviets, who promised to give them due consideration.

Finally, Doug brought up the issue of rejected *zayafkas*. He led off by asking for an explanation behind the Soviet refusal to allow me to witness the most recent elections, back on May 21. Sokolov responded that this was due to the intervention of the deputy mayor, Mr. Kulemin, who had objected to my presence. Doug then brought up the denial of permission for inspectors to go to the *Dom Mody* (House of Fashion). Mr. Tomilov answered by reflecting at length upon the difficulties of getting a dressmaking appointment in the Soviet Union.

Doug then raised the issue of leisure travel in general—with the demise of the former "escort free" zone in the city, facilities that previously could be visited without issue were now being denied to the inspectors. Even something as routine as going into town to buy bread for the inspectors had become difficult. Tomilov noted that the city had deemed many areas of the town closed to inspectors, including neighborhoods that had no relationship with the Votkinsk Factory. In many cases, the Soviets required more than 24-hour notice to make the arrangements necessary to grant the inspector's access. If the inspector's request did not provide enough time for permission to be granted, it was denied out of hand.

The Soviets then presented Doug with a litany of complaints of their own, centering on the conduct of inspections at the Portal Monitoring Facility. The Soviets were insisting on being able to verify the program operation of the computer software in use at the DCC line-by-line at the source code level, noting that the continued operation of the DCC ultimately depended on this happening. Doug responded by noting that this was an issue for the SVC, and that he would pass the Soviet concerns on to OSIA Headquarters for action. Tomilov then complained about the movement of inspectors from the housing and administrative buildings onto what he called the "technical zone"—the DCC, the warehouse, and the CargoScan facility. Tomilov insisted that the Soviets be given control of the inspector badges, ensuring that the inspectors who were on duty would have to check in with them first before conducting their work. Doug rejected this suggestion outright. The issue of inspector movement on site would remain a serious matter for the foreseeable future.

Doug left the meeting with a growing sense of trepidation about the trajectory US-Soviet relations was taking in Votkinsk. His concerns would only be amplified in the days and weeks to come.

As the first anniversary of the arrival of US inspectors in Votkinsk approached, so did the issue of how best to commemorate this event. From the perspective of the US inspectors, it was felt that the best way to do this would be to move the traditional Independence Day celebration from July 4 (which fell on a Tuesday) to July 1 (a Saturday) and treat the event as a joint holiday. Preliminary coordination was carried out between the US inspectors and Department 162 both in terms of the timing and location of the celebration, as well as whom the inspectors planned on inviting to the function (basically a pared-down Open House guest list). Then on June 22, the Soviet shift leader informed the US duty officer that there might be a problem with the US plans regarding the Independence Day celebrations.

With Doug Englund joining General Lajoie and George Connell in Moscow for a meeting with the Soviet Nuclear Risk Reduction Center and Ministry of Defense Industry officials regarding treaty expenses, Chuck Myers, accompanied by Barrett Haver (who oversaw planning the event) stepped in to take the lead on working the Independence Day issue with Alexandr Sokolov (Tomilov was also in Moscow for the treaty expenses conference). Sokolov opened the meeting by stating that as soon as the Votkinsk Factory had learned that the Americans were planning another event at their housing complex, they had forwarded this information to the Ministry of Defense Industry for guidance. Sokolov claimed that the factory was seeking permission to allow Soviet citizens who were not employees access to what the Soviets still considered to be a sensitive military facility. The Ministry of Defense Industry had responded by declaring that only personnel who were directly working at the Missile Final Assembly Plant could attend the festivities. The ban on non-affiliated persons extended even to the families of factory employees.

For Myers and Haver, the Soviet ban on outside visitors was unacceptable. While respecting the Votkinsk Factory's need to safeguard its security, the issue of visitation was a matter of reciprocity—the Soviet inspectors in Magna were allowed to invite anyone they wanted to their living quarters, so long as they notified the US escorts in advance. Myers pointed out that the choice of the housing site had been made by the Soviets, and as such they would have to find a way around this problem.

As an alternative to holding the celebration at the US housing facility, Sokolov instead proposed that the inspectors consider either the House of Culture or the Ustinov Dacha, both of which could be provided with no issues by the Soviet side. Myers responded by reiterating that this was not a matter of practicalities as much as it was a point of principle—the US inspectors should be allowed to invite whomever they wanted into their housing area, so long as they notified the Soviets in advance. This was the arrangement in Magna, and the inspectors were determined that it should apply to them as well. Sokolov noted that the issue of access to the factory grounds was a matter of principle for the Soviets as well.

The two sides adjourned the meeting, agreeing that planning would go forward for the Independence Day celebration while awaiting a final decision of the Ministry of Defense Industry. On the question of how best to celebrate the first anniversary of the US inspectors arriving in Votkinsk, Myers agreed with Sokolov that a small function should be organized at the Ustinov Dacha for General Lajoie and General Medvedev and a select number of other attendees.

However, when Chuck Myers informed Doug Englund and General Lajoie of the Soviet stance restricting access by Soviets invited by US inspectors to the US housing, General Lajoie responded by cancelling the planned gathering at the Ustinov Dacha, and instead proposed that he and General Medvedev make remarks regarding the anniversary at the Independence Day celebrations on July 1. This information was passed on to Alexandr Sokolov on June 25, along with a renewed request for a decision on whether the non-factory affiliated Soviet guests invited by the US inspectors would be permitted to attend the celebration.

On July 28, the Soviets responded with an official decision from the Ministry of Defense Industry. "The factory," the decision read, "which uses in its activities explosive mixtures, based on its safety cannot allow the presence of the vast contingent of guests suggested by you on the territory belonging to the facility and directly adjacent to it. We propose that you shorten the guest list, excluding those people who have no relationship with the activities of the factory." The decision, set forth in a memorandum signed by Anatoli Tomilov, concluded by reiterating the offer of the use of the House of Culture as a fitting location to hold the Independence Day celebration.

Barrett Haver reached out to Colonel Connell, who was in Moscow awaiting a flight back to Izhevsk that evening. Connell made the decision to proceed with the Independence Day celebration at the US housing area as planned, even with a pared down guest list. He indicated that he would meet with Tomilov first thing in the morning to discuss this matter.

Connell's meeting with Tomilov did not go well. The Soviets reiterated the Ministry of Defense Industry directive, indicating that they had no flexibility on this matter. Following the meeting, Connell drafted a memorandum for General Lajoie, who was still in Moscow. "Purposely vague answers were given," Connell wrote, "when asked if this was a universal policy that applied to all visitors to the US housing. Obviously, the probability of reciprocal measures in Magna (we ask you to consider) were not lost on either Mr. Tomilov or Mr. Sokolov. I advised Mr. Tomilov," Connell continued, "that both of the Soviet options (i.e., the use of the Ustinov Dacha or the House of Culture) were unacceptable and further stated that instead the US inspectors would commemorate the 4th by themselves on Tuesday." Connell recommended that "the Soviet side plan some sort of modest ceremony to commemorate passage of the first year on-site."

Connell knew that General Lajoie was going to be accompanied by General Medvedev, Lev Kokurin (a Ministry of Defense Industry official seconded to the SVC), Mr. Rynenko of the Moscow Institute of Thermal Dynamics (the Nadiradze Design Bureau), and Colonel Lebedev, a former Soviet inspection team leader at Magna. Any disruption of the planned schedule of events would be seen as an embarrassment to the Soviets, something Connell hoped would shock them into taking action to reverse the Ministry of Defense Industry policy.

Calmer heads prevailed. General Lajoie, after consultations with General Medvedev, opted to travel to Votkinsk on June 30, where he and his party would spend the night at the US housing facility. The next day would be focused on meetings with the Soviets and US inspectors, including some frank airing of the issues. Lajoie hoped that by exposing the senior Soviet leadership to the pettiness of the Votkinsk Factory dispute (especially Colonel Lebedev, who understood the ramifications of reciprocity only too well), pressure could be brought to bear to bring about a change in attitude.

July 1 came and went. The Independence Day celebration took place as planned, with a dozen or so Soviet personnel from the factory in attendance. General Lajoie and General Medvedev both made statements regarding the one-year anniversary of the arrival of the US inspectors in Votkinsk. But while the US housing facility had the trappings of celebration in full display, with red, white, and blue bunting hung throughout the site, it was but a veneer covering a broader dysfunction that could not be explained by Soviet pettiness alone.

Through Soviet Eyes

THE FACT OF THE MATTER was that the Soviet Union had changed in the intervening year, and not for the better. The pressures brought about by the forces of perestroika weighed heavily on the people of Votkinsk, and the Soviet Union as a whole. Theirs was a life filled with uncertainty and having the US inspectors present to bear personal witness in such an intimate fashion to the discomfort this caused only bred resentment.

Alfred Adler, the noted Austrian psychotherapist best known as the founder of the school of individual psychology, famously observed, "To see with the eyes of another, to hear with the ears of another, to feel with the heart of another. For the time being, this seems to me an admissible definition of what we call social feeling."

In August 1988, having freshly returned from my second deployment to Votkinsk, I was approached by Navy Commander Kendell Pease, the Public Affairs Officer for OSIA. "I have a reporter from *The Boston Globe* who would like to do a story on Votkinsk," Pease said. "You and Major Haver have been volunteered."

The veteran PAO ran Barrett and I through a quick tutorial on what we could and could not say. "Don't lie," he said. "But you don't have to give away the farm. Less is better." He left us with this final piece of advice. "It's still the Cold War. With the Soviets, we're friendly, but not friends."

The resulting article, written by Tom Ashbrook and entitled "Our Men in Votkinsk," ran in *The Boston Globe* on August 31, 1988. It was, to put it mildly, a "fluff" piece. Commander Pease looked over the article, a smile on his face. "Perfect," he said. "Just the right balance of 'feel good' and the banal."

I didn't think about that interview until almost a year later, when I was looking at a translation of a *Leninski Put'* article while on duty in the DCC. Entitled "What they write about us in America: 'The Free Press.' Free of Stereotypes?," the article, published on August 11, 1989, examined how the Soviets, and in particular the citizens of Votkinsk, were portrayed in the American press.

"Imagine for a moment," the article noted, "that you are an average American having his morning coffee in his very own home somewhere in a Washington, DC suburb. In your hands is the morning paper which you have been reading for many years and which you have come to trust. Well now, what's new? Aha," the article exclaimed, "this looks interesting!"

Although peaceful relations have been established between the US and USSR, Kremlin spies still pose a threat to the security of the US. A record number of Soviet students, tourists, businessmen, and emigrees are travelling around the US, and in that way, increasing the number of potential spies.

The newspaper article referred to by *Leninski Put'* was quoting an FBI counterintelligence agent. Other experts, including a former National Security Council staffer, were quoted as depicting perestroika as little more than a front for increased Soviet espionage.

The article continued. "You get in your 'Ford' and roll out to the highway. At the filling station a bright young kid, a newsboy, runs up to you and holds out the latest edition of the *Washington Times*...and suddenly, bang! 'Soviets want to get into the inspector's basements.' How can you not read that?"

The *Leninski Put'* article went on to accurately quote from the Bill Gertz story, including the passage that labeled the Soviet escorts at Votkinsk as KGB agents. The article then explained the reality behind the basement story. But it didn't matter—the prototypical American newspaper reader only had access to what he read in the American press. "Well, how you say," the *Leninski Put'* article declared, "after all this can one not be certain in the opinion that Russian insidiousness knows no bounds?"

Then the article got personal, quoting my interview given to Tom Ashbrook barely a year ago. "'They know who I am and what I present of myself,' said Lieutenant Ritter about his official Soviet hosts. 'They don't ask immodest questions, they don't try to find out anything about my past. They just ask me, for example, "Five years ago, there was the Cold War, and now you're in Votkinsk. What do you think about that?"'"

"So that everything doesn't look a little too comfortable," the *Leninski Put'* article observed, Ritter quickly stressed that he had "'very strict instructions from home regarding how far their relations with the Soviet citizens can go. According to our instructions, we can maintain normal, proper relations with Soviet citizens, be polite and courteous, but separate and reserved,' said Lieutenant Ritter. 'We cannot, under any circumstances, become friends with the Soviet people.'"

I knew the quote was an accurate one, but when I read it in print a year later, I cringed. So, too, must have every Soviet who read it.

"It is understandable," the *Leninski Put'* article concluded, "duty is duty. But after all, it is accepted to repay sincerity and cordiality in kind. Could all the smiles, handshaking, and kind words be 'according to instructions?' One really doesn't want to think so."

Quite a shock, seeing how one is seen by the eyes of another.

For the first time since I began work in Votkinsk, I was compelled by conscience to examine the current state of relations from the Soviet point of view. What I saw was not pretty. The Americans, it seemed, were oblivious to the realities of the Soviet existence. We lived the life of plenty, wanting for nothing, yet complaining about everything. We were friendly enough, and far more sincere than the *Leninski Put'* article suggested. And we were professional. But we lacked a certain gravitas—the lack of attention paid to the issue of documentation for the DCC, cable pull plans, and CargScan more than proved that point.

For the Soviets in Votkinsk, the INF treaty implementation experience was, literally, an existential crisis. The economic, social, and political life blood of the Votkinsk community was under threat because of the disarmament activities being implemented under perestroika. Every day brought a struggle to survive, every morrow a journey into the unknown. Not for the Americans—each day in Votkinsk was just another day at the office. This nonchalance on the part of their American counterparts had to have become off-putting to our Soviet colleagues over time—especially if the sincerity of the persons you were working with was in question.

At the end of the day, all the Soviets had going for them was their individual integrity as humans and the quality of their labor. They didn't enjoy the trappings of comfort that Americans had become accustomed to, and their lives lacked the kind of predictability that Americans demanded. But they did have pride, both in themselves and their organization, the Votkinsk Machine Building Plant. They were tasked with successfully implementing the INF treaty and, when judged by that standard, they were doing yeoman's work.

CargoScan

WHILE THE SOVIETS and Americans prepared for the eventual installation of CargoScan in Votkinsk, the issue of the Stage Measuring Device (SMD) reemerged. The fact remained that, from an actual treaty compliance standpoint, without CargoScan, the only deterrence the US inspectors had against any elaborate Soviet cheating scheme was the eight cannister opening opportunities mandated by the treaty. Even here, however, the inspectors were limited by what they could observe. The only verifiable means of confirming that the second stage inspectors could discern in the shadowy depth of the opened launch cannister, was, in fact, the dimensions claimed by the Soviets was by using a stage measuring device (SMD).

After the failed SMD experiment in Votkinsk on October 12, 1988, the prototype SMD was returned to Moscow, where the SVC took up the issue of how to resolve the discrepancies in its design and function that had been identified during the test. The lack of communication between the SVC and the personnel—American and Soviet alike—in Votkinsk was both telling and trying. The Soviet officials at Votkinsk had stopped asking about the status of the SMD, and on May 10, 1989, the head of Department 162, Anatoli Tomilov, submitted a revision to the existing inspection procedures "for an SS-25 missile in a container with an open lid," emphasizing that "it is not allowed to touch the container or the missile with hands or with any other object." The OSIA Site Commander at the time, Mark Dues, noted in response that the Soviet procedure "needs to take into account the eventual use of a stage measuring device touching both the missile and the container" and submitted modified language to that effect.

Neither side knew what the status of the SMD was. This changed in July 1989. The SVC, it seemed, was ready to move forward on the issue, and a delegation led by Kenneth Huck arrived in Moscow for consultations with a Soviet delegation led by Lev Solomonov, the Chief Designer of the SS-25 missile. John Sartorius and Bill Langemeier were attached to the US delegation to provide an inspector's perspective.

Over the course of a month, the two sides met in a conference room inside the headquarters building of the Moscow Institute of Thermal Technology, going over the technical details of the modifications being made to the SMD. The two delegations worked closely with specialists from AO Optika, an organization that specialized in the manufacture, management, and testing of optical instruments, regarding quality control and safety issues associated with inserting lightbulbs powered by 220 volts of electricity into a cannister loaded with several live solid fuel rocket stages. By mid-August, the joint SMD team reached agreement on a configuration and procedures that could be tested on an actual SS-25.

On August 21, 1989, the joint delegation, led by Huck and Solomonov, travelled to Votkinsk where, later in the day, a locomotive departed the portal pulling a six-axle railcar in which was loaded an SS-25. As had been the case with the previous SMD experiment, the railcar and missile were subjected to a standard inspection protocol, before being sent on to the environmentally controlled inspection building, where a team of Soviet engineers removed the cover of the missile. As had been the case of the previous experiment, the opening of the missile cannister did not count against the eight permitted per year by the treaty.

The Chief Designer of the SS-25 missile and a host of other Soviet and American arms control specialists (including John Sartorius and Bill Langemeier) found themselves crowded onto the concrete inspection pad, dressed in special anti-static coveralls, with anti-static gloves on their hands and anti-static booties on their feet. Each person on the stand had gone through the process of touching a special grounding rod designed to eliminate any residual static charge that may have accumulated. To say that the Soviets were concerned about the dangers associated with an accidental detonation due to exposure of the solid fuel to a static charge was an understatement.

With the missile exposed, the joint SMD evaluation team powered up the SMD device by plugging it into a standard Soviet 220-volt outlet, which drew its power from the factory. The lightbulbs that had been attached to the SMD to illuminate the interior of the launch cannister and the exterior of the second stage of the missile came on, and the device was slowly and very carefully inserted into the missile cannister, with observers carefully tracking its progress. About halfway into the insertion process, the factory experienced a power surge, which caused a lightbulb on the portion of the SMD already inserted into the missile cannister to explode with a loud "pop."

The sound of broken glass settling into the recesses of the loaded missile cannister could be heard by every member of the joint SMD evaluation team as they collectively held their breath, waiting for the explosion that would send them to their doom. After a period of about 30 seconds, a voice called out in Russian, "Well, boys, we're still alive!"

The SMD was removed from the launch cannister, and the joint SMD evaluation team retreated from the environmentally controlled inspection building, leaving the factory technicians with the task of cleaning up the mess they had made. The delegation, with John and Bill in tow, returned to Moscow the next morning, no closer to a solution regarding a usable SMD, but very much lucky to be alive. The SMD issue was once again relegated to the SVC for resolution, leaving CargoScan as the only means of sustained verification when it came to discerning whether the second stage of missiles exiting the Votkinsk portal belonged to an SS-20 or SS-25.

The CargoScan saga had broken down into two separate narratives, one involving the difficulties the US was having in getting the system ready to be shipped to the Soviet Union, and the other the struggle between the inspectors and their Soviet colleagues in preparing the Votkinsk Portal Monitoring Facility to receive it. The responsibility for getting CargoScan assembled, tested, and ready for delivery to Votkinsk rested with the US Air Force Electronic Systems Division (ESD), who had contracted with the Technical On-Site Inspection (TOSI) development project run by Sandia National Laboratory. Testing began on February 10 and was completed on April 3.

One of the problems facing ESD was that the delays in getting CargoScan operational had created a budget shortfall. ESD estimated that it would require $11.6 million dollars to complete its mission of delivering a radiographic imaging system to Votkinsk capable of fulfilling its treaty mandated tasks. However, only $6.2 million in funding had been allocated, leaving a shortfall of $5.4 million. The Secretary of the Air Force was brought in to help squeeze the money out of various agencies. The funding issue became even more acute when, after CargoScan testing was complete, a decision was made not to dismantle it until an actual shipping date had been agreed to. Additional funding had to be allocated to keep CargoScan operational so that OSIA and Hughes personnel could be trained.

The schedule was pushed back even further when the Soviets, during a meeting of the SVC in Geneva, declared that they would not be able to inspect CargoScan and approve its transfer to Votkinsk until they received additional information and documentation, including operator manuals, functional descriptions of hardware and software, block diagrams, and source code. Complicating the matter further was the fact that no money had been allocated for the production of such documentation, forcing the ESD Program Manager, Air Force Lieutenant Colonel John Sovitch, to modify the existing contract vehicles for both Sandia National Laboratory and Hughes Technical Services Company. Sovitch succeeded in expanding the statement of work to allow work to begin on preparing the required documentation, both at Sandia and on-site in Votkinsk. This, of course, cost even more money that ESD had not budgeted for.

By August 1989 the documents requested by the Soviets had been prepared and turned over to their delegation in Geneva. The US delegation proposed that the Soviets send a team of experts to Sandia to participate in a full-scale operational demonstration of CargoScan as the final step needed before breaking the system down and shipping it to Votkinsk. The Soviets turned down the offer of a full-scale demonstration, instead insisting on a software demonstration to be conducted in Moscow during the week of September 15–21, 1989. At the conclusion of the software demonstration, the Soviets presented the US side with a "non-paper" listing a number of unresolved questions that would need to be answered before CargoScan would be allowed to be put into operation.

In the interest of keeping the CargoScan installation on track, however, the Soviets agreed to allow CargoScan to be shipped the Votkinsk, where the various modules could be installed, awaiting final approval to begin operation. ESD had been prepared to fly the CargoScan modules to Izhevsk on giant C-5 aircraft, but the Soviets balked at having aircraft of that size landing on a runway that had not been constructed for that purpose. Instead, they proposed that CargoScan be flown into Izhevsk onboard C-141 aircraft like those that had delivered the furniture shipments in January-February 1989.

The CargoScan modules were flown into Izhevsk on October 2, 3, 5, and 6, where they were inspected by the Soviet side and released for installation on October 8. ESD had done its job. The ball was now in the hands of the US inspection personnel at the Votkinsk Portal Monitoring Facility, both OSIA and Hughes alike. Getting it across the goal line proved much more difficult than anyone could have imagined.[17]

At the Votkinsk Portal Monitoring Facility, the inspectors finalized their cable pulling plan while Anatoli Chernenko, the intrepid construction chief who possessed a seemingly bottomless reservoir of energy, oversaw the concrete pours that, when finished, would become the monolithic structure that would house the giant CargoScan radiographic imaging system. Chernenko and his men were under immense pressure to get the site ready to receive the CargoScan modules.

Basic construction materials, however, were in short supply, and there were competing construction projects at the portal facility itself, including the pouring of concrete footings for the installation of the IR Rail Profiling system. Installation occurred as materials became available; steel beams were put in place over the summer, and by August, the last of the roofing was bolted in place when a shipment of sheet metal arrived. The final construction step—the installation of the railroad tracks leading from the main line into the CargoScan structure—took place at the end of August. All that remained was the completion of the cable pulling plan, and the installation and testing of the CargoScan modules.

OSIA was well within its second year of treaty implementation—enough time for the senior leadership to look at the organizational structure with an eye toward increased efficiency. The looming retirement of OSIA's Chief of Staff, Air Force Colonel Robert McConnell, in November 1989 brought with it the need for a replacement. Rather than going to the Air Force for a replacement, however, General Lajoie decided that Portal Monitoring no longer needed two Colonels working back-to-back rotations. Instead, the decision was made to move Doug Englund to Chief of Staff and keep Colonel Connell on as the

Director of Portal Monitoring. The position of Site Commander would be filled by the experienced Majors and Lieutenant Colonels already resident in Portal Monitoring, with Colonel Connell travelling to Votkinsk on an as-needed basis.

Doug Englund was on the ground in Votkinsk when this decision was made. Roy Peterson would deploy to Votkinsk in early October, where he would have a week-long turnover with Doug, before Doug rotated back to Washington, DC, for a month-long turnover with Colonel McConnell. On paper, early October was the perfect time for such a transition—the drama surrounding the installation of CargoScan appeared to be ending, with most of the outstanding technical issues resolved during the Moscow CargoScan demonstration in September, and the CargoScan modules scheduled to arrive in Votkinsk, where they would be installed and, if all went well, the system made operational by years end.

On October 7, the US inspectors, together with the men and women of Department 162, held a farewell party for Doug Englund at the Café Cosmos. The outpouring of warmth on the part of Americans and Soviets alike attested to the character of the man who, together with George Connell, made the Votkinsk Portal Monitoring Facility what it was. Dinner was served, speeches were made, and gifts exchanged. To everyone present, the event appeared to mark the end of an era, the frontier mindset of the first pioneering year giving way to a more civilized routine of arms control compliance verification. Doug had been a calming influence on Americans and Soviets alike, the voice of reason in a sea of chaos. While there were still improvements that could be made in terms of the relationship between the inspectors and their Soviet hosts, everyone present believed that the toughest days were behind us.

We could not have been more wrong.

The next day, October 8, the Soviet customs inspectors in Izhevsk announced that they had released the CargoScan modules for onward travel to Votkinsk, where Anatoli Chernenko and his crew, together with the Hughes personnel and ESD technicians, were waiting to oversee their installation.

Then Anatoli Chernenko suffered a massive stroke.

The impact of Chernenko being hospitalized was felt immediately by all. Both the Soviet construction team and American inspectors were demoralized, as they had all come to count on Chernenko coming through in a pinch whenever there was a tight deadline or complication. The CargoScan modules were held in Izhevsk while the Soviets regrouped and looked for someone who could take Chernenko's place.

Doug flew out on October 9 with the CargoScan installation in a flux.

Then, on October 10, the Soviets informed the US inspectors that the release of the CargoScan modules came with a caveat. The Soviets would permit the CargoScan modules to be placed on their respective pads but would not permit final installation until all documentation that had been requested in the September 22 non-paper had been provided. This documentation included a schematic of the

CargoScan cable connections, information output about the operating console, a plan for the storage of the imaging tapes produced by CargoScan when imaging a missile, a radiation safety plan, and detailed operating instructions on all aspects of CargoScan operations. The US delegation at the CargoScan software demonstration believed that all these issues had been discussed verbally with the Soviets. It now appeared that the Soviets wanted everything in writing.

Except for the operating procedures, which the Hughes management believed could be written on-site, the other requests were policy questions that had to be addressed at the SVC level. The new Site Commander, Roy Peterson, passed these questions to OSIA headquarters, and then turned to the issue of how the CargoScan modules were going to be transported from Izhevsk to the Votkinsk portal, and then how they would be installed. With no Soviet construction chief available, the US inspectors were left with little choice but to wait.

After a few days, the Soviets cobbled together a team of specialists, led by Boris Solov'ev, the Deputy Chief of Department 162, and Vladimir Polyakov, Chernenko's lieutenant, who would oversee the construction aspects regarding the installation of the CargoScan modules. The Soviets struggled to find a crane large enough to be able to lift the modules over the concrete containment walls, and onto their respective pads. Eventually they were able to obtain the services of an 80-ton KATO crane, and plans were made to have the CargoScan modules moved by rail to the Votkinsk portal on October 27, where they would be installed that same day.

On October 26, Jim Hull, one of the Hughes personnel most experienced on matters regarding the installation of portal monitoring equipment at Votkinsk (he had played a crucial role in the installation of the DCC), fell ill. Joanne Polka, the on-site physician's assistant, suspected appendicitis and immediately had Jim transported to the Votkinsk Factory Hospital. Joanne's diagnosis was confirmed by the Soviets after conducting a white blood cell count, and Jim was scheduled for emergency surgery within the hour. The surgery went well, and Jim was up on his feet within 12 hours. The Soviet doctors insisted that Jim remain hospitalized for 8–10 days, and while Jim stated that it was his intention to remain in Votkinsk once he was released, Joanne overruled him, deeming the risk of infection to be too high. Jim was scheduled to depart on the November 4 rotation. His loss was felt by all.

The CargoScan modules were installed on October 27 as planned, except for the transport module, which was scheduled to be placed on its pad on October 30. The temperature in Votkinsk was already beginning to drop, and while the Soviets continued to insist that further installation would not be permitted until the outstanding questions relating to their September 22 non-paper were addressed to their satisfaction, they did agree to allow the electrical hookups to the heaters in the modules to be connected out of concern that continued exposure to the elements might result in permanent damage. The inspectors were not allowed to hook up power to the module interior lighting, resulting in the final aspects of module installation taking place in the dark. The Soviets reversed themselves on November 3, however, insisting that the electrical hookups to the heaters be disconnected until which time all the Soviet concerns previously outlined to the inspectors were answered to their satisfaction.

The issue of inspector movement on-site was beginning to become an issue with the Soviets. They had, since the moment the US inspectors moved into their permanent housing area, insisted on delineating the Portal Monitoring Facility into "technical" and "administrative" zones, and sought to implement procedures based on these distinctions, which were designed to restrict the movement of US inspectors to and from these two zones. In particular, the Soviets insisted that the inspectors notify the Soviet Duty officer prior to any movement between the zones, and that the inspectors always be accompanied by a Soviet escort.

The Soviets, however, had not permitted the inspectors to install a telephone at the CargoScan facility. The fact that inspectors were required to move between the Roosevelt administrative building, where records were stored and meetings held, and the CargoScan facility, which was located immediately across the road, meant that there was constant movement to and from these locations. While the inspectors could and did telephone the Soviet Duty officer before moving from the Roosevelt building to the CargoScan facility, and would wait until a Soviet escort was provided, once at the CargoScan facility, the inspectors were left with no other option than to inform their Soviet escort that they now would be returning to Roosevelt. The Soviet escort, who was equipped with a radio, would then contact the Soviet Duty officer, and inform him of the movement.

The inspectors believed that they only had to keep the Soviets informed of their movements, and that they did not require the permission of the Soviets to enter the so-called "technical zone." As such, by notifying the Soviet escort, they believed they had fulfilled their responsibilities. In short, the freedom of movement the US inspectors required to do their jobs in an efficient manner was clashing with the Soviet requirement for security and control over a site that was adjacent to a sensitive military installation.

The issue came to a head on November 6. Two days prior, during a meeting with Vyacheslav Lopatin, Barrett Haver, concerned about the buildup of precipitation and debris in the CargoScan detector module, requested permission to connect power to the heaters in that unit in order to prevent permanent damage from occurring. Lopatin agreed, and the power was connected by inspectors, operating under Soviet escort.

The Votkinsk Factory was closed on November 6 for the October Revolution celebration. Unlike the previous year, when the US inspectors had been guests of honor at the parade, the US inspectors were confined to the portal facility, where they continued to focus on issues pertaining to the installation of CargoScan. During an inspection of the CargoScan facility, Lopatin noticed that the power was still connected to the detector module heating element, and protested this fact to the US Duty Officer, accusing the US inspectors of violating the understanding that existed regarding the cessation of CargoScan installation pending the final clarification of outstanding issues. The US inspectors immediately disconnected the electrical hookup, but not before expressing their dismay at Lopatin's behavior.

On November 16, 1989, the Soviet CargoScan Commission arrived in Votkinsk for meetings with the US inspectors, the intention of which were to clarify the outstanding issues so that the installation of CargoScan could be finalized. Upon their arrival, the commission members were given a tour of the CargoScan facility. When Barrett Haver showed the commission members the rusted connections to the detector module and pointed out the deteriorating weather conditions (the temperature had dropped to below freezing, and a light snow was already covering the ground), the commission members immediately authorized the US inspectors to connect electricity to all the heaters used in the CargoScan system, overriding the objections of Anatoli Tomilov.

The arrival of the Soviet CargoScan Commission was a turning point in the installation of CargoScan. Prior to that, the local Soviet authorities (primarily Anatoli Tomilov and Vyacheslav Lopatin) had put a halt to all installation pending the resolution of all outstanding issues. It became clear to the commission members, however, that this approach was putting at risk the operational viability of the CargoScan equipment, and that blame for any such outcome would fall on the Soviet side. Over the course of four days of meetings, the Soviet CargoScan Commission overrode the objections of Tomilov and Lopatin, and gave the green light for the final installation of CargoScan to proceed, with a caveat that CargoScan would not be permitted to be made operational until the Soviet concerns were addressed in full. Tomilov was visibly upset by this decision, as it caused him to lose face in front of the US inspection team. Lopatin was quietly removed from the scene, never again to be seen on-site.

The remainder of November and all of December was taken up by the demands of getting the CargoScan installation finalized. More than 10,000 feet of cable was pulled, enabling all the CargoScan components to be powered up. The Environmental Control Units were up and running in each module. Lighting was installed, and surveillance cameras set up. The Master Control Console was installed, and the control module was hooked up. While the final powering up of the x-ray system was put off pending a radiation safety inspection, all indications pointed to CargoScan being ready for full power up sometime in the first week of January. The Soviet CargoScan Commission planned on returning at that time to assess whether CargoScan could be made operational.

The intervention of the Soviet CargoScan Commission was an extension of a concerted push by Mikhail Gorbachev to be seen as a viable partner for peace by the Bush administration. Gorbachev and his advisors were concerned about the seeming lack of focus on the part of the Bush administration when it came to crafting policy that would assist Gorbachev in fulfilling his goals and objectives under perestroika. Moreover, the geopolitical climate in which such decisions were made was rapidly changing. On November 9, the Berlin Wall came down. The US Military Liaison Mission at Potsdam was put on full alert, dispatched to the field in order to assess what the reaction of the Soviet military stationed in East Germany would be. They got their answer at midnight, when a fax was transmitted to them by the Soviet External Relations Bureau, responsible for coordinating with the Potsdam Mission, that all Soviet soldiers were to be confined to garrison.

"That's when we knew that it was over," Tom Flavia, a driver for the US MLM, noted in an interview years later. That point was driven home the next day, November 10. "It was if someone had hit a switch," Flavia recalled. "From one day to the next, everything had completely changed." Flavia compared the enthusiasm of the East German border guards with the abject terror of the Soviet sentries on duty at the Glienicke Bridge connecting East and West Berlin. The East Germans were friendly, ecstatic, the Soviet soldiers, "terrified."[18]

The fall of the Berlin Wall was seen as a distraction by Soviet experts such as Jack Matlock, who continued to push for improved US-Soviet relations. In a memorandum written for President Bush in mid-November 1989, Matlock declared that "we should be searching for ways in which we can, in a practical way, signal US support for perestroika," adding that "perestroika must succeed or fail on the basis of what the Soviet Union itself is able to accomplish through a thorough reform of its system." The top goal of the US, Matlock argued, should be finding ways to help Gorbachev succeed.[19]

Matlock's memorandum was prepared in support of the Malta Summit between President Bush and General Secretary Gorbachev, which took place onboard the Soviet heavy cruiser, the *Maxim Gorky*, over the course of December 2–3, 1989. Gorbachev had come into the meeting with great expectations. Concerned that the events unfolding in Germany could prove a distraction, the Soviet leader planned on the two heads of state reaching "a common conclusion that the period of Cold War was over and that the emerging era of peace opened up unprecedented opportunities for multilateral and bilateral partnership." Indeed, during his initial conversations with Bush, Gorbachev declared that "First and foremost, the new US president must know that the Soviet Union will not under any circumstances initiate a war. This is so important that I wanted to repeat the announcement to you personally. Moreover, the USSR is prepared to cease considering the US as an enemy and announce this openly."[20]

President Bush wasn't prepared to make any similar grand gesture. He and his advisors viewed the Malta meeting as a precursor to a more decisive summit that was being planned for June 1990. Bush's lack of urgency was shaped in large part by a National Intelligence Estimate prepared specifically for this summit. Entitled "The Soviet System in Crisis: Prospects for the Next Two Years," the estimate had been prepared by Robert Blackwell, the National Intelligence Officer for the Soviet Union.

In the estimate, Blackwell wrote that it was the consensus view of the US intelligence community that, while the current crisis in the USSR would continue even beyond the previously projected two-year timeframe, "the regime will maintain the present course," that Gorbachev was "relatively secure" in his leadership role, and that there was a less likely scenario of "unmanageable" decline that could lead to a "repressive crackdown."[21]

Bush appeared to ignore a more pessimistic dissent put forward in the text of the CIA estimate by John Helgerson, the CIA's Deputy Director for Intelligence. Helgerson predicted that while Gorbachev would continue to pursue a "pluralist—albeit chaotic—democratic system," Gorbachev's political strength would eventually "erode" as he "progressively [lost] control of events."

Too late, President Bush's national security team realized that they had missed a golden opportunity to shape US-Soviet relations at a time when the Soviet leader was prepared to make demonstrable and meaningful changes. While the Soviet leader had emerged from the Malta Summit encouraged by the attention he was getting from the American President, the erosion of Gorbachev's "political strength" predicted by John Helgerson was moving at a rapid pace. Malta, Jack Matlock noted, "didn't make much difference. A bruising session of the Congress of People's Deputies was awaiting him."[22]

The Congress opened upon December 12, 1989, and almost immediately Gorbachev was confronted by an effort on the part of the Interregional Group of Deputies to amend Article VI of the Soviet Constitution which provided for the dominance of the communist party. This confrontation reached a dramatic climax when, on December 13, Andrei Sakharov, the noted Soviet nuclear physicist turned dissident who in 1975 had won the Nobel Peace Prize, approached the dais to speak.

Sakharov had been the first deputy to address the inaugural session of the Congress of People's Deputies in 1988, and was held in high esteem, having been selected as the most popular person in the Soviet Union in 1989 (a designation that certainly irritated Mikhail Gorbachev). On this occasion, however, Sakharov was making the case for the adoption of a motion that would do away with the Article VI domination of the communist party. He was shouted down by Gorbachev, who belittled the 68-year-old physicist before leading an effort to vote down the proposal.[23]

Two days later, while preparing to deliver a speech to the conference in which he would renew his attack on Article VI, Sakharov died of a heart attack. Gorbachev declared four days of national mourning and spoke highly of the man known as the "father of the Soviet hydrogen bomb." But there were no words that could alter the public perception that Gorbachev, through his pointed attack on Sakharov at the Congress of People's Deputies on December 12, had contributed to Sakharov's death. The year 1989 ended with Gorbachev very much on the defensive, and the future of perestroika, and with it, of the Soviet Union, very much in doubt.

The Orakova Girl

SOMETIMES FATE has a way of putting everything into perspective. On August 31, 1989, Olga Orakova, an eight-year-old girl residing in the city of Izhevsk, was admitted to City Children's Hospital Number 2 for a routine tooth extraction. There were complications with the procedure, and as a result she was admitted to the Izhevsk Oncology Center for evaluation. After a thorough examination conducted by doctors from the All-Union Oncological Scientific Center of the USSR Academy of Medical Sciences, Olga was diagnosed as suffering from rhabdomyosarcoma, an exceptionally lethal form of cancer. The doctors began a course of chemotherapy on October 5, 1989, but by October 17 it was apparent to all that the chemotherapy was having little effect on the patient. Her doctors, concerned that Olga would die unless another course of treatment could be found, sent out a call for assistance via the Soviet amateur radio network.

Dr. Andrey Isaev, one of the doctors treating Olga, was an amateur radio enthusiast. In the fall of 1988, he had met Dr. Eugene Walsh at an amateur radio conference in Leningrad, and they exchanged contact details. Dr. Isaev was able to reach Dr. Walsh, who in turn contacted another amateur radio enthusiast, Dr. Harold Maurer of the Viginia Commonwealth University's Medical College of Virginia. Dr. Maurer approached Dr. Saul Kay, a Professor of Surgical Pathology at the same institution. Dr. Saul, who was a leading specialist on rhabdomyosarcoma. Both Dr. Mauer and Dr. Saul agreed to help and requested the Olga's medical history be sent to them.

The problem, now, was how to get these records to Dr. Saul. Dr. Isaev reached out to Dr. Evgeni Odiyankov at the Izhevsk Cardiology Center, whose relationship with the US inspectors in Votkinsk had become public knowledge. Evgeni called the phone number to the inspector's quarters, and got Barrett Haver on the other end. After Evgeni explained the situation to him, Barret responded by saying that the best way forward was to have this request be submitted to the US inspectors from Department 162. Evgeni hung up and contacted Anatoli Tomilov. Based upon that conversation, Tomilov approached the duty officer, who just so happened to be Barrett Haver, with a request for the Americans to use their fax machine to forward Olga's medical records to Dr. Walsh.

Anne Mortenson, a Hughes translator who was on duty at the time, translated the Russian records into English. However, the fax line to Moscow was down and awaiting repairs. The documents were instead transported to

Moscow on October 23 by inspectors making the weekly "mail run," and turned over to Steve Freeman at the ACIU, who transmitted them to Dr. Walsh. Dr. Walsh and Dr. Maurer reviewed Olga's records and concluded that they needed a tissue sample from Olga so they could prepare the stained slides required for laboratory examination. Dr. Walsh communicated this requirement to Dr. Isaev via their amateur radio network.

The tissue sample was prepared, and once again Anatoli Tomilov approached the US inspectors to see if they would be able to hand carry the sample back to the US and see that it was delivered to Dr. Maurer. John Sartorius was the duty officer at the time, and he forwarded the request to Colonel Connell, who was back in Washington, DC. Connell, after consulting with General Lajoie and Ed Pabst, requested that the US Embassy be consulted before any action was taken. If the Embassy approved, then Connell's preference would be for this to become an Embassy action.

The Embassy approved the request for assistance but left the responsibility for action with OSIA. I was scheduled to rotate out of Votkinsk on October 31, 1989, and as such was designated to be the mule for the Orakova package. While waiting to board the outbound flight at Izhevsk airport, I was approached by Dr. Isaev and four of his colleagues, who handed me a package containing histological samples of the tumor tissue encased in paraffin and gauze, along with a letter from Dr. Isaev to Dr. Maurer reasserting the Soviet diagnosis of rhabdomyosarcoma.

The doctors were accompanied by a fifth man, who appeared very worried. This was Olga's father, Vladimir. When I accepted the package, he immediately came up to me and hugged me, thanking me profusely. I did my best to reassure him that everything was going to be just fine.

On November 6 I drove down to Richmond, Virginia, where I delivered the tissue samples and letter to Dr. Maurer, who turned over the materials to Dr. Saul, who conducted an analysis using the slides provided by the Soviet doctors, as well as slides he made using tissue from the sample provided. He concluded that Olga was suffering from a benign lesion known as reparative giant cell granuloma, and not rhabdomyosarcoma.

Dr. Saul provided this diagnosis to Dr. Maurer, who in turn wrote a letter to Dr. Isaev in Izhevsk, forwarding Dr. Saul's findings. "I suggest you stop the chemotherapy," Dr. Maurer wrote. "The treatment for this granuloma is curettage. I am pleased that this is a benign lesion," Dr. Maurer concluded. "Olga should do well."

Dr. Isaev responded that the Soviet doctors would stop Olga's chemotherapy treatments but asked if they could receive written verification of Dr. Saul's findings, together with the slides that were used in his analysis. I reached out to Dr. Maurer with this request, and he sent the requested materials to OSIA headquarters. Unfortunately, the material arrived too late to be shipped out with the inbound Votkinsk rotation on November 19. Instead, the material was given to Team Wurzburger, which was due to travel to Moscow on December 4 to carry out an elimination inspection. Team Wurzburger turned the materials over to Soviet officers from the Nuclear Risk Reduction Center, who in turn passed them onto the ACIU at the US Embassy. On December 5 the Orakova material was turned over by the ACIU to the Votkinsk inspectors conducting their weekly liaison trip, who in turn transferred the material to Department 162, which delivered it to Dr. Isaev that same day.

On December 25, Anatoli Tomilov delivered an envelope to Mark Dues, the site commander. Inside was a letter from Olga Orakova's father. "Esteemed friends!" the letter started.

> *1989 is drawing to a close. This year has brought all of us many experiences, both bad and good. It brought much suffering to our family and all of our friends and relatives, because our older daughter fell ill. The doctors in Moscow diagnosed her with a very serious illness and prescribed a difficult, dangerous treatment. We do now know what the results of this treatment would have been if not for the help of your inspectors, who managed to seek out the opportunity to send samples to Virginia for a more precise analysis in Dr. Maurer's clinic.*
>
> *Now our friends tell us that you have brought us good fortune and we have drawn a lucky card. Dr. Maurer's diagnosis literally brought us back to our feet and provided us hope for our daughter's recovery.*
>
> *It is sad when someone is ill, but that grief is doubled when our children are ill.*
>
> *We are extremely grateful for the assistance the specialists from the United States gave us during a difficult time for us.*
>
> *On the eve of Christmas and as the new year approaches, we would like to wish you and your families happiness and prosperity and good health to all the children!*
>
> > *Merry Christmas and a Happy New Year!*
> > *The Orakova family*

Tucked inside the envelope was a color photograph of a bright-eyed blond girl dressed in a pretty pink dress, a white bow in her hair, holding a doll. That we were able to help save this little girl's life was one of the most heart-warming accomplishments we had as inspectors. All around the Votkinsk Missile Final Assembly Plant the harsh winds of the Siberian winter blew snow whose chill not only permeated the bodies on inspectors and inspected alike, but in symbolic form, the relations between their respective countries. As those who worked at the factory struggled with the complexities of CargoScan installation and the impact of the changes being wrought under perestroika, the knowledge that we—American and Soviet alike—had been able to come together and provide life-saving assistance to the Orakova girl gave us all hope that we would again, together, find a way to resolve our much greater predicament.[24]

CHAPTER SEVEN

The Road to Kapustin Yar

Pro-democracy protesters gather in Gorky Park, Moscow, on February 25, 1990, for a massive demonstration against Gorbachev's perestroika *policies.*

"We find after years of struggle that we do not take a trip; a trip takes us."

JOHN STEINBECK
Travels with Charley in Search of America

The Death of a Legend

ON THE EVENING of December 31, 1989, there were no visits by inspectors to the homes of Votkinsk factory personnel to mark the New Year. 1990 began with a pall over it, cast by the difficult economic and social issues brought on by perestroika, and the chilling impact this had on US-Soviet relations at a portal monitoring facility already laboring under the stresses brought about by the ongoing difficulties with the installation of CargoScan. One of the indicators of the state of relations between inspector and inspected was the status of the various *zayafki* submitted for treaty-permitted social activities. Soviet sensitivities about having 30 Americans living in the heart of what once was a closed city created a built-in reticence regarding freedom of movement on the part of the Americans, with the level of access fluctuating over time.

For the most part the Soviets would cite issues of reciprocity, claiming (almost always without cause) that the US was restricting the movements of Soviet inspectors in Magna, Utah. Such claims were easily refuted, both in terms of up-to-date information in the hands of the US inspectors about the current social activities of the Soviet inspectors, which could (and often were) backed up with direct telephonic communication, facilitated by the inspectors, between the Votkinsk factory officials and the Soviet personnel working at the Hercules plant.

Starting in the spring of 1989, however, *zayafkas* began to be returned for a new reason, one for which there was no issue of reciprocity—our security. Whereas previous Soviet excuses for denying our *zayafkas* often bordered on the petty, when it came to the issue of the deteriorating security situation in Votkinsk and elsewhere, the Soviets were not exaggerating. As the belt-tightening brought on by the new economic reality began to impact a broad swath of the Vokinsk citizenry, the level of anger and acrimony began to bubble to the surface in a society where such acts of socio-economic discontent were almost never manifested in a political manner, especially in a factory town like Votkinsk. The inspectors were able to track the social barometer by reading the local newspaper, *Leninski Put,*' which published several eye-opening articles about the impact perestroika was having on the local population.

In addition to a marked increase in acts of "hooliganism" (robbery, assault, vandalism), the paper addressed a rise in Russian nationalism reflective of a backlash on the part of ethnic Russians against any element of society—in this case the local Udmurt population (a distinct ethnic nationality from the Permian [Finnic] stock comprising close to 27% of the population of the eponymously-named Udmurt Republic), which was deemed to have been provided with preferential treatment. Once again, John Sartorious and Anne Mortenson performed yeoman's work in translating these articles and providing analysis, producing a third volume of their *Perestroika in the Hinterlands* series on "Udmurtiya and the Nationalities Question." Published in September 1989, this volume highlighted the kind of societal issues that the Soviets would have preferred the US inspectors not to see.[1]

By February, the issue of rejected social *zayafkas* began to rival the ongoing CargoScan disagreement in term of US inspector emphasis at the weekly meetings with their Soviet counterparts. Insofar as the treaty called for relative freedom of movement within a 50-kilometer perimeter around the portal monitoring facility, the Soviets could not get away with rejecting every request. The inspectors had put in repeated requests to visit the Café Kosmos, but these were rejected due to a food shortage. To compensate, the Soviets suggested that the inspectors try a different restaurant, the Ural Restaurant near the House of

Culture. I went along on this visit. When we arrived at the restaurant, there were a handful of Soviet couples already seated, their mood gloomy. We were ushered to a separate wing of the restaurant, physically separated from the Soviets but still in their line of vision.

We ordered from the menu and waited for our meals to be served. There had been selections for both chicken and beef main courses, and we had ordered several of each. As the waiting staff brought the food out, however, the mood in the restaurant turned angry. "Why do the Americans get beef and chicken," a young lady cried out, "and we get potatoes!" It quickly became apparent that the factory had stacked the deck in our favor, providing the restaurant with food to feed us. The wild card, however, was a Soviet population fed up with the status quo, and angry at the foreigners who were being given preferential treatment. As the Soviet diners began to rise to their feet and make their way toward our table, our Soviet escorts quickly ushered us out the back door to a waiting Rafik van, which took us back to the portal. We left our meals untouched, feeling lucky to have escaped without a major incident.

On February 17, 1990, *Leninski Put'* published a letter entitled "May Reason Win: Appeal to the Working People of Udmurtia." It was written by a collective of Izhevsk communist party officials, some of whom were candidates running in the March 4 election for Congress of People's Deputies and Supreme Soviet of the Russian SFSR, for the purpose of addressing "what is being discussed with bitterness and indignation at work, home, in lines and on busses."

The authors were concerned about the tone and content of discourse taking place in the leadup to the March 4 elections. "At our enterprises and in our republic, calls to attend rallies and demonstrations, and in some places even to strike, are resounding louder and louder. There are leaflets, various rumors, and appeals, and the party is being slandered groundlessly. People are becoming increasingly agitated and spreading gossip."

Like many communists at the time, the authors were struggling to come to grips with the changes that were sweeping over their country. "In whom and what shall we believe?" they asked. "Who can guarantee that someone is not playing games with people's emotions and the present difficulties? Who is stirring up the pot?" Life in parts of the far-flung Soviet empire was beginning to spin out of control. "We watch television and see the wild throngs of brutal thugs and the events in Baku and Dushanbe. If this is democracy, then spare us. Perhaps they are trying to make our Izhevsk the site of the next slaughter?"

This fear of chaos permeated the letter. "We know that a crowd excited by extremist appeals will do things that one person alone will not do," the authors concluded. "Democracy and anarchy are incompatible."

Such "anarchy," the authors feared, might result from a political rally planned for February 22 in Izhevsk. Many feared that the rally, which was being organized by the "Movement for Democracy," a radical left political organization that was vociferously anti-communist, would be used as a trigger for political violence. However, while more than 10,000 people attended the rally, which lasted 2 ½ hours and involved more than 30 public speakers, there was no violence. "Both sides," an article entitled "The Rally," published in *Udmurtskaya Pravda*, noted, "the protectors and the protected, were at their best."

Many of the speakers were drawn from the stricken working class, who decried "the squalor of life and the squalor of the authorities," empty shelves in stores, deplorable housing situation, and the depressing state of medical care.

Many of the people present, it seemed, had lost faith in the ability and willingness of the "system" to bring about the needed change. As Evgenniy Shumilov, co-chair of the Movement for Democracy, noted, "The problem is not with one odious individual or even a dozen of them. They may replace the rusty screws and wheels on our unwieldy locomotive, which is supposedly going to make a stop at the commune, but even with the new screws we will not reach that brightly shining in a hundred years. We need to replace the entire locomotive."

"The entire locomotive" was all-inclusive. Shumilov and others of his ilk had tired of Mikhail Gorbachev, mocking perestroika as a "pseudo-scientific ideological doctrine." The crowd in attendance was in apparent agreement; they had lost faith in the Communist Party, whose representatives were drowned out with whistling and catcalls when they attempted to address the rally.

The election—the ostensible purpose of the rally—was itself suspect. Over 200 communist party officials had been nominated by the "system" to vie for the 200 seats in the Udmurt Soviet. Demands for the resignation of the entire Udmurt party apparatus were issued by the organizers, to the approval of the majority of those in attendance.

The election of March 4 loomed large, and emotions were running high. As the reporter from *Udmurtskaya Pravda* observed, "The streets are not the best places to make weighty decisions."

On February 24 I travelled to Moscow together with Anne Mortenson, the HTSC translator, for the weekly Embassy liaison trip. Our Soviet escorts cautioned us about being anywhere besides our hotel room or the US Embassy on Sunday, February 25. "If you have to be out," they told us, "stick to the outskirts of the city. But above all else, avoid the city center. There will be a demonstration, and the nationalists and radicals plan to cause trouble. There may be rioting and violence."

Like many of the inspectors with a passion for Soviet affairs, Anne and I had been tracking the political situation in the Soviet Union and were aware of the planned demonstration our escorts were warning us about, and the potential for violence. We had watched as the local Votkinsk authorities had warned about similar unrest in Izhevsk the week prior, only to have the demonstrations unfold peacefully. Anne and I had discussed the Moscow demonstration, and we were both in agreement that we wanted front row seats to the show. I thanked our

Soviet escorts for their concern for our safety and assured them that we would take their warnings into account when conducting ourselves during our Moscow visit.

Early the next morning, Anne and I departed the Ukraina Hotel, and made our way to the nearby Kievskaya Metro Station, where we caught the train to Gorky Park, the site of the planned demonstration. There were two demonstrations being planned for Sunday, both called by the National Democratic Front, a coalition of opposition groups striving for electoral unity in the upcoming March 4 elections. The Gorky Park demonstration—called a "meeting" by the organizers—was the southern grouping of participants. A simultaneous "meeting" was scheduled to take place in northern Moscow at the same time. Upon the conclusion of the speeches, the organizers planned for the two "meetings" to march toward the city center where they would join forces.

The symbolism of the date chosen for the demonstration did not escape anyone with an eye for Russian history—under the old Gregorian calendar, February 25 was the third and final day of massive protests in Saint Petersburg that led to the collapse of the rule of Tsar Nicholas II. The army was called into the streets on February 26 to quell the rioting, before eventually going over to the side of the revolutionaries. Perhaps there were some among the current demonstrators who hoped that history would repeat itself. By the nature of their response, it was certain that at least some among the Soviet authorities feared it would.

Our Soviet escorts had warned us that there could be over a million participants in this demonstration but based upon the ridership on the train to Gorky Park, where there were only a handful of persons carrying rolled-up banners visible, the actual attendance was going to be much smaller. Indeed, Anne and I were struck by the difference in numbers between the demonstrators and the Soviet security forces deployed to contain them. Literally as soon as Anne and I exited the metro, we found ourselves in a veritable sea of police and Interior Ministry troops, all wearing riot gear. At every block, companies of 150–200 riot police were formed up, with hundreds more situated in Gorky Park itself, where the security services had established a command post. Dozens of plainclothes security officers were milling about, and in the adjacent streets ambulances and "paddy wagons" were being pre-positioned.

At around 10.30 am, the first demonstrators began to arrive, consisting primarily of young organizers and old women. Just two weeks ago, on February 7, the Central Committee of the Communist Party, following a tumultuous three-day session, voted to give up the leading role prescribed for it by Article VI of the 1977 Soviet Constitution, which had granted the CPSU a monopoly over the political system. This was part of Mikhail Gorbachev's master plan to transition the Soviet Union away from a single-party system, to one where a strong executive presided over democratic institutions comprised of several different political parties. (This was also the objective of Andrei Sakharov when he tried to speak at the Congress of People's Deputies on December 12, 1989, only to be shouted down by Gorbachev. Major changes in Soviet politics, apparently, could only take place on Gorbachev's timetable.)

Like virtually every aspect of his perestroika-related reforms, however, there was a vast difference between the vision and reality. While the CPSU envisioned that it would play a major role—if not the major role—in helping form and guide these new political parties, it had no mandate to do so. The power was now in the hands of the people who, without any consultation with either the CPSU or central authorities, were acting out as they best saw fit. But this was all new for the vanguard of this experiment in Soviet democracy. An estimated crowd of some 100,000 eventually gathered in Gorkii Park.

Around noon they began to peacefully march down the wide avenues of Moscow's Garden Ring, before marching to Smolensk Square in front of the Foreign Ministry, where a podium had been set up for speeches. There was no riot, no storming of the Kremlin, just the peaceful expression of a population grown weary of a government that no longer seemed to serve their best interests. In the end, the participants eventually dispersed, leaving the riot police and interior ministry troops wondering what all the fuss had been about.

Anne and I returned to Votkinsk the next day, February 26, only to find a city that had been turned upside down. A week after the Izhevsk rally, a rumor surfaced that the Movement for Democracy would hold a demonstration in Votkinsk on Sunday, February 25, timed to coincide with the Moscow "meetings." As had been the case in Moscow, local authorities predicted that there would be wide-spread social disturbances, including "reprisals against certain members of the apparatus." For Vladimir Sadovnikov, the former Director General of the Votkinsk Factory Association, the threat of violence to himself and his family hit home. "They will knock me off first of all," Sadovnikov told his wife. "There are people who want to get even with me."[2]

Since stepping down as the Director General of the Votkinsk Factory, Sadovnikov had settled into a quiet life of semi-retirement. He continued to serve as a deputy in the Supreme Soviet of the Udmurt ASSR, representing Votkinsk, and kept regular meeting hours at the House of Culture to hear the concerns of those he represented. But as the economic situation in Votkinsk worsened, bitterness emerged among those people who sought to shift the blame for their current predicament onto the shoulders of the man who, at a time in the not-so-distant past, had ruled over the town and its inhabitants like a benevolent Lord.

Rumors followed rumors, most (if not all) unsubstantiated: Sadovnikov used the factory car for his personal business (not true—his personal Volga was the same color—white—as the factory Volga), or that the former Director

General fired people without cause (he was the head of a large factory of national importance; terminations certainly occurred, and feelings were invariably hurt). But most of the workforce worshipped the man, a clear indication that he had managed the factory in a fair and balanced manner. Stories about corruption and self-enrichment were belied by the modest reality of his living accommodations and lifestyle. But fact-based truth no longer mattered—if one was a member of the communist elite, as Sadovnikov surely was, then they were, in the minds of the recently empowered working class, automatically guilty of every crime alleged.

On the morning of February 25, fearing the worst, the former Director General of the Votkinsk Machine Building Plant barricaded himself, his wife, and two sons in their modest 3-room apartment in downtown Votkinsk, prepared to fight off any mob that might appear with a Barretta 9mm automatic pistol. Nothing happened; despite the rumors, the streets of Votkinsk were quiet.

The next morning, Sadovnikov woke early, dressed, and hugged his wife before leaving the house. His Baretta pistol was in the pocket of his coat. He promised to call her within the hour. The former Director General was as good as his word. "There is a folder of papers on my desk," he told his wife over the phone. "Read it tomorrow."

At 9.20 am, Vladimir Gennadievich Sadovnikov strode up the stairs of the House of Culture, pulled out his pistol, and shot himself in the temple. He died instantly. In his jacket were found notes to family, colleagues from the Votkinsk factory, and law enforcement.

Sadovnikov blamed Parkinson's disease for the decision to end his life, but his final letter hinted at a man who had lost his place in society. "I ask that those I somehow hurt to forgive me," he wrote. "If I did hurt someone, it was because it seemed to me that I did it for the cause. Matters were complicated and were of great national importance. I ask that I not be considered a coward as regards my fate. I never bent and I reached the end on my own two feet. Sooner or later, everyone meets the same end."

Sadovnikov's suicide exposed fractures in society regarding the man who had once dominated every aspect of life in Votkinsk. The First Secretary of the Udmurt Communist Party, Pyotr Grishchenko, who had called for Sadovnikov's replacement in 1987 (only to be rebuked by the Minister of Defense Industry at the time, Pavel Finogenov) continued his program of personal animosity, refusing to allow the workers of the Votkinsk Factory to republish their obituary for their beloved former Director General in newspapers controlled by the Communist Party. Grishchenko likewise boycotted Sadovnikov's funeral.

The workers of the Votkinsk Machine Building Plant, however, did not. When Vladimir Gennadievich Sadovnikov, the two-time recipient of the gold star of a Hero of Socialist Labor and the man who had more than earned the sobriquet "Father of Votkinsk," was laid to rest in Votkinsk's *Yuzhnii* (southern) cemetery, tens of thousands of men and women who worked at the factory he loved, and lived in the town he helped build, filed past in the cold and snow to pay their final respects.

Life, however, goes on, no matter the tragedy, or how close it hits home. For the workers of the Votkinsk Machine Building Plant, this meant that once they put their long-time Director General in the earth, they had to turn to the very political process which precipitated the changes that helped push Sadovnikov to take his life, in this case the elections scheduled for March 4.

At a meeting of the Votkinsk GorCom on December 28, 1989, the Votkinsk Factory had nominated Boris Mikhailovich Belousov, the Minister of Defense Industry, as their candidate for *Avtozavod* (Automobile Factory) National Territorial District 133 of the Russian Soviet Federative Socialist Republic Council of People's Deputies, which encompassed Votkinsk. Belousov was intimately familiar with both the Udmurt Republic and the Votkinsk region, having spent 24 years working at the Izhevsk Mechanical Plant, starting as a motorcycle mechanic in 1956 and moving up, in 1976, to become Director.

According to an article, "Our Candidates: We are counting on his help," published in *Leninski Put'* on February 7, 1990, Belousov had served on the Udmurt Communist Party's defense industry department since 1969, where he would have been fully briefed on the work done in Votkinsk. In 1980 Belousov was appointed a deputy minister of the USSR Ministry of Defense Industry, and in 1985 made First Deputy Minister. In 1987 Belousov was appointed Minister of the Machine Building Industry, and in 1988, when that ministry merged with the Ministry of Defense Industry, Belousov became the Minister of the newly combined activity.

As the Minister of Defense Industry, Belousov was able to capitalize on his ongoing ministerial work on preparing a law for the conversion of the defense industry into civilian applications. Belousov understood the relationship between factories like the Votkinsk Machine Building Plan and the cities and regions they operated in and emphasized the need for the social development of the populations residing in the district he was seeking to represent.

Under normal circumstances, a candidate with the resume of Boris Belousov would have been a shoo-in for election. But these were not normal times, and Belousov had one resume entry which was to prove his undoing—his membership in the Communist Party. Membership in the Party of Lenin (and Stalin) had been lagging for years, and the situation had worsened considerably under perestroika. Recruitment drives in Votkinsk had come up empty handed, forcing local communist party officials to acknowledge that the party had "simply let time slip away from us." Glasnost and perestroika had caused many young people who would normally be recruited to question the "example of the communist attitude toward life and work" that had motivated those who had gone before them. The question of who would follow the communist party, and how things would be after the communist party was gone, were more important than any notion of reviving what many people believed was a decayed, moribund apparatus.

But the nail in the coffin of Belousov's political fortune was a decision by the Communist Party in early January 1990 to provide a 50% salary increase to party and soviet cadres. While party officials explained this decision as a necessary mechanism to retain membership, which simply brought the salaries of those involved in line with the pay other categories of workers received, for the working population of Votkinsk, it was an unforgivable act. As an article in the January 12, 1990 issue of *Leninski Put'* noted, "those who wished to be considered the leaders of perestroika have used some incomprehensible logic to begin perestroika with an action very typical of the period of stagnation." At a time when many Soviet citizens were questioning whether the Communist Party was capable of supporting the people over its own privileges, the decision to increase the pay of party cadre seemed to provide an answer—M. K. Kokorin, a career prosecutor, won the vote.

While the citizens of the Russian SFSR were engaged in electing their own Congress of People's Deputies, Soviet Premier Mikhail Gorbachev struggled to get the Supreme Soviet, itself a by-product of the 1989 election, to go along with his plan to imbue him with presidential powers, transitioning the Soviet Union away from a system where the Communist Party ruled supreme to one where a representative of the people who was not necessarily a member of the Party could govern the disparate republics that comprised the USSR.

On February 27, two days after the Gorky demonstrations, the Supreme Soviet voted to convene an extraordinary session of Congress of People's Deputies on March 12, where it would be called upon to consider a constitutional amendment calling for the creation of a new presidential system of government. Interestingly, Boris Yeltsin broke ranks with the other members of the Democratic Movement and voted in favor of holding the session.[3]

Agreeing to bring the issue of a presidential form of government up for consideration by the Congress of People's Deputies, and agreeing on who would serve as president, were two different issues altogether. This was especially so when it became clear that Gorbachev had decided to forego a general election and instead would seek his direct appointment through a vote of the deputies. On March 9, Boris Yeltsin told reporters from the Italian newspaper *Corriere della Sera* that "Gorbachev wants to be elected by the Congress of People's Deputies and not by the people, and this is a method I do not approve and will oppose." Yeltsin then added, ominously, "This could change the day on which the president is elected by universal suffrage, perhaps in four years or maybe even in one. If Gorbachev does not change course, his replacement will become necessary."[4]

Yeltsin's words resonated with the US Ambassador to the Soviet Union, Jack F. Matlock, Jr. Matlock had met with Soviet Foreign Minister Eduard Shevardnadze on March 7, at which time he was told by the Soviet Minister that the period between March 10 and March 12 would be "decisive" for the future of the Soviet Union. According to Shevardnadze, there was strong opposition to Gorbachev's plan to create a presidential system of government which would preside over a federation of sovereign states. The nationality issue was seen by Shevardnadze as a trigger for potential civil war, especially if the newly elected Lithuanian Parliament sought to declare independence prior to the convening of the Congress of People's Deputies. In that case, the Soviet military might attempt to seize power in Lithuania, and even remove Gorbachev from power.[5]

On the morning of March 11, the Lithuanian Supreme Council voted 124 to 0, with six abstentions, for the independence of the newly declared "Lithuanian Republic." The Soviet Union was teetering on the brink of collapse. It was in this context that the CargoScan crisis of March 10 unfolded.

Picking up the Pieces

AFTER MORE THAN four months of disagreement between the US and Soviet side over whether or not CargoScan was operational, the issue was brought to a head in early March 1990 when the Votkinsk factory leadership, frustrated over what it viewed as intransigence on the part of the US inspectors, opted to take matters into their own hands. The resulting Soviet decision to transport the three missile-carrying 6-axle railcars from Votkinsk without allowing them to be imaged by CargoScan created a firestorm of diplomatic activity, with US officials reaching out to their Soviet counterparts at every level possible, including the Secretary of State and Foreign Minister. Moscow, however, was distracted with the existential problems presented by the combination of the convening of the Congress of People's Deputies and the looming declaration of Lithuanian independence. What normally would have been a major crisis paled in comparison with the life-or-death issues facing the senior levels of Soviet leadership.

Moreover, far from a black and white case of Soviet cheating, the CargoScan crisis was one of the Americans own making, a fact that soon became clear to US officials as they engaged with their Soviet counterparts. At the US Embassy in Moscow, Eileen Malloy, a State Department official assigned to the Arms Control Implementation Unit (ACIU) responsible for facilitating inspection-related tasks in Moscow, had contacted a duty officer, Mr. Babaevskiy, her opposite number in the Soviet Ministry of Foreign Affairs.

Babaevskiy appeared to be well briefed on the details of the crisis and pointed out that the Votkinsk officials were well within their rights according to the Memorandum of Agreement, given that the CargoScan system was not, in their opinion, operational. Eileen told Babaevskiy that a US delegation, headed by Dr. George Look, was on its way to Votkinsk to resolve the outstanding technical issues, and that the Soviets should hold off on shipping the missiles until after the delegation completed its work. Babaevskiy indicated that he would be in touch with his superiors and get back to Eileen when he had heard something.

At 11.20 am on the morning of March 10, some eight hours after the first missile had left Votkinsk, Ambassador Matlock arrived at the Soviet Foreign Ministry for a meeting with First Deputy Minister. Alexander Bessmertnykh. Bessmertnykh informed Matlock that the decision to ship out the missiles was a purely technical one made by the factory director, Mr. Tolmachev, based upon the needs of the factory. The freezing of missile traffic out of the factory, Bessmertnykh noted, had severely disrupted the factory's carefully planned production schedule.

Bessmertnykh's comments were echoed in a later meeting between Ambassador Matlock, Deputy Foreign Minister Victor Karpov and the Soviet Representative to the Special Verification Committee, Ambassador Strelt'sov. Under no circumstances, Karpov told Matlock, could the actions of the US inspectors in Votkinsk be permitted to disrupt the production schedule of the Votkinsk factory. Ambassador Karpov underscored the fact that the US actions had already held up missile production by nine days, even though the Memorandum of Agreement only allowed for a period of four hours. The Votkinsk factory, Karpov concluded, had complied with every obligation incurred under the treaty. The fault for the crisis, he said, was solely the responsibility of the American side.

It became apparent that the Votkinsk missile crisis was going to have to be resolved by the delegation headed by Dr. George Look, which was scheduled to arrive in Moscow on March 11, and travel to Votkinsk the next day. It was at this juncture that a tactical decision was made on site in Votkinsk that would greatly ease the work of Look and his team. During the back-and-forth conversations between the US Site Commander, Roy Peterson, and the head of Department 162, Anatoli Tomilov, about the technicalities of the dispute, Tomilov had indicated that the time for talking was long past, and that each side would each side should focus on completing the "comments" section of the inspection report with their own narrative.

John Sartorius advised Roy Peterson of the absolute requirement for both the US and Soviet sides to be of one mind on the precise nature of the disagreements over CargoScan, or else risk falling into the trap of competing narratives, the unravelling of which would not only consume a great deal of time, but further cloud the technical issues involved. John was able to cite an earlier incident that had transpired on December 15, 1989, involving the use of cameras to record a dispute over allegations of unauthorized access by US inspectors to the CargoScan facility, which at the time was still under construction. Then, both the US and Soviet sides had provided their own versions of events regarding the incident in question in their respective "comments" section of the inspection report, creating a competing list of charges and countercharges which were viewed by both sides as counterproductive. It was not until the first week of January 1990 that the two sides were able to agree to a common narrative which was then sent on to the Special Verification Commission for resolution.

John had shared his concern over repeating this approach to Colonel Connell, who agreed and instructed John to approach Roy Peterson and get his permission to begin working with their Soviet counterparts to craft agreed upon common language that would be included in both the US and Soviet "comments" section of the inspection reports documenting the treaty "ambiguity" in question, which in this case involved questions pertaining to the operational status of CargoScan.

While the crisis unfolded around him, John, Sam Israelit, and the Soviet escorts sequestered themselves in the OSIA conference room, working on the text of a joint narrative in both English and Russian languages that would be inserted in the "comments" section. This language was critical to delineating the precise nature of the standoff. The precision displayed by John, Sam, and the Soviet escorts in crafting language that captured in exquisite detail the technical issues at stake was to pay huge dividends once the US and Soviet delegations arrived in Votkinsk to negotiate a solution to the CargoScan impasse.

Dr. Look, Karen Lawson, and the other members of the US delegation, along with George Connell, arrived in Votkinsk on the morning of March 12. The Soviet delegation, headed by Lev Kokurin, arrived that same day. The US delegation was quartered at the Ustinov Dacha, while the actual negotiations took place in the US conference room located in the Roosevelt Building. In a memorandum prepared for the Look delegation, Roy Peterson outlined the four "showstopper" issues that needed resolution before the Soviets would agree to allow an SS-25 missile to be imaged by CargoScan. These were shutter attenuation, scan length, detector geometry, and the storage/erasure of image data. Over the course of the next four days, Dr. Look and Lev Kokurin evaluated the respective US and Soviet positions. The common language in the "comments" section of the inspection report greatly facilitated this work, as did the detailed point papers prepared by both John Sartorius and Sam Israelit, explaining the technical details involved.

In the end, Dr. Look agreed to adopt virtually every one of the Soviet recommendations that had been put on the table regarding the operation of CargoScan since December 1989. Regarding the issue of shutter attenuation, it was agreed to power up the Linatron x-ray only one second (versus five seconds) before the imaging began. On the matter of scan length, Dr. Look agreed to adopt the Soviet recommendation that the shutter begin opening 180 milliseconds, versus 200 milliseconds, before imaging begins; on the matter of detector geometry, Dr. Look adopted the Soviet method of calculation, agreeing to have two detectors removed from the array.

The one area where Dr. Look inserted an American solution was on the issue of the storage of magnetic tapes used to record images taken by CargoScan. The Soviets insisted, and Dr. Look concurred, that no magnetic tape would ever leave the Votkinsk site. Moreover, the tapes themselves would be stored in the CragoScan control module using a US lock and Soviet seal. But Dr. Look insisted, and the Soviets agreed, that two hexidecimal data printouts would be made of the image on tape, with one printout given to each side, which would then be included in the Monthly Inspection Report. Dr. Look also required that two polaroid photographs be taken of one view of the CargoScan image, to be selected by the US Duty Officer, which would likewise be shared with both parties and included in the Monthly Report.

Dr. Look and Lev Kokurin agreed to several lesser issues, most of which required locally developed "objective criteria" to be agreed between the US inspectors and the Votkinsk factory representatives, and none of which would prevent CargoScan from being operated. In addition, Dr. Look finally broke the log jam regarding CargoScan documentation, instructing the US inspectors to release all documentation currently stored on site that could be used for the repair and maintenance of CargoScan. Many of these documents had been held back by the inspectors based upon previous policy guidance derived from Defense Technology Security Administration (DTSA) rules and regulations governing the Soviet Union, and their absence had greatly disrupted the CargoScan installation process.

The inspectors who had been involved in the CargoScan crisis received high praise from the OSIA leadership for their performance. General Lajoie sent a formal Letter of Appreciation to all Votkinsk Portal Inspection team members in which he declared that their collective performance "at the front line of INF implementation during a very demanding period" was "highly commendable." Lajoie continued, noting that "[i]n carrying out the inspection process under most challenging circumstances, you have demonstrated the highest degree of professionalism and a comprehensive understanding of the INF Treaty and US rights contained therein."

Roy Peterson, the Site Commander at the height of the crisis, wrote a personal Letter of Appreciation for each of the duty officers that had been on-site during the crisis. "Your tenacity and assistance in delaying final shipment of the [SS-25] missile," Peterson wrote, "was crucial to the success of focusing Soviet interest in permitting a final resolution" to the crisis. "Your help in negotiating with missile factory representatives was of great assistance to me."

The CargoScan crisis was, for all intent and purpose, over. All that was left to do was to test its resilience under operational conditions. On March 21, the

Soviets provided the inspectors with a declaration that an SS-25 missile would be shipped from the portal at around 6.30 PM. In preparation for the inaugural use of CargoScan, the Soviets brought out a rail plow to clear the tracks of snow that had accumulated in the eleven days since they had last shipped a missile. There was a little bit of drama when the plow derailed outside the inspection building, but the Soviets were able to get it back on track using some heavy timbers and muscle. The limit switches inside the CargoScan structure were cleared by a joint team of US inspectors and Soviet escorts using snow shovels.

The actual conduct of the radiographic imaging went off without any issues. Stu O'Neill once again took an inspection "first," serving as the Duty Officer for the event. The procedures agreed to during the Look delegation visit were assiduously adhered to, and the first operational use of CargoScan was in the history books. The ease with which this was accomplished, and the fact that it was done using Soviet solutions that could have (and should have) been adopted back in December 1989, had generated no small amount of angst on the part of the inspectors.

When John Sartorious returned to OSIA Headquarters in late March, he began putting together a detailed after-action report which pointed an acrimonious finger at the bureaucracy of policy oversight which had pushed the CargoScan problem onto the inspectors while providing little or no guidance on how to proceed, and then second-guessed every practical solution offered up by the inspectors, in coordination with their Soviet counterparts, only to finally give in to common sense—but only after engendering a treaty-threatening crisis. John's assessment, which was nicknamed the "Who Shot John" memorandum, was quickly classified, given the political sensitivities associated with the accusatory facts it contained, and handed over to the more seasoned diplomatic hands in the treaty compliance department of OSIA for follow-up discussions with the policy community.

The CargoScan crisis provided grist for the anti-arms control mill operated by David Sullivan on behalf of Senator Jesse Helms. The Director of the Arms Control and Disarmament Agency, Ronald Lehman, had testified before the Senate Foreign Relations Committee on March 7, 1990—prior to the "breakout" of Soviet missiles that occurred on March 10. Senator Helms, in typical fashion, wrote a letter to Lehman on March 12 in which he raised the CargoScan crisis, through a series of questions, in a manner which was both factually wrong and totally devoid of context.

"Has the United States," Helms asked, "used the CargoScan x-ray system at the Soviet Votkinsk missile factory to measure a Soviet missile yet, since we declared the system to be operational on February 9, 1990?" While someone in the policy community had informed David Sullivan, the drafter of the questions, about the decision to make CargoScan operational as of February 9, 1990, this same source failed to inform Sullivan—or Sullivan had chosen to ignore—

the fact that it was the US side which cancelled the agreement which certified February 9 as the official start date for CargoScan operations.

Helms' second question accused the Soviets of insisting "at the last minute" that the US "redesign the shutters on the CargoScan x-ray system, use only one computer tape permanently stored in the USSR for recording missile images, and refrain from making duplicate tapes to be sent back to the United States for further analysis?" Helms then cited these Soviet "conditions" as the source for "a protracted impasse in our first use of CargoScan." The Soviet objections were neither "last minute," nor inconsistent with the agreed upon parameters set forth in the Memorandum of Agreement. Moreover, the blame for the "protracted impasse" regarding CargoScan going operational rested with the US side almost exclusively.

Helms and Sullivan went further down the proverbial rabbit hole when they accused the Soviets of using the CargoScan crisis as an opportunity to ship a "new follow-on to the SS-25, perhaps capable of delivering three MIRVs (multiple independently targetable reentry vehicles—i.e., nuclear warheads), in further violation of SALT II and the already agreed START warhead counting rules?" The level of inaccuracy and baseless speculation present in the Helms letter helped bring an end to the seriousness in which anti-arms control outbursts of this nature were treated by his colleagues in the US Senate. There would be more letters in the future, but they were treated as little more than a sideshow, a distraction from the larger purpose of bringing the strategic nuclear arsenals of the US and Soviet Union under control.

Senator Helms was not the only person engaging in a bit of fanciful writing when it came to the Votkinsk missile crisis. On March 16, 1990, *The Washington Post* published a column written by Rowland Evans and Robert Novak entitled "Missile Crisis," which purported to describe the events of March 10, 1990 at the Votkinsk Portal Monitoring Facility. "Soon after Soviet guards drew their pistols against unarmed US technicians in a standoff at the Votkinsk missile plant last Sunday night," Evans and Novak wrote, "Ambassador Jack Matlock rushed to the Foreign Ministry near midnight in a crisis mood over relations with Moscow not felt since Mikhail Gorbachev took power."[6]

The article was, simply put, pure fiction. "Pistols won the standoff," Evans and Novak reported, "blocking the inspectors a second time from turning on its new x-ray to prevent production of illegal missiles." The crisis, according to the two American writers, was triggered by the Soviets exiting a missile loaded in a railcar. "US technicians tried to turn on the x-ray," Evans and Novak wrote. "They were stunned when the Soviets said no, raising three fresh objections."[7]

For the Soviets reading the pages of *The Washington Post*, the depiction of Soviet guards drawing their weapons while confronting US inspectors had to come as a shock. When asked by a correspondent from *Izvestia* to comment on *The Washington Post* column, the Deputy Minister of Defense Industry, Victor

Schukin, replied "This is the first I've heard of pistols and hostilities in Votkinsk. I'm convinced," Schukin accurately noted, "that this is a fabrication that bears no resemblance whatsoever to reality."

Schukin went on to accurately portray the gist of the missile crisis in Votkinsk, noting that the CargoScan system, as installed, did not "meet three parameters that were agreed upon by the Soviet and American sides." Schukin mentioned the delegation led by Dr. Look, stating that this team had "studied the question" and agreed to adjust the parameters of CargoScan to meet the Soviet demands.

When asked to comment on why the US press was reporting drama where none existed, Schukin replied that "This happened because a lack of knowledge or some other reason," noting that "all items were hauled out of the plant in accordance with the treaty. There were no violations on our part." Underscoring the routine nature of the events, Schukin stated that "the *shlagbaum*, signal light, and the entire control panel are integral and under American control."[8]

It was as if Victor Schukin had read the final entries in the timeline assembled by Roy Peterson detailing the events surrounding the departure of the first missile on March 10:

0219: One final request made to conduct radiographic imaging. Soviet side refuses to consider it. No further questions from US side.

0220: Rail semaphore gate SGA raised, traffic light TLB switched to green.

0221: Traffic light TLB malfunctions—red light will not switch to green.

0223: VPMS Operator Console manually overridden; traffic light TLB switched to green. Railcar 36899565 departs under protest.

Jesse Helms' final question to Ron Lehman was, perhaps, the most relevant to reality. The Soviets maintained that the decision to rush the three SS-25s out of the factory void of CargoScan imaging was purely a matter of economics and production reality. There is no doubting the fact that the Votkinsk factory, like the rest of the Soviet Union, was going through difficult times, and the lack of income brought on by their failure to deliver contracted missiles to their customer was a source of great distress for the factory management. Moreover, the Final Assembly Plant had a finite capacity to store missiles, either as finished products or in various stages of assembly. It is highly plausible that this capacity had been met, and that any continued delay in freeing up space inside the facility brought on by delaying the shipment of assembled missiles would cause the factory to be unable to receive additional missile components due to be delivered by the vendors who supplied them. Seen in this context, the Soviets were not trying to hide anything from the inspectors, and the three missiles that escaped imaging by CargoScan were simply part of the normal production run of SS-25s.

Mitigating against this assessment, however, is the fact that the Soviets had acknowledged that, at the time of the signing of the INF Treaty, the Final Assembly Plant was storing components for some 36 SS-20 missiles. If this statement was correct, then the capacity of the plant to hold missiles and missile components had not been broached by the seven or eight missiles present at the time the decision was made to ship the three missiles on March 10. Likewise, with the delegation led by Dr. Look enroute, the argument that a financial penalty would be accrued by waiting a few more days does not resonate strongly.

The key to the truth behind these three missiles appears to rest with my analysis of "anomalous" missiles, and what, if anything, these anomalies represented. It is possible that my observations were simply a byproduct of misinterpreting the data, drawing conclusions over perceived patterns which bore no relationship to reality, and that my assessment regarding the three "anomalous" missiles, deemed by many to be "deadly accurate," was simply a matter of coincidence.

If, however, my assessments were correct, there remained the mystery of what, if anything, made the three "anomalous" missiles so sensitive that the Soviets would risk an international crisis rather than have them subjected to radiographic imaging by CargoScan. The Helms letter suggests that the missiles were a new version of the SS-25 believed to be under development at the time and assessed as being capable of carrying three independently targeted warheads. However, the SS-25 follow-on, which would become known as the S-27, or *Topol-M*, was still in the design phase at the time of the CargoScan crisis, and as such could not have been the culprit.[9]

There was, however, a unique variant of the SS-25 being shipped from Votkinsk in the winter of 1989–90, one so secret that its potential existence was not on the radar of the analysts in the US intelligence community. The origins of this SS-25 variant lay in a highly classified doomsday system employed by the Soviets, known as "Perimeter" or, more popularly referred to as the "Dead Hand." The purpose of the Perimeter system was to ensure that the Soviets retained a second-strike capability in the case of an all-out nuclear attack by the United States which eliminated the Soviet leadership.[10]

Specially modified MR-UR-100*UTKKh*/SS-17 rockets, equipped with a radio communication system, known as the 15B99, instead of nuclear warheads, were stored in hardened missile silos, where they were connected to an autonomous command and control system. This system collected data from sensors located at strategic locations throughout the Soviet Union which measured flashes of light, radiation concentrations, and seismic activity in order to determine if the Soviet Union had been subjected to a nuclear attack. It also monitored critical national-level communications activity to determine if there was anyone remaining who could order a retaliatory nuclear strike. If the Perimeter system determined that the Soviet command system had, in fact, been taken out by a nuclear strike, it would then launch the modified SS-17 rockets, which would fly over the length of the Soviet Union, broadcasting launch codes which would automatically send all surviving Soviet missiles to their targets in the United States and Europe.[11]

The SS-17 missiles assigned to the Perimeter system became operational in January 1985. Almost immediately, the Soviet high command became worried about their survivability, as the US had developed a new submarine-launched ballistic missile, the Trident D-5, which had a shorter time of flight before reaching their targets (in some scenarios, less than three minutes) and high levels of accuracy which not only made a nuclear surprise attack on Soviet soil possible, but also threatened the very systems—the silo-based SS-17 Perimeter rockets—that were intended to guarantee a viable retaliatory strike.

To supplement the SS-17-based Perimeter system, the Soviets turned to the Nadiradze design bureau to modify the *PioneerUTKKh*/SS-20 so that it could carry a 15B99 radio communication system like the one used by the SS-17 to transmit launch codes to surviving Soviet missiles. The 249th Missile Regiment in Polotsk was selected to operate this new missile, known as the "Gorn."[12] The 249th Missile Regiment stood down in March 1986 and was immediately converted to operate the Gorn command missile, which was undergoing tests at the Plesetsk missile range. On December 26, 1986, the 249th Missile Regiment, equipped with nine Gorn command missiles, went on full duty, with at least three of its mobile launchers always deployed in the field, ready to execute their doomsday mission.

The INF treaty, however, made the Gorn obsolete less than a year after it went online. The 249th Missile Regiment stood down in 1989, its missiles were destroyed under the terms of the treaty, and the regiment was disbanded. Almost immediately, the Soviets began looking for a candidate to fill the gap created by the elimination of the SS-20/"Gorn" command missiles. Once again, the Nadiradze design bureau was called upon to solve the problem, this time by modifying the SS-25 to carry the 15B99 radio communication system instead of a nuclear warhead. Given the experience gained in the development of the Gorn system, the turnaround time for this project was significantly reduced.

At least 13 SS-25s were eventually modified to carry the radio communication system. Four of these were used in flight tests conducted on August 3, October 17, November 26, and December 25 of 1990. All flight tests were successful. On December 26, 1990, the nine remaining modified SS-25 command missiles, known as the "Sirena," assumed full combat duty as part of the 8th Missile Division, operating from the Yurya missile base.[13] At least three of these missiles were deployed in the field at any given time, ready to be called upon to execute their doomsday mission of ensuring that all Soviet intercontinental ballistic missiles that survived a nuclear attack by the US would be able to be launched in retaliation, even if Soviet leadership and command and control capability had been destroyed.

The production timelines that would support the flight test and operational deployment of at least 13 Sirena missiles in the second half of 1990 logically coincided with the observed shipments of the "anomalous" missiles from the Votkinsk Final Assembly Plant in late 1989 and in March 1990. This remains speculation, however—the Soviets have never confirmed that the three missiles shipped out from Votkinsk on March 10, 1990, were affiliated with the Sirena program.

If, however, the "anomalous" missiles were in fact linked to the Sirena program, then the Soviets rush to fill the operational gap in its Perimeter dead-hand autonomous missile launch system created by the INF-mandated elimination of the SS-20/"Gorn" command rocket put the Sirena missile on a collision course with US inspectors seeking to put CargoScan into operation. Given the extremely sensitive nature of the Perimeter program, logic dictates that the Soviets would have preferred a diplomatic crisis over having one of their biggest national security secrets exposed through radiographic imaging that would have detected anomalies in the second stage of the SS-25 that differed from what had been declared in the treaty, and as such would need to be explained.

Team Williams

I RETURNED to OSIA Headquarters while the CargoScan crisis was still raging, and much of my time upon arrival was spent providing a backstop for the technical discussions underway in Votkinsk about resolving the standoff. I was juggling several major projects, including preparing a standard operating procedure for "serendipitous intelligence collection" at Votkinsk, and a paper for ACIS detailing the analytical methodology I had used to make predictions about missile production at Votkinsk that had helped fuel the CargoScan crisis.

Another project involved helping evaluate various options for "tagging" a missile under a future START inspection regime. Under START, missiles would become accountable items, as opposed to prohibited, and any missile exiting a facility subjected to perimeter portal monitoring would need to have a unique identifier attached to it by the inspecting party so that it could be tracked and accounted for as part of an overall verification program.

Perhaps my biggest accomplishment during this time was finalizing a formal curriculum for a solid rocket motor production/assembly course that would become prerequisite training for all future portal monitoring inspectors. I had attended the original course on in-house production designed to familiarize employees and management with the complexity and hazards associated with solid rocket motor production, and found it not only fascinating, but extremely useful for someone like myself who, with no background in missile production, might be thrust into inspecting a Soviet missile final assembly plant.

Originally, I had been tasked to work on this issue with John Sartorius, but his skill set was better needed by those working the Memorandum of Agreement issues, especially when it came to CargoScan. Left to my own devices, I worked with the Hercules course director, Bob Erickson, to pare down the original four-day course, removing overly technical topics of little value to an inspector while focusing on more essential knowledge that could empower an inspector with an understanding of how solid rocket motors worked, how they were produced, and how they were assembled.

An inspector armed with this kind of foundational knowledge, I believed, would be able to make more informed observations during any future missile inspections of Soviet solid-fuel missiles and their production facilities. I also coordinated with the Minuteman ICBM rocket motor storage unit located on nearby Hill Air Force Base to provide attendees of the Hercules course with a tour of the Minuteman III missile assembly facility. Between the Hercules course and the Hill AFB tour, I was able to cobble together a proposal for a two and a half-day course of instruction which, when combined with a specifically tailored intelligence collection standard operating procedure for Votkinsk that I was finalizing, could turn every future inspector into a viable "serendipitous" intelligence collector.[14]

This was a much bigger accomplishment than it appears on paper, in so far as there was little support among some of the field grade officers within the Directorate for Portal Monitoring for this kind of training. From their point of view this training was not essential and took away from what they viewed as the more pressing job of managing portal monitoring activities in both Magna and Votkinsk, which were essential to accomplishing our treaty-mandated mission. I had the support of ACIS, who were pushing the full four-day course—but getting Majors and Lieutenant Colonels who were caught up in complex logistics and contract management details excited about intelligence collection, which was not deemed to be mission essential, was a steep uphill battle.

"Should missile training at Magna be attempted?" was an oft-repeated mantra in the activities schedule prepared each month by the field grade action officers for the Director, Portal Monitoring. In the end, I stopped asking whether a missile course was desirable, and took advantage of approved liaison trips to Magna to engage in a side hustle with Hercules and Hill Air Force Base that produced a finished product. While the field grade officers were debating the merits of a one-day "Missile 101" course, I was able, by the end of March, to deliver a fully vetted two-and-a-half-day curriculum to Colonel Connell as a *fait accompli*. Colonel Connell signed off on it and forwarded it to the Director for Operations for inclusion into the OSIA formal program of training for all future portal monitoring inspectors, much to the chagrin of those opposed to the concept.

Like everyone assigned to the Portal Monitoring Directorate, I blocked out my work schedule at OSIA Headquarters with one eye on the calendar, knowing that in the not-so-distant future I would be rotating back to Votkinsk for a rotation that could last six weeks or more. This meant either working on a project at an accelerated pace, with the goal being to complete it before the next rotation date, slowing things down so that I could find a good point to hit "pause" while I rotated back to Votkinsk, or partnering up with someone so that a project could be handed off without any major interruption brought on by my disappearing for weeks at a time.

When I rotated back from Votkinsk in March, however, this balancing act came to a halt. I was informed that I had new orders and would be leaving OSIA in the summer. There had been a wrestling match between OSIA and Headquarters Marine Corps over the length of my assignment with OSIA—my original orders were ostensibly for two years, but I had blown by that anniversary in February with no hint of any change in the wind. To bring some clarity to the picture, General Lajoie had written to Headquarters Marine Corps, seeking to have my tour extended by 18 months so that I could help prepare for future portal monitoring inspections anticipated under the Strategic Arms Reduction Treaty (START).

I had also submitted a package to be formally trained as a Soviet Foreign Area Officer. In this effort, I had received extremely strong endorsements from General Lajoie, Colonel Englund, and Colonel Connell—three of the most experienced Russian Foreign Area Officers in the US military. "Captain Ritter has already undergone experiences that most FAOs can only aspire to," Colonel Englund wrote. "There will be a critical need for Marines with his talent, drive, and determination in our future dealings with the Soviet Union," Colonel Connell added. "Captain Ritter has already gained unique and critical experience in the East European/Soviet foreign area," General Lajoie noted. "If given the opportunity to add formal, graduate education to this significant experience, he could make many more contributions to the Marine Corps and the Nation in this area of vital importance."

It looked like my acceptance into the program was all but assured, meaning that I could expect to be sent to Monterey California for Russian language training and graduate studies by the end of the summer of 1991. The FAO training request was compatible calendar-wise with the OSIA extension request, and it had been assumed by all that this was how my future was going to unfold.

Headquarters Marine Corps had different plans. While they did, in fact, endorse my FAO package, rather than keeping me at OSIA, it was decided that I would attend Amphibious Warfare School (AWS), the professional-level training for all Marine Captains, before entering the FAO training pipeline. As such, I would be reporting to Quantico, Virginia come early-August 1990. This was an unexpected turn of events, and as such Colonel Connell thought it best that I be pulled out of the Votkinsk rotation cycle and instead focus on closing out all my unfinished work, as well as conducting a thorough turnover with whomever Headquarters Marine Corps sent to replace me. As far as I was concerned, this was welcome news. My plate was full, and it looked as if I had finished my last tour of duty as an inspector implementing the INF Treaty.

Fate, however, had other plans.

In addition to the five types of inspection listed in the original INF treaty text (baseline, closeout, short-notice, elimination, and portal monitoring), there were two other types of on-site inspection that had grown out of treaty implementation requirements unforeseen by the original negotiators. The first of these was the "technical verification" inspection. During the technical talks held in the spring of 1988, the issue of verifying the technical characteristics of the treaty-relevant missile systems that were declared by the possessing party was raised.

On May 12, 1988, following discussions between Secretary of State George Shultz and Minister of Foreign Affairs Eduard Shevardnadze, an agreement was reached which was finalized as an "agreed minute" and incorporated into the treaty. According to this minute, "During baseline inspections, the Parties will have the opportunity, on a one-time basis, to verify the technical characteristics [of missiles listed in the treaty], including the weights and dimensions of SS-20 stages, at an elimination facility. Inspectors will select at random one of each type of item to weigh and measure from a sample presented by the inspected Party at a site designated by the inspected Party."

To accomplish this task, General Lajoie selected Commander John C. Williams, a naval surface warfare officer with several tours of duty in Vietnam, who later trained as a Soviet Foreign Area Officer. Williams had served with Lajoie in Moscow in the early 1980s, where he garnered a well-deserved reputation as an aggressively competent attaché. General Lajoie had originally picked Williams to lead a standard INF inspection team, but when the requirement for "technical verification" inspections arose, it was Williams who got the nod.

Williams commanded a team of INF specialists on six separate technical verification inspections at declared Soviet elimination sites, where they measured the length, width, height, and weight of the six distinct missiles mandated for elimination under the treaty (the SS-20, SS-12, SS-4, SS-5, SS-23, and SSC-X-4 cruise missile). These measurements became the standard for all OSIA inspections. Williams' work was of immense value to OSIA and the US intelligence community, a fact alluded to by General Lajoie in comments he made on my fitness report, where he noted that I was "one of two OSIA officers singled out for commendation by the CIA."

Rumor had it that Commander Williams was the other.

The late admission by the Soviets that the first stage of the SS-25 ICBM was identical to the first stage of the banned SS-20 intermediate-range missile caused more problems than just the issue of portal monitoring. While most SS-20 operating bases were scheduled to be "closed out"—meaning all INF-related systems, along with their support structures and facilities, had been removed and/or destroyed—the Soviets had indicated that some of the former SS-20 operating bases would be converted to SS-25 operating bases. During the negotiations leading up to the signing of the INF Treaty, it was agreed that the US would be able to conduct special inspections of facilities so declared, using radiation detection equipment (RDE) that would be able to differentiate between the fast neutron intensity flux produced by an SS-20 equipped with three nuclear warheads and the single nuclear warhead of the SS-25.

Once again, Williams—who had by this time been promoted to Captain—was called upon to carry out a pair of "special inspections," one at an SS-20 operating base, the other at an SS-25 operating base, where he collected data using a fast-neutron detector, consisting of twelve three-helium (3He) gas proportional tubes in a cadmium-covered polyethylene moderator, which could identify the spatial pattern of neutrons emitted from the nuclear warheads on the two types of missiles, thereby creating a unique signature for each. These inspections were carried out in the summer of 1989, and the data and procedures were turned over to the US and Soviet negotiators in Geneva and subsequently incorporated into the Memorandum of Agreement, which was finalized on December 21, 1989.

In August 1988, the Soviets stood down two SS-20 missile regiments—the 778th Guards in Kansk, and the 382nd Guards in Novosibirsk. The missiles and launchers were scheduled for elimination. Closing out the facilities, however, would have required the destruction of the missile bays where the launchers were housed when in garrison. Instead, the Soviets decided to convert these two units into SS-25 ICBM-equipped regiments, thereby repurposing the respective garrison facilities. The 778th Guards Missile Regiment, newly equipped with nine SS-25 mobile launchers, went on alert status on December 12, 1989, followed by the 382nd on December 22. Both were now eligible under the protocol for a short-notice inspection using the RDE procedures.

Rather than dispatch the original Team Williams to carry out the task, the decision was made to put together a new team comprised of a mix of experienced team chiefs and inspectors who, along with some veterans from the original Team Williams, would form the cadre for an additional two teams capable of conducting RDE inspections. Lieutenant Colonels Nicolas Troyan and John Lohmann, two of OSIA's more experienced team chiefs, were tapped for the mission, along with several linguists and inspectors drawn from their original INF inspection teams. They would join John Williams and several of his RDE development veterans, to carry out the inaugural RDE short-notice inspections.

A short-notice inspection team was comprised of ten members. Given the unique nature of this mission, competition for the few slots on this new composite team not already allocated was high. I was therefore taken aback when I was approached by none other than Captain Williams himself about my willingness to serve as a member of his team.

"Colonel Connell says you might be available for a special inspection I'm putting together. I need a strong guy to carry my bags. Are you available?"

I had heard about the pending RDE inspection, and that Captain Williams was heading it up. I did not have to be asked twice.

In early April, the "new" Team Williams flew to Patrick Air Force Base in Florida, where an SS-25 mock-up had been assembled in a warehouse located on the US space launch complex at Cape Canaveral. We trained on this mock-up over the course of several days, familiarizing ourselves with the RDE equipment and the procedures that would be used during the actual inspection. We had nine missiles to inspect at each site, and a treaty-mandated 24-hour time limit to get the job done. When one factored in the need to do a site walk-around, and a treaty-authorized right to open the cannister of one of the nine missiles at the end of the inspection, there was no room for error. We needed to be able to complete a single missile inspection in no more than two hours. Moreover, we needed to do the task with little or no sleep—the inspection did not stop simply because a notional eight-hour workday had ended.

I was unique among the inspectors on Team Williams in that I had already seen the SS-25 missile as it exited the Votkinsk factory. I was also most probably never going to participate in an RDE inspection again, unlike the rest of the team, who were being trained for just that eventuality. As such, my job was—literally—to "carry the bags," meaning the special Pelican-cases that held the RDE equipment. I was also tasked with mastering the various security mechanisms built into the inspection process, including the use of tamper-resistant tags, tamper resistant shrink wrap, and the cobra seal—a fiber optic cable used to lock the inspection gear when we stored it in the Soviet Union once the inspection was over.

But my primary function was one I had perfected while working in Votkinsk—to conduct "serendipitous" observations, vacuuming up anything I could see during the inspection that might be of intelligence value. On this last point, Captain Williams had some words of caution. "The Soviets will be watching you with an eagle eye," he told me. "They know who you are, and that you're not one of us," meaning the cadre of "normal" INF inspectors. "Understand, we are going to be doing this kind of inspection many more times. If you get caught staring at something of potential interest, then that will probably be the last time anyone will have the chance to see it. You have a notebook. Do not be obvious in your notetaking—walk away and write your observations in a more private setting." He paused, staring at me with the kind of gimlet eye that was the unique purview of senior officers. "Colonel Connell says you are good at this sort of thing, which is why you are here. Don't blow it for the rest of us down the road by being indiscrete."

The days we spent at Cape Canaveral were busy, but there was time for some sightseeing. We were literally surrounded by history—Cape Canaveral was where John Glenn and the other Mercury astronauts got the US space program off the starting ramp, and where the Gemini program got America ready for the ultimate objective—the moon. We toured the memorial for the Apollo 1 astronauts killed in a tragic fire and saw the launch pad where Apollo 11 sent Neil Armstrong and his fellow space explorers on their way to their rendezvous with history. And it was not just history that surrounded us—every day we drove past Launch Pad 17, where a Delta II rocket was being prepared for an April 13 launch of an Australian commercial satellite.

Team Williams would not be present for the Delta II launch—we departed Florida on April 10 for the long flight to Tokyo, Japan, where we were met by the OSIA Gateway personnel. They drove us to Yokota Air Base, some 80 miles west of Narita International Airport, where we checked into the Yakota Inn, a military hotel on base for personnel on temporary assignment. We spent a day getting over the jet lag, and another few days in briefings at the Gateway facility (ACIS had flown in a team from Washington, DC, who provided us a run-down on the two locations we were going to inspect).

According to the provisions of the INF Treaty, the Soviets would be notified 16 hours in advance that a team would be arriving at one of the points of entry (POE). For the Votkinsk inspections, the POE had been Moscow. The sites scheduled for inspection—Novosibirsk and Kansk—were in Siberia, and as such were serviced by the Ulan Ude POE. Ulan Ude was the capitol of the Buryat

Figure Seven: INF Treaty-related Locations visited by the Author, 1988-1990

Autonomous Soviet Socialist Republic, located about 60 miles due east of Lake Baikal, and 150 miles from the border with Mongolia. As a crow flew, Ulan Ude was some 2,000 miles from Tokyo, but because of the need to skirt China, the actual flying distance was over 3,000 miles.

We would be flying into Ulan Ude aboard a US Air Force C-141, with a cruising speed of about 520 miles per hour, putting our time of flight to Ulan Ude at around six hours. Once we landed at Ulan Ude, Captain Williams would notify the Soviets of our intended inspection sight—in this case, the 382nd Guards Missile Regiment in Novosibirsk. The Soviets then had nine hours to get us to the designated site, after which Team Williams would have 24 hours to complete the inspection. The Soviets had already been notified of our pending arrival when we boarded the C-141 scheduled to fly us into Ulan Ude. The inspection clock was ticking.

We tend to take certain things for granted, such as that the aircraft we are flying in will successfully take off and land. But the reality is: nothing can be taken for granted—especially when it comes to aerial flight. On the evening of July 28, 1989, a Soviet Air Force Tu-134 aircraft was attempting a night landing at Ulan Ude Airport. The Tu-134 was deploying to Ulan Ude to provide transportation support for an INF inspection team due to arrive the next day. It undershot the runway by some 300 meters, broke up and caught fire. While the crew escaped unscathed (there were no passengers), the aircraft was a total loss, and its burnt-out frame was clearly visible to other aircraft as they approached the runway—including the C-141 carrying Team Williams.

Our own landing, fortunately, was uneventful, and we were met on the ramp by our Soviet hosts. Our first task upon clearing passport control was to deliver the Pelican containers containing the RDE devices to a storage building near the airfield that was used to hold OSIA inspection-specific equipment. We verified that the tamper resistant seals that had been placed on the door of the storage facility had retained their integrity. Once entry was made into the storage area, we then covered the Pelican case with tamper-evident plastic shrink wrap before securing it with a Cobra Seal—a fiber optic cable which, when applied properly, provided a unique fingerprint generated by the totally random pattern at the ends of the fiber optic bundle which could be photographed using the inspection Polaroid camera, providing a record for comparison when the time came to remove the seal. We then locked and resealed the door to the storage area.

Our inspection equipment secured, we were taken to a hotel in downtown Ulan Ude, where we were able to get a few hours' sleep before flying out the next morning onboard a Soviet Air Force Tu-134—the same make and model as the burned-out airframe on the end of the runway. The Tu-134 was designed to carry 72 passengers. Team Williams comprised 10 inspectors and was accompanied by a team of five Soviet escorts. Although a military aircraft, the Tu-134 was configured like a commercial airliner, with standard overhead storage for carried on luggage. There were plenty of seats available, so every passenger took a row of seats for his exclusive use—meaning to lay down and catch up on our sleep on a flight of a little more than 1,000 miles lasting some 4 hours and 15 minutes.

About an hour into the flight, the door to the cockpit opened, and two members of the Soviet flight crew emerged. I made my way over to where they stood and introduced myself, using my best broken Russian. The Soviet crewmember asked me if I was a pilot, and I tried to explain that while I was not a pilot, I was trained as a Naval Aerial Observer. The crewmember smiled, and invited me into the cockpit, where I was ushered into the navigator's jump seat, situated behind the co-pilot.

The pilot and co-pilot were very genial and pointed out the main features of the cockpit. The aircraft was operating in autopilot mode, so both men were able to give me their full attention. After about 30 minutes or so of polite conversation, the pilot said something to the co-pilot, who got up from his seat. I assumed the tour was over, and I stood up, ready to be escorted out. Instead, the co-pilot gestured to his seat, and told me to sit down. I looked at the pilot, who nodded his head. I was now behind the controls of the Tu-134.

The plane was on direct approach to Novosibirsk, and as we got closer, we could see the airfield off in the distance in front of us. The pilot was talking to the control tower, and then looked at me, pointing to the autopilot controls, and instructed me to begin reducing altitude. This involved dialing in a new altitude, and having the plane respond on its own, leveling off once the altitude indicated was reached. Simple stuff, and I repeated this exercise several times as we approached Novosibirsk. The pilot nodded toward the airfield, nodded at my controls, and gave me a thumbs up. I returned the thumbs up, before using the autopilot to bring about another reduction in altitude. The airfield grew closer and closer, and the pilot kept looking at me as if he expected me to do something.

The realization hit us both simultaneously—he thought I was going to land the aircraft, and I had no intention of doing so because, simply put, I had no idea how to do so. The pilot shouted out "*Yolki Palki*," which loosely translates into "Oh, Shit," and grabbed the controls in front of him, effectively shutting down the autopilot. The co-pilot immediately sat down in the navigator's jump seat, and strapped in. I remained where I was.

The pilot suddenly got busy, executing a series of violent nose-up maneuvers to help bleed off airspeed. He lowered the landing gear at a velocity far greater than it was safe to do in order to create more drag, and thus further slow the aircraft's speed. The ground was approaching fast—too fast. The aircraft was shaking violently from the drag created by the landing gear, and the pilot's face was as white as a ghost. I was convinced we were going to crash and prepared myself for the worst.

The plane hit the runway hard, causing the wings to flap, and then bounced back into the air, before settling down a second time, remaining on the runway and allowing the pilot to hit the reverse thrusters and apply the brakes. The end of the runway was screaming toward us. I was certain we would overshoot it and end up like the Tu-134 that crashed at Ulan Ude, broken up and on fire. Somehow, however, the pilot was able to bring the plane to a halt, with mere feet to spare. Before taxiing in, he gestured with his head that I should exit the cockpit.

As I walked out into the main cabin, I was greeted by chaos—every overhead compartment had sprung open, and the luggage contained there scattered across the interior of the aircraft. If a seat had been occupied by a passenger, it remained upright. Otherwise, every seat had been collapsed forward due to the rapid deceleration and hard braking. Captain Williams took one look at me exiting the cockpit and scowled. "I knew you had something to do with this," he hissed.

My inspection was not starting off on a good foot.

We were driven to the 382nd Guards Missile Regiment in a pair of Rafik vans. Upon arrival we were shown to our quarters—basically the rooms of the unmarried officers which had been requisitioned for our use. My roommate, an interpreter with several short-notice inspections under his belt, watched me eyeball the bunk, and smiled. "Take a good look. You won't be seeing much of it while we are here."

He was right. We were taken to a dining facility, where our hosts provided us with a hot meal, prepared by a group of ladies who were obviously military wives. They stared at us from across the room while we ate. This entire experience had to be mind-bending for them. Their husbands were assigned to a military unit, the mission of which was to deliver nuclear weapons onto targets in the United States. And now, here were a group of Americans, preparing to inspect these very weapons.

The Rafiks took us to the operating base where we did a walk-around, verifying what we saw on the ground with a line diagram of the site that had been prepared by ACIS. The Soviets provided us with a safety briefing, and then we got on with our task. The inspection started at 2.30 PM; we had 24 hours to get the job done.

The regiment had nine SS-25 mobile launchers, each with an SS-25 launch cannister mounted. Each launcher was stored in a dedicated temperature-controlled garage, equipped with a sliding roof that could open, allowing the missile to be raised and fired from that fixed position, if necessary. The SS-25 was intended as a "second-strike" weapon, and its forte was mobile operations— it was designed to be taken out of garrison and dispersed in the forests of Siberia, making subsequent targeting by the US extremely difficult, thereby increasing its chances of survival in any pre-emptive nuclear strike.

To do the RDE inspection, each SS-25 launcher had to be pulled out of its garage and driven to a location in the garrison where the RDE equipment had been set up. The appropriate measurements would be taken, and the data double checked with the Soviet escorts. The launch cannister would then be tagged with a numbered tamper-resistant tape, placed across the where the cap of the cannister joined the main body of the cannister, and then returned to its garage. My job was to escort the launchers to and from their respective garages and conduct periodic inspections to verify that the tamper resistant tags had not been tampered with or removed. This gave me plenty of time to get a close look at the SS-25 launcher and launch cannister.

The inspection itself was straightforward. After the RDE device was calibrated using a standard neutron source, the inspectors set up a 4-meter x 4-meter grid, consisting of a plastic sheet made rigid by a frame of plastic poles. This grid was positioned beneath the front end of the launch cannister. The RDE device was then attached to a tripod and raised to a point where it rested one half meter below the bottom of the launch cannister. Using a plumb bob hanging from the center of the RDE device, the tripod would be positioned, one at a time, over ten points along the grid that were common to measurements taken during the calibration inspections.

At each point, two readings would be taken; if the higher reading differentiated from the lower reading by more than 30%, then a third reading would be taken. If that reading was off, then the RDE device would be recalibrated, and the process started anew. Additional readings would be taken along the top of the cannister (the Soviet escorts would place the device, based on instructions received from the inspectors), as well as at locations extending out to six meters from the front of the cannister. Once satisfactory readings were obtained, the average of the two readings would be recorded for each point as the official reading for the inspection. This would be done for each of the nine missiles belonging to the regiment.

If the value of any of the final readings taken during the inspection differed from the benchmark value by more than 50%, then the inspection team would be able to ask the Soviets to remove the front end of the cannister so that the inspectors would be able to confirm the type of missile inside through visual inspection. In any event, once all nine missiles had been inspected using the RDE device, the inspection team would be able to select one of the nine missiles for visual inspection.

Our inspection went off without a hitch, and shortly after 11 am—some 20 hours and thirty minutes into the inspection—Team Williams finished the last measurements on the last missile. Captain Williams approached me. "Now we get to look inside one of the cannisters. You have the honor of picking which one we will inspect."

I chose missile number four, if for no other reason than the crew had been particularly good natured. At 11.15 am I walked down to the garage where missile number four was located, verified that the tamper resistant tape was still intact, and formally designated the missile for visual inspection. The Soviets pulled the missile out of the garage and brought it to the same spot where the RDE measurements had been taken. A crane mounted on the back of a truck arrived, and the Soviets removed the cap of the launch cannister, exposing the SS-25 missile inside. A five-meter perimeter was established around the exposed cannister, inside of which the inspectors were not permitted. We had five minutes to make our observations. As Captain Williams had warned, the Soviets watched us very closely.

When an SS-25 left the Votkinsk factory, it comprised the first, second and third stages, along with the post-boost vehicle, the equivalent of a fourth stage which allowed the missile to be maneuvered to a precise location before separating the warhead. But the warhead and associated safety and fusing systems were not attached until later, just before the missile was officially turned over to the receiving unit. The cannister lid that was in place when the missile left Votkinsk had been removed, and a launch cap, designed to be blown off prior to launch using explosive bolts, installed. One of the reasons the Soviets were reticent about allowing visual inspections of SS-25 missiles was that the missiles were sealed inside the cannister, surrounded by an inert gas to prevent corrosion. When the inspection was complete, the Soviets would have to go through a lengthy process of evacuating the normal atmosphere and replacing it with inert gas. This, albeit temporarily, took a strategic nuclear weapon out of service, something no nuclear-armed nation desires.

I was intimately familiar with what an SS-25 *sans* warhead looked like, based upon my observations made at Votkinsk during cannister openings. Seeing an SS-25 with its warhead attached was a new experience altogether. I did my best to note specific details but was mindful of the fact that I would be getting a second shot at examining an SS-25 at the next inspection site. I did my best to look as distracted as possible, taking no notes, and casually walking around the perimeter until our time expired.

With the inspection phase completed, the team packed up the inspection equipment, and returned to the main garrison where Captain Williams, Nick Troyan and John Lohmann were working on the inspection report. When they finished, the team was assembled in the main dining facility where Captain Williams and his Soviet counterpart went over the documents before signing them, leaving one copy with each side. At this juncture, the inspection clock stopped. Under normal circumstances, the Soviets would return the inspection team to the POE, where within 24 hours the team would depart using its own aircraft.

However, Team Williams was also tasked with conducting a sequential inspection of the 778th Guards Missile Regiment near the Siberian city of Kansk, some 620 miles due east of Novosibirsk. According to treaty protocol, Captain Williams declared our intent to carry out this inspection, thereby starting the 9-hour clock during which time the Soviets would need to transport us to that facility. We dispersed to our respective bunks, where for the first time in nearly 36 hours we were able to get some sleep. But our rest was short-lived. Soon we were roused from our rest, loaded onto Rafik vans, and driven to the airport, where the same Tu-134 was waiting to fly us to Kansk central airport where we began the process of inspection all over again.

A day and a half later, the same Tu-134 and crew waited for Team Williams on the tarmac at Kansk as we wrapped up our inspection of the 778th Guards Missile Regiment. The weather during the two inspections had been cold but clear. Now that we were preparing to fly back to Ulan Ude, however, clouds were forming on the horizon, a sure sign that a storm was blowing in. Given the strict time requirements set by the treaty, which limited how much time we could spend at a given location, we would be landing at Ulan Ude at night.

As we approached Ulan Ude, the Tu-134 was buffeted by extreme turbulence brought on by a severe thunderstorm, which shredded the sky with sheets of lightning accompanied by driving rain. The aircraft was struck on two separate occasions by lightning, which lit up the wingtips and startled everyone onboard with the accompanying instantaneous thunderclap. Making matters worse, the weather had closed in over Ulan Ude, reducing visibility to near zero and the cloud ceiling to a few hundred feet above ground level. When Captain Williams suggested to the Soviet escorts that consideration be given to landing at another airfield, he was told there was not enough fuel onboard to do anything other than land at Ulan Ude. Moreover, we would only get a few passes at the runway.

The lightning strikes appeared to have disabled the aircraft's navigation instruments, meaning the Tu-134 had to execute a visual flight rules (VFR) landing in conditions that made this nearly impossible. The first order of business was for the aircrew to find the airfield. This was accomplished by slowly reducing altitude under we got below the cloud cover, and then rapidly scanning for any physical feature that could be used to orient the aircrew. On our first attempt, we were able to find Ulan Ude off to our right, but we were so close to the ground that the Tu-134 was compelled to climb back into the clouds before trying to reorient toward where the airfield should be. A subsequent pass put us over the airfield, but not aligned with the runway.

The navigator came back and briefed us that he needed everyone to keep their eyes peeled as the aircraft came back under the clouds, as given the lack of altitude, decisions would have to be made extremely fast. I was resigned to the fact that I was going to be a grease stain decorating the fields of the Buryat

ASSR when, over the right wing, I saw the lights of the runway. I shouted to the navigator, who in turn shouted to the pilot, and the Tu-134 made an aggressive maneuver, lining up with the runway. But now the pilot had another problem—extremely high cross winds caused him to point the nose of the aircraft at an extreme 40-degree deviation from the direction of landing, meaning we were crabbing toward the runway nearly sideways. As we crossed the runway proper, the pilot tapped his rudder, swinging the nose around and touching down in a near-perfect landing.

The Soviet aircrew came out of the cockpit to bid us farewell. After my performance while landing at Novosibirsk, the aircrew had ignored me, with neither the pilot nor co-pilot even making eye contact while I was onboard. Now they were all smiles, shaking my hand and offering me their pilot's wings. Even Captain Williams warmed to me. "Better than the first try," he said. "Much better."

We repeated the process of securing the inspection equipment, and then were driven to our hotel, where the team settled in for the night. In the morning, the Soviets gave us a quick tour of Ulan Ude before taking us to the airport where a C-141 was waiting to fly us back to Yokota. Much to my surprise, when I boarded the aircraft, I was greeted by several of the analysts from ACIS who had helped brief us back in Yokota. Once the plane was in the air, the analysts proceeded to take each inspector aside and conduct a thorough debriefing about what they had seen and experienced at each of the SS-25 sites. When my turn came, I saw that the ACIS debriefers had brought a drafting kit, which could be used to make drawings of the missile and the TEL. Between my notes and my memory, I was able to make a series of detailed drawings full of tiny technical details, including various markings that had been stenciled on the missile cannister. From what I could see, the ACIS debriefers were pleased with my work.

When I returned to OSIA, I found a copy of a note on my desk from the Director for Operations, Colonel Ronald Forrest, to Colonel Connell. "Captain Williams reports that Captain Ritter did a super job on his recent inspection. Williams said he was a team player and a valuable asset to have along." This meant a lot coming from a man of Captain William's stature and experience.

Later, the Chief of the Treaty Monitoring Center within ACIS, John Bird, sent a letter of commendation to General Lajoie about my work at OSIA over the course of the past year. Bird singled out my efforts during the two RDE inspections. According to Bird, I had been able to relate what I had learned at Votkinsk to what I observed at the two operational bases in a manner that made me the "most valuable member" of the inspection team. Given the fact that I was in the company of people like John Williams, Nick Troyan, John Lohmann and other veteran inspectors, Bird's compliments were high praise indeed.

The events surrounding the CargoScan crisis and my experience with Team Williams only underscored the surreal nature of the work myself and the other

US inspectors were involved in while implementing the INF Treaty. It was part and parcel of what General Lajoie described as the "Road to Kapustin Yar," an inspection-laced journey which, in August 1988, had found him standing inside an empty SS-20 launch cannister to avoid the rain while observing the Soviet elimination of SS-20 missiles at a missile test facility in Kapustin Yar. As General Lajoie later noted, "Four years ago, as an Army attaché in Moscow, had I been within 100 miles of that facility, I would have found myself in a very, very difficult situation. And yet," Lajoie continued, "here we were, a group of American inspectors, not only on a secret military test facility, but blithely stepping into a missile cannister to get out of the rain as though it were the most natural thing to do."[15]

I was having my own "Road to Kapustin Yar" experience. Three years ago, I was training to execute the classic Marine Corps mission of closing with and destroying Soviet military forces through firepower and maneuver. Now I was inspecting missiles designed to facilitate the nuclear destruction of the United States, using the information gleaned from this experience to help further the verification of future arms control agreements. This journey was taking place within the context of Mikhail Gorbachev's efforts, under perestroika and glasnost, to transition the Soviet Union away from being an enemy of the United States to one that peacefully coexisted with its former adversary.

I was on the cusp of a major career move, preparing to leave OSIA and enter the training pipeline to become a Soviet Foreign Area Officer (FAO). But the allure that this status once held over me was no longer there. The Military Liaison Mission in Potsdam, once the proving ground for frontline Soviet FAOs, had stopped performing the kind of aggressive intelligence collection "tours" it was known for, instead assuming a more passive monitoring posture, observing Soviet forces as they withdrew from their former East German bases into Poland on the eve of the formal reunification of Germany.[16] The operational environment that allowed military attachés like George Connell to carry out legendary intelligence collection exploits while assigned to the US Embassy in Moscow no longer existed. The "Road to Kapustin Yar," no matter how exciting the journey proved to be, was always going to be a dead end for then-aspiring Cold War warriors like myself.

CHAPTER EIGHT

A Changing of the Guard

Boris Yeltsin delivers his speech denouncing the attempted coup by Communist hardliners, August 19, 1990. Photo Credit: Itar-TASS

*"Be ashamed to die until you
have won some victory for humanity."*

HORACE MANN

The Long Goodbye

I WAS IN RECEIPT of orders that had me reporting to the Marine Corps Amphibious Warfare School (AWS) in early August 1990. The game plan was for me to spend May and June clearing out my in-basket and conducting an orderly turnover with my replacement (who had yet to materialize), and then take 30 days leave (basically the month of July) to recharge my batteries before returning to the life of an active-duty Marine Corps officer. The month of May turned out to be relatively low-key; the highlight was when I joined Roy Peterson and Mark Dues as the Portal Monitoring representatives at the OSIA exhibit on the National Mall that had been set up as part of the Public Service Recognition Week exhibition. Over the course of two days, we shared our experiences as inspectors to several members of the public who stopped by. I had by this time resigned myself to a quiet departure from OSIA.

It was not to be.

Portal Monitoring had always been OSIA's red-headed stepchild when it came to manpower allocation. The original manning document for OSIA had Votkinsk working a "Blue-Gold" rotation like that used on US Navy submarines—one team of five OSIA inspectors, led by a Colonel, working in Votkinsk, while a second team of five worked at the OSIA Headquarters. The initial manning provided by the Department of Defense, however, provided only two Colonels and four field-grade officers, a shortfall of four personnel.

The allotment of three Company Grade counterintelligence billets, along with the arrival of Roy Peterson in the fall of 1988, brought Portal Monitoring up to full strength—on paper, at least. However, the need to support both the SVC talks in Geneva and START planning quickly stripped two of the deputy site commander positions, and the consolidation of the Colonel billets, with one taken away to serve as Chief of Staff, and the other remaining as the non-deploying Director of Portal Monitoring, meant that there were only seven OSIA bodies to fill ten billets.

It was decided early on that the Site Commander would not serve as a duty officer at the portal under anything other than the most extenuating circumstances, as it conflicted with his overall responsibilities. While it was possible to sustain a watch schedule with only three deputy site commanders, the requirement to have one OSIA officer accompany the Hughes personnel on the weekly Moscow run, and the strains put on manning created by rotations, had the OSIA personnel assigned in Votkinsk officers burning the candle at both ends.

"We are rapidly wearing people out," Colonel Connell noted in a January 15, 1989, memorandum to General Lajoie concerning government manning at Votkinsk. The three-officer rotation left the OSIA personnel working in Votkinsk with "virtually no time to do anything but stand watch and discharge essential administrative duties." This schedule left limited time to build team rapport with the Hughes inspectors (an essential aspect of on-site leadership) or carry out the critical representational mission of interacting with the Soviets in Votkinsk.

Things didn't improve when the portal monitoring staff returned to Washington, DC—the demands of backstopping the Votkinsk portal, supporting Magna, managing the contractual aspects of the portal monitoring operation, and the numerous liaison and coordination responsibilities that attach to serving in the Soviet Union during a critical time in Cold War history, meant that there was no down time. "What rest they get," Connell wrote, "is in Votkinsk, not Washington; but it isn't much and it isn't a substitute for having a family and a personal life." If measures weren't taken to rectify the situation, Connell noted, "no one will believe that we care about our people."

By the end of 1988, the manning situation had reached crisis proportions, with only six officers available to fill five Votkinsk slots. A temporary solution was found by bringing in government personnel from other agencies to serve as "guest inspectors," enabling Portal Monitoring to run a three-man port-and-starboard rotation. This solution, Connell pointed out to General Lajoie in a second memorandum, written on November 14, 1989, "cannot be sustained over the long term without serious damage to family life and to the sustained, professional functioning of [the Directorate of Portal Monitoring]. We already have problems because we have had this surge mentality for too long."

For 1989, the average time away from Washington, DC for an officer assigned to Portal Monitoring was 240 days. (Indeed, from June 19, 1988, through December 31, 1989, I had been away from Washington, DC for a total of 385 days, 353 of which were spent in Votkinsk. In 1990, I would spend 110 days between January 1 and July 10 deployed in the Soviet Union.) "The result," Connell said, "is permanent crisis and continuous reaction. We habitually change officers at meetings that cry for continuity and reassign important actions in mid-course."

General Lajoie had questioned what he viewed as Portal Monitoring's excessive use of "guest inspectors" as duty officers. "Although borrowing duty officers," Connell responded, "is similar to putting band aids on major injuries," unless the permanent manning of the Portal Monitoring Directorate was increased to 16 full-time officers, there was no other choice.

There was no more manpower available. General Lajoie acceded to the continued use of "guest inspectors."

When a "guest inspector" arrived in Votkinsk, they were given a day to acclimatize, and then another day for training, before being allowed to stand their first shift under the supervision of an experienced OSIA officer. While this could be managed if there were two OSIA duty officers available, the reality of supporting the Moscow mail run, and the demands of rotations, meant that often there was only one OSIA duty officer. This meant that instead of the normal 12-hour duty shift, these officers were called upon to stand duty for 36, 48, and even 72 hours straight on a regular basis.

At the end of May 1990, the inevitable happened—Portal Monitoring ran out of experienced OSIA duty officers. A new Portal Monitoring officer, Army Major Tom Michaels, had arrived in Votkinsk in early April and, after a two-week turnover with Roy Peterson, took over as Site Commander. Tom Michaels was due to rotate out at the start of June, but neither Roy Peterson nor Mark Dues were available to replace him. Chuck Myers, who was serving as the START Treaty planning officer, was pulled from his duties to serve as Site Commander until someone became available. John Sartorius was the only experienced OSIA duty officer in Votkinsk—the remainder were "guest inspectors," many of whom were on their first tour. My replacement had yet to arrive, and Stu O'Neill, Barrett Haver, and Rich Kurasiewicz were all committed to other projects. As the only experienced OSIA duty officer available for deployment, I was taken out of semi-retirement to serve one last rotation in Votkinsk as Chuck's deputy.

In Votkinsk, even though the CargoScan crisis was over, the US inspectors and Soviet factory escorts continued to circle each other like punch-drunk prize fighters. While the first use of CargoScan had gone off without any significant difficulty, the question remained as to whether that was a sustainable outcome. When the next two missiles exited the Votkinsk portal on April 5 and 6, it soon became apparent that there was some work left to be done before both sides were comfortable with the imaging process.

The April 5 imaging took a whopping eight-and-a-half hours to complete. The Soviets had mismarked the leading edge by 20mm, which meant that a second scan was necessary to bring the trailing edge of the image in line with the technical requirements of the Memorandum of Agreement (MOA). During the imagery interpretation phase of the inspection, the Soviets brought in extra people. The result was an extra 30 minutes of questioning by the Soviets before they requested an extended (i.e., one hour and ten minute) break while they consulted with one another before requesting that a second scan be conducted. The Soviets then spent another half an hour getting the railcar properly positioned. The subsequent scan, the weekly report from Votkinsk noted, "was almost perfect."

Things went better for the April 6 CargoScan imaging—the Soviets positioned the railcar properly, the US inspectors made a single scan, which satisfied the Soviets, who subsequently reduced the number of persons they needed in the control module. The April 6 inspection took five hours and 32 minutes, a three-hour improvement over April 5.

The Soviets and US inspectors had yet to formalize a procedure for the two-lock arrangement for securing the storage box where the imaging tapes and disks were kept. The US side proposed using a flexible rubber belt, which was placed through the hasp, and then secured with the US and Soviet locks. The Soviet duty officer agreed to this procedure, but later the Site Commander, Roy Peterson, was informed by Anatoli Tomilov that this method was unacceptable. Tomilov also formally complained about the amount of time it took the US inspectors to review an image, stating that the US side was using an actual inspection event for training purposes.

Roy Peterson was able to appease Tomilov's concerns about the dual locks simply by demonstrating the process to him in person. As for the issue of time, Peterson noted that it was important to ensure that the image taken was, in fact, a good one, and that there was no treaty limited item in the railcar; this took time. Tomilov forwarded both of his complaints as written protests to the Soviet Ministry of Foreign Affairs.

The extent to which relations between the US inspectors and their Soviet escorts had deteriorated was highlighted during a tense meeting between Colonel Connell and Alexandr Sokolov on April 21, 1990. Connell protested the Soviets having placed a lock on the electrical panel in the basement of the Roosevelt building. The Soviets responded that the Americans had installed equipment not envisioned in the original functional description of the basements, which the Soviets claimed was exclusively for plumbing, electrical, and heating systems. The US inspectors were using the basements for storage and had converted one basement into an informal lounge/poker room/sauna that was very popular with off-duty inspectors.

The Soviets claimed that what the US inspectors were doing violated Soviet safety standards. Connell responded by noting that the basements in question were diplomatically inviolable. The discussion ended when Connell informed the Soviets that the US would place American locks on the electrical panel and provide the Soviets with keys.

Connell then brought up the unsatisfactory performance by the Soviets when it came to maintenance support, citing as examples the Soviet delay in helping the US install a water filtration system and sump pumps. Tomilov responded that the issue was political in nature. Connell then demanded that in the future, the Soviets needed to provide written notice one day prior if they wanted to enter a basement, specifying the exact nature and purpose of the visit. Tomilov responded that the Soviets could only give the US side a one-hour notice.

Connell next raised the issue of leisure activities, noting that relations were at their worst point ever. Sokolov responded that the US inspectors were ignoring the legal demands of their escorts—for example, the Soviets had told the inspectors that they needed to leave a party with the Izhevsk cardiologists at midnight but were ignored by the inspectors. As result, the Soviets were denying inspector leisure requests as a means of retaliation. Such had been the case of an inspector request to attend Easter Mass. Sokolov then went on to state that the hooligan problem in Votkinsk had increased "catastrophically," and that many requests were being turned down for security reasons.

The next issue concerned the US request to use image tapes produced during an inspection for training purposes. Tomilov rejected this, saying that the treaty set limits on how a radiographic image could be used. Connell noted that if both sides agreed to look at an image, then there would be no treaty violation. Tomilov countered by offering to construct a missile mock-up that could be used for training purposes. Both sides agreed to give the matter further consideration.

The next issue brought up by George Connell was the condition of the perimeter, noting that the Soviets had agreed back in April 1989 to fix it. Connell noted that the appalling conditions around the perimeter were impacting inspector safety—indeed, just the previous week, an inspector had badly sprained an ankle while conducting a perimeter patrol. Tomilov responded that the Soviets had done as much as they could, but that there were financial constraints. Connell threatened to cancel perimeter patrols altogether and declare the Soviets to be in violation of their treaty obligations to create safe conditions for the conduct of treaty-mandated tasks. Tomilov responded by telling Connell to go ahead— maybe by getting Geneva involved, resources might be provided.

Tomilov then requested that the US side clean up the area around their warehouse because the Soviets were bringing in a tractor and bulldozer to level the ground around the warehouse. Connell noted that if the Soviets were looking for work for the tractor and bulldozer, "perhaps they could do something on the perimeter."

The final issue dealt with inspector movements between the housing area and the warehouse. Connell noted that the US had a treaty right to unimpeded access to its facilities, including the warehouse, and that, other than CargoScan or perimeter inspections, there was no need for US inspectors to notify the Soviets before moving to and from the housing area and warehouse. Sokolov responded by saying if this were to happen, then the Soviets would be compelled to construct a barrier separating the US housing area from what the Soviets called the "technical zone"—the DCC, warehouse, and CargoScan facilities. The issue was left unresolved.

The unusual level of terseness on the part of Colonel Connell must have resonated with the Soviets. When the missile backlog created by the CargoScan crisis was finally cleared out of the factory (the last missile exiting on April 21, and inspection procedures streamlined so that an inspection now took just over three hours to complete), the Soviets provided an empty railcar for OSIA to use to train new inspectors on the use of the CargoScan system. One benefit of this training was that the Hughes personnel were able to modify the procedures used to install the bar code and bar code holder, reducing the time from between 30–45 minutes to 10–15 minutes.

The Soviets allowed the inspectors to attend the grand opening of the Chaikovsky Estate as part of the 150th celebration of the famous composer's birthday, and to visit the Izhevsk automobile factory. Sokolov also informed the inspectors that funding "had been made available" for the factory to begin work to improve the perimeter.

By the end of May, the tension that had gripped the Votkinsk Portal Monitoring Facility had begun to ease. When the Soviets shipped out four SS-25s between May 12–18, they joked with General Lajoie and Lev Kokurin that they had done this "as a special present" for the two officials so they could experience a live missile scan.

Inspectors were allowed to resume jogging in downtown Votkinsk, a practice that had been halted when the inspectors moved out to their permanent quarters in April 1989. Slowly but surely, the Soviets were easing up their previous restrictions regarding leisure activities. By the time Chuck Myers and I arrived in Votkinsk in early June, an equilibrium had been reached where the US and Soviet sides continued to spar about limitations imposed on leisure activities, but also where the Soviets showed signs of trying to reach an accommodation with the US inspectors on issues the US side deemed important.

One such issue was the issue of the inspector's ability to invite non-factory personnel to official functions hosted at the US housing area. The July 4th Independence Day celebration was approaching, and neither side wished for a repeat of the animosity of the previous year. In a meeting with Alexandr Sokolov, Chuck Myers was informed that the Soviets were inclined to permit a limited number of outside guests, as well as the family members of factory escorts, to attend the July 4th celebration. Their main concern, Sokolov noted, was to avoid the kind of "large crowd" that had been present during the Open House in June 1989.

There was still a treaty to be implemented. Four SS-25 missiles exited the Votkinsk portal during my June rotation and at long last, I had the opportunity to conduct an inspection of the SS-25 using the CargoScan radiographic imaging system. CargoScan turned out to be quite "Marine-proof"—the scans went off without a hitch. Moreover, whether for my benefit or not, ACIS instructed that one of the SS-25 cannisters be opened for visual inspection. I had to admit to more than a little bit of nostalgia as I made my way down the confined spaces between the cannister and the railcar, the air smelling of fresh paint and grease. I had a similar experience doing my last perimeter inspection, trying to take in the sights and sounds of the Votkinsk factory which, as always, I viewed from the outside looking in.

The June rotation, however, was not a case of "all work, no play." On June 17—two days before my scheduled departure—I joined Chuck Myers and several Hughes inspectors on a leisure excursion to the town of Sharkhan, a rural farming community nestled in the hills north of Votkinsk, where we attended a summer festival. Shortly after we arrived, I was approached by a Soviet Colonel who had accompanied us, and asked if I, as a Marine, would like to participate in the local "triathlon." When I responded that I was not dressed for the occasion, having not brought any athletic gear, the Colonel produced a pair of running shorts he said would fit me, and offered the use of the Rafik van as a changing room. No sooner than I had emerged from the van, wearing only the shorts (which did, in fact, fit), I heard a starter's pistol go off.

"The race has started," the Colonel said, pointing toward a boat landing on a nearby lake, where scores of competitors were already entering the water, beginning what amounted to about a half-mile swim to the other side. I handed the Colonel my running shoes. "Meet me when I get out of the water," I said, before jogging about 400 yards to the starting line. I dove into the water, having spotted the other competitors enjoying a couple of minutes head start.

Swimming was not my forte, and about mid-way across the lake I realized that I would be better off worrying about not drowning than trying to catch up with the others. I managed to make my way out of the lake, which required wading through some 20 yards of knee-high water, my feet sinking into a foot or so of slimy mud with each step. About five meters from the shore, I stepped onto a sharp object—either a rock or piece of glass—which punctured the sole of my right foot right at the instep.

The Colonel was waiting for me when I exited the water, holding my shoes in one hand, and supporting a rickety old bike with the other. I sat down to put on my shoes, and took the time to examine my foot, only to find a nasty looking three-inch gash, packed with mud. When I opened the wound to see how deep it went, I was met by a spurt of blood. I quickly pulled on a sock, and then put on my shoe, which I laced up tight. I did the same with the other shoe, and then grabbed the bike from the Colonel. "What next?" I asked. He pointed up a hill. "Head that way. There will be people to direct you once you get to the top."

The bike had but one gear, and there was no way I was going to make it up the hill peddling it, so I grabbed it by the handlebars and seat and began running, my right foot exploding in pain with every step. By the time I got to the top, blood was seeping out of my shoe. I climbed onto the bike and started peddling down a path indicated by one of my guides. This went on for about five miles, with me peddling the bike on the level and downhill portions of the course and dismounting and running with the bike on the uphill portions. After what seemed an eternity, I arrived at a spot where other bikes were scattered on the ground. A smiling local grabbed my bike, and pointed down a road, indicating the start of my three-mile run. By this time, my foot felt like someone was sticking a red-hot poker into it. But running in pain was what the Marine Corps did for a living, so I just lowered my head, and started forward at a modest clip, my blood-filled right shoe making a discernable "splat" sound with every footfall.

The local crowd had been told that an American inspector—a Marine, none the less—was competing in the race. With my late start, punctured foot, and less-than-race-worthy bike, I was running dead last—not very impressive. But a crowd had formed along the side of the road leading into a natural amphitheater created by a bowl-like depression in the hills, cheering me on. By the time I got to the finish line, there were hundreds of people gathered, applauding me. The Colonel was there, too, smiling. "I came in last," I said, embarrassed. "Why are they cheering?"

"They love the fact that you participated," the Colonel said. "That matters more than anything. You showed them great respect." I now had greater insight into his insistence that I run the race—and the fact that he had a pair of swim trunks that fit!

The rest of the afternoon was spent eating shashlik, drinking vodka (for the pain), and having a good time with the locals, most of whom worked on the local collective farms. Chuck Myers came up to me, a smile on his face. He had a bandage on his head, covering a wound created a few days ago when, during a volleyball game we were both playing in, a loose basketball from a pick-up game on the neighboring court came rolling across in front of me as I was preparing to set the volleyball. I sought to kick it off the court, only to send the ball directly into Chuck Myers head, knocking him to the ground and opening a cut in his head. He looked at my foot and shook his head. "Karma is a bitch."

When I got back to the portal, I was taken to Joanne Polka, who examined the wound. "This is pretty bad," she said, angry at me for not coming straight to her after I was injured. "If this gets infected, you could lose the foot." She spent the better part of an hour cleaning the wound, scooping out gobs of mud while probing for any pieces of glass or rock that might have broken off inside. This was done without pain killers, with a pair of inspectors holding me down while Joanne made a point of digging deep. Afterwards I was given a handful of antibiotics and instructions to see a doctor as soon as I got to Frankfurt to check for infection.

I was scheduled to rotate out on June 19, which just so happened to be the second anniversary of my and Chuck Meyer's arrival in Votkinsk with the Advance Party back in 1988. Chuck and I celebrated it in quiet fashion with several Soviet escorts who had been there at the start. Chuck was scheduled to rotate out on June 26. "With our departure," Chuck noted in the weekly report, "we have passed into the very fine print footnotes of Votkinsk history (US version only). Several escorts were visibly saddened by Captain Ritter's departure. I have the impression the management wishes us both good riddance."

I returned to Washington, DC on June 22, a Friday. On Monday, June 25, I arrived at the Portal Monitoring offices in Dulles Airport, looking forward to spending the next week checking out of OSIA, and beginning my 30-day leave before reporting to AWS.

Fate once again intervened. On Thursday, June 28, I was told to pack my bags—I was headed back to Votkinsk. Stu O'Neill's father had fallen ill, and Stu was heading home on emergency leave. I was to remain in Votkinsk until Stu was able to return.

The vagaries of Portal Monitoring's manpower shortages had struck again. I cancelled one set of airline tickets (I was supposed to fly to Europe on July 6 to start my long-planned vacation) and picked up another which had me flying direct into Moscow's Sheremetyevo Airport, before transferring to Vnukovo

Airport, where I caught the Aeroflot Yak-42 flight into Izhevsk, arriving in the afternoon of June 30. Nikolai Vyuzhanin, the Department 162 official who coordinated transportation for the inspectors, was there to greet me. We climbed into the Rafik van and headed north toward Votkinsk. Nikolai turned from where he was seated in the front passenger seat. "Welcome back," he said, smiling.

I slipped back into the duty schedule as if I had never left. Any notion that I would get to experience the visceral pleasures of inspecting another SS-25 missile, however, were quickly quashed. On the morning of July 3, we were preparing to conduct a test of the CargoScan system in anticipation of a demonstration that we were going to provide to a delegation led by Colonel. Connell's delegation was due in later that evening, and we were looking to do the demonstration sometime on the morning of July 4, prior to the Independence Day celebration kicking off.

The Soviets had provided us an empty 6-axle railcar to use in the demonstration. As the locomotive pulling the railcar positioned itself to back into the CargoScan facility, the inspectors opened the access gate, which normally would automatically swing open. However, as chance would have it, Soviet construction workers had dumped a load of dirt near the gate just as the train began to back in, preventing the gate from fully opening. Despite the frantic efforts of the Soviet workers (who only too late realized what they had done) to remove the dirt, it was soon obvious to all that the train was not going to clear the gate. A Hughes inspector began waving his arms and yelling for the engineer to stop. The train kept going, striking the right side of the gate, crushing it and folding it nearly in half. The train continued for another 20 feet before stopping.

Fortunately, no one was hurt, and the CargoScan interlock mechanism was not damaged. But until the gate could be replaced, CargoScan was out of service. According to the Memorandum of Agreement, since the damage to the gate was clearly the fault of the inspected party, no missiles would be allowed to exit the Votkinsk portal until satisfactory repairs had been made. The Soviets indicated that they would be able to repair the damaged gate by July 9, and that until then, no missiles would exit the facility.

With CargoScan down and inspections halted, we turned to preparing the site for the arrival of Connell's delegation and celebration of Independence Day. In 1988, the US inspectors had celebrated the July 4th holiday by holding a round-robin touch football tournament in the Votkinsk stadium, The 1989 festivities had had a damper put on them as the Soviets put the permanent US housing area off limits to anyone who was not an employee of the factory or present on official business. This year both sides were hoping for a more equitable outcome. In the spirit of compromise, the Soviets permitted the US inspectors to invite a small number of outside guests, as well as members of Department 162 and their immediate families to a modest celebration, which included a barbeque and games.

My contribution to the festivities was to deliver the official OSIA speech to our Soviet guests, ably translated by Mike Schultz, a Hughes linguist. A small crowd, consisting of the senior factory and escort personnel, the doctors from the Izhevsk Cardiology Center, and select guests, squeezed into the TV lounge of the Roosevelt building to hear the presentation. I was pleased to see Anatoli Chernenko seated in the back of the room. His recovery from his heart attack had been touch and go, but here he was, accompanied by his daughter.

"Dear Guests," I began, reading from prepared remarks. "I would like to thank you all for attending our little celebration here today, and in doing so take a few moments to explain the significance that this day holds to us as Americans, and why we feel compelled to gather together in this place so far from our home in order to mark its passing." I went on to outline the history behind the Declaration of Independence, and the subsequent effort to form "a more perfect union," the work for which was still ongoing to this day.

The United States is a nation of immigrants, of people drawn to our shores by the hope of a better life in which they can live as free people. Among the US inspectors here today you will find a considerable cross section of ethnic backgrounds, proof of our diverse heritage. But rather than be fractured by our diversity, we are strengthened by it, for we are united in the concepts that our forefathers set forth 214 years ago, that all men are created equal.

I continued. "Each year American all around the world…gather together to celebrate the concept of freedom." Such gatherings, I noted, involved "family and friends, in which a meal is shared, and life and freedom celebrated quietly." I then invited the assembled guests "to join our small family here" to help us celebrate this occasion.

The speech was well received, and as I made my way out of the room, I found myself standing next to Anatoli Chernenko, who reached up and grabbed my hand, pulling me down so that he could speak int my ear.

"*Zayabis!*" he said, smiling.

The rest of the day was spent enjoying the company of friends and colleagues alike, people I had spent the better part of the past two years toiling with to make the Votkinsk Portal Monitoring Facility a reality. The relationship between the permanent OSIA officers and the Hughes inspectors was always somewhat tenuous, relying more on personal relationships than the official chain of command. The Site Commander and his deputies were contractually obligated to go through the Hughes Site Manager when it came to direct tasking of Hughes personnel. The only exception to this was when the Hughes inspectors were on duty in the "inspector" capacity, at which time they worked at the direction of the Duty Officer—but only when it came to specifically delineated inspection tasks.

Some OSIA personnel rankled at this arrangement, and quickly drew the ire of the Hughes personnel, who made it clear from the start they were not in the military (although many were veterans) and they weren't there to obey orders from some overbearing martinet. Whenever a situation like this developed, site performance and moral plummeted. Fortunately, most OSIA officers understood the reality of their situation, and adjusted accordingly. Doug Englund was famous for putting everyone at ease, and George Connell was noted for his hands-on approach toward leadership—when the Hughes inspectors were laboring in the snow and sub-zero temperatures of a Votkinsk winter, one knew they could find George Connell out there among them, working as a regular member of the team to get the job done.

I did my best to strike a balance between the leadership styles of Doug and George, trying to be "one of the guys (and gals)" without compromising my role as a leader. When Justin Lifflander opened his "hole in the wall" lounge in the basement of the Lincoln Building, I joined the other inspectors in playing what seemed to me to be a permanent poker game. When OSIA Headquarters balked at the idea of a poker room ("There's gambling in Casablanca!"), I joined the other junior officers in successfully defending Justin's creation as an essential part of the Votkinsk inspector social fabric.

Justin Lifflander was one of the most unique characters who worked at the VPMF. Justin had been an employee of the US Embassy when Doug Englund encouraged him to apply to Hughes for a position in Votkinsk. A permanent nonconformist, Justin ran afoul of the "system" (American and Soviet) from day one. His engaging personality and ability to get things done, however, provided (barely) enough job security to prevent his termination. Justin's poker room was but one of several forays testing the limits of what authority would accept.

The poker room survived. Others, such as Justin's attempt to fly a locally purchased radio controlled airplane over the factory, his acquisition of a boat (which the Soviets would not let him sail for safety reasons), and his efforts to bring a goat he bought at the local market onto the VPMF (the goat made it to the site, but was unceremoniously removed when it escaped the American compound and was almost struck by the factory director's car), had less auspicious outcomes. In the end, Justin became a fixture at the VPMF, tolerated by Americans and Soviets alike through the sheer magnetism of his personality.

Morale was always an issue at the VPMF, especially during the long, cold winters, when leisure opportunities were few and far between. On one particularly dreary stretch, I was joined on duty in the DCC by Joe O'Hare, Hal Longley, and Hien Trang. I remember looking around at the sullen faces of the Hughes inspectors and thinking something needed to be done. I grabbed the "boom box" that the inspectors used to play quiet background music and cued up some Guns and Roses. With the volume turned up full, I woke the trio of Hughes inspectors up with a roaring rendition of "Welcome to the Jungle." Soon

Hal Longley was at the light switches, turning the lights to the DCC on and off in time with the music. Joe O'Hare and I were spinning around on the floors in our chairs, crashing into one another while playing air guitar. Hien Trang just watched us, a giant smile on his face.

As the song reached its conclusion, and with the inspectors in their most compromising poses, the door to the DCC opened. In walked Nikolai Shadrin, Alexandr Fomin, and Vladimir Kupriyanov—the Soviet duty shift. In Shadrin's hand was a declaration for the exit of a missile. In quick order, Hal turned on the lights, Joe turned down the music, and I came to my feet as if nothing had occurred. Hein Trang just continued to sit there, taking it all in. Shadrin had a quizzical smile on his face as he handed me the document, trying not to let the spectacle he had just witnessed interfere with the conduct of his official duties. But it was Kupriyanov who broke the ice. "Guys," he said in his thickly accented English. "I want to party with *you!*"

Hal Longley was one of the Hughes all-stars, an intelligent, quiet professional with California surfer-good looks and an easy-going manner. He also had a wonderful sense of humor. In the summer of 1989, Hal and I conspired to write a rap song which, thankfully, was only performed once in front of a crowd of Soviet escorts, following a closely fought soccer match with the Votkinsk factory team (they won, 4–3). Sung to the tune of Ice-T's hit song, "Colors," our version ("Missiles") focused on the work of inspectors as opposed to LA gangs. "SS-20, SS-25, we want to see what you've got inside…we're searching for missiles, missiles, missiles….," the song started. There were a few more verses before the song concluded: "If you launch those babies into the sky, don't you know we're all gonna die…from…missiles, missiles, missiles…"

The song was well-received, our hip-hop dancing less so. Hal and I both agreed that it was best to end our rap careers on a high, and "Missiles" was retired, never to be performed again.

Fortunately for the Votkinsk community, the issue of musical talent didn't die with "Missiles." In 1989 Hughes hired Thom Moore as one of their on-site interpreters. Prior to coming to Votkinsk, Thom, a US Navy veteran who served from 1962–1965, had worked as a linguist-escort with OSIA, helping escort Soviet INF inspection teams that passed through Travis Air Force Base in California. Thom was an accomplished Russian linguist, having received a bachelor's and master's degree in Slavic Languages and Literature from the University of California, as well as completing a Russian language refresher course prior to beginning his work with OSIA.

But Thom had other talents as well, including a knack for writing and performing songs inspired by traditional Irish music. In the 1970s Thom had settled near Sligo, Ireland, where he formed a band, *The Pumpkinheads*, that served as an outlet for his creative talents. Thom returned to the US in 1979 and spent the '80s teaching English at a stenographers' school while performing part-time with his new band, *Train to Sligo*. Some of his songs were picked up and performed by the noted Irish singer, Mary Black. Thom was torn between returning to Ireland to try and rekindle his music career or pursue his passion of Slavic studies by taking advantage of a once-in-a-lifetime opportunity to live and work in the Soviet Union.

Like most Hughes personnel, Thom had a fiercely independent streak which did not lend itself to military discipline and other martial shenanigans. He was an artist, with an artist's eye and heart. He was also a solid Russian linguist, and soon became enamored with the technical and social aspects of live and work in Votkinsk. Thom quickly fell in with a pair of like-minded free spirits, Justin Lifflander and Jim Stewart, and the trio formed the nucleus of what passed for a counter-culture movement on site.

The three OSIA company grade officers—me, Stu O'Neill, and John Sartorius—were outcasts from the rarified world of Majors, Lieutenant Colonels, and Colonels, and quickly found common cause with these rebels. Our headquarters was Justin's Poker Room, from which numerous conspiracies were hatched between hands of cards, Cuban cigars, and ice-cold beer. We were often joined by Sam Israelit, Jim Luscher, and Jim Hanley, the real brain trust behind whatever technical success we enjoyed in Votkinsk.

And Thom brought his guitar. At first, Thom would regale us with covers of popular songs, or his own Irish-themed work. Sometime in late 1989, however, Thom began working on something new. Whether in Justin's basement, the Roosevelt TV lounge, or in the DCC during shift, Thom could be found picking out a tune, humming lyrics, and writing it all down on pieces of paper that he would periodically crumple up into a ball and throw away. This song ate at Thom, and one had the perception that he was seeking perfection.

He found it.

Slowly but surely, a tune was developed and mastered, followed by lyrics which Thom worked over like a worn bone. On occasion he would bounce an idea off those of us fortunate enough to watch him at work, seeking feedback and reinforcement. By the time the song was finished, many of us found more than a little of ourselves in the words he had written, given our proximity to their creation.

The song, *A Prayer for Love*, was publicly unveiled during a gathering of US inspectors and the doctors and nurses of the Izhevsk Cardiology Center at the center's conference hall in Izhevsk. The hall was packed with American inspectors and their hosts. The lights dimmed, and a solitary figure—Thom Moore—strode out on stage, guitar in hand, and began singing his haunting ode to love and romance. It was, simply put, a magical moment that was seared into the minds of those who were fortunate enough to witness it, leaving not a dry eye in the house. He got a well-deserved standing ovation.

My last memory of Thom was while seated on the steps of the Roosevelt building on that Independence Day in 1990. I watched the Irish American bard, a cigarette dangling from the side of his mouth, roam the grounds, guitar in hand, serenading everyone—Soviets and Americans alike—with ballads performed from the heart. It was quintessential Thom Moore. For those of us who knew him, Thom represented the ideal of what US-Soviet relations could be.

I rotated out of Votkinsk for the last time on July10. Following the debrief at Gateway, I partook in what had become a post-rotation tradition of sorts—a short cab ride out the front gate of Rhein Main Air Base to the German village of Schwanheim, where a fantastic little restaurant called the Frankfurter Hof was located. Going on two years, I had joined my fellow inspectors for a hot meal, cold beer, and good conversation before we headed our separate ways— the Hughes personnel off on their months-long breaks, and the government personnel back to their home offices. I had the same meal each time—Hungarian Goulash served in a bowl of fresh baked bread, Jaeger Schnitzel with Spätzle, and a tall glass of ice cold Hefeweizen beer. I did so once again. As usual, the company was great, and the food delicious.

Back at OSIA, I was able to get in a few days of turnover with my replacement, Marine First Lieutenant Henry Gaab, but it wasn't a very thorough one, as I was tied up with the administrative requirements associated with signing out of an organization. My last day of duty at the agency was Friday, July 20. The OSIA Weekly Bulletin gave me a nice sendoff:

> Unfortunately, this week we have to bid farewell to Captain Scott Ritter, USMC. Scott is one of the original "Buzzards," hit the ground running from the first day, and will maybe stop running when he leaves the Fairchild Building for the last time. Not only have his operational contributions to OSIA been immeasurable, he provided a clear definition of the word "officer" for all of us. Good luck, Scott— we'll miss you.

OSIA held an awards ceremony that morning, where General Lajoie presented me with a medal for services rendered. The next day I joined Colonel Connel at the home of Karen Schmucker, where the ACIS staff gave me a very nice farewell party. I had worked closely with Karen and her crew over the past two years, either from their offices at CIA Headquarters, or alongside them in Votkinsk when they rotated through as "guest inspectors." They were good people, professionals all, and together we helped turn Votkinsk from an INF afterthought into one of the stars of the ACIS intelligence constellation.

And then, like that, it was over.

Farewell, Communism

ON JUNE 11, 1990, while in Moscow as part of the VPMF weekly "mail run," Chuck Myers and Thom Moore met with Chief Cardiologist Yevgeni Odiyankov over dinner at the Glazur Restaurant in central Moscow. In March, Odiyankov had been elected to the Congress of People's Deputies for the Russian Soviet Federative Socialist Republic (RSFSR) and, once the Congress convened, was further elected to the RSFSR Supreme Soviet. He was in Moscow attending a session of the Supreme Soviet and had extended an invitation to the inspectors when he heard they were travelling.

Over the course of dinner, Odiyankov provided the two inspectors with insight into the workings of the new Russian legislative organ. The Izhevsk cardiologist-turned-politician expressed regret that the work of the Congress was proceeding so slowly. Odiyankov blamed the newness of the Russian experiment in democracy, with the newly elected deputies simply lacking experience in how to organize political work in an efficient manner. In a way, Odiyankov viewed the inefficiencies of the Congress as a blessing in disguise, since its inherent political incompetence helped slow down the pace of reform, something Odiyankov believed was essential if the system was to be changed without the system revolting against the changes.

When it came to the Chairman of the RSFSR Congress of People's Deputies, Boris Yeltsin, Odiyankov admitted that his initial negative opinions had been replaced by admiration over his drive and work ethic when it came to generating genuine reform in Russia. Odiyankov expressed hope that Yeltsin and Gorbachev would be able to get along, opining that "two intelligent men in positions of such responsibility" should logically be able to reach an agreement that was best for all.

The problem facing both Yeltsin and Gorbachev, Odiyankov noted, was they were facing an existential economic crisis which boiled down to one thing—a lack of money to pay for things. Central to resolving that issue, Odiyankov felt, was the drive by Boris Yeltsin to make Russian laws have primacy over Soviet laws—the Russian budget, for instance, should be drafted by Russian legislators, not Soviet. "How can the RSFSR make any progress toward an improved economic situation," Odiyankov asked rhetorically, "without having control of its own budget?"

Odiyankov also discussed the worsening state of relations between the US inspectors and the Soviets in Votkinsk. He told them that he had approached the Udmurt office of the KGB in an official capacity about why relations were so bad. The KGB replied that they were not to blame, adding that every aspect of US-Soviet relations at Votkinsk was the responsibility of the Ministry of Defense Industry. (Indeed, on July 13, the US inspectors conducted a meeting with the local KGB office in Votkinsk, where the KGB officers present told the inspectors the very same thing—they had no control over the relationship between the inspectors and the Votkinsk Factory. This was the sole purview of the Ministry of Defense Industry.)

Odiyankov's concerns about the economy came on the heels of a presentation by the Chairman of the USSR Council of Ministers, Nikolai Ryzhkov, to the Soviet Congress of People's Deputies, on May 25, 1990. The "shock therapy" Ryzhkov proposed would impact the Russian economy first and foremost, and yet the plan had not been considered by the representatives of the Russian people.

Concerning the Russian people, if the reaction of the citizens of the Udmurt Republic were any judge, the Ryzhkov report did not impress. "The concept of converting to a regulated market," a reporter from *Udmurrtskaya Pravda* noted, "made me and my comrades from work feel like we had been drenched with ice water."[1] Having been told by the Soviet leadership a mere five years ago that the economy was going through a period of acceleration, to be now informed that "for the first time in many decades the absolute size of social production and its efficiency is falling" hit many readers hard.

One issue that readers of the Ryzhkov plan had to wrestle with was the fact that Ryzhkov's report gave them nothing to chew on while considering its merits. "Current prices," Ryzhkov wrote, "neither reflect actual expenditures nor correspond to supply and demand. It is impossible to use these prices even to perform a serious analysis of the state of the economy." Ryzhkov's proposal would significantly lower the standard of living for the average Soviet worker. Odiyankov's observation over the lack of money wasn't just a problem for the government, but a reality for the Soviet citizen. For example, while a lathe worker's salary may have increased by 30–40 rubles a month, the relative cost of living had increased by some 70–80 rubles a month. In short, a Soviet factory worker needed 500 rubles a month to survive but was only receiving 350–370. And this was before Ryzhkov's belt-tightening proposals would come into effect.

The collective uncertainty that was gripping the Soviet Union, and the citizens of the Udmurt Republic in particular, was captured in a letter to the editor written by Viktor Chirkov, an engineer at the Chepetskii Mechanical Factory in Izhevsk, who had been a member of the Communist Party since 1982. Likening Chirkov's letter to that written by Nina Andreevna back in 1988, during the time of the 19th All-Union Conference and Gorbachev's initial push for structural changes in the way the Soviet Union was governed, the *Udmurtskaya Pravda* editors noted that its message was "unpleasant," and while the editorial board may not agree with its content, "everyone should have the right to express his opinion."[2]

Chirkov's letter asked the questions many Soviets were thinking: "Can we be satisfied with the direction and results of perestroika and economic and political reform? Are we moving backwards? Who is responsible for the growing crisis? And, finally, what is the [communist] party today, a discussion club or a real political force? Is it capable of preventing society from sliding into an abyss of chaos?"

"We needed perestroika," Chirkov declared, "as much as we need air to breath, because it was impossible to continue to live as we did during the years of stagnation." However, from Chirkov's perspective, the noble goals of perestroika were little more than a pretense for a massive effort designed to "discredit the Soviet State." Chirkov quoted Gorbachev himself where, in a September 25, 1988 speech, the Soviet leader declared that "much more must be done to shake the old tree loose from its roots, uproot it, and then raise a new forest and harvest the fruit." Nearly two years later, Chirkov noted, "we see where this led to." Anyone who dared speak out against the Gorbachev reforms was labeled an "enemy of perestroika," the end result being the "ideological imprisonment" of the Soviet people.

Projecting perestroika as little more than political cover for Gorbachev and his political allies to destroy the "achievements of the Great October Revolution," Chirkov declared that "the slogan 'The Socialist Fatherhood is in danger' stands before us. This slogan," Chirkov concluded, "should sound like an alarm bell appealing to each and every person to be vigilant and uncompromising in the struggle against counter-revolution."

When Boris Yeltsin led the movement in the Russian Supreme Soviet to have the Russian Federation declared sovereign, thereby undermining the centralized authority of the Soviet State and its leader, Mikhail Gorbachev, observers began to interpret his moves as an act of political reprisal for Yeltsin's past mistreatment at the hands of Gorbachev and his allies. When Yeltsin made a similar move to form a Russian Communist Party that would be separate from the Soviet Communist Party, these same observers began to believe that Yeltsin's goal was the destruction of the Communist Party as an institution, and with it the dilution of Gorbachev's authority, given that his leadership position was solely derived from his status as the General Secretary of the Communist Party of the entire Soviet Union. These fears became reality when, in June 1990, the Russian Communist Party was organized on the eve of a meeting of the Central Committee of the CPSU. At the time, Jack Matlock, the US Ambassador to the Soviet Union, asked Yeltsin if he were worried about the anti-reform tendencies of the Russian Communist Party. Yeltsin answered that question when, in July 1990, he stormed out of the Russian Communist Party Congress. The Russian Communist Party was no longer a political powerhouse. Neither was the CPSU. Chirkov's concerns about who would defend the accomplishments of the Great October Revolution were well founded. The answer, it seemed, was no one.[3]

Toward an Inspection "Normal"

AS PORTAL MONITORING began to feel the impact that comes with the loss of experienced personnel, the arrival of Captain Robin Cantwell as a Deputy Site Commander helped soften the blow. Robin was an Air Force intelligence officer who, at the time the INF treaty was signed and implemented, was working at the Pentagon as a Strategic Forces Analyst, providing customized intelligence analysis for senior military and civilian decision makers. Robin's specialty was Soviet Strategic Forces, a skill set she earned the hard way, as one of the first Air Force females assigned to the USNS *General Hap H. Arnold*, a range instrumentation ship that had been extensively modified for intelligence data collection.

Robin served off and on over the course of a five-year assignment with the National Security Agency, as a member of the ship's crew, deploying on numerous occasions between 1977 until shortly before the ship was decommissioned in 1982. The work done aboard the *Hap H. Arnold* was, at the time, considered to be among the most sensitive intelligence missions conducted by the military. Robin was always circumspect with the other inspectors about what she had done while serving as a member of the "Air Force's Navy," telling anyone who asked that she studied the effect of ionization in the atmosphere.

The National Security Agency, which oversaw the intelligence data collection conducted onboard the *Hap Arnold*, has since declassified aspects of its mission. According to these documents, the Hap Arnold "provided radar signature data and collected telemetry data from Soviet ICBMs that impacted on the Kamchatka peninsula or in the Pacific Ocean when they were tested to their full range," as an NSA brochure discussing Cold War intelligence operations noted. The *Hap Arnold* "deployed on Pacific Ocean intelligence missions several times per year when Soviet ICBM tests were anticipated."

Robin's self-professed status as a student of atmospheric ionization disguised the real purpose of her mission—to track targets entering the atmosphere using a 40-foot X and L radar dish capable of tracking a 15-inch spherical object to a range of 1,500 miles. The US had an understanding with the Soviet Union, tied to both the SALT I and SALT II treaties, that allowed for the use of "national technical means" to collect telemetry data relating to ballistic missile launches. Between August 10, 1979 and August 14, 1980, the Soviets had conducted ten flight tests of the *PioneerUTKKh* (an improved version of the SS-20, with three 150 kiloton warheads possessing improved accuracy and greater warhead dispersal capability than the earlier versions).

The *Hap Arnold* provided the United States with the best means of monitoring the capabilities of this new system. (Later, once Robin had served on a launch to destruct missile elimination inspection, where she was able to observe the Soviets launch several SS-20 missiles, those in the know would tease her that she was the only American who got the watch the SS-20 during both the launch and re-entry phases of its operation.)

The operations of the *Hap Arnold* weren't for the faint-hearted—in addition to dealing with the heavy seas of the northern Pacific, the crew had to cope with the reality of serving on an aging ship which began service as a troop transport, launched in April 1944. On at least one occasion during an ICBM monitoring mission, the ship lost power and began floating toward Soviet waters. US Forces in the Pacific began scrambling in response, fearing a repeat of the *USS Pueblo* incident, where a US Navy intelligence gathering ship and its crew were captured by the North Koreans. Fortunately, the crew was able to get the engines back up and running and keep the *Hap Arnold* in international waters.

Robin was not selected as a primary candidate for the initial INF teams (her employers at the Pentagon were loathe to let her go), but when Colonel McConnell, an OSIA Team Chief, made the rounds looking for "reserve" inspectors, Robin took the interview, and was subsequently assigned to one of the part-time Baseline Inspection teams. Robin and I first met when she arrived in Votkinsk as a member of the initial supplemental portal monitoring inspection team on July 1, 1988.

Robin went on to serve on several OSIA inspection teams, including a launch-to-destruct mission in Kansk, as well as an SS-20 elimination inspection in Kapustin Yar, the latter in the company of George Connell, who was by then serving as the Director of Portal Monitoring. Connell was so impressed with her performance and capabilities that he personally recruited her in early 1990 to become a permanent member of the Portal Monitoring staff.

Robin arrived in Votkinsk on July 10, 1990. Inspections and inspector leisure activities had assumed a friction-free routine, where the most stressful thing to happen was the malfunction of the CargoScan fire alarm in August 1990. There was no fire, the cause of the alarm being attributed to a sensor malfunction in the transport module. It took a few tries to finally fix the problem, however, resulting in the local fire department, a military unit stationed outside the factory gates, having to respond a few times.

The biggest issue for the Votkinsk factory in the summer and fall of 1990 was not the presence of US inspectors outside its gates, or even the functioning of CargoScan. Like every other Soviet ministry-run industrial enterprise, the Votkinsk Machine Building Plant was struggling with a new and confusing economic reality imposed by a system seeking to transition away from the previous model of centralized planning to the new cost accounting (*khozrashet*) methods imposed under perestroika.

In June 1990 the Supreme Soviet passed a new law, "On Enterprises in the USSR," which replaced the State Enterprise Law of 1987. The primary purpose of this law was to replace the Council of Labor Collectives (STK) system created in 1987 with a new "Enterprise Council," which was responsible for establishing the work priorities of the establishment as well as resolving management-worker disputes.

Additional new legislation passed in October 1990 set forth wage reforms, while another law passed in December 1990 regulated investments involving State enterprises, with an eye toward protecting shareholder assets while paving the way for eventual privatization. This legislative minefield impacted how Votkinsk was renumerated for its work, and by extension, how the workers at the Votkinsk factory were compensated for their labor.

The change in legislation prompted the factory leadership to delay the shipment of five SS-25 missiles originally scheduled to exit the factory in November and December of 1990. By delaying the exit of these missiles until January 1991, the Votkinsk Factory was buying time for its leadership to navigate the new rules and regulations to make sure they were fully and fairly compensated in an environment where many State enterprises were seeking to gain access to a shrinking pool of State-controlled financial resources.

From the perspective of the US inspectors in Votkinsk, the shipment of five missiles in one week was a blessing, as it allowed the inspectors to demonstrate their various inspection procedures to the new inspectors replacing Ed Curran and Colonel Connell. They were able to witness a cannister opening and the visual inspection of its interior, while taking note at the continued lack of a stage measuring device to conduct treaty-mandated measurements of the second stage.

One of the major projects ongoing at the Votkinsk Portal Monitoring Facility focused on the issue of maintaining the CargoScan system. As Doug Englund had pointed out back in July 1988, there were no Radio Shack stores in Votkinsk, and any repairs had to be done by the personnel available on site using the resources that had been stockpiled in the warehouse. In late January 1991 a representative from Varian arrived in Votkinsk to provide guidance to the Hughes personnel on the operation of the Linatron system used in CargoScan, as well as identifying potential system failures and the spare parts that would be needed on hand to permit a rapid repair. Based upon this visit, the Hughes personnel on site began to take inventory of the CargoScan spares on hand and segregating them in the warehouse so they could be located when needed.

The focus on maintenance soon proved fortuitous. On February 5, 1991, a delegation from the Soviet CargoScan Commission, headed by Lev Kokurin, arrived in Votkinsk as part of a routine visit. On February 7, the Soviets declared that an SS-25 missile would be leaving the site, providing an opportunity for the Soviet Commission members to observe CargoScan in action. A failure in the CargoScan transportation system, however, prevented the missile from being imaged and, after the expiration of the treaty-mandated four-hour maintenance period with the system still down, the US inspectors released the missile from the CargoScan inspection area with no radiographic image having been taken. A second missile departed the Votkinsk factory on February 8, with the same result.

The Hughes inspectors troubleshooting the failure of the transportation system quickly identified the problem as coming from the Inverter Drive Panel. The previous work on inventorying spare parts quickly permitted the inspectors to identify what parts they had on-site, and those that would be needed to be brought in to effect the needed repairs. A "SWAT" team was set up on site which coordinated closely with Hughes personnel back in the United States, as well as representatives from Bechtel, the company responsible for the transportation system.

The Soviets continued to ship missiles out of the Votkinsk Factory, with four departing between February 11–14. None of these missiles were subjected to CargoScan imaging due to the continued problems with the transportation system. A shipment of CargoScan spare parts arrived in Moscow from Germany on February 14, but the part numbers on the various devices did not match those on the accompanying documentation, causing a delay while Soviet customs officials conducted a more thorough review. The parts were finally released and forwarded to Votkinsk that evening on the Aeroflot flight from Vnukovo to Izhevsk. The Hughes "SWAT" team worked through the night and into the next day installing a new Inverter Drive Chassis, and by 5 PM on February 15, 1991, CargoScan was declared fully operational—but not before six missiles mandated by the treaty for radiographic imaging had departed the portal without having been inspected.

The issue with the malfunctioning CargoScan transportation system was the last Votkinsk adventure for Lieutenant Colonel Mark Dues, who rotated out of Votkinsk for the final time on February 23, 1991. His replacement as Site Commander, however, was no newcomer to OSIA or the Soviet Union. Lieutenant Colonel Nick Troyan was one of the original inspection team leaders hand-picked by General Lajoie to implement the non-portal inspections mandated by the INF Treaty. A legendary Soviet FAO in his own right, Troyan had served with the USMLM from 1974 until 1976 where he pioneered the exploitation of Soviet trash dumps for intelligence value, beginning a program called SANDDUNE which ended up producing nearly 50% of the intelligence produced by USMLM. Troyan also had volunteered to serve as the first USMLM officer to participate in the "Larkspur" aerial reconnaissance program around West Berlin. His Russian language skills were second to none, as was his acumen when it came to collecting intelligence on the Soviet target.

Troyan was one of the most experienced OSIA inspectors; his five-week inspection mission in August-October 1988 stands as a case study or professionalism and endurance. Troyan first deployed with his 10-person team to Ulan Ude, in the Soviet far east, in mid-August. From there they travelled to Saryozek, in Kazakhstan, where they spent two weeks monitoring the elimination of SS-12 missiles. At the completion of that task, Troyan took his team to Kansk, in central Siberia, where they spend another two weeks monitoring the launch-to-destruct elimination of SS-20 missiles. Troyan then took his team to the Soviet Pacific Maritime Province where, on October 1, 1988, they conducted a closeout inspection of the Novosysoyevka SS-12 missile base. By the time their mission was complete, Team Troyan had logged in over 23,000 miles in travel.[4]

Nick Troyan and a few of his inspectors were part of the first RDE inspections conducted in April 1990, and a month later, Team Troyan oversaw the final elimination of Soviet SS-4 missiles in Lesnaya. Even after his initial stint as Site Commander in Votkinsk in February-March 1991, OSIA sought to tap Troyan's experience further. In May 1991, Troyan accompanied Team Williams to Kapustin Yar where, in front of a group of VIPs which included Major General Robert Parker (who had taken over from General Lajoie as the Director of OSIA in January 1991), Soviet General Medvedev, and Colonel Doug Englund, he oversaw the elimination of the final SS-20 missiles. The last SS-20 launchers were destroyed later that month under the supervision of a different team, completing the Soviet destruction phase of the INF Treaty.

Troyan was the last "Buzzard" (a term given to the original members of OSIA who had worked in the Coast Guard Headquarters facility at Buzzard's Point in Washington, DC) to serve as a Site Commander in Votkinsk. When he rotated out at the end of March, 1991, his replacement, Army Lieutenant Colonel Warren Wagner, represented part of the "new breed" of portal monitoring Site Commanders, people who only knew the Votkinsk Portal Monitoring Facility as a finished product, not having experienced the Wild West days when the portal consisted of little more than a hand-written cardboard stop sign and a pair of inspectors with a tape measure, flashlight, and clipboard.

Soviet paranoia about CargoScan continued unabated, nonetheless. One problem that continued to occur was that the Soviets kept placing their shielding device in the wrong place, resulting in altered images that often required a re-scan. This problem had originally arisen during the scan of an SS-25 missile on September 14, 1990. The missile was held by the Soviets until September 17, after which time the Soviets inspected the interior of the railcar. A second scan was subsequently conducted to the satisfaction of both sides.

"In an attempt to resolve the shielding intrusion issue," a weekly report in mid-May 1991 noted, "a test scan with the shielding device purposely placed 3–4 pixels into the imaged area, was conducted on May 6." This test was proposed by John Sartorius, and agreed to by Lieutenant Colonel Wagner, the Site Commander, after consulting with the Soviet side.

"The test illustrated to the Soviets where they needed to place the shielding device in future missiles, so as to avoid a comment on the intrusion in the inspection report," the report stated, adding that "[i]t should be noted that the three missiles which exited the Portal following this test scan have contained no intrusion into the imaged area."

A new problem emerged with the settling of the train tracks due to the winter freeze and subsequent thawing. The detector array and x-ray head centerline were recalibrated using a test rail car without a missile. However, during the May 6 test scan the Soviets requested that the US side return to the pre-recalibration settings, suggestive of the fact that the Soviets were using the old US settings when calibrating their own. Subsequent centerline height measurements were virtually perfect in succeeding scans.

The issue of insufficient documentation continued unabated. On May 15, 1991, the US inspectors removed two spare circuit boards from the warehouse and tested them in the CargoScan system. When the inspectors sought to return the spare circuit boards to the warehouse, however, the Soviets blocked them, noting that they lacked any specific documentation for the individual chips contained in the circuit boards that would permit them to determine whether they had any memory capability. This matter was eventually clarified when the US provided the necessary documentation.

Refinements of the operation of CargoScan continued. On May 15, the Soviets requested that the US conduct a test of the CargoScan system using a dummy railcar for the purpose of checking the scan start time. The test subsequently showed that the actual imaging was starting some 36mm into the area that was designated to be scanned, indicating that all previous missile scans had been mismarked. Given that all previous radiographic images conducted by the inspectors using CargoScan had successfully imaged the scan length and area required by the treaty, it was clear to the US inspectors that the Soviets had been aware of the discrepancy and had adjusted on their own when it came to marking the railcar to compensate.

During this test, the Soviets noticed that the laser offset measurement was some 35mm shorter than the setting used on previous scans. This test was repeated by the US inspectors on May 16, confirming the findings.

More than a year into the operation of CargoScan, the Soviets appeared to have become aware that the hexadecimal printouts that were produced as part of each CargoScan imaging and subsequently attached to the inspection report could be reverse engineered to produce an "image" of the second stage, thereby sidestepping their concerns over memory and the storage of images. This realization resulted in an increased level of concern about multiple scans and retained images.

The US inspectors had been trying to get the Soviets to pre-mark their railcars, and then make any adjustments only if the scan failed to meet inspection criteria. The Soviets, however, were keen on the scan succeeding the first time, eliminating the need to do multiple scans. In this light, the Soviets requested in a meeting on May 17 that the US return to its original measurements regarding the centerline height.

The US inspectors made the requested adjustments to CargoScan, but in turn requested that the Soviets stop making their own adjustments. Despite this request, on May 28, the Soviets shipped an SS-25 missile from the factory, the scan of which, on the first try, was deemed to be unusable due to the excessive speed of the railcar going through CargoScan. A review of the image also indicated that the Soviets had not made the requested adjustments. Rather than fix the problem at the time, the Soviets asked that the missile be held in the Environmental Inspection Building overnight while they discussed the issue internally. The next day, the Soviets adjusted their marking per the US request, and the missile was successfully scanned without any issue.

On May 30, the Soviets shipped another SS-25 missile. The initial image was unusable due to the Soviets failing to adjust their marker, resulting in a bad scan. After the Soviets made the necessary adjustments, a second scan was conducted. While the second scan was a success, it did show that the Soviet marker intruded some 6mm into the image.

To the US inspectors, it appeared that the Soviets were deliberately trying to create an issue regarding the quality of the CargoScan images. These concerns were reinforced when, on May 30, 1991, Lev Kokurin, a member of the Soviet CargoScan Commission, forwarded a proposal to the US inspectors for analyzing a test tape to determine the extent/source of the intrusion during affected scans. The Soviets followed this proposal with a request that the US provide them with copies of all tapes which contained a shielding intrusion. On June 29, 1991, the Soviets modified this request—now they only wanted a tape of a test object, not an actual missile.

The reasoning behind the Soviet requests became clear when, on July 8, in a meeting with Aleksandr Sokolov, the request for a tape of a test object was renewed. According to Anatoli Tomilov, the Soviets needed the tape to help them build an apparatus to read the tapes as an alternative to both sides trying to segregate tapes showing shielding intrusion. According to the Soviets, such a machine would eliminate the need for a printout of missile scans, enabling both sides to independently review the tapes and compare notes on the source of any obstruction.

The US inspectors forwarded the Soviet request to OSIA headquarters, which responded with a paper detailing the official US position on the need for rescans. The image area, the paper noted, was determined by where the Soviets mark the railcar, together with the height of the missile centerline above the railbed. Based upon the data provided by the Soviets, the US inspectors would adjust the Linatron and detector arrays prior to a scan being made using the data provided by the Soviets. From the US perspective, errors occurred only if the Soviets provided the wrong data, by either mismarking the railcar or providing incorrect height data. Moreover, the image would be erased only if the imaged zone exceeded the area authorized by the MOA—i.e., an area larger than 339 cm.

If CargoScan imaged the wrong area (i.e., if the data was wrong), the paper stated, then the scan would be repeated. This was a treaty requirement. There was, however, no requirement for the data to be erased from the tape—the MOA allowed for all images to be retained on site. In any event, the image had to be examined by both sides to determine if an error had been made. As such, the US inspectors intended to examine each image after a scan, and before making any determination if it was acceptable or not.

This response was provided to the Soviets in early August 1991. On August 18, 1991, Master Sergeant Gary Marino, an Army linguist assigned to the VPMF and one of the first noncommissioned officers used by OSIA in a deputy site commander role, together with Joe Murphy, a recent hire by Hughes, arrived in Moscow for the weekly mail run.

By the time they returned to Votkinsk two days later, the world had turned upside down.

Political Chaos and Arms Control

THE COLLAPSE of the Russian Communist Party as a viable political institution in the summer of 1990 led to a crisis within the CPSU which resulted in the purging of the Politburo, leaving Gorbachev hanging onto his position of General Secretary by a thread. At the center of Gorbachev's problems was the issue of economic reform. In his discussions with Chuck Myers and Thom Moore in June 1990, Evgeni Odiyankov had stated that "a change in property relationships was required" before any meaningful economic reform could commence. As the US Ambassador to the Soviet Union, Jack Matlock, explained, "Unless the state could find a way to divest itself of control over most income-producing property, reform could not take hold since no real market system of economic interchange would be possible."[5]

Gorbachev was in a political bind—the declaration of sovereignty by Russia had been followed by a similar declaration by most of the other Soviet Republics of the Soviet Union, which, according to Ambassador Matlock, "were no longer willing to have their economic fate decided by bureaucrats in Moscow." Control over these Soviet bureaucracies, however, was the last vestige of political power wielded by Gorbachev, who refused to relinquish it to others. "By clinging to the power over property," Matlock noted, "he [Gorbachev] doomed his own office and the state he headed."[6]

While the need for economic reform was real, there were no political institutions capable of carrying it out. When the Russian Parliament passed an economic reform plan and forwarded it to the Supreme Soviet of the Soviet

Union for approval, Gorbachev responded by instead having the Supreme Soviet pass a separate economic reform plan, resulting in policy chaos. Gorbachev then doubled down by proposing a significant restructuring of Soviet presidential institutions, consolidating power in an ever-tightening circle of advisors surrounding the presidency. Included in the restructuring was the creation of the office of the Vice President, which Gorbachev filled by naming Gennady Yanayev, a relatively unknown trade unionist who presented no political challenge to the Soviet President. Gorbachev pressured the Congress of People's Deputies to approve Yanayev's appointment, as well as new laws which granted the president the ability to govern by decree.

That last move was too much for Eduard Shevardnadze, Gorbachev's long-time Foreign Minister, who resigned in a speech delivered before the Soviet Congress of People's Deputies in December 1990, citing the growing danger of "dictatorship." And, for the first time, rumors began circulating around Moscow of a coup to oust Gorbachev.

When Gorbachev used his new decree powers to begin passing laws governing economic reform, Boris Yeltsin responded by declaring Russian law to have primacy. Gorbachev then signed a decree declaring Soviet law to be supreme. The issue came to a head when Russia refused to turn over taxes collected on Russian soil to Soviet authorities, effectively bankrupting the Soviet economy. As 1990 ended, the Soviet Union was wracked by political chaos and economic confusion.

On October 15, 1990, Mikhail Gorbachev was awarded the Nobel Peace Prize in recognition of his role in ending the Cold War between the Soviet Union and the United States. What Gorbachev had not achieved, however, was the kind of far-reaching arms control treaty which reflected this contention.

One of the reasons for this delay was a growing rebellion within the ranks of the Soviet military that Gorbachev was giving away too much to the US when it came to the arms reductions proposed under the START Treaty. These concerns ballooned into a genuine crisis over arms control, leading to the Soviet negotiating position being hardened to the point that there was a complete breakdown in the negotiations during critical meetings held in Washington, DC in April 1990. To get the Soviet military to yield, it took the personal intercession of Gorbachev, who demanded the resignation of anyone who did not agree with his position on arms control. By May 1990 Gorbachev had a new negotiating position, which served as the final basis of what was to become the START Treaty.

The "crisis in arms control" that gripped the Soviet Union in the spring of 1990 helped set in motion events that impacted the work of the Votkinsk Factory. These events would in no small way lead to the downfall of the Soviet Union. To structure its strategic nuclear posture to support the anticipated demands of the START Treaty, the Soviet military opted to embrace single-warhead mobile ICBMs over heavy, silo-based multiple-warhead carrying missiles.

One reason for this was to seek to retain mobile ICBMs (the US negotiating position sought their outright elimination) by trading away multiple-warhead missiles. Another was a decision by the Soviet military to undertake what it called an "asymmetric response" to the US Strategic Defense Initiative (SDI, better known as Star Wars). The *Kourier*, along with a follow-on to the SS-25 known as the *Topol-M*, had been designed with operational characteristics designed to defeat SDI. However, by 1989 the Soviet concern over SDI had diminished, and the Soviet military began to sour on the project. In 1989, just as the *Kourier* entered its initial operational testing phase, the Ministry of Defense ordered the project put on hold, with about three-quarters of its budget having been spent.[7]

The Minister of Defense Industry, Boris Belousov (the same person nominated by the Votkinsk Production Association to represent them in the March 1990 elections) opted to keep the *Kourier* in production to keep desperately needed funding flowing to the Votkinsk Factory. Belousov was supported in this decision by Yuri Masluykov, the head of the Military Industrial Commission of the USSR (VPK). Masluykov had stepped in as the principal supporter of the Nadiradze Design Bureau/Votkinsk Factory ballistic missile partnership following the death of Dmitri Ustinov and was a major proponent of the road-mobile ballistic missile niche that these organizations had created for themselves.

Boris Belousov's decision to keep the *Kourier* in production despite reticence on the part of the Defense Ministry led to a showdown in the summer of 1990, when the missile was declared ready for initial flight testing. The Minister of Defense, Dmitri Yazov, threatened to fire the Chief of the Soviet General Staff, Mikhail Moisev, for failing to follow an order regarding the shutting down of the *Kourier* program when ordered to do so back in 1989. Moreover, the internal domestic competition between the Nadirazde and Yuzhnoe design bureaus for resources created a situation where Yuzhnoe's allies prevailed upon the Foreign Ministry to declare that any flight test of the *Kourier* missile would undermine the Soviet position in the ongoing negotiations over a strategic arms reduction treaty (START). The decision was made to postpone any flight test of the *Kourier* until more was learned about the American intent regarding its own small ICBM, the *Midgetman*.[8]

Economic chaos, combined with the ongoing political feud between Mikhail Gorbachev and Boris Yeltsin, had created a climate of crisis among the Soviet Union's Communist Party hardliners, many of whom continued to hold positions of power. They saw Gorbachev's willingness to yield to US demands when it came to reducing the ultimate symbol of Soviet power and prestige—its strategic nuclear force—as problematic and began to organize in response. On February 7, 1991, the Soviet military began joint patrols with the civilian police in cities and towns across Russia. This maneuver was seen by many as a naked power grab by the Soviet Minister of Defense, Dimitri Yazov, and the Minster of Internal Affairs, Boris Pugo. Gorbachev's approval of these patrols took many observers by surprise.

When, in March 1991, the Russian Communist Party attempted to remove Boris Yeltsin as the head of the Russian Supreme Soviet, pro-democracy parties organized a massive demonstration in response, scheduled for March 28. Gorbachev, in discussions with Yazov and Pugo, ordered the military into Moscow to protect both the Kremlin and the Russian Parliament from being overrun by a mob of anti-Soviet protesters. More than 100,000 people demonstrated—peacefully. Not only was the show of force not needed, but it backfired. When the Russian Congress of People's Deputies found the Russian Parliament surrounded by Soviet troops—part of a force of some 50,000 soldiers from the Army and Interior Ministry deployed in the streets of Moscow—instead of voting down a motion moving to create the position of a Russian President (which would fall to Boris Yeltsin), the measure was passed overwhelmingly, more as a vote against Soviet power than a vote in support of Yeltsin.

The state of political crisis in the Soviet Union continued. Yeilding to economic and political realities, Gorbachev held a series of meetings with the heads of the newly sovereign republics that comprised the Soviet Union, reversing many of his emergency decrees concerning taxation, and setting the stage for the signing a document which would create a new constitutional basis for their union. For members of the CPSU, this was too much. On April 24, 1991, Gorbachev was confronted by a rebellion from within the ranks at the plenary session of the Central Committee of the Communist Party. The plenum continued into the next day, leading to Gorbachev, frustrated and angered at the vicious criticism being pointed at him, declaring his intention to resign. Recognizing that Gorbachev's resignation could very well lead to the dissolution of the CPSU, the plenum called a recess, and then convened an emergency session of the Politburo, which decided to back Gorbachev and end the rebellion.

As Gorbachev was facing down opposition in the CPSU, the CIA was presenting President Bush with a dark assessment detailing the possibility of a coup designed to topple both Gorbachev and Yeltsin. A nine-page estimate entitled "The Soviet Cauldron," written by George Kolt, the director of the CIA's office of Soviet analysis, warned that the Soviet "centrally planned economy had broken down irretrievably" and that a "situation of growing chaos" existed which could produce "explosive events." Kolt warned that "reactionary leaders, with or without Gorbachev, could judge that the last chance to act had come and move under the banner of law and order," noting that the military, Ministry of Internal Affairs and the KGB, were leading "a premeditated, organized attempt to restore a full-fledged dictatorship," and were "making preparations for a broad use of force in the political process."[9]

"[W]ith or without Gorbachev," Kolt concluded, "with or without a putsch, the most likely prospect for the end of this decade, if not earlier, is a Soviet Union transformed into some independent states and a confederation of the remaining republics, including Russia."

Kolt backed this warning up with testimony before the Joint Economic Committee on May 17, 1991. "There is no doubt that 1991 will be a worse year for the Soviet economy than 1990, and it is likely to be radically worse,'" Kolt testified, adding that "tough economic times are in store for the Soviets." Kolt emphasized the importance of economic reform, noting that void of such, "the economic future will be totally bleak" leading to a downward spiral where "decline could eventually equal or exceed the 30 percent drop in GNP and the 25 percent unemployment rate experienced in this country during the Great Depression from 1930 to 1933."[10]

Kolt's testimony provided clear evidence that perestroika had run its course. While the term was touted around in diplomatic circles and foreign capitals as the defining movement justifying continued support for both Gorbachev and the Soviet Union, in practice the politics of reform had run into a brick wall. Every aspect of the Soviet economy was feeling the pinch—even sacred cows such as the Ministry of Defense Industry and mobile missile programs such as the *Kourier* small ICBM.

The intervention of the Foreign Ministry in the summer of 1990 to halt the *Kourier* flight test program should have killed the program. Rather than placing a nail in the coffin of the *Kourier* program, however, the collusion between the Foreign Ministry and *Yuzhnoe* served to compel the Ministry of Defense Industry to double down on the *Kourier*, ordering an acceleration of the program with an eye on conducting an initial operational flight test in August 1991, fully a year ahead of schedule.[11]

The fact that the Ministry of Defense Industry was able to make this decision in the face of concerted opposition from both the Ministry of Defense and the Foreign Minister is a testament to the level of independence and lack of oversight the ministry enjoyed, as well as the overall state of dysfunction that existed within the Soviet system at the time. This turned the *Kourier* program into a symbol of Soviet power, relevance, and economic capability. Yazov was won over and authorized the military to continue supporting the *Kourier* development program.

The flight testing of a missile represented the final stage of development before a missile could be declared operational. Before a missile could be flight tested, however, there were extensive preliminary tests that had to be conducted, all of which required a unique test object (i.e., missile) manufactured by the Votkinsk Factory. Overseeing this effort was General Colonel Alexander P. Volkov, the First Deputy Commander in Chief of the Soviet Strategic Rocket

Forces, who had been appointed chairman of the "State Commission for the Adoption of the Missile Small Mobile Ground Complex *Kourier*."

Between March 1989 and May 1990 more than 90 tests of the *Kourier* cold-launch system (so-called "throwing tests") were conducted at the 53rd Scientific Research Proving Ground (NIIP) test site in Plesetsk using inert missiles with lightweight first stages and dummy upper stages launched from both silos and mobile launchers. In addition, four actual launches from a mobile launcher were conducted using a lightweight first-stage engine with a reduced charge of fuel. The first of these took place on March 16, 1989. Two more launches occurred in 1990, and the last on May 30, 1991.

While the *Kourier* was being put through its paces, political crises continued to abound in Moscow. Following his election as president of Russia on June 12, Yeltsin had travelled to Washington, DC, where he was scheduled to meet with President Bush (although elected, Yeltsin had yet to be inaugurated). On June 17, 1991, with Yeltsin out of the country, Prime Minister Valentin Pavlov formally asked the Supreme Soviet of the Soviet Union to grant him presidential powers. Pavlov made this request without consulting with Gorbachev.

The Supreme Soviet immediately went into executive session, where KGB Chairman Kryuchkov, Defense Minister Yazov, and Minister of Internal Affairs Pugo all supported Pavlov's request. Gorbachev appeared before the Supreme Soviet the next day, rejected Pavlov's proposal, and helped organize an overwhelming defeat for the motion. However, Pavlov's move had raised several red flags, prompting President Bush to instruct Ambassador Matlock to meet with Gorbachev in person and warn him of the possibility of a coup led by Pavlov.

On June 21, Gorbachev, flanked by Kryuchkov, Pugo, and Yazov, spoke to the Russian press, confidently announcing that "The coup is over."[12]

Gorbachev was wrong. The coup had only just begun.

On July 10, 1991, Boris Yeltsin was sworn in as president of Russia. Alexii II, the Russian Orthodox Patriarch for all of Russia, blessed the newly installed Russian president. It was the first time since the accession of Tsar Nicholas II in 1894 that the Russian Church had anointed a leader of Russia.

The Great October Revolution had been defeated.

The Death of Perestroika

PRESIDENT BUSH had been hoping to conclude a Moscow Summit with Gorbachev before summer's end, after which a START treaty could be signed. Gorbachev, too, was desirous of this summit. However, American and Soviet negotiators continued to haggle over critical details of the treaty, with President Bush's National Security Advisor, Brent Scowcroft, proving to be particularly tough minded on several critical details. By mid-July, things were at a crisis point. A date of July 31 had been set for a treaty signing ceremony, to be held in Saint Vladimir's Hall, in the Kremlin. Time was running out.

Bush and Gorbachev were scheduled to have a lunch in London on July 17, prior to Gorbachev meeting with the Group of Seven nations about the need for foreign assistance in bailing out the Soviet economy. For Gorbachev, it was critical that the negotiators conclude the deal prior to any meeting relating to financial assistance, lest he be accused of selling out the Soviet military in exchange for money. In the end, a final deal was reached; Gorbachev had his "tin cup" meeting, and Bush had his summit.

The START treaty was signed on July 31, 1991. Presidents Bush and Gorbachev exchanged the pens used to sign the documents, which had been crafted from metal taken from missiles destroyed under the INF treaty. Bush celebrated the fact that the US and Soviet sides were reversing a "half century of steadily growing strategic arsenals," adding that "neither side has acquired unilateral advantages over the other."[13]

The Soviet Defense Minister, Dmitri Yazov, praised the treaty, telling a Soviet reporter that the START treaty "makes it possible to lower the level of nuclear confrontation between the USSR and the United States, strengthen strategic stability, and thereby reduce the likelihood of a nuclear conflict. It is a treaty," Yazov said, "that for the first time ever not only limits, but reduces, strategic nuclear arms."[14]

The treaty, however, had come at a cost to Soviet military prestige, with many senior Soviet officials believing that Gorbachev had given away too much to get his deal. For these officials, projects like the *Kourier* missile were important not only from a strategic capability standpoint, but also as a weapon of prestige, something that would demonstrate to the Americans that the Soviet Union was still a power to be reckoned with.

Following the second flight test of the *Midgetman* missile by the US in April 1991, the proponents of the *Kourier* missile sent a memorandum to Gorbachev requesting permission to begin operational flight testing of the *Kourier* in August 1991. The signatories of this request included Dmitri Yazov and Vladimir Kruychkov (the KGB Chief), as well as Boris Belousov, Alexander Bessmertnykh (the Foreign Minister), and Yuri Masluykov.[15]

For the Ministry of Defense Industry, the *Kourier* was seen as a vehicle of economic survival in the age of cost-cutting brought about by Gorbachev's policies of perestroika. This was especially true for factory towns like Votkinsk, whose viability rested on the continued production of missiles like the *Kourier*—between January 15 and August 31, 1991, 15 "partitioned railcars" carrying *Kourier* missiles had exited the Votkinsk portal, bringing the total to 62 since entry into force of the INF Treaty. The economic value of this missile program to the Votkinsk Factory and by extension, the people of Votkinsk, cannot be overstated—a fact that was not lost on the signatories of the letter.

Following the signing of the START Treaty on July 31, 1991, Viktor Karpov, the head Soviet negotiator for START, interceded. Arguing that any flight test of the *Kourier* missile less than one month after the signing of START could put the entire treaty at risk, Karpov prevailed upon Bessmertnykh to abandon the *Kourier* flight test planned for mid-August. Instead, it was decided that flight tests of the *Kourier* ICBM would be postponed until the START treaty entered into force, which was at that time estimated to be sometime in late 1991–early 1992. Bessmertnykh drafted a new letter for Yazov's signature that, if approved by Gorbachev, would have dealt a lethal blow to the prospects of the *Kourier* missile.[16]

In the minds of the old-guard Soviets who supported the program, the *Kourier* small ICBM had become a symbol of relevance in terms of Soviet strategic power, and in doing so, the decision regarding its operational testing had taken on a political dimension. The planning for a coup to overthrow Gorbachev had been ongoing for some time, and the reasons behind the coup were complex and deep seated, involving far more than just arms control or the fate of a single missile program. However, when Bessmertnykh's letter reached Yazov's desk, it proved to be the proverbial straw that broke the camel's back.[17]

Planning for what eventually became a coup to oust Gorbachev began on August 4, 1991. A few days prior, on July 29, Gorbachev met with Yeltsin and the Kazakh President, Nursultan Nazarbayev, to discuss the timing for signing a union treaty. Recognizing the need for major changes in the Soviet government, Gorbachev informed Yeltsin and Nazarbayev that he would be replacing Chairman of the KGB Vladimir Kryuchkov, Interior Minister Boris Pugo, and Premier Valentin Pavlov once the treaty was signed. The signing ceremony was set for August 20, after Gorbachev returned from vacationing in Crimea.

Gorbachev and his wife, Raisa, left for Crimea on August 4. That afternoon, Kryuchkov organized a team of KGB officers for the purpose of planning a coup. Recognizing the reality that his authority would be ended on August 20, Kryuchkov pushed for action prior to that day. By August 16 the KGB had finalized an operational plan, and had begun to deploy resources to implement it, including the dispatch of a team to Crimea charged with cutting off all communications links between Gorbachev and the outside world.[18]

Kryuchkov organized a meeting with fellow hardliners on August 17 for the purpose of outlining his plans for a coup and lining up their support. Attendees included Pavlov, Yazov, First Deputy Chairman of the Defense Council of the USSR Oleg Baklanov (responsible for oversight of defense industry) and importantly, Valery Boldin, Gorbachev's Chief of Staff. After an alcohol-soaked meeting, the coup plotters agreed to send a delegation, headed by Baklonov and Boldin, and which would include General Valentin Varennikov, the commander of Soviet ground forces, to Crimea to confront Gorbachev and pressure him into supporting the imposition of a state of emergency. This delegation flew to Crimea on August 18, but their efforts were rebuffed by an angry Gorbachev. The delegation returned to Moscow empty handed. Gorbachev remained in Crimea under house arrest, cut off from the rest of the world.[19]

On the morning of August 19, 1991, the Minister of Defense of the Soviet Union, Marshall Dmitri Yazov, together with Vice President Gennady Yanayev, Pavlov, Pugo, Kryuchkov, Baklanov, Chairman of the Peasants' Union of the USSR Vasily Starodubtsev, and President of the Association of State Enterprises Aleksandr Tizyakov, formed what they called the State Committee on the State of Emergency (GKChP). A state of emergency was declared and some 4,000 troops from the Tamanskaya and Kantemirovskaya divisions, together with paratroopers and special forces, entered Moscow, accompanied by hundreds of tanks and armored personnel carriers.

The real coup had begun.

The Votkinsk weekly mail run was underway when the coup began. Gary Marino, a military linguist, and Joe Murphy, a Hughes contractor, were just exiting the US Embassy when they were confronted by a column of tanks making its way toward the Kremlin. Marino and Murphy eventually made their way to the streets surrounding the Russian Parliament Building, where they witnessed Russian President Boris Yeltsin mounting a tank, and delivering a decree rejecting the actions of the Emergency Committee.[20]

"In connection with the acts of a group of people who have declared themselves the State Committee on the State of Emergency," Yeltsin said, speaking from a piece of paper he held in his hand, "I hereby decree that the committee's announcement violates the Constitution, and the actions of its organizers constitute a coup d'état and a state crime."

While the image of Yeltsin on the tank resonated around the world, the image that most Russians saw was that of Vice President Yanayev's hand, shaking like a leaf on a tree, as he read the announcement regarding the establishment of the emergency committee live on Russian television. Yanayev was scared, and his demeanor did nothing to inspire a population that was predisposed to oppose authoritarian displays of this nature—especially those conducted outside the framework of the rule of law.[21]

The Russian people saw and heard something else as well. When questioned by reporters outside his vacation home in Kennebunkport, Maine about the fate of Gorbachev, President Bush remarked "Coups can fail." Wayne Merry, who was responsible for political reporting coming out of the US Embassy in Moscow at the time, later called Bush's statement "three of the words that George Herbert Walker Bush ever said in public."[22]

"Coups can fail."

On August 20, faced with a growing wave of popular support for the anti-coup position taken by Boris Yeltsin, the Emergency Committee ordered the Soviet military to storm the Russian Parliament. These orders were not obeyed. By the end of the next day, Gorbachev had returned to Moscow.

The coup had, indeed, failed.

None of the signatories of the April 1991 request regarding the *Kourier* flight test survived the aftermath of the coup; all were either arrested or forced to resign. As for the *Kourier* missile, Gorbachev terminated it for good on October 5, 1991. The "partitioned railcar," it seemed, had served as a trigger for a conspiracy to take down the Soviet government, and paid the price.

Gorbachev never recovered politically from the damage to his prestige done by the coup. While Yeltsin had rallied to Gorbachev's defense in the face of the coup plotters, it was the defense of the rule of law over dictatorship, rather than the defense of an individual or institution, that motivated the Russian President.

Talks to form a union which would serve as a state for Gorbachev to govern also collapsed. In the end the Soviet Union dissolved into a commonwealth of independent states composed of sovereign constituents, none of whom owed their loyalty to a higher authority. The Soviet Union was dead, leaving Gorbachev no choice but to resign, which he did in a televised speech on December 25, 1991.

Shortly after Gorbachev's resignation speech, the Soviet flag was lowered from the Kremlin, and replaced by the tricolors of the Russian Federation. At the Votkinsk portal, the factory personnel found themselves overcome by events—with no Russian flag available, the Soviet colors continued to fly over their administrative building. The US Site Commander, Stephen Zolock, tasked the weekly mail run to purchase some Russian flags and bring them back to the VPMF, where they were handed over to Department 162. The Soviet flag was removed, and the Russian flag raised in its stead.

The Votkinsk Portal Monitoring Facility, conceived as a function of Cold War reality, and weaned through the socio-economic pressures of perestroika, would be left to mature within the new geopolitical framework of US-Russian relations.

Russia, as Jack Matlock, the former US Ambassador to the Soviet Union, observed, must either reform, or fall apart.[23] This truism, however, existed independent of the policies of perestroika which came to define the tenure of Mikhail Gorbachev as the leader of the Soviet Union. Whatever transpired in the way of reform post-December 25, 1991, however, cannot be equated to perestroika. Perestroika was a creation of Mikhail Gorbachev, and its conception and implementation were unique to the Soviet experience. When Gorbachev resigned, perestroika as an idea died.

Disarmament, however, continued, as did the work of Russian defense industry, including the Moscow Institute of Thermal Technology and the Votkinsk Factory. Missiles continued to be produced, albeit at rates of production significantly reduced from Soviet times. The context of this continued production, and of the continued disarmament talks between the United States and Russia, however, had changed dramatically from that which governed both the INF and START treaties.

On December 25, 1991, the world changed. The Cold War was over. During his time as the leader of the Soviet Union, Mikhail Gorbachev understood the need to reform the Soviet economy, inclusive of defense industry. Gorbachev understood, too, that defense conversion and the socio-economic impact this conversion had on the lives of the people who were engaged in the business of producing missiles, was tied to the way the Soviet Union was governed, especially the top-down aspect of decision making.

Perestroika represented a process designed to change this system. As such, the internal Soviet struggle to implement perestroika was inextricably linked both to the inception and conception of the INF treaty, and the way the treaty was implemented. In short, without perestroika, there would not—and indeed, could not—have been an INF treaty, at least not in the form that it was eventually constituted and implemented.

The INF treaty continued to be implemented after the resignation of Mikhail Gorbachev, and the START treaty was eventually ratified and implemented as well. But the processes and context of these activities differed from what had transpired prior to Gorbachev's resignation.

Disarmament in the time of perestroika was a unique phenomenon, never again to be replicated.

Castles in the Air

*Paul Copeland receives the US flag from Jonathan Sachar after it was lowered
for the last time from the Votkinsk Portal Monitoring Facility, December 4, 2009.
Photo Credit: Valeri Yakolev*

> *"If you have built castles in the air, your work
> need not be lost; that is where they should be.
> Now put the foundations under them."*

HENRY DAVID THOREAU
Walden

Striking the Colors

VOTKINSK PORTAL MONITORING FACILITY, December 4, 2009—It was a
solemn ceremony, repeated daily on US military installations around the world
at 5 PM sharp—the lowering of the colors. The only thing missing was the sound
of a bugler playing "Retreat" and "To the Colors," music familiar to anyone who
has ever served in the armed forces of the United States.

The American flag had been flying over the Votkinsk Portal Monitoring
Facility (VPMF) continuously since July 1988, when the first INF inspectors

arrived. The INF treaty's inspection phase had ended in 2001. After that, the US inspectors working in Votkinsk operated under the mandate of the START treaty. The treaties may have changed, but the flag had remained the same.

The US flag had flown side by side with that of either the Soviet Union or Russia from a flagpole mounted on the Data Control Center, the center for monitoring operations. When the DCC was dismantled in early November 2009 and shipped off to Germany, the flagpole was moved to a position over the entrance to the Roosevelt administrative building, one of four structures that gad provided living quarters and administrative offices for the US inspectors in Votkinsk since 1989. Here, the inspection team maintained their watch, with the telephone switchboard from the dismantled DCC moved into the former office for the Raytheon Site Manager, which had been converted into a temporary duty office.

The team implemented their treaty-mandated tasks up until the last moment. When the DCC was operational, the inspectors used a network of sensors, traffic lights, and gates to control the flow of traffic in and out of the monitored missile assembly facility. With the DCC gone, the semaphore gates were locked into the "up" position, and power was disconnected to the traffic lights, making vehicle traffic control difficult. Rail traffic was still declared by the Russians and the treaty-mandated inspection tasks were still conducted. The inspectors were reduced to using tape measurers, clipboards, and flashlights to do their work— the same basic tools that their predecessors had relied upon in the early days of the INF treaty back in July-August 1988, before the portal monitoring facility had been constructed.

Under the watchful eyes of the assembled American inspectors and Russian factory escorts, a trio of US personnel approached the flag. Leading the team was Air Force Lieutenant Colonel Kelley Easler. Assisting Lieutenant Colonel Easler with the flag lowering detail was Jim Hanley, a civilian technician with Raytheon Technical Services Company (RTSC). Watching from the sidelines, along with the rest of the team and a handful of Russian officials from Department 162 (the Votkinsk factory organization responsible for escorting the US inspectors), was Air Force Colonel Tom Summers, the START Division Chief at DTRA, and Scott Yoder, the head of the Votkinsk Support Office for RTSC.

The third person on the flag lowering detail was Marine Corps Lieutenant Colonel Jonathan Sachar. Jonathan Sachar was a CH-53 pilot and Eurasian Foreign Area Officer (FAO). During Operation Iraqi Freedom, then-Major Sachar served as the CH-53 detachment commander assigned to Marine Helicopter Squadron HMM-264, onboard the USS Iwo Jima, as part of the 26th Marine Expeditionary Unit, where he participated in combat operations in northern Iraq. Jonathan Sachar had been recently assigned to the START Monitoring Branch, and this was his first—and only—rotation into the VPMF.

Jonathan Sachar supervised the handling of the flag, working with Jim Hanley and Kelley Easler to fold it into a triangle consisting of a field of blue with white stars. The task completed, Jonathan took the flag, and turned to face the Site Commander, Air Force Lieutenant Colonel Paul Copeland. Jonathan Sachar presented Paul Copeland with the flag, and then snapped to attention. The deed was done—after 21 years of flying proudly from what had become a little slice of Americana in a far-off corner of Russia, the US flag would never again be unfurled over the VPMF.

Lieutenant Colonel Paul Copeland was a veteran ICBM operator, having previously served as the deputy commander of the 91st Operations Group, in Minot, North Dakota, and as the commander of the 323rd Training Squadron at Lackland Air Force Base, in Texas. He also had previous joint assignments with Joint Strategic Target Planning Staff, and at Strategic Command. He joined DTRA in 2006, where he served as a Site Commander at the VPMF, before assuming command of the START Monitoring Branch in June 2009.

Paul Copeland headed up the Votkinsk Closeout Team, which won a DTRA Director's Award for excellence in 2009. Work on the closeout effort had begun two years prior, when Paul's predecessor, Army Lieutenant Colonel Norman Fuss, began formal meetings with Department 162 (by this time headed by Aleksandr Fomin, the former Bureau Chief who, together with Nikolai Shadrin and Vladamir Kupriyanov, had walked in on the impromptu DCC light show back in 1989), to create a framework for planning site closure. One of the critical issues was how much material would have to be removed from the VPMF, and how much could either be turned over to the Russians, who were quite enthusiastic about having the furnishings of the housing units and the contents of the warehouse remain behind.

Closing out the VPMF, however, was easier said than done, especially when the bar kept changing as US arms control negotiators in Geneva, Switzerland tried to obtain a last-minute extension of the START treaty, or else negotiate a continued presence at Votkinsk into a replacement treaty. The US inspectors were instructed to stop coordinating closeout operations with the Russians out of concern such talks could compromise the US negotiating position in the ongoing talks over the possible extension of the START treaty.

By October 2009, however, the writing was on the wall, and the VPMF Site Commander was instructed to resume closeout coordination with the Russian factory personnel. The US inspectors, however, had to remain diligent; even on this last tour, Paul Copeland was prepared to reverse the closeout operations and continue the monitoring mission if circumstances changed.

They did not.

Besides the flag, there was not much left at the VPMF for the US inspectors to take away. The DCC had been broken down and loaded onto three trucks for delivery to a Raytheon warehouse in Darmstadt, Germany. Various gifts and souvenirs that the US inspection team had acquired over the years were similarly packaged up and shipped via DHL to the DTRA Headquarters in Fort Belvoir, Virginia for safekeeping and eventual display. Everything else was to be handed over to the Russians, including the furniture and furnishings in the four buildings that comprised the US inspector housing and administrative quarters.

On November 18, 2009, a final official function was organized by Department 162, bidding the US inspectors farewell. The event was held at the Café Versailles, adjacent to the School of Arts, in downtown Votkinsk. The geopolitics involved in leisure activities never abated, even though issues of reciprocity kept things from spinning out of control. An uneasy equilibrium was eventually reached which gave the inspectors continued access to specific locations within the treaty-mandated 50-kilometer leisure zone, as well as by-exception access to the city of Izhevsk. The spontaneous interactions between Americans and the residents of Votkinsk that had marked the first year of the VPMF's existence, however, no longer existed.

Social restrictions, however, could not derail the camaraderie that existed between the US inspectors and their factory counterparts from Department 162. While many of these relationships were defined by the tour length of the individual Americans, there were a select few who could claim a relationship that ran the entire 21-year history of the VPMF. These included Barrett Haver, Scott Yoder, and Jim Handley on the American side, and Aleksandr Fomin, Vladimir Kupriyanov, and Valerey Yakovlev from Department 162.

The inspectors maintained a duty shift throughout the night, ceasing monitoring operations at 5 am sharp on the morning of December 5, 2009. At that point they were taken by bus to Izhevsk airport, where they flown to Moscow's Sheremetyevo onboard a Russian air force aircraft. The team made its way to the commercial terminal, where the boarded a Lufthansa flight to Frankfurt, Germany.

The last rotation completed, America's 21-year experiment in continuous portal monitoring came to an end.

Back at the Votkinsk Final Assembly Plant, the buildings that once housed the American inspectors were empty, standing watch over a monument to the INF treaty that the Votkinsk factory had built back in 2001, when inspections under that treaty ended. The monument had been popular among inspectors as a setting for team photographs. Now it stood alone, a memento of a time long past, unnoticed by anyone who was not specifically looking for it.

There was another statue.

On September 10, 2010, the Votkinsk Production Association erected a bust of Vladimir Gennadievich Sadovnikov in downtown Votkinsk. The installation was a collaboration between Votkinsk artist Alexander Sorochkin and Izhevsk artist Pavel Medvedev and placed on a parcel of land belonging to the Votkinsk Production Association located not far from 20 Dzerzhinsky Street, the site of the temporary quarters of the US inspectors. In an accompanying ceremony, Sadovnikov was proclaimed an "honorary citizen of Votkinsk." Technical schools so vital to the training of a new generation of worker at the Votkinsk Factory were also named in his honor.

Sadovnikov had put Votkinsk on the Soviet map by transforming a factory known for steel working into the centerpiece of Soviet ballistic missile manufacturing and, later, when the changes brought on by perestroika caused some to cast blame on him for the sad state of the Soviet economy, had gone on to take his own life. The people had not forgotten the man they lovingly called "the father of Votkinsk."

Monument to Vladimir Gennadievich Sadovnikov, the "Father of Votkinsk."
Photo Credit: Valery Yakovlev

The Last Cowboy

THE DEPARTURE of Lieutenant Colonel Copeland's team from Russia was the culmination of a treaty relationship between the US and Russia which was born at the commencement of the collapse of the Soviet Union. The repetitive nature of portal monitoring did not change once the Soviet flag was replaced by that of the Russian Federation. A *New York Times* reporter who visited the VPMF in January 1992 noted that "life has slowed to a crawl. Weeks pass between missile checks, so inspectors often fill their days skating, cleaning dormitories, meeting with schoolchildren and, in winter, skiing around the 4-mile fenced perimeter of the missile factory."

The Site Commander at the time, Air Force Lieutenant Colonel Stephen Zolock (who first rotated into Votkinsk in December 1990), observed that "the splash of the original treaty is gone and it's a greater challenge to keep everybody motivated." Unlike his predecessors, Zolock bristled at being characterized as a Cold Warrior, noting that the VPMF mission "is more of a peacemaking role than warfighting role."[1]

A second reporter, writing for the *Wall Street Journal*, visited the site in early December 1993, and noted that "[t]here is little to do, and the boredom is intense. Life here seems to be part country club, part detention center." Gary Marino, the long-time OSIA military linguist who had been in Moscow on August 19, 1991, during the abortive coup against then-Soviet President Gorbachev, likened the VPMF to "a minimum-security prison with frills." Tack Lim, one of the original Hughes inspectors, declared "[t]he novelty has worn off." The Site Commander, Air Force Lieutenant Colonel William Friese, was more worried about weeds growing along the perimeter path than any missiles coming out of the factory.[2]

The missiles, however, continued to be shipped out the Votkinsk Missile Final Assembly Plant, including types that had not existed when the INF treaty entered into force in 1988. Even though the START treaty had been signed in July 1991, it had yet to be ratified, and as such its provisions were not enforced. However, missiles that were covered under START, but which were not part of the INF monitoring framework, were being produced and were ready to be shipped out. The START treaty created a body, known as the Joint Compliance and Inspection Commission, or JCIC, which now served in the same capacity as the Special Verification Commission (SVC) had for the INF treaty.

One of these missiles was the RS-12M/*Topol-M,* known in the West as the SS-27. While the initial flight test of the SS-27 did not take place until December 20, 1994, like all other missiles under development, numerous test and training missiles were manufactured prior to actual operational testing. Since the SS-27 was assembled at the Votkinsk Missile Final Assembly Plant, this meant that it would be subject to inspection under the terms of the INF Treaty, which included radiographic imaging using CargoScan.

In April 1993, the JCIC promulgated procedures which sought to identify training models of the SS-25 and SS-27 so that they could avoid being imaged by CargoScan. These procedures included the drilling of two holes in the launch cannister in the region of the first stage motor and coaxially related to one of these two holes, another hole drilled through the casing of the first stage rocket motor and into the inert propellant.

On December 25, 1993—Christmas day—the Russians exited what it declared to be a training model of the RS-12M Variant 2 ICBM for silo launching—designated by the US as the SS-27. Unlike previous training missiles, this one did not have the holes drilled into it, suggesting that it was meant for operational testing. The Russians refused to allow the missile to be imaged by CargoScan, and shipped it under protest by the US inspectors, who declared an inspection anomaly.[3]

On July 18, 1994, the Russians shipped a railcar carrying an empty, cannister-like cylinder. Under the procedures agreed to regarding the shipment of empty SS-25 cannisters, the object should have been allowed to have been measured by inspectors. This time the Russians, claiming that the object was not related to the SS-25 and, as such, not covered by those procedures, denied the inspectors request to measure the cylinder in question. The US inspectors again declared an inspection anomaly.[4]

The inspectors were now operating in an environment that existed in the nether regions of policy linking the INF and START treaties. In October 1994, the SVC reached an agreement which declared that "as a matter of policy," the US "will direct its inspectors in Votkinsk not to exercise the US right to image the contents of the launch cannister of up to five missiles." In short, the terms had been reversed. Whereas under the INF treaty the inspectors could designate up to eight SS-25 cannisters to be opened for visual inspection, the Russians, under these new procedures, would be able to designate up to five SS-27 launch cannisters per year that would *not* be subjected to radiographic imaging using CargoScan.[5]

Additionally, after extensive negotiations, including the conduct of several test scans using CargoScan, procedures were established by the JCIC that allowed US inspectors to use CargoScan to image a narrow slice of the first and second stages of an SS-27 that had not been designated for exclusion by the Russians.

The role played by the Hughes inspectors in adapting CargoScan to meet the new demands created by the presence of the SS-27 cannot be overstated. While the Russians had grown skeptical of the arms control role played by having Americans parked outside the gates of their preeminent missile assembly factory, the record of demonstrated integrity and professionalism of the Hughes contractors when it came to CargoScan operations, born from the experiences of Sam Israelit and Jim Lusher during the CargoScan Crisis of March 1990, allowed the changes to be made without generating a whole new crisis. As Air Force Lieutenant Colonel Michael Krimmer, a veteran of Votkinsk, noted, "Negotiating changes to the CargoScan system required to perform inspections of the new SS-X-27 ICBM exiting the Votkinsk plant would have been dramatically more difficult without the technical expertise and reputation of the contract engineers."[6]

These procedures, however, were not fool-proof. As late as 1998, SS-27 missiles inspected using CargoScan revealed "anomalies" which the Russians refused to acknowledge, leading to a number of "treaty anomalies" being declared by the US inspectors.

Other procedures were put in place regarding a modification of the SS-25 missile used for civilian space launches known as the "Start." In this case, the missile was shipped out as two separate cannisters, one containing the first two stages, the second the third stage and a new, fourth stage unique to the space launch vehicle.

Another unresolved inspection-related matter was that of the stage measuring device. On April 4, 1991, the Americans and Soviets signed an amendment to the December 1989 Memorandum of Agreement regarding what was now termed the "Stage Measuring System," or SMS. The Soviets would manufacture the SMS, and the US would purchase no fewer than three of the devices. The US was in negotiations with the Soviets about the purchase of the SMS when the Soviet Union collapsed on December 31, 1991. The issue of the SMS went into limbo, and once the START treaty entered into force in 1994, the plethora of missile types exiting the Votkinsk portal, each with its own unique measurements, made the SMS impractical. It was dropped, leaving CargoScan and the visual inspections as the sole means available to inspectors in Votkinsk for distinguishing between an SS-20 and an SS-25.

The INF treaty's inspection phase was limited to 13 years. After all the angst and drama associated with the installation of CargoScan in Votkinsk, its departure was, by comparison, simple and free of controversy. On May 31, 2001, the INF inspection protocol expired. At the VPMF, the Americans and Russians held a ceremony marking the occasion. On June 1, 2001, the VPMF became a START-only facility. CargoScan was disassembled, its modules put on a train and shipped to Germany, where they were turned over to the Department of Defense for disposal. A key aspect of the agreement between the US and the Soviets that allowed CargoScan to be made operational in March 1990 concerned the storage of the magnetic disks and tapes containing data derived from the CargoScan imaging processes. Under the term of the agreement, these materials were not allowed to leave the site. The US inspectors and their Russian escorts jointly destroyed the disks and tapes by burning them in a barrel.

While CargoScan may have been a thing of the past, the work of a START portal monitor was no less challenging post its removal. In addition to carrying out technical inspections involving visual evaluation and physical measurements, the personnel at the VPMF were now required to record information relating to a "unique identifier" (a non-repeating alpha-numeric designator) that was affixed to the launch cannister or missile prior to exiting the Votkinsk Missile Final Assembly Plant. These numbers were recorded and integrated into a data base that would be used by other US inspectors to keep track of the Russian ballistic missile inventory.

These provisions were not above the occasional controversy. The Russians conducted a flight test on October 22, 2008 of an extended range SS-25. The missile in question had exited the VPMF a few weeks before. The Soviets had painted the launch cannister red and declared its contents to be a test missile "of a new design." From the Soviet perspective, because the missile would not be entering the operational inventory, there was no need to mark the launch cannister with a "unique identifier." From the perspective of the US inspectors however, the only thing that differentiated this launch cannister from any other SS-25 launch cannister was its color. There was no way for an inspector to confirm that the contents of the cannister was, indeed, a modified SS-25. To qualify as a "missile of new design," there needed to be a discernable physical difference in the launch cannister in terms of length and width, but there was not. The Russians refused to mark the cannister or provide another means for the inspectors to confirm its contents, so when the cannister was shipped from the portal, the inspectors reported it as a treaty anomaly.

As with any organization, while the positions that constituted the manning chart remained relatively constant, the people who filled these positions were in a constant state of flux. Starting in 1991, OSIA increased its staffing in anticipation of the increased responsibilities that would accrue when the START treaty entered into force. Portal Monitoring received several new officers who were tasked with preparing to open a second continuous portal monitoring facility in Pavlograd, Ukraine. The Pavlograd Mechanical Plant, which was part of *Yuzhmash* Production Association, was producing the SS-24 rail-mobile ICBM from this location. Under the terms of the START treaty, the US was planning on exercising its option to establish a continuous perimeter portal monitoring facility at that location. The new officers were tasked with preparing for that mission. The collapse of the Soviet Union put the entry into force of the START treaty on hold. By 1993–94, many of these officers were due to depart OSIA, their tours of duty ending without ever fulfilling their assigned mission. Many of these officers were rotated through Votkinsk to gain experience in portal monitoring operations.

The Votkinsk experience, circa 1993–94, was completely different than that of the early years, so much so that there was a clash of cultures between the original OSIA "Buzzards" and the new generation of portal monitoring inspectors. Stu O'Neill had left OSIA in 1992, reassigned to the Air Force Office of Special Investigations. In 1994 he was tasked with returning to OSIA to help set up the Pavlograd Portal Monitoring Facility. When the mission slipped by a few months, Stu returned to Votkinsk to help train some of the newer personnel. In preparing for his rotation into Votkinsk, Stu met with several of them, including an Army Major who proceeded to lecture Stu on the new reality that existed in Votkinsk. "Votkinsk has changed," the Major noted. "It is not like when cowboys like you and Ritter were there. There are rules and procedures that have to be followed."

Stu O'Neill had been part of the first team of portal monitors to arrive in Votkinsk back in July 1988. He was part of the first team of inspectors to inspect an SS-25 launch cannister. He was with Colonel Englund when the first opening of an SS-25 launch cannister took place for visual inspection. Stu was the duty officer on March 1, 1990, when the CargoScan Crisis began, and he was the duty officer on March 10, 1990, when the Soviets shipped three missile-carrying railcars out of the portal without allowing them to be imaged by CargoScan. Stu was also the duty officer overseeing the first operational use of CargoScan. Stu had helped write the rules and procedures used at Votkinsk. The idea of Stu being lectured to by an officer whose list of accomplishments in Votkinsk paled in comparison was laughable.

There was still a need for cowboys. When the first team of US inspectors flew into Ukraine in January 1994 to set up from scratch the new Pavlograd Portal Monitoring Facility (PPMF), Stu O'Neill was there, lending his unique experience in building a portal facility from scratch to the "new breed" of OSIA inspectors. Joining Stu in this new adventure were Scott Yoder and Mike Wilking, two of the original contingent of Hughes personnel involved in making the Votkinsk Portal Monitoring Facility (VPMF) operational, Scott as an on-site technician, and Mike as the field Operations-Europe manager supporting Votkinsk operations from his offices in Frankfurt, Germany. Tom Michaels, who served as Site Commander at the VPMF in 1990–91, was selected to be the first Site Commander for the PPMF. (The PPMF was closed on May 31, 1995, after Ukraine declared that no SS-24 production was taking place at the facility, allowing the facility to be converted to a site subject to suspect site inspections.)

But Stu was a dying breed. There was a shift in organizational mindset that was occurring within OSIA. The departure of General Lajoie in January 1991 marked the end of the dominance of a Russian Foreign Area Officer as the desired experience base for a US inspector. The "patrol leader" mindset that was attractive to officers such as Roland Lajoie and Larry Kelley, where independent thinking under stressful situations, bred through assignments with the US Military Liaison Mission in Potsdam, East Germany, or as a military attaché assigned to the US Embassy in Moscow during the height of the Cold War, and considered a

Stu O'Neil (fifth from left) with the initial team of portal monitors at the Pavlograd Portal Monitoring Facility, January 1994. Photo Credit: Paul Gwaltney

necessary attribute, had been replaced by a more structured, methodological approach to inspections. The appointment of Major General Robert Parker, a career ballistic missile operations officer with no experience in Russian affairs, to replace General Lajoie underscored this shift in organizational emphasis.

To Kill a Dragon

WHEN OSIA WAS absorbed into a new umbrella organization, the Defense Threat Reduction Agency (DTRA), on October 1, 1998, the primacy of Russian-area expertise for assigned personnel was even further diluted. The Votkinsk Portal Monitoring mission was able to benefit from the institutional knowledge of pioneers like Doug Englund, who had served as the Director of DTRA prior to his retirement in 2007, and George Connell, who had overseen portal monitoring contract management issues for HTSC and later RTSC before retiring in 2004. But the role played by the two men most responsible for the creation of the VPMF was peripheral at best—there was a new breed of Site Commander in charge, men whose life experience was not defined by the exigencies of the Cold War, but rather the mundane realities of peacetime routine.

Moreover, while the actual job of inspecting a missile remained challenging, the opportunity to do so diminished considerably in the summer of 2000, when Russian President Vladimir Putin, who took over after Boris Yeltsin resigned at the end of 1999. Putin conducted a review of Russia's nuclear posture and, in the interest of budget cuts, radically reduced the number of missiles to be procured from the Votkinsk Factory. Whereas the initial plans for 2000 called for the purchase of 20 SS-27 missiles per year, this number was cut to six, and then four. This meant that the drudgery of life as a portal monitor was made even more so through a lack of work.

Then, starting in 2005, the Russian Ministry of Defense began buying more missiles, increasing the number per year to be purchased to 13.

This was good news for the Votkinsk plant, which had been functioning well below even its minimal capacity, meaning the factory had been operating at a significant loss for close to four years straight. The factory's economic outlook was boosted even further with the production of the RSM-56 *Bulava* submarine-launched ballistic missile, which began in 2005. Even with this increased level of production, however, the inspection of one or two missiles per month was hardly the kind of workload needed to justify the expense of maintaining 30 inspectors on full-time duty in the heart of Russia. When the time came to extend the START treaty, it was instead allowed to lapse with the consent of both parties, ending 21 years of continuous portal monitoring at the Votkinsk Missile Final Assembly Plant. The decision to let START expire was made at the end of the administration of George W. Bush, which was opposed to Cold War-style arms control agreements it viewed as too constraining when it came to America's nuclear posture. Bush was, by this time, a lame duck President, and the decision was made to let his successor, Barack Obama, craft a new arms control relationship. While a follow-on treaty, known as "New START," was eventually signed, ratified, and implemented, it did not include provisions for portal monitoring inspections.

The INF treaty had played a crucial role in shaping the course of US and Soviet (and later, Russian) nuclear arms control. But enforcing it had become far more problematic since on-site inspections were no longer integral to the treaty's verification system. Portal monitoring inspections did not come cheap—the annual operating expense for Votkinsk in the 1990s was $9.2 million. This figure did not include the $32 million that the Air Force and Department of Energy spent on CargoScan and the other unique equipment that comprised the technical on-site inspection concept as deployed to Votkinsk (some of which, like the IR rail profiler, never worked and was eventually dismantled and done away with).[7]

The alterations to the "verification equation" that on-site inspections brought back in the 1980s, allowing the standard to be changed from "adequate" to "effectively verifiable," were no longer in place. Once again, arms control verification became conducted almost exclusively by spy satellites that, despite their many capabilities, lack the in-person human element inherent in rigorous inspections.

The consequences of this lack of "effective verification" capability were highlighted when, post-2009, questions about compliance with the INF treaty were raised by Americans and Russians alike. The US concerns rose from an allegation that the Russians had tested a ground-launched cruise missile with a range of 500 to 5,500 kilometers—an act prohibited by the treaty. The Russians vehemently denied the charge and repeatedly pointed out that the US had failed to provide specific data to sustain the allegation.

In turn, Russia levied its own battery of claims against the US for INF treaty violations. The most serious centered on US plans to deploy the Navy's Aegis missile defense system and Standard Missile-3 interceptors using a vertical launch system in Romania and Poland. The launcher in question was a multi-missile, multi-mission system designed for use aboard ships and capable of launching both the SM-3 interceptor and the Tomahawk cruise missile. The Russians contended that this would give the US the capability of launching the Tomahawk in an aggressive ground-launch configuration, a violation of the INF treaty.

Historically, compliance issues such as these were dealt with through on-site inspections, but after the expiration of the INF treaty's inspection phase on May 31, 2001, treaty verification became the exclusive purview of spy satellites. Data collected using so-called "National Technical Means" (NTM) is by its very nature incomplete and subject to interpretation, making it unreliable as a means of verifying compliance. This is especially true in the two cases of alleged non-compliance, one American, one Russian, that were levied post-2009.

On-site inspections conducted within the framework and context of the INF treaty would have allowed for the investigation and resolution of these kinds of treaty compliance issues. And even though on-site inspections were, at the time of the allegations, no longer integral to the INF treaty, they could have been brought back under certain circumstances by the Special Verification Commission, the organization established by the treaty to "resolve questions relating to compliance" and "agree upon such measures as may be necessary to improve the viability and effectiveness of the treaty."

The SVC's intervention in the 1990 CargoScan crisis helped resolve a dispute over the installation and operation of a controversial treaty-mandated inspection capability that threatened to derail the treaty. This intervention set a precedent that could—and should—have been used to resolve the post-2009 allegations of treaty noncompliance lodged by the US and Russia.

The Russian event in question probably involved a test of a sea-launched cruise missile utilizing a fixed, land-based launcher used solely for test purposes—an activity which was permitted by the treaty. An on-site inspection could have verified that the launcher was physically different from those used for ground-launched cruise missiles, as required by the treaty. Likewise, the US admits that the structural components of its land-based vertical launchers in Romania and Poland were like the ship-borne version but contends that the electronics and software used by the land-based systems are incapable of launching a Tomahawk. These claims can only be verified by up-close, in-person on-site inspection.

The need for on-site inspection as a verification tool is as great today as it was when the INF treaty came into force back in 1988. But the SVC was not called upon to make full use of the versatility and utility of trained inspectors to breathe new life into on-site inspections as a treaty compliance tool and, in doing so, imbue the INF treaty with a credibility it had been lacking for many years. The mistrust created by the lack of an "effective verification" capability ultimately led to the US withdrawing from the INF treaty in August 2019.

The loss of the VPMF has left a gaping hole in the ability of the US to effectively and reliably monitor Russian missile production. Given the recent proliferation in missile types being produced by Russian (most of which are still being assembled at the Votkinsk Missile Final Assembly Plant), this creates a confidence gap when it comes to assessing Russian capability and intention regarding its strategic nuclear forces. Likewise, with the US on the cusp of initiating a program designed to replace the ageing Minuteman III ICBM with a new "Ground Based Strategic Deterrent," Russia, too, would benefit from having inspectors able to monitor the production of these new missiles.

Even more problematic than the lack of on-site monitoring of ballistic missile production, however, is the fact that, with the demise of the INF treaty, the specter of the proliferation of missile systems that had been completely eradicated under the INF treaty has once again reared its ugly head.

Zurab Tsereteli's statue commemorating the INF Treaty and the destruction of nuclear missiles still stands where it was installed, outside the United Nations Headquarters in New York City. But what once was a symbol of "good" (arms control) defeating "evil" (intermediate-range nuclear missiles) has instead been transformed into a reminder of the even more urgent need to revisit nuclear disarmament and kill the nuclear dragon once and for all.

Glossary of Terms

ACDA – Arms Control and Disarmament Agency

ACIS – Arms Control Intelligence Staff

ACIU – Arms Control Implementation Unit

Buzzards Point – Washington, DC neighborhood, location of Coast Guard Headquarters

CIA – Central Intelligence Agency

CPSU – Communist Party of the Soviet Union

Department 162 – Soviet INF treaty escort organization in Votkinsk

DIA – Defense Intelligence Agency

DIC – Defense Intelligence College

DIS – Defense Investigative Service

DCC – Data Control Center

DLI – Defense Language Institute

DOD – Department of Defense

DOE – Department of Energy

DPM – Directorate for Portal Monitoring

DTRA – Defense Threat Reduction Agency

EPB – Environmentally Protected Building

ESD – Electronics Systems Division

FAO – Foreign Area Officer

FBI – Federal Bureau of Investigation

FOE – Field Office-Europe

GAN – Great American Novel

Gateway – Joint OSIA/CIA facility in Frankfurt, Germany and Yokota, Japan

GLBM – Ground Launched Ballistic Missile

GLCM – Ground Launched Cruise Missile

GorIsPolKom – City Communist Executive Committee

GorKom – City Communist Party Committee

HTSC – Hughes Technical Services Company

ICBM – Intercontinental Ballistic Missile

INF – Intermediate Nuclear Force

ISO – designation for standard US army container.

JCS – Joint Chiefs of Staff

KGB – Committee for State Security (Komitet Gosudarstvennoy Bezopasnosti)

Komsomol – Communist Youth League

Kourier – Soviet experimental small intercontinental ballistic missile

M1022 – US Army wheeled trailer used to transport DCC shelters

MFA – Soviet Ministry of Foreign Affairs

MITT – Moscow Institute of Thermal Technology

MoA – Memorandum of Agreement

MOP – Soviet Ministry of Defense Industry

MoU – Memorandum of Understanding

NRRC – Nuclear Risk Reduction Center

NSA – National Security Agency

OSD – Office of the Secretary of Defense

OSI – US Air Force Office of Special Investigations

OSIA – On-Site Inspection Agency

Pershing II – US intermediate range ballistic missile

PM – Portal Monitoring

PO-RTO – Radio Technological Production Administration

PPM – Perimeter Portal Monitoring

RDE – Radiation Detection Experiment

SABRE – NATO designation for the SS-20 missile

SCALEBOARD – NATO designation for the SS-12 missile

SICKLE – NATO designation for the SS-25 ICBM

Sirena – Soviet designation for SS-25 missiles used in Perimeter system

Skorost – Soviet experimental intermediate range ballistic missile

SMD – Stage Measuring Device

SMS – Stage Measuring System

SNL – Sandia National Laboratory

SPIDER – NATO designation for the SS-23 missile

START – Strategic Arms Reduction Treaty

SVC – Special Verification Commission

Temp-S – Soviet designation for the SS-12 ballistic missile

Temp-2S – Soviet designation for the SS-16 ballistic missile

TBE – Tick-borne encephalitis

TMC – Treaty Monitoring Center

TMMO – Treaty Monitoring Management Office

Topol – Soviet designation for the SS-25 ballistic missile

Topol-M – Russian designation for the SS-27 ballistic missile

TOSI – Technical On-Site Inspection

USAIAREES – US Army Institute for Advanced Russian and East European Studies

USAMRIID – US Army Medical Research Institute of Infectious Diseases

USARI – United States Army Russia Institute

USMLM – United States Military Liaison Mission

USSR – Union of Soviet Socialist Republics

UTTKh – Improved Tactical and Technical Characteristics

VMBP – Votkinsk Machine Building Plant

VPMF – Votkinsk Portal Monitoring Facility

Endnotes

PROLOGUE

1. Judith Miller, "Ex-CIA Aide's Role Spurs Controversy," *The New York Times,* January 4, 1981.

2. The National Academies, in a proposal in support of "Risk-Based Approaches for Securing the DOE Nuclear Weapons Complex," provides a biography of Dr. Osias which notes that he was detailed to the Director of Central Intelligence (DCI) "to manage intelligence community activities to monitor and implement the Intermediate-Range Nuclear Forces (INF) treaty," and that for this work he was awarded the Department of Defense Distinguished Civilian Service Award.

3. Memorandum from Chief, Arms Control Intelligence Staff to Director of Central Intelligence, "Intelligence Capabilities for Monitoring Arms Control" (ER 83-6069), December 19, 1983.

4. Don Shannon, "Helms asks CIA to Check if Soviets Cheated on INF," *Los Angeles Times,* January 24, 1988.

CHAPTER ONE

1. Seth Mydans, "Ustinov's Funeral Rites Adhere to Fixed Pattern," *The New York Times,* December 23, 1984.

2. Eric Pace, "Ustinov had Key Roles in Military and Politics," *The New York Times,* December 22, 1988.

3. "Narkom's Essays," *Znamya magazine,* 1988:1–2. Vannikov was later rehabilitated and went on the head up the bureaucracy responsible for building the Soviet atomic bomb.

4. A. Z. Vorotov (editor), *Votinsk: Letopis', Sobuitiy, i Faktov* (Udmurtia Publishing House: Ustinov, 1985).

5. Walter S. Dunn, Jr., *Stalin's Keys to Victory: The Rebirth of the Red Army* (Praeger: London, 2006), p. 30.

6. Steven J. Zaloga, *The Kremlin's Nuclear Sword: The rise and fall of Russia's strategic nuclear forces, 1945–2000* (The Smithsonian Institution Press: Washington, DC, 2002), p. 30.

7. See Steven J. Zaloga, *Scud Ballistic Missile and Launch Systems 1955–2005* (Bloomsbury Publishing: London, 2013).

8. Zaloga, *The Kremlin's Nuclear Sword,* op. cit., pp. 90–94.

9. Nikolai Sokov, *Russian Strategic Modernization, Past and Future* (Rowman and Littlefield Publishers, Inc: New York, 2000), p. 38.

10. Sokov, *Russian Strategic Modernization,* p. 39.

11. Sokov, *Russian Strategic Modernization,* pp. 39–40.

12. Arthur Cox, *Russian Roulette: The Superpower Game* (Times Books: New York, 1982), p. 10.

13. Statement by Soviet Minister of Defense, Dmitry Ustinov at the Extraordinary Session of the Committee of Defense Ministers of Warsaw Pact Member States, Berlin, German Democratic Republic, October 20, 1983, "Highly Confidential." (Source: Federal Archives of Germany, Military Branch (BA-MA), Freiburg i. B. Call Number DVW 1/71/1040).

14. Dmitri Ustinov, "To Struggle for Peace, To Strengthen Defense Capability," *Pravda,* November 19, 1983.

15. Roy A. Medvedev, *Neizvestnii Andropov* (The Unknown Andropov), (Rostov: Feniks, 1999), 379–382.

16. Preliminary INF negotiations had begun in October 1980, with formal negotiations commencing on November 30, 1981.

17. Svetlana Savranskaya and Thomas Blanton, "Gorbachev's Instructions to the Reykjavik Preparation Group," October 4, 1986, *The Last Superpower Summits* (Budapest: Central European University Press, 2016), p. 163.

18. Serge Schmemann, "Defense Minister of Soviet Union is Dead at 76," *The New York Times,* December 22, 1984.

19. Schmemann, "Defense Minister of Soviet Union is Dead at 76."

20. "Excerpts from Gorbachev's first speech as USSR leader," UPI, March 11, 1985.

21. Bill Keller, "Upstaged by Soviet Events, Geneva Arms Talks Fade," *The New York Times,* March 14, 1985.

22. Nikolaev Yu. M., Panin S. D., *Basics of designing solid-fuel guided ballistic missiles (part 2)* (Moscow State Technical university: Moscow, 1998).

CHAPTER TWO

1. "Fraley Faces Soviets in Working Group," *Lab News,* Vol. 41, No. 8, Sandia National Laboratories, April 21, 1988, p. 7. (Note: Stan Fraley received the Secretary of Defense Medal for Outstanding Public Service for his work on the INF Treaty.)

2. "Fraley Faces Soviets in Working Group."

3. Adapted from Howard Stoertz, Jr., "Monitoring a Nuclear Freeze," *International Security,* Vol. 8, No. 4 (Spring 1984): 95.

4. In his memoirs, published in 1967, Kennan argued that containment was not an exclusively military concept, and that the US government use of his arguments to justify the Cold War model of militarized containment was flawed. See George Kennan, *Memoirs: 1925–1950* (Boston: Little, Brown and Company, 1967).

5. Scott Ritter, *Scorpion King: America's Suicidal Embrace of Nuclear Weapons from FDR to Trump* (Clarity Press: Atlanta, Georgia, 2020), p. 287.

6. Kevin Costelloe, "Army Training Facility in W. Germany: Just Don't Call It a 'Spy School,'" *Los Angeles Times,* May 7, 1989.

7. "Samuel V. Wilson, Army lieutenant general and spymaster, dies at 93," *Bangor Daily News,* June 13, 2017.

8. Annual Historical Review, US Army Intelligence and Security Command, 1979 (History Office, US Army INSCOM: Arlington, Virginia, September 1979).

9. "The US Army's Russia Institute," *Stars and Stripes* (European Edition), June 8, 1978, p. 8.

10. Charles Stuart Kennedy, "Oral Interview: Phillip C. Brown," The Association for Diplomatic Studies and Training, *Foreign Affairs Oral History Project,* January 18, 2012, p. 102.

11. Anthony Austin, "US Army Attache Called Target of Soviet Plot to Compromise Him," *The New York Times,* February 17, 1981.

12. Edward T. Pound, "An Informer Helped FBI's Agents Trap Soviet Army Attache," *The New York Times,* February 2, 1982.

13. John F. Burns, "Moscow ousts a US Diplomat, Calling Him a Spy," *The New York Times,* March 11, 1983.

14. David E. Hoffman, *The Billion Dollar Spy: A True Story of Cold War Espionage and Betrayal* (Doubleday: New York, 2015), pp. 159–160.

15. Ruth Quinn, "US Military Liaison Mission Ends October 3, 1990," army.mil, September 25, 2013.

16. Thomas Wyckoff, *Mission: A Cold War Remembrance* (Dorrance: Pittsburgh, 2018), pp. 1–4.

17. David Rising, "30 years after Cold War killing, US officer is remembered," Associated Press, March 16, 2016.

18. "US Vehicle is Hit in East Germany," *The New York Times,* July 17, 1985.

19. Mike Duff, "4WD Diplomacy: We Retrace US Intelligence Cold War Routes in a Mercedes G-Wagon and SRT Jeep," *Car and Driver,* May 2, 2017.

20. Liz Dee, "The Embassy Moscow Fire of 1977," The Association for Diplomatic Studies and Training, August 18, 2014.

21. The history of Detachment "A," and Stu O'Neill's participation, can be found in James Stejskal's *Special Forces Berlin: Clandestine Cold War Operations of the US Army's Elite, 1956–1990* (Philadelphia: Casemate, 2017.)

22. Wykoff, *Mission,* p. 47.

23. James F. Peltz, "25 Technicians 'Willing to Sacrifice' Will Go to the Soviet Union: Hughes to Monitor Treaty Compliance," *Los Angeles Times,* June 24, 1988.

CHAPTER THREE

1. "Remarks on Signing the Intermediate-Range Nuclear Forces Treaty December 8, 1987," National Archives and Record Administration of the Ronald Reagan Presidential Library and Museum.

2. "Sandians Serve on Soviet Site," *Lab News,* Vol. 41, No, 8, Sandia National Laboratories, April 21, 1988, p, 7.

3. Maynard Glitman, *The Last Battle of The Cold War. An Inside Account of Negotiating the Intermediate Range Nuclear Forces Treaty* (Palgrave McMillan: New York, 2006), p. 231. According to Ambassador Maynard Glitman, the Chief US INF negotiator, the Soviets were talking about "a new missile with dimensions that had more girth, but less length, than the SS-20. But in any case," Glitman noted, "it was not an SS-20."

4. While written comments in fitness reports are usually best ignored, given the tendency on the part of reporting seniors to inflate the worth of those being reported on, I was proud of one line in particular Colonel Connell wrote in my initial report while assigned to OSIA: "Unmatched ability to accomplish the mission, whatever it takes."

5. "Sandians Serve on Soviet Site," pp. 7– 8.

6. Richard Trembley, "Logistics Support for U.S. Perimeter and Portal Monitoring Sites in the Soviet Union," Air Force Institute for Technology: Wright Patterson Air Force Base, Ohio, September 1990.

CHAPTER FOUR

1. Yulia Afanasyenko, "The State Kremlin Palace: An ambitious project in the heart of Russia," *Russia Beyond,* January 27, 2021.

2. Bruce Weber, "Ekaterina Maximova, Ballerina, Dies at 70," *The New York Times,* April 29, 2009.

3. Jack F. Matlock, *Autopsy on an Empire: The American Ambassador's Account of the Collapse of the Soviet Union* (Random House: New York, 1995), pp. 109–110.

4. "Excerpts from Gorbachev's Talk at Party Parley," *The New York Times,* January 28, 1987.

5. Charles Mitchell, "Gorbachev says reform program at crucial phase," *United Press International*, October 13, 1987.

6. Matlock, *Autopsy...*, pp. 114–115.

7. "Excerpts from TASS account of Gorbachev talk on Yeltsin," *The New York Times*, November 13, 1987.

8. "Gorbachev's Ex-Protégé Yeltsin Loses Politburo Job," *Los Angeles Times*, February 18, 1988.

9. Gerald Nadler, "Soviet parliament ousts Yeltsin," *United Press International*, May 25, 1988.

10. "Yeltsin Must Defend His Criticism of Politburo Member—Gorbachev," *Los Angeles Times*, June 1, 1988.

11. Robert G. Kaiser, "Red Intrigue: How Gorbachev Outfoxed His Kremlin Rivals," *Washington Post*, June 12, 1988.

12. Kaiser, "Red Intrigue...."

13. Anatoly Chernyaev, *My Six Years with Gorbachev* (Penn State Press: University Park, 2000), p. 160.

14. Chernyaev, *My Six Years...*, p. 161.

15. All quotes from Gorbachev are taken from "Key Sections of Gorbachev Speech Given to Party Conference," *The New York Times*, June 29, 1988.

16. "Excerpts from Remarks by Yeltsin and Ligachev," *The New York Times*, July 2, 1988.

17. Chernyaev, *My Six Years...*, pp. 169–170.

18. Alyans Sabirov, "Prams Instead of Missiles: About a US Inspection and the Fate of a Military Factory in Votkinsk," *Sovetskoye Voyennoye Oborzrenniye (Moscow)*, No. 3, 1989.

19. Alexei Kireyev, "Disarmament Economics," *Pravda*, August 20, 1988.

20. G. K. Khromov, "Problems of Conversion from Military to Civilian Production Following the Soviet-US Treaty on the Elimination of Intermediate-Range and Shorter-Range Nuclear Forces: The Example of the Votkinsk Plant," presented at the Informal Meeting on Defense Expenditure and Local Employment (Geneva), May 18–19, 1989, International Labor Office Working Document WEP 2-41-03-01 (Document number 2).

21. William S. Ritter, Jr., "Defense Conversion in Votkinsk," *Problems of Communism*, September-October 1991, p. 51.

22. Khromov, "Problems of Conversion...."

23. Chernyaev, *My Six Years...*, p. 160.

CHAPTER FIVE

1. "New Year's Messages of President Reagan and President Mikhail Gorbachev of the Soviet Union," January 1, 1989, www.reaganlibrary.gov.

2. Bill Gertz, "US balks at giving Soviets high-tech INF software," *Washington Times*, January 24, 1989.

3. Nikolai Brusnitsin, *Openness and Espionage* (Military Publishing House: Moscow, 1990), p. 31.

4. N. Burbyga, "What does military counterintelligence do?," *Izvestiya*, April 26, 1990.

5. I. Baranovsky, "KGB without secrets," *Rabochnaya Tribuna*, April 29, 1990.

6. Burbyga, "What does military counterintelligence do?"

7. The early blueprints of the four structures show that the original name for the administrative building was "Fillmore," after the 13th President, Millard Fillmore.

Indeed, internal memoranda from OSIA continued to use this name well into November 1988. George Connell thought it would be fascinating to have Udmurt school children compelled to study one of the least known Presidents and learn the history of the Whig Party and other details of a period of American history unknown to most US students. General Lajoie quashed this experiment in radical propaganda, ordering the structure renamed as "Roosevelt," ostensibly to complete the Mount Rushmore theme. But Theodore Roosevelt was deemed too obscure a President, so in the end the decision was to name the administrative building after the Roosevelt best known by the Soviet people, their war-time ally, Franklin Delano.

8. I. Yeremin, "Business Trip from North Carolina," *Izvestiya,* January 14, 1989.

9. My dealings with Lopatin were almost exclusively in the realm of treaty-mandated inspections, which meant our interactions were virtually void of controversy. I did challenge him once to an arm wrestling contest, which he handily won. Chagrined, Colonel Connell demanded I redeem my honor, and the honor of the Marine Corps, which I did by besting Lopatin in a pull-up contest.

10. Bill Gertz, "The Soviets want access to the inspector's basements," *Washington Times,* February 24, 1989.

11. "On the way to strengthening trust; Housewarming at the American village," *Leninski Put',* June 14, 1989.

CHAPTER SIX

1. John M. Broder, "Cheney Predicts Gorbachev Will Fail, Be Ousted," *Los Angeles Times,* April 29, 1989.

2. Michael R. Beschloss and Strobe Talbott, *At the Highest Levels: The inside story of the end of the Cold War* (Little Brown: New York, 1993), pp. 54–55.

3. "Bush Rejects Cheney View on Gorbachev," *Los Angeles Times,* May 1, 1989.

4. Nikolai Sokov, *Russian Strategic Modernization: Past and Future* (Rowman & Littlefield: New York, 2000), p. 46.

5. Beschloss and Talbott, *At the Highest Levels,* p. 64.

6. Michael Dobbs, "Gorbachev announces troop cuts of 500,000," *Washington Post,* December 8, 1988.

7. Dobbs, "Gorbachev announces troop cuts...."

8. Robert Gates, *From the Shadows: The Ultimate Insider's Story of Five Presidents and How They Won the Cold War* (Simon & Shuster: New York, 1996) pp. 430–431.

9. Sokov, *Russian Strategic Modernization...,* p. 61.

10. Thomas L. Friedman, "Baker plans visit to Moscow in May to discuss summit," *The New York Times,* March 8, 1989.

11. Beschloss and Talbott, *At the Highest Levels,* p. 60.

12. George C. Wilson, "NATO 'shooting itself in the foot,' Nunn says," *Washington Post,* May 8, 1989.

13. Beschloss and Talbott, *At the Highest Levels,* pp. 66–68.

14. Beschloss and Talbott, *At the Highest Levels,* pp. 70–71.

15. Matlock, *Autopsy...,* pp. 224–226.

16. Nikolai Brusnitsin, *Openness and Espionage* (Military Publishing House: Moscow, 1990), p. 31.

17. John Sovitch and his team of technicians and contract specialists from ESD, Sandia and ASEC put together a work/travel schedule that would have the appropriate technical expertise in Votkinsk while CargoScan was being installed. Sovitch's goal was to be able to conduct a Program Management Responsibility Transfer of the CargoScan

system from ESD to OSIA by the end of December 1989. As things turned out, this date slipped further, to mid-February. John Sovitch was able to keep pace with a fluid schedule that often changed daily. He and his team deserve a great deal of credit for making CargoScan a reality.

18. Interview with Tom Flavia, *Cold War Conversations,* June 20, 2021.

19. Jack Matlock, Cable for Secretary of State James Baker, "Preparing for Malta: US Trade Policy Towards USSR," November 14, 1989.

20. Soviet Transcript of the Malta Summit, December 2–3, 1989, Gorbachev Foundation, Fond 1, Opis 1.

21. National Intelligence Estimate 11-18-89, *The Soviet System in Crisis: Prospects for the Next Two Years.*

22. Matlock, *Autopsy...,* p. 274.

23. Matlock, *Autopsy...,* p. 275.

24. Olga Orakova survived her childhood ordeal and went on to become a doctor. Today she runs a successful clinic in Barcelona, Spain.

CHAPTER SEVEN

1. Violence based on nationalism was becoming an unfortunate reality in Gorbachev's Soviet Union. In July 1989, simmering tensions between the Georgian and Abkhazian populations of the Soviet Georgian city of Sukhumi erupted into fighting that left 18 persons dead; only the intervention of thousands of Interior Ministry troops prevented more violence. From January 12, 1990, a seven-day pogrom broke out in the Soviet Republic of Azerbaijan against the Armenian civilian population in Baku during which scores of Armenians were beaten, murdered, and expelled from the city. On January 20, the Soviet Army and Interior Ministry forces occupied Baku to stabilize the situation. Similar unrest broke out in the capitol of Soviet Tajikistan from 10–11 February involving thousands of protesters. The Soviet Army eventually intervened, but not before some 25 people were killed, many of them Russians.

2. The entire narrative regarding Sadovnikov is derived from an article "Tikhii Vystrel (The Quiet Gunshot)," written by Anatoliy Golovkov, which appeared in the Russian magazine *Ogonek,* No. 30, July 1990, pp. 22–24.

3. Matlock, *Autopsy...,* p. 321.

4. Matlock, *Autopsy...,* p. 336.

5. Matlock, *Autopsy...,* p. 323.

6. Rowland Evans and Robert Novak, "Soviets block nuclear missile inspection," *Washington Post,* March 16, 1990, p. 23.

7. Evans and Novak, "Soviets block nuclear missile inspection," p. 23.

8. N. Burbyta, "Votkinsk Missile Crisis: The American Version," *Izvestia,* March 17, 1990.

9. Sokov, Russian Strategic Modernization, p. 74.

10. Nicholas Thompson, "Inside the Apocalyptic Soviet Doomsday Machine," *Wired,* September 21, 2009.

11. Michael Peck, "Russia's 'Dead Hand' Nuclear Doomsday Weapon is Back," *The National Interest,* December 12, 2018.

12. Oleg Odnokolenko, "Colonel-General Viktor Yesin: 'If the Americans do start to deploy their missiles in Europe, we will have nothing to do but abandon the doctrine of retaliatory strike and switch to the doctrine of preemptive strike'," *Zvezda,* November 8, 2018.

13. Pavel Povdig, "Tracking down road-mobile missiles," *Russian Strategic Nuclear Forces,* January 13, 2015.

14. My perseverance in making this course a reality, along with several other Portal related projects I was responsible for bringing to fruition, prompted Charles Myers, a Navy Commander whom I held in the highest regard, to write that I excelled at leading "from below, demonstrating what he developed to often skeptical superiors and stealthily enticing them to do it right." Coming from a man of his caliber, this was good praise indeed.

15. Roland Lajoie, "The INF Treaty: A Status Report on INF Inspections," *Challenges for the 1990s for Arms Control and International Security* (National Academy Press: Washington, DC, 1989), p. 36.

16. On October 3, 1990, the US Military Liaison Mission ceased to exist, having been redesignated as the Combined Analysis Detachment-Berlin (CAD-B), which assumed joint intelligence exploitation of former Soviet military facilities together with the German intelligence services. This mission lasted until 1992.

CHAPTER EIGHT

1. "On the market economy: Problems remain," Udmurtskaya Pravda, June 6, 1990.

2. Viktor Chirkov, "A Step Backward," *Udmurtskaya Pravda,* June 15, 1990.

3. Matlock, *Autopsy...,* pp. 377–378.

4. Joseph P. Harahan, *On-Site Inspections under the INF Treaty* (US Government Printing Office: Washington, DC, 1995), pp. 127–131.

5. Matlock, *Autopsy...,* p. 400.

6. Matlock, *Autopsy...,* p. 400.

7. Sokov, *Russian Strategic Modernization,* p. 71

8. Sokov, *Russian Strategic Modernization,* p. 72.

9. Richard Kerr, "CIA's Track Record Stands Up to Scrutiny," *The New York Times,* October 24, 1991.

10. Terry Atlas, "Soviet economy near collapse, CIA says," *Chicago Tribune,* May 17, 1991.

11. Sokov, *Russian Strategic Modernization,* p. 72.

12. Beschloss and Talbott, *At the Highest Levels...,* p. 400.

13. Yevgeniy Shashkov, "START Made," *Pravda,* August 2, 1991.

14. Viktor Litovkin, "Marshal of the Soviet Union D. Yazov: It is a Balanced Treaty," *Izvestiya,* August 2, 1991.

15. Sokov, *Russian Strategic Modernization,* p. 73.

16. Sokov, *Russian Strategic Modernization,* p. 73.

17. Sokov, *Russian Strategic Modernization,* p. 73.

18. Matlock, *Autopsy...,* pp. 578–579.

19. Matlock, *Autopsy...,* pp. 581–582.

20. Harahan, *On-Site Inspections....,* pp. 158–159.

21. Charles Stewart Kennedy, "Interview with E. Wayne Merry," The Association of Diplomatic Studies and Training, *Foreign Affairs History Project,* 2013, p. 190.

22. Kennedy, "Interview with E. Wayne Merry," pp. 191–192.

23. Matlock, op. cit., p. 739.

EPILOGUE

1. Eric Schmitt, "At Cold War's End, Whither the Missile Monitors?," *The New York Times,* January 26, 1992.

2. Adi Ignatius, "The Best Part of Life for These Americans Is Not Paying Taxes," *The Wall Street Journal,* December 6, 1993.

3. *Adherence and Compliance with Arms Control Agreements,* 1995, ACDA, May 30, 1995.

4. *Adherence and Compliance with Arms Control Agreements,* 1995.

5. Letter from Ambassador Steven E. Steiner to Ambassador Mikhail N. Streltsov, October 6, 1994.

6. Michael Krimmer, *Comrades in...Arms Control: The Contractor's Role in Implementing On-Site Inspections* (Air University: Maxwell Air Force Base, 1998), p. 11.

7. "Arms Control: Intermediate-Range Nuclear Forces Treaty Implementation," United States General Accounting Office report, September 12, 1991, pp. 56–57.

Index